LIVING LANGUAGE®
ULTIMATE
ITALIAN
ADVANCED

Available from LIVING LANGUAGE®

ULTIMATE COURSES. This comprehensive program covers conversation, grammar, reading, writing, and culture. Each of the 40 lessons begins with a dialogue and includes explanations of grammar and usage, vocabulary, and notes on customs and culture. Unique to this course are two sets of recordings: four hours in the target language only for use with the manual, and four bilingual recordings, ideal for learning on the go. Basic–Intermediate. French, German, Inglés, Italian, Japanese, Russian, Spanish, and Chinese (1999).

ULTIMATE ADVANCED COURSES. Sequels to the Basic–Intermediate program, these courses include sections on business vocabulary and etiquette, in addition to the dialogue-based lessons. Advanced. French, German, Inglés, Italian, Japanese, Russian, and Spanish.

COMPLETE BASIC COURSES (Level 1). The original, best-selling Living Language program developed by U.S. government experts in 1946, revised and updated in 1993, includes three hours of recordings on cassette or compact disc, a manual, and a two-way 20,000-word dictionary. Featuring a proven speed-learning method, the course progresses from words to phrases to complete sentences and dialogues. Recordings are all in the target language. Beginner–Intermediate. French, German, Inglés, Italian, Japanese, Portuguese, Russian, and Spanish.

INTERMEDIATE COURSES (Level 2): A Conversational Approach to Verbs. This course teaches more than 150 conjugations through practical phrases and dialogues. Four 60-minute bilingual cassettes and a 384-page text with 40 dialogues, exercises, and verb charts. Intermediate. French, German, Italian, and Spanish.

ADVANCED CONVERSATION COURSES (Level 3). Four 60-minute cassettes in the target language only feature more sophisticated dialogues, idiomatic expressions, and grammar. The accompanying 350-page conversation manual also includes the transcript with English translations, plus verb charts, culture notes, and exercises to check one's progress. Advanced. French and Spanish.

Books also available separately.

ULTIMATE
ITALIAN
ADVANCED

WRITTEN BY

SALVATORE BANCHERI, PH.D.

MICHAEL LETTIERI, PH.D.

MARIA D. IOCCO, M.A., M.ED.

LUCY DIROSA, M.A.

EDITED BY

ANA SUFFREDINI AND

CHRISTOPHER A. WARNASCH

LIVING LANGUAGE®
A Random House Company

ACKNOWLEDGMENTS

Many thanks to Crown Publishers' Living Language™ team: Kathryn Mintz, Lisa Alpert, Helga Schier, Alexia Brue, and Tony Distefano. Special thanks to Renata Rosso, Roberto Severino, Remo Trivelli, Jim Walsh, John Sharp, Lenny Henderson, *Oggi, Ulisse 2000,* Edigraf Cosentina, Pino Nano, Carlo Santoro, and the Italy-America Chamber of Commerce, Inc.

Random House, Inc. New York, Toronto, London, Sydney, Auckland

www.livinglanguage.com

Living Language and colophon are trademarks of Crown Publishers, Inc.

Printed in the United States of America

Library of Congress Cataloging-in-Publication Data is available upon request.

ISBN 0-517-88503-4

10 9 8 7 6 5 4 3 2 1

First Edition

CONTENTS

INTRODUCTION

Living Language™ Ultimate Italian: Advanced is a continuation of the beginner–intermediate *Ultimate Italian™* program. If you have already mastered the basics of Italian in school, while traveling abroad, or with other *Living Language™* courses, then *Ultimate Italian: Advanced* is right for you.

The complete course includes this text, along with eight hours of recordings. However, if you are confident of your pronunciation, you can also use the manual on its own.

With *Ultimate Italian: Advanced* you'll continue to learn how to speak, understand, read, and write Italian. The program will also introduce you to some of the more interesting aspects of Italian culture and business. You'll be able to participate in engaging conversations about a variety of topics, as well as recognize and respond to several styles of formal and informal speech.

The course will take you everywhere, from Chianti's vineyards to the glassworks of Murano to a trade show in Milan, while teaching useful vocabulary and expressions. You'll also learn about subtle cultural distinctions in personal interaction, such as how to use proper eating etiquette in both social and business settings, that will help smooth your way abroad.

COURSE MATERIALS

THE MANUAL

Living Language™ Ultimate Italian: Advanced consists of twenty lessons, four reading passages, and two review sections. The reading passages appear every five lessons. There are review sections after Lesson 10 and Lesson 20. It's best to read and study each lesson in the manual before listening to it on the recordings.

DIALOGO (DIALOGUE): Each lesson begins with a dialogue in standard, idiomatic Italian presenting a realistic situation—using the internet, searching for a first job, taking a trip in a car—set in various locales. All dialogues are translated into colloquial English.

IN BREVE (IN BRIEF): The notes in this section refer to specific expressions and phrases in the dialogue. They'll introduce you to the cultural and historical background relevant to a particular expression, and allow you to see grammar rules and vocabulary "in action."

GRAMMATICA E SUOI USI (GRAMMAR AND USAGE): After a brief review of basic Italian grammar, you'll concentrate on the more advanced grammatical forms and their usage. You'll learn how to express yourself more accurately and appropriately by using idiomatic Italian. For easy reference, the heading of each topic corresponds to its listing in the table of contents.

PAROLE! PAROLE! PAROLE! (WORDS! WORDS! WORDS!): This section focuses on idiomatic expressions in Italian. You'll learn how to express yourself in Italian the way a native speaker would, using some of the more colorful Italian idioms and maxims. This in-depth vocabulary study will improve your idiomatic usage of Italian and help you avoid common linguistic pitfalls.

L'ANGOLO DEGLI AFFARI (BUSINESS CORNER): In this section you'll explore different areas of the Italian economy, as well as cultural and historical information relevant to business etiquette and procedures. Discussing topics such as table etiquette, transportation and shipping, and the mass media, this section will enable you to do business in Italy with confidence.

ESERCIZI (EXERCISES): This section allows you to review the grammar and vocabulary covered in the lessons. You can check your answers in the *CHIAVE PER GLI ESERCIZI* (ANSWER KEY) appearing after lesson 20.

DA LEGGERE (READING): The four reading passages—appearing after lessons 5, 10, 15, and 20—are not translated. The material covered in the preceding lessons, along with the vocabulary notes on the more difficult words and phrases, will enable you to infer the meaning, just as you would when reading a newspaper article or business report abroad.

RIPASSO (REVIEW): The two review sections appear after lessons 10 and 20. Similar in structure to the *ESERCIZI,* these sections will allow you to integrate and test your mastery of the material covered in the preceding lessons.

APPENDIXES: There are a number of helpful appendixes: Abbreviations and Measurements, a Grammar Summary, Regular and Irregular Verb Charts, Sections on special verbs and expressions, and Letter Writing.

GLOSSARY: The extensive two-way glossary will prove an invaluable reference as you work through this program and as you apply your knowledge when communicating with Italian speakers and traveling abroad.

INDEX: The manual ends with an index of the major grammar points covered in the lessons.

The appendixes, glossary, and index make this manual an excellent source for future reference and study.

RECORDINGS (SETS A & B)

This program provides you with eight hours of audio instruction and practice. There are two sets of complementary recordings: the first is designed for use with the manual, while the second may be used independently. By listening to and imitating the native speakers, you'll improve your pronunciation and comprehension while learning to use new phrases and structures.

RECORDINGS FOR USE WITH THE MANUAL (SET A)

This set of recordings gives you four hours of audio practice in Italian only, featuring the complete dialogues of all 20 lessons. The recorded material appears in **boldface** in your manual. You'll first hear native Italian speakers read the complete dialogue without interruption at normal conversational speed. Then you'll have a chance to listen to the dialogue a second time and repeat each phrase in the pauses provided.

If you wish to practice your comprehension, first listen to the recordings of the dialogue without consulting the translations in the manual. Write down a summary of what you think the dialogue was about, and then listen to the recordings a second time, checking how much you understood with the translations in the manual.

After you study each lesson and practice with Set A, go on to the second set of recordings (Set B), which can be used on the go—while driving, jogging, traveling on a plane, or doing housework.

This set of recordings gives you four hours of audio instruction and practice in Italian and English. Because they are bilingual, the Set B recordings may be used "on the go" without the manual, wherever it's convenient to learn.

The 20 lessons on Set B correspond to those in the manual. A bilingual narrator leads you through the four sections of each lesson.

The first section presents the most important phrases from the original dialogue. You will first hear the abridged dialogue without interruption at normal conversational speed. You'll then hear it again, phrase by phrase, with English translations and pauses for you to repeat after the native Italian speakers.

The second section reviews and expands upon the most important vocabulary introduced in the lesson. You will practice words and phrases collected from the *DIALOGO* (Dialogue), *IN BREVE* (In Brief), *PAROLE! PAROLE! PAROLE!* (Words! Words! Words!), and *L'ANGOLO DEGLI AFFARI* (Business Corner). Additional expressions show how the words may be used in other contexts. Again, you are given time to repeat the Italian phrases after the native speakers.

In the third section you will explore the lesson's most important grammatical structures. After a quick review of the rules, you can practice with illustrative phrases and sentences.

The conversational exercises in the last section integrate what you've learned and help you generate sentences in Italian on your own. You'll take part in brief conversations, ask and respond to questions, transform sentences, and occasionally translate from English into Italian. After you respond, you'll hear the correct answer from a native Italian speaker.

The interactive approach on this set of recordings focuses on the idiomatic spoken word and will teach you to speak, understand, and *think* in Italian.

Now let's begin.

LEZIONE 1

A. DIALOGO

DA NEW YORK A ROMA

Il signor Anderson, un uomo d'affari americano,[1] telefona[2] all'ufficio Alitalia di New York.

AGENTE ALITALIA: **Alitalia. Good morning! Buon giorno!**

DAVID ANDERSON: **Scusi, signorina,[3] parla[4] l'italiano?[5]**

AGENTE ALITALIA: **Sì, parlo l'italiano e l'inglese.**

DAVID ANDERSON: **Beh, visto che vado[6] in Italia, è meglio iniziare subito a parlare in italiano. Vorrei fare una prenotazione[7] per Roma,[8] per favore.**

AGENTE ALITALIA: **Quando desidera partire e quanto tempo si ferma in Italia?**

DAVID ANDERSON: **Dovrei partire il mese prossimo e vorrei restarci almeno un mese.**

AGENTE ALITALIA: **Un biglietto escursione costa $878.00 più le tasse. Da New York ci sono tre voli al giorno, sette giorni alla settimana. Per il weekend c'è una tariffa supplementare.**

DAVID ANDERSON: **Allora, mi prenoti, per cortesia,[9] un posto per il 12 aprile.[10] Se possibile, nel volo del pomeriggio.**

AGENTE ALITALIA: **Controlliamo nel computer.[11] Vediamo . . . sabato 12 aprile, volo AZ 611, New York—Roma, partenza ore 17:30, arrivo a Roma domenica, alle 7:35 ora locale. Va bene?**

DAVID ANDERSON: **Va bene, grazie.**

AGENTE ALITALIA: **Preferisce un posto vicino al finestrino o al corridoio?**

DAVID ANDERSON: **Vicino al finestrino.[12]**

AGENTE ALITALIA: **Zona fumatori o non fumatori?[13]**

DAVID ANDERSON: **Zona fumatori. E al ritorno, ci sono dei posti liberi per il 12 maggio?**

AGENTE ALITALIA: **Aspetti che controllo un momento . . . Sì, ci sono dei posti liberi. Le prenoto un posto. Il costo totale è di $1,068.00. Il pagamento deve essere effettuato entro sette giorni . . . Solo così potremo confermare la prenotazione. Il posto Le è stato già assegnato. Non Le rimane che presentarsi al banco di accettazione Alitalia per il check-in.**

DAVID ANDERSON: **Benissimo. Posso pagare ora con la carta di credito?**

AGENTE ALITALIA: **Certamente. Mi dia il Suo recapito . . .**

All'uscita.

IMPIEGATO: **Il biglietto, per favore.**

DAVID ANDERSON: **Eccolo. Il volo è in orario?**

IMPIEGATO: **Sì, oggi è in orario. Ha il passaporto?**

DAVID ANDERSON: **Eccolo! Sa quale film fanno vedere a bordo?**

IMPIEGATO: **Credo *Caro diario* di Moretti.[14] Comunque controlli l'elenco dei film in programma nella rivista[15] di bordo.**

DAVID ANDERSON: **Grazie. Il volo è pieno?**

IMPIEGATO: **No, ci sono ancora diversi posti liberi.**

DAVID ANDERSON: **C'è posto nella Business Class?[16]**

IMPIEGATO: **Mi faccia vedere, signor Anderson. Sì, c'è ancora posto. Se desidera, La metto allora nella Business Class.**

DAVID ANDERSON: **Grazie. Fantastico! Scusi, che tipo di aereo è? Un Boeing 747? Un Airbus?**

IMPIEGATO: **È un Jumbo 747. Ecco a Lei[17] il biglietto, il passaporto e la nuova carta d'imbarco. L'imbarco è previsto fra qualche minuto.**

DAVID ANDERSON: **Grazie.**

Sull'aereo.

ASSISTENTE DI VOLO: **Signore e signori, buona sera. L'Alitalia vi augura il benvenuto a bordo del volo AZ 611 per Roma. Siete** pregati di prendere posto, di prepararvi per il decollo e di fare attenzione alle seguenti norme di sicurezza. Le uscite di sicurezza sono anche indicate nell'opuscolo situato nella poltrona davanti a voi.

Dopo aver dormito per un paio d'ore, il signor Anderson si rivolge ad un'assistente di volo.[18]

DAVID ANDERSON: **Scusi, signorina, potrei avere un giornale, per favore? Ha il** *New York Times*[19] **o il** *Corriere della Sera?*[20]

ASSISTENTE DI VOLO: **Li abbiamo distribuiti qualche tempo fa . . . Comunque mi faccia vedere se posso trovargliene uno . . .**

DAVID ANDERSON: **Grazie.**

ASSISTENTE DI VOLO: **È fortunato. Gliene ho procurata una copia di tutti e due. Gradisce qualcosa da bere? Un Campari, un Cognac, una birra? Sono offerti gratuitamente.**

DAVID ANDERSON: **No, grazie, non bevo. Potrei avere un altro cuscino, per favore?**

ASSISTENTE DI VOLO: **Ma certamente! Eccolo.**

DAVID ANDERSON: **A che ora è previsto l'arrivo?**

ASSISTENTE DI VOLO: **Fra due ore,**[21] **alle 7:35 ora locale.**

DAVID ANDERSON: **Scusi, ma . . . come si chiama l'aeroporto di Roma?**[22] **Il nome ce l'ho proprio sulla punta della lingua, ma non lo ricordo.**

ASSISTENTE DI VOLO: **Leonardo da Vinci, a Fiumicino.**[23]

Prima dell'atterraggio un'assistente di volo annuncia:

ASSISTENTE DI VOLO: **Un attimo di attenzione, per cortesia. Stiamo iniziando la discesa verso Fiumicino. Siete pregati di allacciare le cinture di sicurezza, di mettere i bagagli a mano sotto la poltrona davanti a voi e di porre lo schienale in posizione verticale. Oggi a Roma il cielo è sereno. La temperatura è di 25 gradi centigradi. Sono le sette e venticinque ora locale. Vi ringraziamo per aver volato Alitalia e vi auguriamo un piacevole soggiorno in Italia. I passeggeri in transito sono pregati di contattare un agente Alitalia.**

FROM NEW YORK TO ROME

Mr. Anderson, an American businessman, calls Alitalia's New York office.

ALITALIA AGENT: Alitalia. Good morning! Buon giorno!

DAVID ANDERSON: Excuse me, Miss, do you speak Italian?

ALITALIA AGENT: Yes, I speak Italian and English.

DAVID ANDERSON: Well, since I'm going to Italy, I should probably start speaking Italian right away. I would like to make a reservation for Rome, please.

ALITALIA AGENT: When would you like to leave, and how long will you be staying in Italy?

DAVID ANDERSON: I should be leaving next month, and I would like to stay there at least one month.

ALITALIA AGENT: A round trip ticket costs $878.00 plus tax. From New York there are three flights daily, seven days a week. There is an additional charge for weekend travel.

DAVID ANDERSON: Well then, would you please make a reservation for me for April 12? On the afternoon flight if possible.

ALITALIA AGENT: Let's check the computer. Let's see . . . Saturday April 12, flight AZ 611, New York—Rome, departure time 5:30 p.m., arrival in Rome on Sunday, 7:35 a.m., local time. Is that okay?

DAVID ANDERSON: That's fine, thank you.

ALITALIA AGENT: Do you prefer a window or an aisle seat?

DAVID ANDERSON: Window.

ALITALIA AGENT: Smoking or non smoking?

DAVID ANDERSON: Smoking. And for the return flight, are there seats available for May 12?

ALITALIA AGENT: One moment, please, and I'll check . . . Yes, there are seats available. I'll make the reservation. Your total cost is $1,068.00. Your payment is due within seven days in order to keep these reservations. You'll need to check in at one of the Alitalia counters prior to departure, but your seats are already assigned.

DAVID ANDERSON: Great! Can I pay now, by credit card?

ALITALIA AGENT: Of course. Let's start with your billing address . . .

At the gate.

EMPLOYEE: Your ticket, please.

DAVID ANDERSON: Here you go. Is the flight on time?

EMPLOYEE: Yes, today it's on time. Do you have your passport?

DAVID ANDERSON: Here it is! Do you know what movie they'll be showing on board?

EMPLOYEE: I believe it's *Caro diario* by Moretti, but you can check the program listing in the inflight Alitalia magazine.

DAVID ANDERSON: Thanks. Is the flight fully booked?

EMPLOYEE: No, there are plenty of seats available.

DAVID ANDERSON: Are there seats available in Business Class?

EMPLOYEE: Yes, there are some seats available. If you'd like, I'll upgrade you to Business Class.

DAVID ANDERSON: Thanks! Great! Oh . . . what type of plane is it? A Boeing 747? An Airbus?

EMPLOYEE: It's a Jumbo 747. Here are your ticket, your passport, and your new boarding pass. We'll begin boarding shortly.

DAVID ANDERSON: Thank you.

On board.

FLIGHT ATTENDANT: Ladies and gentlemen, good evening. Alitalia would like to welcome you on board flight number AZ 611 to Rome. Please take your seats as we prepare for take-off, and pay attention to the following emergency procedures. You'll also find a brochure indicating all emergency exits in the pocket in front of you.

After having slept for a few hours, Mr. Anderson speaks to a flight attendant.

DAVID ANDERSON: Excuse me, Miss, may I have a newspaper, please? Do you have the *New York Times* or the *Corriere della Sera*?

FLIGHT ATTENDANT: We handed them out a while ago, but let me see if I can find one for you.

DAVID ANDERSON: Thank you.

FLIGHT ATTENDANT: You're in luck. I got you a copy of both. Would you like something to drink? A Campari, a Cognac, a beer? There is no charge.

DAVID ANDERSON: No, thank you, I don't drink. May I have an extra pillow, please?

FLIGHT ATTENDANT: Yes, of course. Here you are.

DAVID ANDERSON: What time are we expected to land?

FLIGHT ATTENDANT: Within two hours, at 7:35 local time.

DAVID ANDERSON: By the way, what's the name of the airport in Rome? I have it on the tip of my tongue but I can't remember it.

FLIGHT ATTENDANT: Leonardo da Vinci, at Fiumicino.

Before landing, a flight attendant announces:

FLIGHT ATTENDANT: May I have your attention, please? We are beginning our descent to Fiumicino. Please fasten your seatbelts, store all handbags beneath the seat in front of you, and place the back of the seat in the upright position. Today is a clear day in Rome. The temperature is 25 degrees Celsius. It is seven twenty-five local time. We thank you for flying Alitalia, and we wish you a pleasant stay in Italy. Passengers in transit are kindly requested to contact an Alitalia agent.

B. IN BREVE (In Brief)

1. Remember that nationalities are capitalized only when used as nouns that refer to people. *Gli Americani amano viaggiare.* (Americans like to travel.) When used as adjectives, or when referring to a language, they are not capitalized: *Lavoro per un'impresa giapponese.* (I work for a Japanese company.) *Parlo l'italiano.* (I speak Italian.)

2. In Italian, unlike in English, the verb *telefonare* (to phone) is always followed by the preposition *a* (to): *Telefono a Maria tutti i giorni.* (I phone Maria every day.)

3. There is no direct equivalent in Italian for "Ms." Instead *signorina* (literally: "Miss") is used. Other common titles include: *signora* (Mrs., ma'am), *signore* (Mr., sir), *signori* (ladies and gentlemen, gentlemen), *signore* (ladies). Notice that *signore* drops the final *-e* when it precedes a name and that in Italian titles are not capitalized (except at the beginning of a sentence). *Ecco la Sua carta d'imbarco, signor Rossi.* (Here is your boarding pass, Mr. Rossi.)

4. The *Lei* form (3rd person singular) is used to address someone in a formal setting. The *tu* form (2nd person singular) is reserved for close friends, family members, and children. When addressing a group, the *voi* form (2nd person plural) is preferred, and the *Loro* form is generally used only when addressing people very formally.

5. For the use of articles with languages, see *Grammatica e suoi usi* in this lesson.

6. Subject pronouns are generally omitted in Italian, as the verb endings reveal the person and number of the subject. However, they may be used for emphasis or clarity, or when preceded by one of the following words: *perfino, anche, solo, pure, nemmeno, neppure, neanche. Anch'io ho richiesto un posto vicino al finestrino.* (I also asked for a window seat.)

7. Words ending in *-ione* are usually feminine: *una prenotazione* (a reservation), *un'escursione* (an excursion), *una destinazione* (a destination), *una stazione* (a station). For more on the gender of nouns, see *Grammatica e suoi usi* in this lesson.

8. Rome, with a population of approximately three million, has been the capital of unified Italy since 1871. Former capitals were Turin and Florence. Founded in 753 B.C. according to the legend, it is called the Eternal City for its role in shaping Western civilization. Rome is also the seat of the papacy and the Roman Catholic church.

9. In Italian there are three ways of saying "please": *per piacere, per favore,* and *per cortesia.* They can be used interchangeably, but the first two are more popular.

10. Days of the week and months of the year are never capitalized in Italian, unless they begin a sentence.

11. In Italy the English term "computer" is more popular than its Italian equivalent, *elaboratore elettronico.*

12. Note that the ending *-ino* usually implies smallness or endearment: *il gatto* (cat) → *il gattino* (kitten), *la mano* (hand) → *la manina* (small hand). However, it can also be used to form new words, as in the word *finestrino* which is not a diminutive of *finestra* (window) but refers to a car or plane window.

13. Nouns ending in *-ore* are usually masculine: *fumatore* (smoker), *direttore* (director), *attore* (actor), *liquore* (liquor). When referring to people (usually professions) they generally have feminine counterparts ending in *-trice: fumatrice, direttrice, attrice.* Two common exceptions are: *dottore—dottoressa,* and *professore—professoressa.*

14. Nanni Moretti, one of Italy's best-loved film directors, won the Best Director Award at the Cannes Film Festival in 1994. *Caro Diario* was the first of his films to be released in the United States. In this cinematic simulation of a diary, Moretti, playing himself, makes a series of witty and insightful observations about contemporary culture and life in general. The film features three episodes: a personal tour of Rome by scooter, a visit to a number of Italian islands in search of inspiration, and a funny but dark battle against incessant itching.

15. Beware of "false friends"—words that sound alike in Italian and English but have different meanings. The Italian word for "magazine" is *rivista:* L'Espresso, Panorama, Epoca *e* Oggi *sono le riviste più popolari in Italia.* (*L'Espresso, Panorama, Epoca* and *Oggi* are the most popular magazines in Italy.) *Magazzino* means "warehouse" or "store": *Ho comprato questo vestito ai grandi magazzini.* (I bought this suit at a department store.)

16. The gender of foreign words used in Italian is determined in one of two ways. If the word comes from a language that distinguishes grammatical gender, it will have the same gender in Italian as in the original language, e.g., *la brochure* (Fr.)→ *la brochure* (It.). If, on the other hand, the word comes from a language which does not clearly distinguish grammatical gender, it will take the gender of a related Italian word, e.g., business class (Eng.)→ *la business class* (It., based on *la classe*).

17. *Lei* and *Loro,* meaning "you," are capitalized to distinguish them from *lei* meaning "she" and *loro* meaning "they."

18. Note that *assistente di volo* or *assistente di bordo* can be masculine or feminine, depending on whether the flight attendant is male or female. Related terms include: *hostess* (stewardess), *equipaggio* (crew), and *pilota* (pilot, captain).

19. Note that the article here is masculine because the word *giornale* (newspaper) is masculine. Similarly, the names of mountains, rivers, lakes, seas, oceans, languages, days of the week, months, trees, colors, and metals are all masculine because the words describing the category to which they belong—*monte, fiume, lago, mare, oceano, idioma, giorno, mese, albero, colore,* and *metallo*—are masculine. *Dal finestrino a sinistra vedrete il Po, il più grande fiume d'Italia.* (From the window on the left you will see the Po, the largest river in Italy) The names of cities, nations, regions, and fruits are usually feminine because the corresponding Italian words—*città, nazione, regione,* and *frutta*—are all feminine: *La Francia è una nazione leader nell'industria aerospaziale.* (France is a leader in the aerospace industry.)

20. *Il Corriere della Sera,* published in Milan, is one of the most widely read newspapers in Italy. Other popular dailies include *La Stampa* (Turin), *il Giorno* (Milan), *La Repubblica* (Rome and Milan), *La Nazione* (Florence), *Il Messaggero* (Rome), *Il Tempo* (Rome), and *Il Mattino* (Naples).

21. Notice that "in two hours" can be translated as *fra due ore* or *in due ore,* depending on context. To indicate when an action will take place, use *fra;* to indicate the duration of an action, use *in.* Compare: *L'aereo parte fra due ore.* (The plane leaves in two hours.) *Hanno finito il lavoro in due ore.* (They finished the job in two hours, i.e., it took two hours of work to complete the job.)

22. The Italian equivalent for the possessive -'s or -s' is *di: Leonardo da Vinci è l'aeroporto di Roma.* (Leonardo da Vinci is Rome's airport.) For more on possessives, see *Grammatica e suoi usi, Lezione 3.*

23. Rome's Leonardo da Vinci International Airport at Fiumicino is ranked fourth in Europe in number of passengers served.

C. GRAMMATICA E SUOI USI
(Grammar and Usage)

1. *IL GENERE E IL NUMERO DEI NOMI*
(THE GENDER AND NUMBER OF NOUNS)

All Italian nouns have gender. Nouns ending in -*o* are generally masculine and form their plural in -*i* *(biglietto, biglietti; aeroporto, aeroporti);* those ending in -*a* are usually feminine and form their plural in -*e* *(ditta, ditte; partenza, partenze);* those ending in -*e* can be either masculine or feminine and must be learned on a case by case basis. They form their plural in -*i*.

	SINGULAR	PLURAL
MASC.	-*o*	-*i*
MASC./FEM.	-*e*	-*i*
FEM.	-*a*	-*e*

Da New York ci sono sette voli settimanali.
From New York there are seven flights a week.

Potrei vedere queste cravatte blu?
May I see these blue ties?

Gli assistenti di volo dell'Alitalia sono molto preparati.
Alitalia's flight attendants are well trained.

Some nouns undergo spelling changes during plural formation. Here are the most common patterns:

a) Feminine nouns ending in -*ca* and -*ga* form their plural in -*che* and -*ghe:*

bank	*banca*	*banche*	banks
ruler	*riga*	*righe*	rulers

b) Masculine nouns ending in *-go* form their plural in *-ghi*.

lake	*lago*	*laghi*	lakes
magician	*mago*	*maghi*	magicians

c) Masculine nouns that end in *-ologo* and indicate a profession form their plural in *-ologi*.

psychologist	*psicologo*	*psicologi*	psychologists
biologist	*biologo*	*biologi*	biologists

d) Masculine nouns ending in *-co* form their plural in *-ci* or in *-chi* according to the following pattern: if *-co* is preceded by *-e* or *-i,* the plural ends in *-ci;* otherwise the plural ends in *-chi*.

friend	*amico*	*amici*	friends
Greeks	*greco*	*greci*	Greeks
desk	*banco*	*banchi*	desks
fire	*fuoco*	*fuochi*	fires

e) Nouns ending in *-io, -cia, -gia* will drop the *-i* in the plural form unless it is stressed.

UNSTRESSED *-I*

piece of luggage	*bagaglio*	*bagagli*	luggage
province	*provincia*	*province*	provinces
beach	*spiaggia*	*spiagge*	beaches

STRESSED *-I*

uncle	*zio*	*zii*	uncles
pharmacy	*farmacia*	*farmacie*	pharmacies
lie	*bugia*	*bugie*	lies

Nouns ending in *-i, -ie,* or an accented vowel are generally feminine and are invariable in the plural.

series	*la serie*	*le serie*	series
crisis	*la crisi*	*le crisi*	crises
company	*la società*	*le società*	companies

Nouns of one syllable are invariable in the plural.

tea	*il tè*	*i tè*	teas
king	*il re*	*i re*	kings
crane	*la gru*	*le gru*	cranes

Foreign words do not change in the plural.

computer	*il computer*	*i computer*	computers
film	*il film*	*i film*	films

Puoi cambiare i soldi ad una delle banche dell'aeroporto.
You can exchange money at one of the banks at the airport.

I miei amici arrivano stasera con il volo delle sei.
My friends arrive tonight on the six o'clock flight.

Due caffè e due tè, per favore.
Two coffees and two teas, please.

Note also the following irregular plurals: *moglie → mogli; uomo → uomini.*

Molti uomini d'affari viaggiano in prima classe.
Many businessmen travel first class

Ecco Carlo e Ivo con le loro mogli.
Here are Charles and Ivo with their wives.

2. *GLI ARTICOLI* (ARTICLES)

Italian articles agree with the nouns to which they refer in gender and number. The spelling of the word they precede also determines which form to use according to the following pattern:

	SINGULAR		PLURAL	
	DEFINITE	INDEFINITE	DEFINITE	INDEFINITE
Masculine:				
before most consonants	*il*	*un*	*i*	*dei*
before *s* + consonant,	*lo*	*uno*	*gli*	*degli*
z-, ps-, pn-, gn-, i + vowel				
before vowels	*l'*	*un*	*gli*	*degli*
Feminine:				
before consonants	*la*	*una*	*le*	*delle*
before vowels	*l'*	*un'*	*le*	*delle*

Remember that *lo/uno* and *gli/degli* are used not only with words that begin with a *z-* or an *s* + consonant, but also with words beginning with *ps-, pn-, gn-,* and *i* + vowel. For the forms *ps-, pn-,* and *gn-*, however, the use of *il/un* and *i/dei* is becoming more accepted: *il psicologo, dei gnocchi.*

Il passeggero ha perso una valigia e uno zaino e vorrebbe presentare un reclamo.
> The passenger lost a suitcase and a knapsack and he would like to file a claim.

Gli assistenti di volo cominceranno a servire il pranzo fra quindici minuti.
> The flight attendants will begin serving dinner in fifteen minutes.

Gli aeroporti italiani sono molto sicure.
> Italian airports are very safe.

Remember that the form of the article is determined by the word immediately following it, which may not always be a noun. Compare:

l'aeroporto di Roma
> Rome's airport

il bell'aeroporto di Roma
Rome's beautiful airport

In a list, the article is often used before each item, but it is not mandatory. It does not make any difference if the items are singular or plural.

Ecco il biglietto, il passaporto, gli scontrini per i bagagli e la carta d'imbarco.
Here is the ticket, the passport, the luggage tags, and the boarding pass.

Nella boutique troverà profumi, abbigliamento, liquori e tante altre cose.
In the boutique you'll find perfumes, clothing, liquor, and many other things.

When a noun follows *parlare, studiare,* or *insegnare,* the article is often used but is not mandatory.

Gli agenti dell'Alitalia parlano (l')italiano molto bene.
Alitalia's agents speak Italian very well.

The definite article is required with titles preceding last names, when referring to someone in the third person. When addressing someone directly, the article is omitted.

Il signor Sullivan arriva domani.
Mr. Sullivan arrives tomorrow.

Signor Sullivan, c'è un volo sabato.
Mr. Sullivan, there is a flight this Saturday.

The definite article is required with dates, seasons, and the time. It is used with days of the week only to indicate that something regularly occurs on a particular day.

C'è un volo il 12 maggio alle tre e mezzo.
There is a flight on May 12 at three thirty.

La primavera è la migliore stagione per andare in Italia.
Spring is the best season to go to Italy.

Sabato il volo è stato cancellato a causa di uno sciopero dei controllori di volo.
> The flight on Saturday was canceled due to an air-traffic controllers strike.

Il mercoledì non ci sono voli per Milano.
> There are no flights to Milan on Wednesdays.

Contrary to English, the definite article is required with the adjectives *prossimo* (next) and *scorso* (last).

Da quanto tempo manchi dall'Italia? —Dall'anno scorso.
> How long have you been away from Italy? —Since last year.

Noi partiamo il mese prossimo perché possiamo usufruire dei prezzi di bassa stagione.
> We'll leave next month because we can take advantage of off-peak fares.

The definite article is required with the names of countries, regions, states, provinces, rivers, mountains, lakes, continents, oceans, colors, newspapers, as well as the names of some islands.

Secondo un sondaggio del Corriere della sera, *la Sicilia è la più bella regione d'Italia.*
> According to a survey by the *Corriere della sera,* Sicily is the most beautiful region of Italy.

L'Italia è tra le sette nazioni più industrializzate del mondo.
> Italy is among the seven most industrialized nations in the world.

Il verde è il colore della speranza.
> Green is the color of hope.

The definite article is required with possessive adjectives and pronouns, except with singular nouns denoting family members.

Mio fratello mi ha dato il suo computer portatile per il mio viaggio.
> My brother gave me his laptop for my trip.

Mia cugina è una hostess dell'Alitalia.
> My cousin is an Alitalia hostess.

The definite article is required with abstract nouns and "general" statements.

Gli assistenti di volo si vestono sempre alla moda.
Flight attendants always dress fashionably.

L'amore è cieco.
Love is blind.

3. *LA POSIZIONE E L'ACCORDO DEGLI AGGETTIVI* (THE POSITION AND AGREEMENT OF ADJECTIVES)

In Italian an adjective generally follows the noun it modifies* and always agrees with it in gender and number. Adjective endings are the same as those for nouns. Note, however, that the ending of the adjective may not necessarily match the ending of the noun it modifies, e.g., *un aeroporto internazionale* (an international airport).

	SINGULAR	PLURAL
MASC.	*-o*	*-i*
MASC./FEM.	*-e*	*-i*
FEM.	*-a*	*-e*

Gli articoli elencati sono in vendita solo sui voli internazionali.
The products listed are for sale only on international fights.

Accettiamo anche bancanote estere.
We also accept foreign currency.

Sua madre è una signora molto gentile.
His mother is a very kind lady.

Il signor Anderson lavora per una ditta americana.
Mr. Anderson works for an American firm.

La settimana prossima Carlo va in Italia.
Next week Carlo is going to Italy.

* Some very common adjectives such as *buono, grande, santo, brutto,* and *caro* can be placed before or after the noun but their meaning may vary. We will introduce these adjectives in *Lezione 7.*

La nostra compagnia ha appena comprato due computer portatili.
    Our firm has just bought two laptops.

Remember that when more than one adjective modifies the same noun, one adjective generally precedes the noun, and the others follow it.

Signor Bonetti, Le abbiamo prenotato una bellissima camera elegante e spaziosa in uno stupendo albergo medievale.
    Mr. Bonetti, we reserved for you a beautiful, elegant, and spacious room in a stupendous, medieval hotel.

If an adjective modifies two nouns of different gender, then the masculine plural form must be used.

Carlo e Luisa sono molto alti.
    Carlo and Luisa are very tall.

The adjectives *blu, rosa,* and *viola* are invariable.

Vorrei vedere quelle cravatte blu.
    I would like to see those blue ties.

Numeric, possessive, demonstrative, and indefinite adjectives precede the noun.

Nella lista d'attesa ci sono solo quattro persone prima di Lei.
    There are only four people ahead of you on the waiting list.

Mi dispiace, ma questo è il mio posto.
    I'm sorry but this is my seat.

Questo aeroplano è un Boeing 747.
    This airplane is a Boeing 747.

C'è un altro volo Roma-New York nel pomeriggio?
    Is there another Rome-New York flight in the afternoon?

Whenever an adjective is preceded by an adverb such as *molto* (very), *troppo* (too), *poco* (a little), or *tanto* (too), it must follow the noun.

Questo è un aereo molto veloce.
    This is a very fast plane.

Questo è un film troppo violento.
This film is too violent.

4. *IL PRESENTE INDICATIVO* (THE PRESENT INDICATIVE)

Italian verbs are divided into three groups, according to their infinitive endings: *-are, -ere,* and *-ire.* To form the present indicative of regular verbs* simply drop the infinitive ending and add the appropriate personal ending to the stem (e.g., *parlare → parl → parlo*). Note that there are two different models for conjugating *-ire* verbs (one with an extra *-isc-* syllable** and one without). There is no way to determine which is appropriate simply by looking at the infinitive. Instead, the correct conjugation pattern must be learned on a case by case basis. Following are four model regular verbs.

	LAVORARE	VEDERE	PARTIRE	FINIRE
io	*lavoro*	*vedo*	*parto*	*finisco*
tu	*lavori*	*vedi*	*parti*	*finisci*
lui/lei/Lei	*lavora*	*vede*	*parte*	*finisce*
noi	*lavoriamo*	*vediamo*	*partiamo*	*finiamo*
voi	*lavorate*	*vedete*	*partite*	*finite*
loro/Loro	*lavorano*	*vedono*	*partono*	*finiscono*

Tu capisci l'italiano?—Sì, lo capisco, lo leggo e lo parlo molto bene.
Do you understand Italian?—Yes, I understand it, read it, and speak it very well.

Il signor Townsend arriva all'aeroporto di Roma. Scende dall'aereo e sale in un autobus.
Mr. Townsend arrives at Rome's airport. He gets off the plane and gets on a bus.

---

* For the conjugation of irregular verbs, including *essere* (to be), *avere* (to have), *dire* (to say), *sapere* (to know), *fare* (to do, to make), *dare* (to give), *venire* (to come), *andare* (to go), *bere* (to drink), *dovere* (to have to), *potere* (to be able to), *volere* (to want), *piacere* (to like), *tenere* (to keep, to hold), *rimanere* (to stay, to remain), and *uscire* (to go out), please refer to verb charts in Appendix C.
** Some very common verbs conjugated with *-isc-* include: *capire* (to understand), *chiarire* (to clarify), *finire* (to finish), *preferire* (to prefer), *pulire* (to clean), *sostituire* (to substitute), *spedire* (to mail), and *ubbidire* (to obey). For a complete list, please refer to Appendix C, section 3.

Stabiliscono rapporti d'affari con società italiane.
They are establishing business relationships with some Italian companies.

Some regular verbs undergo spelling changes in conjugation. Following are the most common.

Verbs ending in *-care* and *-gare* add an *-h-* in the second person singular and in the first person plural forms in order to retain the hard *c* and *g* sounds.

Da quanto tempo manchi dall'Italia?
How long have you been away from Italy?

Oggi paghiamo noi il conto!
Today, we will pay the bill!

Verbs ending in *-ciare, -giare, -gliare,* and *-sciare* generally drop the final *i* from the stem in the second person singular and the first person plural forms.

Noi viaggiamo per affari.
We travel for business purposes.

Ogni primo lunedì del mese ci svegliamo alle cinque perché dobbiamo prendere il volo Roma-Milano delle sette.
Every first Monday of the month we get up at five to make the seven o'clock flight from Rome to Milan.

However, some verbs ending in *-iare* retain the double *-i* in the second person singular form if that vowel is stressed.

Invii tu il fax al signor Giannini?
Will you send the fax to Mr. Giannini?

The present indicative is used to describe an action in the present and translates into English as "I speak," "I am speaking," or "I do speak." The present indicative can also be used:

a) to express an immediate future action.

Mi fermo in Italia circa un mese.
I'll stay in Italy about a month.

Quando mi sveglio, mi faccio sentire io.
When I wake up, I'll call you.

b) to express an action that began in the past but continues in the present. The verb is then followed by *da* or introduced by *sono/è* + time expression + *che.*

Manco dall'Italia da due anni.
I have been away from Italy for two years.

È un anno che aspetto di fare questo viaggio in Italia.
I have been waiting one year for this trip to Italy.

Sono dieci minuti che è partito l'aereo.
The plane left ten minutes ago.

c) to render more vivid and immediate a past event, a historical fact, or a story.

Nel 1492 Colombo scopre l'America.
In 1492 Columbus discovered America.

Il principe vede Cenerentola e se ne innamora.
The prince saw Cinderella and fell in love.

D. PAROLE! PAROLE! PAROLE!
(Words! Words! Words!)

Even in your native language you may sometimes have trouble remembering a word. If it happens in Italian you can say:

Ce l'ho proprio sulla (punta della) lingua!
It's on the tip of my tongue!

La parola non mi viene in mente.
The word doesn't come to mind.

Non ricordo la parola.
I do not remember the word.

In questo momento mi sfugge la parola.
At this moment the word escapes me.

Here are other examples of words or expressions that help smooth out a conversation.

Dunque . . . come dicevo prima . . . è importante confermare la partenza.
So, as I was saying, it is important to confirm your departure.

Allora . . . allora . . . quando parte l'aereo?
So, when is the airplane leaving?

Allora, ti aspettiamo questa estate in Italia? —Beh . . . forse . . . non so . . . vediamo . . .
So, will we be seeing you this summer in Italy? —Well . . . maybe . . . I don't know . . . we'll see . . .

Ho fatto un viaggio fantastico e ho dormito come . . . come . . . come un angelo.
I had a fantastic trip and I slept like . . . you know . . . like a baby!

All'aeroporto ho chiesto a un . . . um! . . . come si chiama/dice in italiano? . . . a un portabagagli di aiutarmi con le valige . . .
At the airport I asked a . . . um . . . what's the word in Italian? . . . a porter to help me with the suitcases.

E. L'ANGOLO DEGLI AFFARI (Business Corner)

QUADRO PANORAMICO DELL'ITALIA (FACTS ABOUT ITALY)

The republic of Italy is a peninsula in southern Europe that extends into the central Mediterranean Sea. It spans an area of 116,303 square kilometers. Its terrain is mostly rugged and mountainous, with some plains and coastal lowlands. Its climate is predominantly Mediterranean in the Southern areas and alpine in its northern regions. It is comprised of twenty regions, and its capital is *Roma* (Rome). Other major cities include *Milano* (Milan), *Torino* (Turin), *Venezia* (Venice), *Genova* (Genoa), *Firenze* (Florence), *Napoli* (Naples), and *Palermo*.

Italy has a population of close to 60 million and low population growth. Italy was traditionally homogenous, with 98% of the population being of Italian origin and having Italian as its native language. The remaining 2% comprised small groups of German-, French-, Slovene-, and Albanian-Italians. In recent times, Italy has experienced waves of immigration from African and Eastern European countries. The principal religion is Roman Catholicism. The literacy rate is high at 98%. The lira is the official currency.

Italy has few natural resources. Much of the land is unsuitable for farming. As a consequence, the country is a net food importer. There are no substantial deposits of iron, coal, or oil. Exploitation of natural gas reserves, mainly in the Po Valley and offshore in the Adriatic, has increased in recent years and constitutes the country's most important mineral resource. Most raw materials needed for manufacturing, and more than 80% of the country's energy sources, are imported. Italy's economic strength is in the processing and manufacturing of goods, primarily in small, family-owned firms. Its major industries are precision machinery, motor vehicles, chemicals, pharmaceuticals, electrical goods, and fashion and clothing.

The Italian economy has changed dramatically since the end of World War II, from an agriculturally based economy to an industrial one. Italy is a member of the UE or *Unione Europea* (the EU or European Union) as well as the OECD, the Organization for Economic Cooperation and Development.

Italy is the United States' fourth largest trading partner in Western Europe, with office machinery and aircraft being the principal U.S. exports to Italy. Among the United States' primary imports from Italy are garments, leather goods, furniture, and precision machinery. (For more information on Italian industry and trade, please see the *Angolo degli affari* of *Lezione 13*.)

The growing trade relationship between Italy and the United States has potential for further development. Italians are, by far, Europe's best savers, and they are enjoying a period of newly acquired wealth. U.S. businesses selling in Italy should concentrate on high added-value, high-quality products, which are less vulnerable to exchange rate variations, and ensure a long-term commitment on the part of the importer. The ongoing liberalization of exchange controls should allow easier payment terms for Italian importers.

ESERCIZI

A. *Completare con l'articolo determinativo e volgere al plurale.* (Fill in the blanks with the appropriate definite article; then write the plural form of each article and noun.)

il 1. *un* biolog *o* _____ (masc.) _____

  2. _____ sportell _____ _____

il 3. *un* compute *r* _____ _____

il 4. *un* lag *o* _____ _____

lo 5. *un'* amic *o* _____ (masc.) _____

la 6. *una* societ *à* _____ _____

lo 7. *un* psicolog *o* _____ (masc.) _____

la 8. *una* banc *a* _____ (fem.) _____

il 9. *un* grec *o* _____ (masc.) _____

il 10. *un* fuoc *o* _____ _____

  11. _____ bagagli _____ _____

  12. _____ valig _____ _____

  13. _____ bugi _____ _____

  14. *la* *une* seri *e* _____ _____

  15. _____ cris _____ _____

B. *Completare in modo opportuno.* (Fill in the blanks appropriately.)

1. *Il* signo *re* _____ Paolo Rossi, rappresentant *e* _____ di _____ ditt *a* _____ american *a* _____, telefon *a* _____ all'ufficio Alitalia.

2. Vorrei fare *una* prenotazion *e* _____ per Roma.

3. Devo partire *il* *della* mes *e* _____ prossim *o* _____. Vorrei restare in Italia *il* *del* mes *e* _____. *almeno un mese.*

4. Signorin *a* _____, mi prenoti *un* post *o* _____ per *il* 16 maggio, *molte*

5. Ci sono *dei* post *e* _____ liber *i* _____ per *il* 24 aprile?

6. Che tip *o* _____ di aere *o* _____ è? *Un'* Airbus?

7. Ecco *il* bigliett *o* _____, *il* passaport *o* _____, *i* scontrini e *il* cart *e* _____ d'imbarco.

8. Con me ho anche _____ mio computer portatil _____.

9. _____ attimo di attenzion _____, per cortesi _____.

10. Siete pregati di mettere _____ schienale in posizion _____ vertical _____.

C. *Completare le seguenti frasi usando il presente indicativo di uno dei verbi elencati.* (Choosing from the following list, fill in the blanks with the present indicative of the appropriate verb.)

pagare	*parlare*	*partire*	*ricordare*
vedere	*preferire*	*viaggiare*	*dimenticare*

1. *Signorina, Lei _____ italiano?*
2. *Domani noi _____ per l'Italia.*
3. *Noi _____ sempre con la carta di credito.*
4. *Signori, come _____, questi articoli sono in vendita in questo negozio.*
5. *Loro _____ viaggiare con l'Alitalia.*
6. *Ma tu _____ sempre con l'American Airlines?*
7. *Tu _____ sempre di confermare il tuo volo.*
8. *Io non _____ come si chiama l'aeroporto di Roma.*

D. *Tradurre.* (Translate.)

1. Mr. Verdi, is there a flight tomorrow? —No, there is a flight next month, on August 2.
2. When are you leaving for Italy? —I am leaving in five days.
3. Will you phone Diana tonight? —No, I will phone her Saturday.
4. Which Italian magazine do you like to read? —I like *L'Espresso* and *Panorama.*
5. Is there a flight to Milan tomorrow? —No, there are no flights to Milan on Mondays.
6. Is it true that Sicily is the most beautiful region in Italy?
7. We have reserved for Mr. Giannini a beautiful and elegant room in a stupendous medieval hotel.
8. I would like to see those blue ties, please.
9. What's the word in English for *"decollo"*? —Well . . . it is . . . I'm sorry, but the word isn't coming to me either. Wait, I remember now. It's "take-off."
10. We have to hurry up! We have to be at the airport at 5:00. Departure is at 6:00, and it's already 4:30.

LEZIONE 2

A. DIALOGO

DALL'AEROPORTO ALL'ALBERGO

Il signor Townsend arriva all'aeroporto Linate di Milano. Scende dall'aereo e sale su un autobus che lo porta all'aerostazione. Si mette in fila[1] davanti allo sportello "controllo passaporti."

FINANZIERE: **Buon giorno. Il passaporto, prego.[2]**

VINCE TOWNSEND: **Eccolo.**

FINANZIERE: **Qual è[3] lo scopo del Suo viaggio? È in Italia in vacanza?**

VINCE TOWNSEND: **No, è un viaggio d'affari.**

FINANZIERE: **Quanto tempo pensa di fermarsi in Italia?**

VINCE TOWNSEND: **Circa un mese.** *indiret formal*

FINANZIERE: **Bene. EccoLe i documenti. ArrivederLa.**

Il signor Townsend ritira i bagagli e va a passare la dogana.[4]

DOGANIERE: **Buon giorno. Quanti bagagli ha?**

VINCE TOWNSEND: **Ho due valige e una borsa a mano. Qui dentro c'è il computer.**

DOGANIERE: **Che cos'ha da dichiarare?**

VINCE TOWNSEND: **Una stecca di sigarette.**

DOGANIERE: **Soltanto una?**

VINCE TOWNSEND: **Sì.**

DOGANIERE: **Viaggia da solo?[5]**

VINCE TOWNSEND: **Sì, sono qui in viaggio d'affari.**

DOGANIERE: **Bene. Buona permanenza in Italia.**

VINCE TOWNSEND: **Grazie. ArrivederLa.**

29

All'uscita della dogana incontra il suo amico e collega[6] Paolo Giannini. I due si salutano e si abbracciano.[7]

PAOLO GIANNINI: **Ciao, Vincenzo. Benvenuto in Italia. Come stai?**

VINCE TOWNSEND: **Benone.[8] E tu come stai? Che bello rivederti![9]**

PAOLO GIANNINI: **Finalmente ci vediamo. Da quanto tempo manchi dall'Italia?**

VINCE TOWNSEND: **Ci manco da due anni. Allora, hai ricevuto il mio fax?**

PAOLO GIANNINI: **Sì, l'ho ricevuto proprio[10] ieri. È anche arrivato il tuo pacco con tutto il campionario. Allora, hai fatto un buon viaggio?**

VINCE TOWNSEND: **Sì. Fortunatamente, il volo è partito in orario ed[11] è arrivato in orario. A bordo ho fatto molto lavoro. Ho scritto qualche[12] lettera e mi sono organizzato il programma per la settimana. E per di più, mi sono fatto una bella dormitina.**

PAOLO GIANNINI: **Nessun problema in dogana?**

VINCE TOWNSEND: **No, no. Tutto è andato bene . . .**

PAOLO GIANNINI: **Queste sono le tue valige?[13]**

VINCE TOWNSEND: **Sì. Abbiamo bisogno di un portabagagli?[14]**

PAOLO GIANNINI: **No, ho qui un carrello.**

VINCE TOWNSEND: **Tu pensi sempre a tutto!**

PAOLO GIANNINI: **Allora andiamo alla macchina. Ti accompagno in albergo.**

Arrivano in albergo e il signor Townsend va al banco accettazione.

VINCE TOWNSEND: **Buon giorno! Ho prenotato una camera singola.**

IMPIEGATO: **Ha un documento?**

VINCE TOWNSEND: **Sì, ho il passaporto e la mia patente di guida.**

IMPIEGATO: **Mi dia il passaporto, per favore . . . Ah, il signor Townsend! Abbiamo per Lei una camera bellissima, spaziosa e** con tutti i comfort. E che veduta! Naturalmente la prima colazione è inclusa.[15]

VINCE TOWNSEND: Bene, grazie. Senta, è possibile chiamare in interurbana dalla mia camera?

IMPIEGATO: Certo. Troverà le istruzioni necessarie sul telefono stesso. Al secondo piano abbiamo anche sale riunioni con telefoni, fotocopiatrici, telefax, computer e servizi di segreteria a disposizione degli uomini d'affari.

VINCE TOWNSEND: Grazie delle informazioni. Vorrei chiederLe ancora una cortesia. Avrei bisogno di una spina per le prese italiane.[16] Potrebbe procurarmene una?

IMPIEGATO: Sì, senz'altro. Gliela faccio portare in camera.

VINCE TOWNSEND: Un'ultima cosa. Vorrei lasciare questi documenti nella cassaforte[17] dell'albergo. È possibile?

IMPIEGATO: Certamente. Ah, dimenticavo:[18] questo messaggio è per Lei.

VINCE TOWNSEND: Grazie.

IMPIEGATO: Prego. Questa è la chiave della camera e questa la chiave del frigo-bar. ArrivederLa.

VINCE TOWNSEND: Paolo, grazie di tutto.

PAOLO GIANNINI: Ma figurati![19]

VINCE TOWNSEND: Vuoi prendere qualcosa al bar?

PAOLO GIANNINI: No, no. Prima sistemati un po', poi possiamo vederci a cena.

VINCE TOWNSEND: Non vedo l'ora. Non mangio come si deve da ieri mattina!

PAOLO GIANNINI: E riposati!

VINCE TOWNSEND: Ti chiamo quando mi sveglio.

FROM THE AIRPORT TO THE HOTEL

Mr. Townsend arrives at Milan's Linate airport. He gets off the plane and gets on a bus that brings him to the terminal. He gets in line in front of the "passport control" window.

IMMIGRATION OFFICER: Good morning. Passport, please.

VINCE TOWNSEND: Here you go.

IMMIGRATION OFFICER: What is the purpose of your trip? Are you here on vacation?

VINCE TOWNSEND: No, I'm on a business trip.

IMMIGRATION OFFICER: How long are you thinking of staying in Italy?

VINCE TOWNSEND: Approximately one month.

IMMIGRATION OFFICER: Okay. Here are your documents. Goodbye.

Mr. Townsend gets his luggage and goes to customs.

CUSTOMS OFFICER: Good morning. How many bags do you have?

VINCE TOWNSEND: I have two suitcases and one carry-on bag. My computer is in here.

CUSTOMS OFFICER: Do you have anything to declare?

VINCE TOWNSEND: A carton of cigarettes.

CUSTOMS OFFICER: Only one?

VINCE TOWNSEND: Yes.

CUSTOMS OFFICER: Are you travelling alone?

VINCE TOWNSEND: Yes, I'm here on a business trip.

CUSTOMS OFFICER: Okay. Have a good stay in Italy.

VINCE TOWNSEND: Thank you. Goodbye.

At the customs exit, he meets his friend and colleague, Paolo Giannini. The two greet one another and hug.

PAOLO GIANNINI: Hello, Vincenzo. Welcome to Italy. How are you?

VINCE TOWNSEND: I'm okay. And you? It's so good to see you again.

PAOLO GIANNINI: We finally get to see each other again. How long have you been away from Italy?

VINCE TOWNSEND: I haven't been here in two years. Well then, did you receive my fax?

PAOLO GIANNINI: Yes, I just got it yesterday. Your package also arrived with all the samples. So then, did you have a nice trip?

VINCE TOWNSEND: Yes. Luckily, the flight left on time and arrived on time. I got a lot of work done on the plane. I wrote a few letters and organized my schedule for the week. Best of all, I had a nice nap.

PAOLO GIANNINI: And no problems at customs?

VINCE TOWNSEND: No, no. Everything went well . . .

PAOLO GIANNINI: Are these your bags?

VINCE TOWNSEND: Yes. Do we need a porter?

PAOLO GIANNINI: No, I got a cart.

VINCE TOWNSEND: You always think of everything!

PAOLO GIANNINI: Let's go to the car then. I'll take you to the hotel.

They arrive at the hotel, and Mr. Townsend goes to the reception desk.

VINCE TOWNSEND: Good morning! I reserved a single room.

HOTEL EMPLOYEE: Do you have any identification?

VINCE TOWNSEND: Yes, I have my passport and my driver's licence.

HOTEL EMPLOYEE: May I have the passport, please . . . Ah, Mr. Townsend! We have a lovely, spacious room for you with all the amenities. And just wait till you see the view! Breakfast is included, of course.

VINCE TOWNSEND: Great, thank you. Can I make long-distance calls from my room?

HOTEL EMPLOYEE: Certainly. You'll find all the necessary instructions on the telephone itself. On the second floor, we also have conference rooms with telephones, photocopy and fax machines, computers, and secretarial services available for the convenience of business travelers.

VINCE TOWNSEND: Thanks for the information. I would like to ask you another favor. I need an adaptor for the electrical outlet. Would you be able to get one for me?

HOTEL EMPLOYEE: Yes, of course. I'll have it brought to your room.

VINCE TOWNSEND: One last thing. I'd like to leave these documents in the hotel safe.

HOTEL EMPLOYEE: Of course. Ah, I almost forgot: this message is for you.

VINCE TOWNSEND: Thank you.

HOTEL EMPLOYEE: You're welcome. Here's your room key, and this is your mini-bar key. Bye for now.

VINCE TOWNSEND: Paolo, thanks for everything.

PAOLO GIANNINI: Don't mention it!

VINCE TOWNSEND: Would you like to have a drink at the bar?

PAOLO GIANNINI: No, no. I'll let you get settled in first and we can meet for dinner.

VINCE TOWNSEND: I'm looking forward to it. I haven't had a decent meal since yesterday morning!

PAOLO GIANNINI: And get some rest!

VINCE TOWNSEND: I'll call you when I wake up.

B. IN BREVE

1. *La fila* has two plural forms corresponding to two different meanings. The plural of *la fila,* meaning "line," is *le file*. *Al "Controllo passaporti" c'erano due file lunghissime di persone.* (At "Passport Control" there were two very long lines of people.) The irregular plural form *le fila* is used in the expression *le fila del discorso* (train of thought). *Cosa stavo dicendo? Tutto ad un tratto ho perso le fila del discorso.* (What was I saying? All of a sudden I lost my train of thought.)

2. *Prego* can mean "please" or "you're welcome." *Il passaporto, prego.* (Your passport, please.) *Grazie del passaggio.—Prego* (Thanks for the ride.—You're welcome.) It is commonly used in the expression *Prego, s'accomodi* which can mean "Please, make yourself comfort-

able/at home," "Please sit down," or "Please, come in." Finally, Italians say *prego* (After you!) when they allow someone to pass.

3. Note that *qual* never takes an apostrophe *(qual è, qual era)*.

4. At Rome's airport, the customs *(la dogana)* area is divided into two sections, one marked by a green arrow for passengers who have nothing to declare *(nulla da dichiarare)*, the other marked by a red arrow for passengers who have goods to declare *(merci da dichiarare)*.

5. There is no difference between *Viaggia da solo* (Are you traveling by yourself?) and *Viaggia solo?* (Are you traveling alone?)

6. *Collega* can be masculine or feminine *(il/la collega)*. The masculine plural form is *i colleghi* and the feminine is *le colleghe*.

7. A hug and a kiss are common forms of greeting among Italian men and women.

8. Compare with *benino* which means "pretty well." For more on suffixes, see *Grammatica e suoi usi, Lezione 11*.

9. The construction *che* + adjective + noun or *che* + noun/adjective is used to express surprise, admiration, or disgust. *Che bel panorama!* (What a beautiful view!) *Che spettacolo!* (What a show!) *Che ingiustizia!* (What an injustice!)

10. In addition to meaning "just, really," *proprio* can also be a possessive adjective meaning "one's own." *Farà del proprio meglio per venire alla riunione.* (He will do his best to come to the meeting.) For emphasis, it can be used in conjunction with other possessive adjectives. *L'ho visto con i miei propri occhi.* (I saw it with my own eyes.)

11. The letter *d* may be added to the conjunction *e* or *o* and to the preposition *a* if the following word begins with a vowel: *Gianni ed Elena non hanno telefonato.* (John and Helen didn't phone). *Va giù ad aprire!* (Go down and open the door!).

12. *Qualche* and *alcuni/e* both mean "some," but *qualche* is always followed by a singular noun and *alcuni/e* always takes a plural noun.

Al duty free ho comprato qualche regalo per la mia famiglia. (At the duty-free shop I bought some gifts for my family.) *Alcuni passeggeri sono arrivati all'aeroporto dieci minuti prima della partenza.* (Some of the passengers arrived at the airport ten minutes before take-off.)

13. The plural of *valigia* may be spelled *valige* or, less commonly, *valigie.*

14. Another word for *portabagagli* is *facchino. Hai dato la mancia al facchino?* (Did you give the porter a tip?)

15. A typical Italian *colazione* (breakfast) includes coffee (*cappuccino, caffellatte, espresso,* or *caffè macchiato*) and a pastry *(brioche, cornetto, pasta).*

16. Italian voltage is generally 220V AC 50Hz, and occasionally 115–125V. Some cities, like Rome, have both. It is best to check the current before you plug in your appliance.

17. Note that the plural of *cassaforte* is *casseforti.*

18. *Dimenticavo* is here equivalent to "I almost forgot." Compare: *Ho dimenticato le chiavi della macchina a casa.* (I forgot the car keys at home.) *Quasi quasi dimenticavo di telefonargli.* (I almost forgot to phone him.)

19. *Figurati* is a common colloquial expression. Its translation varies according to context. *Mio figlio è contento perché gli ho comprato una bicicletta. Figurati se gli compravo una macchina!* (My son is happy because I bought him a bicycle. Just imagine if I had bought him a car!) *Ti dispiace se accendo la radio?—Figurati!* (Do you mind if I turn on the radio?—Of course not.)

C. GRAMMATICA E SUOI USI

1. *I VERBI PRONOMINALI* (PRONOMINAL VERBS)

In the infinitive, a pronominal verb ends in *-si*. It is conjugated like a regular verb, but it is always accompanied by an additional pronoun that corresponds to the subject.

	FERMARSI	*METTERSI*	*VESTIRSI*	*PULIRSI*
io	mi fermo	mi metto	mi vesto	mi pulisco
tu	ti fermi	ti metti	ti vesti	ti pulisci
lui/lei/Lei	si ferma	si mette	si veste	si pulisce
noi	ci fermiamo	ci mettiamo	ci vestiamo	ci puliamo
voi	vi fermate	vi mettete	vi vestite	vi pulite
loro/Loro	si fermano	si mettono	si vestono	si puliscono

Si dirigono verso la zona doganale.
They go toward the customs area.

Ci fermiamo in Italia circa un mese.
We'll stay in Italy for about a month.

Il signor Townsend si mette in fila davanti allo sportello "controllo passaporti."
Mr. Townsend gets in line in front of the passport control window.

Mi rinfresco e mi riposo un po'. Quando mi sveglio, mi faccio sentire io.
I'll freshen up and I'll rest a while. When I wake up, I'll call you.

Ci vediamo stasera.
See you tonight. (lit.: We will see each other tonight.)

There are three categories of pronominal verbs (reflexive, reciprocal, and apparent reflexive verbs), but grammatically they all follow the same rules. A verb is called reflexive if the subject acts on itself (the subject is identical to the object): e.g., *lavarsi* (to wash), *vestirsi* (to get dressed). Reciprocal verbs convey the idea "(to) one another, (to) each other," and the subjects (always plural) act on each other: e.g., *amarsi* (to love each other), *conoscersi* (to know each other), *vedersi* (to see each other). Apparent reflexive verbs are reflexive only in grammatical form but not in meaning: e.g., *svegliarsi* (to wake up), *recarsi* (to go).

Quando viaggio mi metto sempre la giacca sportiva e un paio di jeans.
When I travel I always wear my sports jacket and a pair of jeans.

Mia moglie ed io ci siamo conosciuti durante un viaggio aereo in Italia. Mi sono innamorato di lei a prima vista.
My wife and I met on a flight to Italy. I fell in love with her at first sight.

Ci siamo recati in Belgio per una conferenza.
We went to Belgium for a conference.

A few verbs such as *dimenticare* (to forget) and *ricordare* (to remember) have a reflexive and a non-reflexive form with the same meaning.

Io (mi) dimentico sempre di telefonarti.
I always forget to phone you.

(Ti) ricordi dove abita Maria?
Do you remember where Maria lives?

With modal verbs *(dovere, potere, volere)* the reflexive pronoun can either precede the conjugated verb or be attached as a suffix to the infinitive.

Carlo, ti devi sbrigare perché è tardi.
Carlo, devi sbrigarti perché è tardi.
Carlo, you must hurry up because it is late.

Mamma, mi puoi svegliare alle cinque?
Mamma, puoi svegliarmi alle cinque?
Mom, can you wake me up at five?

2. *IL PASSATO PROSSIMO* (THE PRESENT PERFECT)

The present perfect *(passato prossimo)* is used to indicate a completed action and translates into English as "I have spoken", "I spoke", or "I did speak." It is formed with the present tense of *avere* or *essere* and the past participle of the main verb. Remember that the past participle of verbs conjugated with *essere* always agrees in gender and number with the subject. When a verb is conjugated with *avere*, the past participle usually remains unchanged.* Regular past participles are formed by dropping the infinitive *-are, -ere,* or *-ire* ending and replacing it with *-ato, -uto,* and *-ito,* respectively (e.g., *parlare > parl<u>ato</u>; credere > cred<u>uto</u>; dormire > dorm<u>ito</u>).* * *

	LAVORARE	ANDARE
io	ho lavorato	sono andato/a
tu	hai lavorato	sei andato/a
lui/lei/Lei	ha lavorato	è andato/a
noi	abbiamo lavorato	siamo andati/e
voi	avete lavorato	siete andati/e
loro/Loro	hanno lavorato	sono andati/e

Most verbs require the auxiliary *avere.*

Ti ho mandato i nuovi campionari.
    I sent you the new samples.

Ho prenotato una camera singola.
    I reserved a single room.

A bordo io ho conosciuto un uomo d'affari americano.
    On the plane I met an American businessman.

Noi abbiamo telefonato a Marco e gli abbiamo dato il numero del volo e l'orario d'arrivo.
    We phoned Marco and gave him the flight number and the arrival time.

Loro hanno ritirato i bagagli prima di passare la dogana.
    They got their bags before going to customs.

Verbs that require the auxiliary *essere* include:

a) intransitive verbs that relate to motion: *andare, venire, uscire, arrivare, entrare,* etc., as well as the verb *stare.*

---

* For agreement of the participle with direct object pronouns, please refer to *Grammatica e suoi usi, Lezione 4.*
** For irregular past participles, see Appendix C, section 5.

Il volo è partito in orario ed è arrivato in orario.
   The flight left and arrived on time.

Alla dogana tutto è andato bene.
   At customs everything went well.

Sono già stato in questo hotel e le tariffe erano ragionevoli.
   I've stayed at this hotel before and the rates were reasonable.

   b) pronominal verbs.

A bordo non mi sono affatto annoiato, anzi mi sono divertito.
   On the plane I did not get bored at all; as a matter of fact I had a good
   time.

   c) verbs that relate to psychological or physical processes: *nascere* (to
   be born), *arrossire* (to blush), *impazzire* (to go crazy), *dimagrire* (to
   become thin), *invecchiare* (to grow old), etc.

Mia figlia è nata nel 1985.
   My daughter was born in 1985.

   d) all linking verbs (i.e., verbs that simply link a subject with a predi-
   cate): *essere, sembrare* (to seem), *apparire* (to appear), *diventare* (to
   become), etc.

Il viaggio mi è sembrato corto.
   The trip seemed short to me.

   e) the verb *piacere,* and other verbs that follow the same grammatical
   structure (sometimes referred to as "indirect object verbs"): *mancare,
   costare,* etc. (see *Lezione 6*).

Le cravatte mi sono piaciute, ma erano troppo costose.
   I liked the ties, but they were too expensive.

I miei bambini mi sono mancati molto.
   I missed my kids a lot.

f) verbs used in their passive form.

La partita è stata vinta dall'Italia.
    The game was won by Italy.

Some verbs can be conjugated with either *essere* or *avere,* depending
on the function of the verb: The verbs *finire, cominciare, aumentare,*
guarire, scendere, salire, maturare, and *terminare* are conjugated with
avere when they take a direct object, and with *essere* if they do not.
Compare:

Gianni ha cominciato il lavoro.
    Gianni started the job.

Il lavoro è cominciato ieri.
    The job started yesterday.

Note that when these verbs are followed by a preposition + infinitive,
they take *avere.*

Abbiamo finito di lavorare.
    We finished working.

Ho cominciato a studiare.
    I started studying.

Some action verbs, like *correre* and *saltare,* are usually conjugated with
avere, but take *essere* when they indicate the direction of the movement
(i.e., from one place towards another).

Ho corso due ore.
    I ran for two hours.

Siamo corsi all'aeroporto.
    We rushed to the airport.

Certain verbs can be conjugated with both *essere* or *avere.* There are
no rules to identify them. Here are some of the most common: *nevi-*
care (to snow), *piovere* (to rain), *tuonare* (to thunder), *grandinare* (to
hail), *decollare* (to take off), *atterrare* (to land), *durare* (to last), *vivere*
(to live), *squillare* (to ring), and *inciampare* (to stumble, to trip).

La riunione è durata tre ore e non abbiamo concluso niente.
La riunione ha durato tre ore e non abbiamo concluso niente.
   The meeting lasted three hours and we accomplished nothing.

È piovuto tutto il giorno e Giovanna aveva paura di prendere l'aereo.
Ha piovuto tutto il giorno e Giovanna aveva paura di prendere l'aereo.
   It rained all day and Giovanna was afraid to take the plane.

   Modal verbs *(dovere, potere, volere)* that introduce an infinitive take
   the auxiliary required by the infinitive. Compare:

Il presidente della ditta ha voluto incontrare tutti gli impiegati.
   The company president wanted to meet all his employees.

Io sono voluto andare a Milano un paio di giorni prima dell'inizio dell'esposizione.
   I wanted to go to Milan a few days before the start of the exhibition.

   In current spoken Italian, however, the auxiliary *avere* may be used in
   both cases.

3. *LA PREPOSIZIONE DA* (THE PREPOSITION *DA*)

   The preposition *da* generally means "from." *Da dove viene il vostro rappresentante di vendita?* (Where is your sales representative from?)
   However, it can also be used:

   a) with a person's name, a pronoun, or a noun that refers to a person
   to indicate "at the house of," "at the office of," "at the restaurant of,"
   etc.

Si è fermato dall'avvocato per discutere la vendita della casa.
   He stopped off at the lawyer's office to discuss the sale of the house.

Domani vado dal dentista.
   Tomorrow I'm going to the dentist.

Sono da Paolo.
   I'm at Paolo's house.

b) to indicate what something is used for.

Poche persone usano ancora la macchina da scrivere.
Few people still use the typewriter.

Ho messo la crema da barba nella borsa a mano.
I put the shaving cream in the carry-on bag.

c) before an infinitive to indicate necessity or purpose.

Ho un sacco di lavoro da finire.
I have a lot of work to finish.

Non abbiamo tempo da perdere oggi perché abbiamo due riunioni.
We don't have time to waste today because we have two meetings.

Ho tutti questi campioni da distribuire.
I have all these samples to distribute.

d) following *qualcosa, niente, nulla, molto, poco, troppo,* and *tanto* to introduce an infinitive.

Mi dispiace, ma oggi non posso venire con te perché ho troppo da fare.
I'm sorry, but today I can not come with you because I have too much to do.

Ha qualcosa da dichiarare?
Do you have anything to declare?

Noi non abbiamo niente da dirci.
We have nothing to say to each other.

e) to indicate a place of origin.

Non capiva le nostre usanze perchè veniva dal Sud Africa.
He did not understand our customs because he came from South Africa.

f) with nouns and adjectives to denote age.

Da piccola accompagnavo spesso mio padre al lavoro.
When I was small often I accompanied my father to work.

43

Da bambino andavo sempre in Italia.
As a child, I always went to Italy.

g) to denote worth.

Mi hanno regalato un oggetto da poco.
They gave me something of little value.

h) in expressions of time to indicate how long an action has been going on.

I ricercatori cercano un nuovo vaccino da tre anni.
The researchers have been looking for a new vaccine for three years.

i) in past-tense statements to indicate an action that continued until a given point of time in the past.

L'aereo era già partito da dieci minuti quando sono arrivati all'aeroporto.
The plane had already left ten minutes before they arrived at the airport.

j) in the following adverbial expressions with *da: da lontano* (from far away), *da vicino* (from nearby), *da parte* (aside).

Ieri ho preso il cliente da parte e gli ho spiegato la procedura.
Yesterday I took the client aside and explained the procedure to him.

Da lontano quell'aereo sembra un giocattolo.
From afar that plane looks like a toy.

D. PAROLE! PAROLE! PAROLE!

In Italian, "to chat" is expressed by *fare due chiacchiere* or *fare quattro chiacchiere:*

Verremo a vederti per fare quattro chiacchiere.
We'll come to see you and have a chat.

Other similar expressions are *scambiare due/quattro parole* or simply *parlare un po'*.

Perché non vieni a trovarmi, così scambiamo quattro parole?
Why don't you come to see me so that we can chat?

Chiacchiera also has the meaning of "rumor."

Non è vero. È una chiacchiera.
It's not true. It is a rumor.

Note also the following expressions:

Mario è buono solo a chiacchiere.
Mario is only good at talking.

Loro si perdono sempre in chiacchiere.
They always waste time in idle chatter.

Poche chiacchiere: chi ha nascosto le chiavi della macchina?
Stop the nonsense: who hid the car keys?

E. L'ANGOLO DEGLI AFFARI

SPEDIZIONE E TRASPORTO MERCI
(TRANSPORT AND SHIPPING)

Italy's transportation infrastructure is very well developed. There are over 7,700 miles of railroad, almost 6,200 of which are state owned (*Ferrovia Statale* or *FS,* State Railroad). Most parts of the peninsula are also easily accessible by the almost 115,000 miles of highway. For transport by way of water, there are 925 miles of inland waterways for various kinds of commercial traffic.

As far as international transportation is concerned, Italy is easily reachable by sea as well as by air. The country's major *porti* (ports) are located at Cagliari (Sardinia), Genoa, La Spezia, Livorno, Naples, Palermo (Sicily), Taranto, Trieste, and Venice. As for air transportation, there are 137 airports in Italy. The country's two largest international airports are Rome's Fiumicino and Milan's Malpensa. However, during peak travel periods, international flights are routed to many smaller airports throughout the country, including Venice, Turin, Palermo, Naples, Cagliari, Bologna, Lamezia Terme, Rome's Ciampino, and Milan's Linate. Air transportation to Italy from the U.S. is offered by many major U.S. airlines, by Alitalia (Italy's official airline), and by many international airlines. While many destinations outside of major centers are not on the direct routes of major airlines, Alitalia and its affiliates provide adequate transportation between smaller cities and major airports, and between smaller centers.

When shipping from the U.S. to Italy, it is important to keep in mind that shipping by air is the most expensive method, and is usually recommended for cargo that is fairly compact and light, or extremely valuable. Typically, delivery time is around 72 hours or less. For large shipments, the best method of transport is by sea *(via marittima)*.

Container space aboard cargo ships is sold by specialized freight consolidators. Rates to Italy vary greatly, so it is prudent to compare prices. Prices may be calculated according to volume or mass. It is advisable to purchase insurance *(assicurazione)* for surface shipments; generally speaking, insurance rates are 0.5% of the value of the merchandise. For shipping and insurance purposes, it is also advisable to prepare a packing list (in English), describing the contents and value of each individual box. Be advised that consolidators will not ship to all Italian cities, but only to those with a customs office. Consequently, if you are shipping merchandise to a location a distance away from a customs office, you must make further arrangements to have your cargo transported via surface to its final destination. Remember that goods are the responsibility of the importer, not the shipping company. It is therefore important to plan well in advance to avoid delays, as there is generally a fee charged for goods left unclaimed at the point of arrival for a period usually exceeding three days.

Clearing customs *(la dogana)* in Italy is relatively hassle-free as long as all required documentation is in place. It is useful to consult an Italian consulate and the U.S. Chamber of Commerce well in advance of shipping a certain type of item to ensure that all necessary permits can be obtained before merchandise is transported to Italy. If all documentation is in order, clearing customs at the point of destination should take only a few days. In general, to ship merchandise to Italy and other countries belonging to the EU, one should prepare the following documents: a bill of lading or airway bill *(una polizza di carico)*, a certificate of origin *(un certificato di origine)*, and a commercial invoice *(una fattura)*. Certain goods, such as plants, animals, and produce, may require additional documents. For detailed information regarding the shipping of agricultural products, it is best to contact the U.S. foreign agricultural service.

To ensure proper handling of merchandise, you may want to label your shipments with one or more of the following terms, as is appropriate: *urgente* (urgent); *fragile* (fragile); *deperibile* (perishable); *non capovolgere* (this side up).

ESERCIZI

A. *Completare usando il presente indicativo di uno dei seguenti verbi.* (Choosing from the verbs listed below, complete each sentence using the present indicative.)

mettersi	*abbracciarsi*	*rinfrescarsi*	*tenersi*
riposarsi	*fermarsi*	*salutarsi*	*prepararsi*

1. *Voi quando _____ per il viaggio in Italia?*
2. *Loro _____ in fila davanti allo sportello "controllo passaporti."*
3. *Marco _____ in Italia due settimane.*
4. *Prima di partire Gianni e Teresa _____ e _____.*
5. *A bordo io _____ sempre impegnato: scrivo qualche lettera, leggo il giornale, lavoro con il computer, metto a posto le pratiche, chiacchiero con gli assistenti di volo . . .*
6. *Vado in camera. _____ e _____ un po'. Poi ti telefono io.*

B. *Completare usando il passato prossimo di uno dei seguenti verbi.* (Choosing from the verbs listed below, complete each sentence using the present perfect.)

salire	*arrivare*	*partire*	*piacere*	*viaggiare*
scrivere	*durare*	*costare*	*vedersi*	*fermarsi*
leggere	*andare*	*volere*	*dichiarare*	*scendere*

1. *Il volo _____ in orario ed _____ in orario.*
2. *Io _____ dall'aereo e _____ su un autobus.*
3. *Voi quanto tempo _____ a Roma?*
4. *In dogana noi _____ una stecca di sigarette e una bottiglia di whisky.*

5. *L'anno scorso Claudia* _____ *da sola. La sorella non* _____ *accompagnarla.*
6. *Io e Gianni* _____ *in albergo e insieme* _____ *a prendere un caffè.*
7. *Sull'aereo noi* _____ *alcune cartoline e* _____ *una bellissima rivista.*
8. *Il mio biglietto aereo* _____ *$1500.*
9. *Il volo* _____ *quasi otto ore.*
10. *Roberto, ti* _____ *viaggiare con l'Alitalia?*

C. *Transformare i verbi del seguente paragrafo dal presente al passato.* (Change the verbs from the present to the past.)

La signorina Smith entra in albergo, dà il passaporto all'impiegato, si prende la chiave e lascia dei documenti nella cassaforte dell'albergo. Prima di salire in camera, si ferma a scambiare quattro parole con un amico. Poi va in camera, si rinfresca e si riposa un po'. Quando si sveglia, si fa la doccia, si mette dei vestiti più comodi e scende giù al bar a prendere un caffè. Infine va a fare una bella passeggiata per le strade della città.

D. *Tradurre.* (Translate.)

1. At the duty-free shop we bought some gifts for the children.
2. —Do you mind if I smoke? —Of course not!
3. On the plane I didn't get bored and in customs everything went well.
4. Last night we rushed to the airport.
5. —Sir, do you have anything to declare?
6. I prefer traveling with my family. I don't like to travel alone.
7. It's a rumor; it's not true!
8. John, you must hurry because it's late.
9. Miss, what is the purpose of your trip? Are you here on vacation?
10. It snowed all day and they were afraid to fly.

LEZIONE 3

A. DIALOGO

Il signor Young, impiegato presso un'impresa di import ed export[2] americana, appena[3] arrivato a Milano,[4] decide di telefonare ad alcuni suoi amici italiani.

MARK YOUNG: *(a sé[5] stesso)* **Vediamo con chi dovrei cominciare? Con Marco! Oh, dimenticavo . . . Marco in questo momento è all'estero.[6] Vediamo se c'è Monica . . .**

Il signor Young compone il numero di telefono di Monica.

GIANNI: **Pronto![7]**

MARK YOUNG: **Pronto! C'è Monica, per favore?**

GIANNI: **No, non c'è. È fuori.**

MARK YOUNG: **Buon giorno, sono Marco Young, un suo amico americano. Scusi, con chi parlo?**

GIANNI: **Io sono Gianni, il fratellino di Monica.**

MARK YOUNG: **Potresti darle un messaggio?[8]**

GIANNI: **Sì, certamente. Un attimo, per favore che prendo una penna. Dimmi . . .[9]**

MARK YOUNG: **Bene . . . Sono all'albergo Executive. Ti lascio il numero di telefono: trentaquattro, sessantuno, ventisette, otto.[10]**

GIANNI: **Va bene. Appena sarà arrivata, le comunicherò il messaggio.**

MARK YOUNG: **Grazie. Arrivederci.[11]**

GIANNI: **Ciao.**

Il signor Young riaggancia e compone un altro numero.

MARK YOUNG: **Buon giorno. La Signora Pozzi?**

VOCE: **No, mi dispiace. Ha sbagliato numero.**

MARK YOUNG: **Oh . . . Chiedo scusa . . .**

VOCE: **Non si preoccupi. ArrivederLa.**

MARK YOUNG: **ArriverderLa.** *(fra sé)* **Ah, ecco perché! Ho dimenticato di fare il prefisso. I Pozzi non abitano a Milano.** *(Il signor Young rifa il numero)* **Pronto, signora Pozzi?**

SIGNORA POZZI: **Sì . . .**

MARK YOUNG: **Signora, sono Mark Young, un amico di Suo figlio Andrea.**

SIGNORA POZZI: **Oh, sì . . . Andrea mi ha parlato tanto di Lei. Come sta Andrea?**

MARK YOUNG: **Andrea sta bene e L'abbraccia. Mi ha chiesto anche di portarLe un pacchettino e una lettera.**

SIGNORA POZZI: **Molto gentile. Se mi dice dove si trova, verrò personalmente a ritirarli.**

MARK YOUNG: **Signora, glieli porterò io. Ho il Suo indirizzo.[12] Posso passare domani pomeriggio. Va bene?**

SIGNORA POZZI: **Benissimo. La ringrazio. A domani, allora.[13] L'aspetto.**

MARK YOUNG: **ArrivederLa. A domani![14]**

Il signor Young fa un'altra telefonata alla Camera di Commercio di Milano, dove lavora il suo amico Gino Tellini.

MARK YOUNG: **Beh, è ora di mettermi al lavoro!**

CENTRALINISTA: **Buon giorno. Camera di Commercio di Milano.**

MARK YOUNG: **Buon giorno. Vorrei parlare con il dottor Tellini. Interno 340.[15]**

CENTRALINISTA: **Chi parla, scusi?**

MARK YOUNG: **Sono il signor Young.**

CENTRALINISTA: **Come, scusi?[16]**

MARK YOUNG: **Mark Young.**

CENTRALINISTA: Il dottor Tellini è sull'altra linea . . . Può attendere un momento o preferisce richiamare?

MARK YOUNG: Preferisco attendere. Grazie.

CENTRALINISTA: Bene . . . La linea ora è libera. Le passo il dottor Tellini.

MARK YOUNG: Grazie . . . Pronto! Gino, sono Mark.

SIGNOR TELLINI: Mark, che bella sorpresa! Quando sei arrivato?

MARK YOUNG: Ieri. Come stai?

SIGNOR TELLINI: Benissimo, e tu?

MARK YOUNG: Bene. Bene. Grazie.

SIGNOR TELLINI: Allora, quando possiamo vederci?

MARK YOUNG: Quando vuoi tu. Dovrei chiederti delle informazioni.[17] La mia azienda desidera stabilire dei rapporti[18] d'affari con delle società italiane. Vorrei poter conoscere meglio ed essere in grado di analizzare il mercato[19] italiano.

SIGNOR TELLINI: Certamente. Sono a tua disposizione. Il mio ufficio offre diversi supporti informativi e assistenziali. Quando ci vediamo, ti porto degli opuscoli[20] informativi. Ma hai già telefonato a tua moglie e ai tuoi?

MARK YOUNG: Ovviamente. È la prima cosa che ho fatto. Ho telefonato in teleselezione[21] dall'albergo.

SIGNOR TELLINI: Un consiglio: la prossima volta telefona all'operatore americano.[22] Il numero è 172-1011. In questo modo la telefonata sarà addebitata alla tua carta di credito telefonica, usando le tariffe americane che sono molto inferiori a quelle italiane.

MARK YOUNG: Grazie per il consiglio. Allora, quando ci vediamo?

SIGNOR TELLINI: Che ne dici di stasera? Incontriamoci per cena.

MARK YOUNG: Ottima idea. Dimmi dove e quando.

SIGNOR TELLINI: Alle otto al *Piatto*. Sai dov'è?

MARK YOUNG: È in via Mazzini, vero?

SIGNOR TELLINI: Sì.

MARK YOUNG: **Va bene. Ci vediamo alle otto. Gino, ti ringrazio. A presto, allora.**

SIGNOR TELLINI: **Non c'è di che, Mark. Ciao.**

Il signor Young, prima di telefonare a New York, fa un'ultima telefonata a Roma.

MARK YOUNG: *(fra sé)* **Dovrei telefonare anche a Walter. Ma . . . sarà a casa? Risponderà sicuramente la segreteria telefonica. Walter va sempre in giro. Proviamo, comunque.**

Il signor Young fa il numero e . . .

SEGRETERIA TELEFONICA: **Questo è un messaggio automatico. In questo momento non sono in casa. Lasciate il vostro nome e numero di telefono e vi richiamerò il più presto possibile. Parlate dopo il segnale acustico.**[23]

MARK YOUNG: **Ciao, Walter**[24] **Sono Mark. Mi trovo a Milano, all'Hotel Executive. Ti richiamerò domani.** *(fra sé)* **Lo sapevo. Questo qui non è mai a casa. Il lupo perde il pelo ma non il vizio.**[25] **Chissà dove sarà andato.**

ON THE PHONE

Mr. Young, an employee at an American import and export company, having just arrived in Milan, decides to phone a few of his Italian friends.

MARK YOUNG: (to himself) Let's see . . . who should I start with? Marco! Oh, I almost forgot . . . Marco's abroad right now. Let's see if Monica's in . . .

Mr. Young dials Monica's telephone number.

GIANNI: Hello!

MARK YOUNG: Hello! Is Monica in, please?

GIANNI: No, no she's not. She's out.

MARK YOUNG: Good morning. This is Mark Young, her friend from America. And who's this, please?

GIANNI: It's Gianni, Monica's little brother.

MARK YOUNG: Could you give her a message, please?

GIANNI: Sure. Just a second and I'll get a pen . . . Okay, go ahead.

MARK YOUNG: Okay . . . I'm at the Executive Hotel. Here's my telephone number: thirty-four, sixty-one, twenty-seven, eight.

GIANNI: Okay. I'll give her the message as soon as she gets in.

MARK YOUNG: Thanks. Bye.

GIANNI: Bye.

Mr. Young hangs up and dials another number.

MARK YOUNG: Good morning. Mrs. Pozzi?

VOICE: No, I'm sorry. You have the wrong number.

MARK YOUNG: Oh . . . I'm sorry . . .

VOICE: Don't worry about it. It's okay. Goodbye.

MARK YOUNG: Goodbye. (to himself) Ah, here's why! I forgot to dial the area code. The Pozzis don't live in Milan. (Mr. Young dials the number again) Hello, Mrs. Pozzi?

MRS. POZZI: Yes . . .

MARK YOUNG: Ma'am, I'm Mark Young, a friend of your son, Andrea.

MRS. POZZI: Oh, yes . . . Andrea has told me so much about you. How is Andrea?

MARK YOUNG: Andrea is fine, and he sends his love. He also asked me to bring you a small package and a letter.

MRS. POZZI: That's very kind of you. If you tell me where you are, I will come personally to pick them up.

MARK YOUNG: Ma'am, I'll bring them to you. I have your address. I can come by tomorrow afternoon. Is that okay?

MRS. POZZI: Excellent. Thank you. Till tomorrow, then. I'll be waiting for you.

MARK YOUNG: Goodbye. See you tomorrow.

Mr. Young makes another phone call to the Milan Chamber of Commerce, where his friend Gino Tellini works.

MARK YOUNG: Okay, time to get to business.

OPERATOR: Good morning. The Milan Chamber of Commerce.

MARK YOUNG: Good morning. I would like to speak to Dr. Tellini. Extension 340.

OPERATOR: May I ask who is speaking?

MARK YOUNG: Mr. Young.

OPERATOR: I beg your pardon?

MARK YOUNG: Mark Young.

OPERATOR: Dr. Tellini is on the other line . . . Would you like to hold or would you prefer to call back?

MARK YOUNG: I'll hold. Thank you.

OPERATOR: Okay . . . The line is free now. I'll put you through to Dr. Tellini.

MARK YOUNG: Thank you . . . Hello! Gino, it's Mark.

MR. TELLINI: Mark, what a nice surprise! When did you arrive?

MARK YOUNG: Yesterday. How are you?

MR. TELLINI: Great, and you?

MARK YOUNG: Fine. Fine. Thanks.

MR. TELLINI: So, when can we see each other?

MARK YOUNG: Whenever you want. I have to ask you for some information. My company would like to establish business relations with Italian firms. I would like to better understand and be able to analyze the Italian market.

MR. TELLINI: Certainly. I am at your disposal. My office provides information and assistance. When we get together, I'll bring you some pamphlets. So, have you called your wife and family yet?

MARK YOUNG: Of course. It was the first thing I did. I dialed direct from my hotel.

MR. TELLINI: Listen, you should call the American operator next time. The number is: 172-1011. That way, the call will be charged to your telephone credit card, using American rates, which are much lower than the Italian rates.

MARK YOUNG: Thanks for the tip. So, when can we meet?

SIGNOR TELLINI: How about tonight? Let's go for dinner.

MARK YOUNG: Sounds great. Just tell me when and where.

SIGNOR TELLINI: Eight o'clock at *Il piatto.* Do you know where it is?

MARK YOUNG: It's on Via Mazzini, right?

SIGNOR TELLINI: Yes.

MARK YOUNG: Okay. See you there at eight. Thanks, Gino. See you soon, then.

SIGNOR TELLINI: No problem, Mark. Bye.

Mr. Young, before calling New York, makes one last call.

MARK YOUNG: (to himself) I should call Walter too. But . . . will he be at home? I bet the answering machine is on. Walter's always out. Let's try anyway.

Mr. Young dials the number and . . .

ANSWERING MACHINE: This is a recorded message. I am not home right now. Leave your name and number and I'll call you back as soon as I can. Speak after the tone.

MARK YOUNG: Hello, Walter. It's Mark. I am in Milan at the Executive Hotel. I'll call you again tomorrow. (to himself) I knew it. This one is never home. You can't change a leopard's spots. I wonder where he went.

B. IN BREVE

1. Notice that "on the phone" is rendered with the preposition *a,* as in *al telefono.*

2. Although Italians often use the English terms "import" and "export," these two words also have Italian equivalents: *importazione* and *esportazione.*

3. *Appena* may be repeated for emphasis. *Ha fatto appena appena in tempo a vedere il suo amico.* (He barely made it in time to see his friend.) *Appena* can also mean "only" or "as soon as." *È appena l'una.* (It is just one o'clock.) *Appena sarà arrivato ti telefonerà.* (As soon as he arrives, he'll phone you.)

4. Milan, capital of the Lombardy region, is the second largest Italian city, with a population close to 1.5 million inhabitants. It is the nation's industrial, financial, and commercial center.

5. When *sé* is followed by *stesso* it may also be written without the accent *(se stesso)*.

6. *Estero* can also be used as an adjective. *Quel giornalista si occupa di politica estera.* (That reporter writes on foreign politics.)

7. There are several common ways to answer the phone in Italian: *Pronto!* (Hello!); *Sì . . .* (Yes . . .), *Buon giorno!* (Good morning!); *Sì, mi dica!* (Yes, go ahead/tell me!). Note also that the English "speaking" is rendered as *Sono io.* *C'è il signor Wilkinson? —Sì, sono io.* (Is Mr. Wilkinson there? —Yes, speaking.)

8. To leave a message you can also say: *Potrebbe/potresti farle/fargli avere un messaggio?*

9. To take a message you can also say: *Dica pure.*

10. Note that in Italy phone numbers are generally given in pairs. If it is composed of an odd number of digits, the last number is said on its own. The number of digits in both the area code and the telephone number may vary.

11. When saying "good-bye" to someone formally you can also say *buongiorno* (morning/early afternoon) or *buonasera* (late afternoon/evening).

12. A synonym for *indirizzo* is *recapito*. *In caso di mancato recapito rispedire al mittente.* (In case the item cannot be delivered, return to sender.)

13. *Allora* is commonly used as a transitional expression meaning "so, then." It can also be used literally to mean "at that moment" or "at that time" *Allora non sapevo cosa fare.* (At that time I didn't know what to do.) *Allora viaggiavamo molto.* (At that time we used to travel a lot.) When repeated it means "just." *Paolo era entrato in camera allora allora.* (Paul had just entered the room.)

14. Other similar expressions for saying "good-bye" to someone are: *A più tardi!* (See you later!); *A presto!* (See you soon!); *Ci vediamo!* (See you!).

15. *Interno* can refer to a telephone extension or an apartment number. *Abita in Via Nazionale, numero 81, interno 9.* (He lives at 81 Via Nazionale, Apt. 9.) *Pronto, vorrei parlare con il signor Agostini, interno 203.* (Hello, I would like to speak to Mr. Agostini, extension 203.)

16. When you want someone to repeat what they said you can also ask: *Come ha/hai detto?* or *Può/puoi ripetere, per piacere?* The informal equivalent of *Scusi?* is *Scusa?*

17. In Italian the plural form *informazioni* is used frequently. The singular *informazione* is used when referring to a single piece of information. *Mi mancava quell'informazione per completare il modulo.* (That piece of information was missing to complete the application.)

18. The plural form *rapporti* refers to "relations, dealings"—e.g., *rapporti d'affari* (business relations), *rapporti commerciali* (trade relations), *rapporti sindacali* (labor relations). The singular form *rapporto* means "report, account" or "relationship": *rapporto finanziario* (financial report), *rapporto mensile* (monthly report), *il rapporto manager-imprenditore* (the manager-owner relationship).

19. *Mercato* means "market" or "market place". Note also the following: *il Mercato Comune Europeo* (the European Common Market), *mercato di libera concorrenza* (free market), *i mercati esteri* (foreign markets), *mercato favorevole agli acquisti* (buyers' market), *mercato favorevole alle vendite* (sellers' market).

20. The French terms *brochure* (f.) and *dépliant* (m.) can also be used instead of *opuscolo. Troverete tutte le informazioni necessarie nella brochure.* (You will find all the necessary information in the brochure.)

21. In Italian, a collect call is *una telefonata con addebito a carico del destinatario*. The expression *telefonare collect* is also sometimes used.

22. The telephone operator is also known as *il/la centralinista* or *il centralino*.

23. Another typical answering machine greeting is *Questo è un avviso registrato. In questo momento non sono in casa. Vi prego di lasciare un messaggio dopo il segnale acustico.* (This is a recorded message. I am not at home right now. Please leave a message after the tone.)

24. The *w* in English words like "Walter" is often pronounced as *v* in Italian.

25. Lit: "The wolf may lose his fur but not his habit."

C. GRAMMATICA E SUOI USI

1. *IL FUTURO E IL FUTURO ANTERIORE* (THE FUTURE AND THE FUTURE PERFECT)

a. *Il futuro* (the future)

The future tense of regular verbs is formed by dropping the final -*e* from the infinitive and adding the appropriate personal ending: -*ò, -ai, -à, -emo, -ete,* or -*anno.* For the first conjugation, the -*a-* in the infinitive ending changes to -*e-*. Here are three model regular verbs.

	LAVORARE	PRENDERE	PARTIRE
io	lavorerò	prenderò	partirò
tu	lavorerai	prenderai	partirai
lui/lei/Lei	lavorerà	prenderà	partirà
noi	lavoreremo	prenderemo	partiremo
voi	lavorerete	prenderete	partirete
loro/Loro	lavoreranno	prenderanno	partiranno

Remember that verbs ending in -*care* and -*gare* add an -*h-* after the -*c* and -*g* in order to keep the hard sound, and that verbs ending in -*ciare,* -*giare,* and -*sciare* drop the -*i*.

Cercherò di dargli il messaggio questo pomeriggio.
I'll try to give him the message this afternoon.

Signorina Carlini, mi indicherà Lei dove comprare una carta telefonica prepagata?
Miss Carlini, will you tell me where to buy a prepaid phone card?

Naturalmente pagheremo noi le spese di viaggio!
Of course, we will pay your travel expenses!

Se non è in casa, le lascerò un messaggio.
If she is not at home, I'll leave her a message.

A che ora cominceremo ad intervistare i candidati per il nuovo posto?
At what time are we going to start interviewing the candidates for the new position?

Stasera mangeremo all'albergo con i nuovi clienti.
Tonight we'll eat at the hotel with our new clients.

Verbs ending in *-rre* drop the final *-e* and take the regular future endings. For example, the conjugation of *tradurre* (to translate) is *tradurrò, tradurrai, tradurrà, tradurremo, tradurrete, tradurranno.*

L'interprete tradurrà simultaneamente dall'inglese all'italiano.
The interpreter will translate simultaneously from English to Italian.

Verbs that are irregular in the future tense have irregular stems, but take the regular endings. Note that some irregular stems are formed by simply dropping both vowels from the infinitive ending. For example, *andare → andr-, avere → avr-, dovere → dovr-, potere → potr-, sapere → sapr-,* etc.

Il prossimo anno andremo in Italia.
Next year we will go to Italy.

Lo saprò domani tramite telegramma.
I'll find out tomorrow by telegram.

Se tu andrai in Italia, verrò anch'io.
If you go to Italy, I'll come too.

Noi rimarremo a New York tutta l'estate per aiutare mio zio con l'azienda.
We will stay in New York all summer to help my uncle with the company.

The simple future also conveys the idea of probability, supposition, or conjecture about the present.

Chi chiama così tardi? —Sarà tua madre.
Who could be calling so late? —It must be your mother.

Dove ha lo studio il signor Antonucci? —L'avrà fuori città, vicino a quello dei suoi colleghi.
Where does Mr. Antonucci have his office? —It must be just outside of the city, near his colleagues'.

As in English, the present indicative is often used in place of the simple future when referring to an action that will take place shortly or to a scheduled event:

Trovami l'interno e gli telefono/telefonerò al lavoro.
Find the extension for me and I will phone him at work.

Abbiamo deciso che ci sposiamo/sposeremo tra due anni.
We have decided that we're getting married in two years.

Ti telefono/telefonerò mercoledì prossimo.
I'll phone you next Wednesday.

The simple future may also be used to translate the English present progressive:

Quando telefoni/telefonerai a tua moglie?
When are you going to phone your wife?

The present indicative or the simple future may be used after secondary clauses introduced by *se, quando, appena, non appena, dopo che,* if the future is implied. In Italian, both the main verb and the secondary verb must be in the same tense. Notice that while the future may be used in Italian the present is always used in English.

Quando arrivo alla stazione, ti chiamo.
Quando arriverò alla stazione, ti chiamerò.
When I arrive at the station, I'll call you.

Appena lo so, ti telefono.
Appena lo saprò, ti telefonerò.
As soon as I know, I'll phone you.

b. *Il futuro anteriore* (the future perfect)

The future perfect tense is formed by using the past participle with the future form of *avere* or *essere*.

	LAVORARE	ANDARE
io	avrò lavorato	sarò andato/a
tu	avrai lavorato	sarai andato/a
lui/lei/Lei	avrà lavorato	sarà andato/a
noi	avremo lavorato	saremo andati/e
voi	avrete lavorato	sarete andati/e
loro/Loro	avranno lavorato	saranno andati/e

It is used: to express an action or event that will be completed prior to a specified time in the future.

Ritelefoni alle tre. A quell'ora il dottor Scala sarà già uscito dalla riunione.
Phone back at three o'clock. By then Dr. Scala will have already returned from the meeting.

Io avrò già completato il rapporto prima che tu mandi il fax con tutti i dati.
I will have already completed the report by the time you fax me all the information.

following the conjunctions *quando, dopo che,* or *(non) appena che* to express an action that will have taken place prior to another future action. Notice that in English the present or the present perfect is used instead.

Dopo che avrò rivisto i documenti, farò una passeggiata.
After reviewing the documents, I'll go for a walk.

(Non) appena sarò arrivato, ti telefonerò.
As soon as I arrive, I'll phone you.

Quando avrai finito di battere a macchina questa lettera, ti prego di spedire questo fax al signor Marini.
When you've finish typing this letter, please send this fax to Mr. Marini.

to express probability, supposition or conjecture about a past action.

Come mai Carlo non ha ancora telefonato? —Non sarà ancora arrivato.
Why hasn't Carlo called yet? —He probably hasn't arrived yet.

Chi era al telefono? —Nessuno. Qualcuno avrà sbagliato numero.
Who was on the phone? —Nobody. Someone must have dialed the
wrong number.

Ho chiamato ma non ha risposto nessuno. Avrò sbagliato numero!
I called but nobody answered. I must have dialed the wrong number.

2. *GLI AGGETTIVI E I PRONOMI POSSESSIVI* (POSSESSIVE ADJECTIVES AND PRONOUNS)

Possessive adjectives and pronouns have the same form in Italian.

	MASCULINE		FEMININE	
	SINGULAR	PLURAL	SINGULAR	PLURAL
my/mine	*il mio*	*i miei*	*la mia*	*le mie*
your/yours (fam. sg.)	*il tuo*	*i tuoi*	*la tua*	*le tue*
his, her/hers, its	*il suo*	*i suoi*	*la sua*	*le sue*
your/yours (formal sg.)	*il Suo*	*i Suoi*	*la Sua*	*le Sue*
our/ours	*il nostro*	*i nostri*	*la nostra*	*le nostre*
your/yours (formal/fam pl.)	*il vostro*	*i vostri*	*la vostra*	*le vostre*
their/theirs	*il loro*	*i loro*	*la loro*	*le loro*
your/yours (formal pl.)	*il Loro*	*i Loro*	*la Loro*	*le Loro*

a. *Gli aggettivi possessivi* (Possessive Adjectives)

In Italian, possessive adjectives are generally preceded by the definite
article and always agree in gender and number with the noun they
modify. *Loro,* however, is invariable.

Il mio numero di telefono è 568-8493.
My telephone number is 568-8493.

La mia ditta ha una filiale in Italia.
My firm has a branch in Italy.

I miei amici sono tutti uomini d'affari.
    My friends are all businessmen.

Le loro aziende hanno rapporti d'affari con l'Italia.
    Their companies do business with Italy.

When the possessive adjective accompanies a singular, unmodified noun denoting a family relationship,* the definite article is omitted. With *mamma, papà, nonno,* and *nonna,* however, the use of the article is optional. The article is always used with *loro.* Remember that words like *fratellino, sorellina, cuginetto, sorellastra,* etc. are considered modified, so the article is not omitted.

Suo cugino è venuto a ritirare il pacco.
    His/her cousin came to pick up the package.

Quello stilista ha invitato mia sorella a sfilare a Parigi.
    That designer invited my sister to model in Paris.

Mio fratello Le telefonerà non appena sarà rientrato a casa.
    My brother will call you as soon as he comes back home.

La vostra sorellastra lavora in un'agenzia di pubblicità.
    Your stepsister works at an advertising agency.

Note that the *suo* forms can mean "his," "her," "its," or "your" (formal). In writing it is possible to distinguish between "his/her" and "your" (formal) by capitalizing the latter. To avoid ambiguity, use *di lui* (his) and *di lei* (her).

È il suo indirizzo.
    It is his/her address.

Arriverò con i suoi zii.
    I will arrive with his/her/your uncles.

Ottavio ha una Fiat e Carla una Lancia. La macchina di lui è bianca. La macchina di lei è rossa.
    Ottavio has a Fiat and Carla a Lancia. His car is white. Her car is red.

Qual è il Suo numero di telefono?
    What is your telephone number?

* Nouns like *bambino/a, fidanzato/a* (child, fiancé/e) do not actually refer to a family relationship and therefore require an article if preceded by a possessive.

63

Possessive adjectives are often omitted when ownership is understood, especially with articles of clothing and parts of the body.

Si è messo il cappello.
He put on his hat.

Lo studente ha alzato la mano per rispondere alla domanda.
The student raised his hand to answer the question.

Il bambino ha aperto la bocca quando ha visto la caramella.
The child opened his mouth when he saw the candy.

Note that there are two different ways to express the English construction "of mine/of yours," etc.

Alle nove ho un appuntamento con un mio collega.
At nine o'clock I have a meeting with a colleague of mine.

Dottor Cecchin, è arrivato uno dei Suoi clienti.
Dr. Cecchin, a client of yours has arrived.

The adjective *proprio* (one's own) may also be used in conjunction with the possessive adjectives for emphasis. It is always accompanied by the definite article.

Devi farcela con le tue proprie forze.
You must make it with your own strength.

L'ha fatto con le sue proprie mani.
He made it with his own hands.

Si comporta così per motivi propri.
He behaves this way for his own reasons.

s.p.m. (= sue proprie mani)
Delivered by hand.

Proprio is also used in impersonal sentences or with an indefinite subject.

La gente deve occuparsi dei fatti propri.
People must mind their own business.

With certain idiomatic expressions, the possessive adjective follows the noun and the definite article is omitted. Such expressions include: *Mamma mia!* (Dear me!), *Dio mio* (My God!), *a casa mia* (at my house), *è colpa mia/tua* (it's my/your fault).

Dio mio! Che cosa è successo?
My God! What happened?

L'affare è andato male. È colpa tua!
The deal did not go through. It's your fault!

b. *Pronomi possessivi* (Possessive Pronouns)

Possessive pronouns have the same forms as the possessive adjective and are generally preceded by the definite article.

L'indirizzo? Il mio è sul modulo.
The address? Mine is on the form.

Ho bisogno di una valigia. Potresti prestarmi la tua?
I need a suitcase. Could you lend me yours?

When the possessive pronoun follows the verb *essere* the article may be omitted.

Quest'indirizzo è mio.
This address is mine.

Sono sicura che quel messaggio è suo.
I'm sure that message is his/hers.

D. PAROLE! PAROLE! PAROLE!

The word *aspettare* can be used in many different ways.

Ai clienti non piace dover aspettare in fila per ore.
Customers hate having to wait in line for hours.

Marianna, non aspettarmi prima delle undici.
Marianne, don't expect me before eleven.

Aspettate gente a pranzo oggi?
Are you expecting people for lunch today?

Tutti si aspettano troppo da noi.
Everyone expects too much of us.

C'era da aspettarselo!
It was only to be expected!

Sua moglie aspetta un bambino.
His wife is expecting a baby.

Ragazzi, avete un bell'aspettare!
Boys, it's no use waiting!

Loro si fanno sempre aspettare.
They're always late.

Io me l'aspettavo!
I was expecting it!

Quando meno te l'aspetti . . .
When you least expect it . . .

Qui ti aspettavo!
I thought I'd catch you on that!/Now let's see what you do!

Aspettiamo le vostre istruzioni.
We await your instructions.

Aspetto con ansia la vostra risposta.
I am anxiously awaiting your reply.

I suoi progressi si fanno aspettare.
His progress is slow in coming.

Now let's take a look at some proverbs with *aspettare.*

Chi la fa l'aspetti.
As we sow so do we reap/We reap as we sow.

Chi ha tempo non aspetti tempo.
Strike while the iron is hot.

Aspetta cavallo che l'erba cresca.
While the grass is growing the horse starves.

E. L'ANGOLO DEGLI AFFARI

I MEZZI DI COMUNICAZIONE (TELECOMMUNICATIONS)

In Italy, telephone services are regulated by the *Ministero delle Poste e Telecomunicazioni* (the ministry of postal services and telecommunications). *Telecom Italia* (SIP) held a monopoly over Italian communications systems until very recently. With the move towards a common European market and a global economy, there has been a strong push towards deregulation. The growing demand for more sophisticated telecommunications equipment along with increased competition are driving Italian telecommunications forward, approaching the American level.

For example, Italian phone lines are changing rapidly from the pulse system to a tone system, as the demand for products and services such as pagers and system-based answering services is growing. Services such as *avviso di chiamata* (call waiting), *documentazione traffico teleselettivo da utente* (call display), *conversazioni a tre* (three-party calls), and *trasferimenti di chiamata* (call transferring) are more and more common.

Since the early nineties Italians have had access to an extremely sophisticated and advanced video-telephone service called VIDEOTEL. It allows users to make bank transactions, rail and other reservations, monitor stock markets, play video games, access meteorological forecasts and travel information, and utilize a variety of other services, including an electronic mail system. VIDEOTEL may be accessed with the use of a video phone produced by Telecom Italia or even with a personal computer via modem.

Telephone rates are generally much higher in Italy than the United States. Local calls can become quite expensive, as charges are incurred based on the duration of the call, i.e., the number of *scatti* accumulated. (Literally, *scatti* are clicks; they are the units by which telephone charges are tabulated). As in the States, the rate at which units are calculated on the *bolletta* (telephone bill) varies depending on the time of day of the phone call. For international and overseas calls, units are accumulated at a faster pace; the farther the distance, the more quickly the units accumulate, in seconds rather than minutes.

The cellular phone has become the most sought after means of communication in Italy, not only in business, but also, and perhaps primarily, for personal use. Many Italians are flocking to purchase their own *telefonini* (cellular phones; literally, "little phones"). In fact, the *telefonino* has become an important status symbol during the nineties.

Pay phones are abundant in major cities. A *carta telefonica prepagata* (prepaid phone card) is a wise investment if you plan to use pay phones on a regular basis in Italy. They can be purchased at tobacco shops, post offices, and at automatic dispensers at railway stations, airports, and Telecom Italia retail outlets. The phone cards come in values of 5,000, 10,000, and 15,000 Lire.

It is useful to learn some common telephone phrases if you intend to spend some time in Italy. Here is a list of useful phrases:

Pronto?
Hello?

Chi è che parla?/Chi parla?
Who's speaking?

Qui parla Daphne./Sono Daphne.
This is Daphne.

C'è il signor Rosso?
Is Mr. Rosso there?

Vorrei parlare con la signora Guarini.
I would like to speak to Ms. Guarini.

È occupato/a in questo momento.
He/she is busy at the moment.

È uscita.
She is out.

Non è disponibile.
He is not available.

Glielo/la passo subito.
I'll let you speak to him/her right away.

Di che cosa si tratta?
What is this in reference to?

Potrei lasciare un messaggio?
Could I leave a message?

Attenda in linea, per piacere.
Please wait on the line

Richiamerò domani.
I'll call back tomorrow.

Gli/le lascerò il messaggio.
I'll leave him/her the message.

Even with all the technological advances in the industry, the telegram continues to be a common means of communication in Italy. Telegrams are often sent when one wishes to acknowledge an event such as a wedding, the birth of a child, or a funeral. Some common idiomatic expressions used in telegrams are:

Vivissimi auguri ai novelli sposi.
Auguri di felicità infinita!
Warmest congratulations to the newlyweds.

Vi inviamo le nostre condoglianze.
Sentite condoglianze!
Vicini in questo momento di dolore!
We send you our condolensces.

Congratulazioni/felicitazioni/auguri!
Congratulations!

If you will be sending a telegram while in Italy, there is a nationwide number you can call that provides information on all telegraph (as well as postal) services: 26435. Other useful numbers to remember when visiting Italy are for emergencies, 113 (equivalent to 911), 176 (for information regarding international telephone calls), 170 (to place telephone calls with phone cards, including American ones.)

ESERCIZI

A. *Cambiare le seguenti frasi al futuro.* (Change the following sentences to the future.)

1. *Se ci dici dove abiti, veniamo a trovarti.*
2. *Gino, andate in Italia quest'estate?*
3. *Quando ci vediamo, ti porto degli opuscoli.*
4. *Il mio ufficio offre diversi supporti informativi ed assistenziali.*
5. *Ha detto che non appena sanno la notizia, ve la comunicano.*

B. *Completare le frasi con il futuro di uno dei seguenti verbi.* (Complete the following sentences with the future tense of one of the verbs below.)

cercare   essere   incominciare   potere   venire

1. *Domani non _____ venire con te perchè ho un appuntamento d'affari.*
2. *Se vengo in Italia, _____ sicuramente a trovarti.*
3. *Ingegner Carli, quando _____ il Suo nuovo progetto?*
4. *Come mai la segretaria non è venuta al lavoro oggi? —_____ malata.*
5. *Signorina, non riesco a trovare i documenti. —Non si preoccupi, dottore, li _____ io.*

C. *Completare le frasi con la forma appropriata del futuro o del futuro anteriore dei verbi fra parentesi.* (Complete the following sentences with the appropriate form of the simple future or future perfect of the verbs in parentheses.)

1. *Il tuo partner ti (telefonare) dopo che (arrivare) in ufficio.*
2. *Quando loro (rientrare), io gli (dare) il messaggio.*
3. *Il direttore è ancora al telefono? —No, a quest'ora (finire) già.*
4. *Signorina, ha già spedito il pacco? —No, lo (spedire) domani.*
5. *Appena la linea (essere) libera, Le (passare) il dottor Vivona.*

D. *Completare con la forma appropriata del possessivo tra parentesi, usando, se necessario, gli articoli.* (Complete the following sentences with the appropriate form of the possessive in parentheses. Use the appropriate article, if necessary.)

1. *Abbiamo telefonato ai* (our) *amici italiani.*
2. *Signorina, potrebbe prendermi* (their) *pratica?*
3. *Io ho già telefonato a* (my) *moglie. E tu, hai telefonato alla* (yours)?
4. *Ragionier La Motta, non ho il* (your) *indirizzo.*
5. (His) *azienda desidera stabilire dei rapporti d'affari con delle società italiane.*

E. *Rispondere alle seguenti domande, usando l'aggettivo possessivo.* (Answer each question logically, using the appropriate possessive adjective.)

ESEMPIO: Chi è la madre di tuo padre?
    È mia nonna.

1. *Chi sono i fratelli di tua madre?*
2. *Chi è il figlio di tuo figlio?*
3. *Chi è il marito di tua sorella?*
4. *Chi è la figlia di tua zia?*
5. *Chi è la moglie di tuo padre?*

F. *Tradurre.* (Translate.)

1. Are their friends Italian? —No, they're American.
2. Where do your parents live? —They live on Bloor Street. Not too far from here.
3. Is this your book? —No, this is Teresa's book.
4. Dr. Green isn't in? May I leave a message, then?
5. I'm sorry. I've dialed the wrong number.
6. For long distance phone calls, don't forget to dial the area code.
7. May I speak with Miss Bonomo? Extension 5543.
8. I am not at home. Please leave a message after the signal.
9. Who was on the phone? —It was John. He hung up on me!
10. John just phoned me. He told me that his wife is expecting a baby.
11. Would you like to hold?
12. I am expecting an important phone call.

LEZIONE 4

A. DIALOGO

Loredana entra in casa di Roberta. Roberta è sposata, ha due bambini ed è in cerca del primo lavoro.

LOREDANA: **Ciao, Roberta. Dov'è il bambino?**

ROBERTA: **Nella culla. Sta dormendo.**

LOREDANA: **Ogni volta che vengo qui, dorme sempre come un ghiro. Sei proprio fortunata! Non piange mai!**

ROBERTA: **Sì, è proprio un'angioletto.**

LOREDANA: **E tu, cosa stai facendo?** [1]

ROBERTA: **Sto sfogliando il giornale. Cerco** [2] **un lavoro. Non sarà facile trovarne uno! Di questi tempi è come cercare un ago in un pagliaio.**

LOREDANA: **Non essere così pessimista . . . Vedrai che qualcosa** [3] **troverai . . . C'è un opuscolo che voglio farti vedere. Ce l'ho proprio qui nella borsetta. Lo vuoi vedere?**

ROBERTA: **Certo, lo vedo volentieri.** *(legge il titolo)* **Hmm . . . "Donne e lavoro: consigli ed informazioni". Vediamo un po' cosa mi consigliano.**

LOREDANA: **Dovresti leggerlo tutto e attentamente. È molto interessante e mi ha aiutato tanto.**

ROBERTA: **Dunque . . . "È necessario innanzitutto controllare la situazione del mercato, studiare le esigenze attuali . . . "** [4]

LOREDANA: **C'è proprio tutto. Ridammi un momento l'opuscolo così ti mostro subito quello che ti interessa.** *(si riprende l'opuscolo)* **Prova a leggere qui: "È importante essere «elastiche», pronte ad accettare qualsiasi lavoro e a sottoporsi a periodi di riqualificazione . . . " Qui parlano del libretto di lavoro . . .**

ROBERTA: **Leggi un po' . . . Dove lo rilasciano?**

LOREDANA: **È possibile averlo recandosi all'ufficio anagrafe** [5] **del comune di residenza . . .** [6] **Devi presentare un documento di identità** [7] **ed un titolo di studio . . .** [8]

ROBERTA: **E a che cosa ti serve?**

LOREDANA: **Beh, ad ogni assunzione lo devi consegnare al datore di lavoro, il quale registra sul libretto il tipo di lavoro svolto, le mansioni e le qualifiche ricoperte . . . Sai che dovresti anche iscriverti** [9] **ad un ufficio di collocamento . . .**

ROBERTA: **No, non lo sapevo.** [10]

LOREDANA: **Sì, infatti per un'assunzione pubblica** [11] **occorre il nullaosta dell'ufficio di collocamento in cui si è iscritti.**

ROBERTA: **E quali sono i documenti richiesti per poter iscriversi?**

LOREDANA: **Te lo dico subito . . .** *(sfoglia l'opuscolo)* **È necessario un documento d'identità, il libretto di lavoro, lo stato di famiglia,** [12] **il codice fiscale,** [13] **il titolo di studio . . .**

ROBERTA: **Qui ti danno veramente tutte le informazioni . . .**

LOREDANA: **Hai pensato al curriculum vitae? A come prepararlo? Cosa metterci?**

ROBERTA: **No, mi devi dare una mano anche tu. Non l'ho mai** [14] **fatto prima.**

LOREDANA: **Devi includere nome, cognome,** [15] **indirizzo, numero di telefono, descrizione degli studi, lingue straniere parlate e scritte, esperienze di lavoro, tipo di diploma . . . Te lo posso fare io sul mio computer.**

ROBERTA: **Mille grazie! Puoi aiutarmi anche a prepararmi per il colloquio?**

LOREDANA: **Certo. Ma ricordati che se anche il colloquio ti va bene, prima di firmare il contratto di assunzione è sempre bene rivolgersi al sindacato per informarsi sul tipo di contratto** [16] **e sulla retribuzione . . .** [17]

ROBERTA: **Mi sembra tutto così complicato. E anche se tutto va bene mi rimane comunque un problema. Come farò a far coincidere gli orari di lavoro con quelli dei bambini?**

LOREDANA: Eh . . . lo so. Non è una cosa facile, ma ho sentito alla radio[18] che ultimamente un'azienda ha trovato una soluzione a questo problema.

ROBERTA: E di cosa si tratta?

LOREDANA: È stato stilato questo accordo, con l'approvazione del sindacato,[19] principalmente per le neomamme. Quest'accordo permette loro di lavorare quattro ore invece di sei, come normalmente prescritto per il periodo di allattamento . . . E tutto questo grazie al programma job sharing.

ROBERTA: Job sharing?

LOREDANA: Sì. Due donne si dividono il posto di lavoro per avere più tempo per i figli . . . La neomamma deve trovare un collega o una collega che divida con lei i turni di lavoro . . .

ROBERTA: Ma tutto questo è perfetto! E tu sei . . . un'artista!

LOREDANA: Veramente, lo sono le aziende e i sindacati. Con queste iniziative le aziende potranno fornire nuovi posti di lavoro . . .

ROBERTA: Sì, proprio così! Grazie di tutto. Stasera, quando andiamo al cinema, offro io!

IN SEARCH OF A FIRST JOB

Loredana enters Roberta's house. Roberta is married with two kids, and is looking for her first job.

LOREDANA: Hi, Roberta. Where's the baby?

ROBERTA: In the crib. He's asleep.

LOREDANA: Every time I come here, he's always sleeping like a log. You're really lucky! He never cries!

ROBERTA: Yes, he's an angel.

LOREDANA: And you, what are you doing?

ROBERTA: I'm looking through the newspaper. I'm looking for a job. It won't be easy to find one. Nowadays, it's like looking for a needle in a haystack.

LOREDANA: Don't be such a pessimist. You'll see, you'll find something . . . There's a pamphlet I want to show you. I have it right here in my purse. Would you like to see it?

ROBERTA: Sure, I'll be happy to look at it. (Reads the title.) Hmm . . . "Women and Work: Tips and Information." Let's see what they advise.

LOREDANA: You should read it all carefully. It's very interesting, and it helped me a great deal.

ROBERTA: Now then . . . "It is necessary, first of all, to survey the market, to study current demands . . ."

LOREDANA: It has everything. Give me back the pamphlet for a moment, and I'll find what you need right away. (She takes the pamphlet back.) Look at what it says: "It is important to be flexible, prepared to accept any position, and willing to undergo periods of re-training . . ." Here they write about the official Employment Record.

ROBERTA: Read some more . . . Where do you get one?

LOREDANA: It's possible to get one by going to the City Hall registration office . . . You have to show identification and a diploma . . .

ROBERTA: And what do you do with the Employment Record?

LOREDANA: Well, at every job you give it to your employer, who will then record the type of work done, the duties, and the skills required . . . Do you know that you should also register at an employment office . . .

ROBERTA: No, I didn't know that.

LOREDANA: Yes, in fact for a state position, you need authorization from the employment office where you're registered.

ROBERTA: And what do I need to register?

LOREDANA: I'll tell you right away . . . (Leafs through the pamphlet.) Here: identification papers, the Employment Record, marital status, Social Security number, diploma.

ROBERTA: They really do give you all of the information here . . .

LOREDANA: Have you thought of the curriculum vitae? How to prepare it? What to put in it?

ROBERTA: No, you have to help me. I've never done it before.

LOREDANA: You have to include your first name, last name, address, phone number, description of your studies, foreign languages spoken and written, work experience, education . . . I can do it for you on my computer.

ROBERTA: Thank you so much! Can you help me prepare for the interview, too?

LOREDANA: Of course. But remember that even if the interview goes well, before signing the contract, it's always best to inquire at the union on the type of contract and the payment . . .

ROBERTA: This seems so complicated. And even if everything goes well, I still have a problem. How will I coincide the work hours with the children's schedule?

LOREDANA: I know. It's not easy, but I heard on the radio that a local company has recently found a solution to this problem.

ROBERTA: What is it?

LOREDANA: An agreement was reached with the trade union, mainly for new mothers . . . The agreement allows mothers to work four hours instead of six, as is normally the rule for the breastfeeding period . . . And all of this thanks to job sharing.

ROBERTA: Job sharing?

LOREDANA: Yes. Two women divide their work load to have more time for their children . . . The new mother must find a colleague who is willing to split his or her shift . . .

ROBERTA: That's perfect! And you are . . . a genius!

LOREDANA: Actually, I guess the companies and the unions are. With all of these initiatives, the firms will be able to provide more jobs.

ROBERTA: Yes, exactly! Thank you for everything. Tonight, the movies are my treat!

B. IN BREVE

1. In Italian *stare* + the gerund is used instead of the present indicative to emphasize that an action is currently in progress. Note, however that the English present progressive ("to be" + "-ing") can be trans-

lated into Italian with the present indicative or with *stare* + gerund, depending on how much you want to emphasize the process of the action. *Cosa fai? —Sto leggendo gli annunci di lavoro./Leggo gli annunci di lavoro.* (What are you doing? —I am reading the Help Wanted classifieds.)

2. Note that the Italian verb *cercare* (to look for) does not require a preposition, unlike its English equivalent.

3. *Qualcosa* is a contracted form of *qualche cosa. Cerco qualcosa di interessante da fare.* (I'm looking for something interesting to do.) Note that the expression "something/anything else" may be rendered in two ways: *Vuoi qualche altra cosa?/Vuoi qualcos'altro?* (Do you want anything else?)

4. The word *attuale* is a "false friend" and means "current, of the moment" *L'attuale presidente del consiglio di amministrazione ha bisogno di un assistente.* (The current chairman of the board needs an assistant.) "Actual" is generally translated as *vero. Questo film è basato su una storia vera.* (This movie is based on an actual/true story). *La data vera e propria della riunione è il 30 novembre, ma vorremmo che tu venissi il 29.* (The actual date of the meeting is November 30th, but we'd like you to come out on the 29th.) Likewise, *attualmente* means "at the present time, currently." *Attualmente tutto va bene.* (At present everything is going well.) "Actually" is translated as *infatti, a dire il vero,* or *in realtà. A dire il vero, non riesco a trovare un impiego.* (Actually, I can't find a job.)

5. The *ufficio anagrafe* is under municipal jurisdiction and records the vital statistics of all of the residents of a municipality. It issues all documents, such as identification cards, birth and death certificates, marriage certificates, etc.

6. The term *comune* refers either to the notion of borough or municipality, or to the actual place where the offices of the municipality are located, i.e., a town hall or city hall. All Italians must be registered residents of a borough, i.e., they belong to a particular *comune di residenza* (municipality of residence).

7. This official document is used as the primary photo identification in Italy. It is roughly the equivalent of an American birth certificate,

but it is only issued on request on or after the age of fifteen. It contains information about the bearer's residence and place and date of birth. Italians may legally travel throughout the EU with the *carta d'identità* as their only means of identification.

8. In Italy a *titolo di studio* is issued upon completion of high school or college. A high school student who graduates, for example, from an *Istituto Tecnico Commerciale* (the commercial or business secondary school), receives *il diploma di ragioniere,* and with it the title of *ragioniere.* University students receive *la laurea* and the title of *dottore/dottoressa.*

9. *Iscriversi* means "to register, to enroll." *Ti sei iscritto al corso di stenografia?* (Did you register for the stenography course?) The Italian verb *registrare* means "to record, to tape" as on a cassette player or VCR. *Ti ho registrato un programma su come trovare un impiego.* (I taped a program on job-hunting for you.)

10. Remember that *sapere* (to know) means "to find out" if used in the *passato prossimo* (present perfect). Compare: *Sapevamo che Lucia era sposata.* (We knew that Lucia was married.) *Abbiamo saputo che Lucia si è sposata.* (We found out that Lucia got married.) For more on *sapere,* please refer to *Lezione 10.*

11. In Italy many sectors of industry and institutions (such as universities) are state-run. The state is therefore directly involved in hiring workers. Hiring practices include a *concorso* (competition), in which all applicants must undergo lengthy and often complicated exams to establish competency in their field. Competition in these *concorsi* is often fierce.

12. *Lo stato di famiglia* refers to a legal document listing all the members of one's nuclear family (spouse and children).

13. The *codice fiscale* is the equivalent of a Social Security number.

14. Normally *mai* is placed either between the auxiliary and the past participle or after the past participle. However, it can be placed before the auxiliary for emphasis *In quattordici anni non ho perso mai un giorno di lavoro e mai sono stato sotto malattia.* (In fourteen

years I have never missed a single day of work and never have I been on sick leave.)

15. In Italy, when women marry and take their husband's family name, they nevertheless remain registered at their municipality under their maiden names.

16. Contract law is quite complex in Italy, as it is in most countries. The categories of possible contracts are numerous. Italian legislation provides parties entering into a mutual agreement with the opportunity to design very specific contracts which may not fall under any of the existing categories; these are known as *contratti innominati* (unnamed contracts). Alternatively, parties may choose to design a contract which includes elements from different types of contracts. These are known as *contratti misti* (mixed contracts). The flexibility of Italian contract law gives parties entering into a contractual agreement the freedom to design a contract that is tailor-made for the intended transaction. Some common types of contracts include: a *contratto di compra-vendita* (contract of sale); a *contratto di lavoro* (contract of employment), a *contratto collettivo* (collective agreement). Here are some related expressions which may be useful: *sotto contratto* (under contract); *come da contratto* (as per contract); *fare un contratto con* (to enter into a contract with); *condizioni del contratto* (terms of contract); *lavorare in appalto* (to work on contract); *fare un'offerta per ottenere un contratto* (to tender for a contract); *ottenere un contratto* (to secure a contract).

17. Under Italian law, wages must be calculated and set based on the number of hours worked or the quantity produced. Salaries in both the public and private sectors tend to be distributed monthly, not weekly or bi-weekly as in the United States.

18. Note that the expression "on the radio" is rendered as *alla radio*.

19. As in much of Europe, unions in Italy are in large part associated with left-wing political parties, although many have integrated into the capitalist system very well. Unions have a very long history in Italy, and are very powerful. Some of the larger unions are actually umbrella organizations that smaller trade unions can join and look to for support. These include the *CISL* or *Confederazione Italiana*

Sindacati Lavoratori (Italian Confederation of Unions and Workers), the *CGIL* or *Confederazione Generale Italiana del Lavoro* (Italian General Confederation of Labor), and the *UIL* or *Unione Italiana del Lavoro* (Italian Labor Union).

C. GRAMMATICA E SUOI USI

1. *PRONOMI OGGETTO* (OBJECT PRONOUNS)

a. *Pronomi oggetto diretto* (direct object pronouns)

Direct object pronouns replace direct object nouns and generally precede the verb.

	SINGULAR	PLURAL	
me	*mi*	*ci*	us
you (sg.)	*ti*	*vi*	you (fam. and formal)
him it	*lo*	*li*	them (m.)
her, it	*la*	*le*	them (f.)
		Li	you (formal m.)
you (formal, m. and f.)	*La*	*Le*	you (formal f.)

Vuoi vedere questo opuscolo? —Certo che lo voglio vedere.
Would you like to see this brochure? —Of course I want to see it.

Mi hanno chiamato per un colloquio.
They called me for a job interview.

Scusi, ha il libretto di lavoro? —Mi dispiace, ma non l'ho portato.
Excuse me, do you have your employment card? —I'm sorry, but I didn't bring it.

Note that the third-person pronoun *lo* can take the place of entire phrases and refer to actions as well as objects or people:

Sai che devi presentare anche la carta d'identità? —No, non lo sapevo.
Do you know that you also have to produce a piece of identification? —No, I didn't know (it).

Tu compri il libro di Moravia? —Sì, lo compro.
Are you buying Moravia's book? —Yes, I am buying it.

When *lo, la, li* and *le* precede a verb in a compound tense, the past participle must agree with the pronoun in gender and number. With *mi, ti, ci,* and *vi* this agreement is optional.

Hai trovato i documenti che cercavi? —Sì, li ho trovati.
Did you find the documents that you were looking for? —Yes, I found them.

Roberta, ti ha chiamata/chiamato il tuo direttore.
Roberta, your boss called you.

The pronouns *lo* and *la* require an apostrophe before a vowel or an *h.* On the contrary, *li* and *le* are never elided.

Chi ti ha dato quell'opuscolo? —L'ho prelevato all'ufficio di collocamento.
Who gave you that brochure? —I picked it up at the employment office.

Hai riempito tutti i moduli per la domanda di lavoro? —Sì, li ho riempiti.
Did you fill out all the forms for the job application? —Yes, I filled them out.

Direct object pronouns can be attached as a suffix to infinitives, gerunds, and familiar forms of the imperative.

Ho perso la mia busta paga. Dobbiamo trovarla subito.
I lost my pay check. We have to find it right away.

Vorrei comprare questo vestito per l'intervista. Che ne pensi? —Sì, compralo!
I would like to buy this suit for the interview. What do you think?
—Yes, buy it!

Leggendolo, capirai quali documenti devi presentare.
By reading it, you'll know what documents you have to submit.

With modal verbs *(dovere, potere, volere)* the object pronoun can either precede the modal or be attached to the infinitive as a suffix.

Queste istruzioni sono importanti. Dovresti leggerle anche tu.
Queste istruzioni sono importanti. Le dovresti leggere anche tu.
These instructions are important. You, too, should read them.

Object pronouns are always attached to *ecco:*

Alida, ti ho portato un opuscolo. Eccolo!
   Alida, I brought you a pamphlet Here it is!

Ho trovato la mia busta paga! Eccola!
   I found my pay check. Here it is!

Note that some verbs that take an indirect object in English, such as *ascoltare* (to listen to), *aspettare* (to wait for), and *pagare* (to pay for), take a direct object in Italian.

Lei aspetta una telefonata per un colloquio di lavoro.
   She's waiting for a telephone call for a job interview.

Io ascolto la radio ogni giorno.
   I listen to the radio every day.

Quanto hai pagato quel vestito?
   How much did you pay for that dress?

b. *Pronomio oggetto indiretto* (indirect object pronouns)

Indirect object pronouns replace indirect objects and they, too, usually precede the verb, except *loro,* which always follows the verb.

	SINGULAR	PLURAL	
to me	*mi*	*ci*	to us
to you (sg)	*ti*	*vi*	to you (fam. and formal)
to him	*gli*	*gli/loro*	to them (m.)
to her	*le*	*gli/loro*	to them (f.)
to you (formal, m. and f.)	*Le*	*Loro*	to you (formal m. and f.)

Enzo, scrivi tu al cliente che abbiamo visto ieri? —Sì, gli scrivo io.
   Enzo, are you writing to the client we met yesterday? —Yes, I'll write to him.

Hai spiegato le condizioni di lavoro alla candidata? —Sì, le ho spiegato tutto.
   Did you explain the work conditions to the candidate? —Yes, I explained everything to her.

Questo lavoro non gli interessa?
   This job doesn't interest him?

Non scriviamo loro da due anni.
We have not written to them for two years.

Remember that there is no agreement between the indirect object pronouns and the past participle in compound tenses.

Dottor Vizini, ieri Le ho spedito la mia domanda di lavoro.
Dr. Vizini, yesterday I sent you my job application.

Indirect object pronouns can also be attached as a suffix to infinitives, gerunds, and the familiar forms of the imperative.

Digli di vestirsi bene per il colloquio di lavoro.
Tell him to dress well for the job interview.

Parlandole, ho capito che era la persona adatta per il lavoro.
Talking to her, I understood that she was the right person for the job.

Ho voluto scrivervi io personalmente.
I wanted to write to you personally.

With modal verbs *(dovere, potere, volere)* the indirect object pronoun can either precede the modal or be attached to the infinitive as a suffix.

Lidio, puoi darle una mano a preparare il curriculum vitae?
Lidio, le puoi dare una mano a preparare il curriculum vitae?
Lidio, could you help her prepare her curriculum vitae?

Note, however, that *loro/Loro* always follows the infinitive.

Non ho potuto scrivere loro perché sono stato molto occupato.
I could not write to them because I have been very busy.

Some verbs, such as *telefonare* (to telephone, to call), *dire* (to say), *rispondere* (to answer), *insegnare* (to teach), *chiedere* (to ask), take an indirect object in Italian but a direct object in English.

Telefona a Roberta e dille che i clienti arriveranno domani alle undici.
Phone Roberta and tell her that the clients will arrive tomorrow at eleven o'clock.

Gli hanno detto di venire subito.
They told him to come right away.

Le abbiamo risposto immediatamente.
We answered her immediately.

c. *Pronomi tonici* (disjunctive pronouns)

Direct and indirect object pronouns also have emphatic forms.

	SINGULAR	PLURAL	
me	*me*	*noi*	us
you	*te*	*voi*	you (fam. and formal)
him	*lui*	*loro*	them (m.)
her	*lei*	*loro*	them (f.)
you (formal, m. and f.)	*Lei*	*Loro*	you (formal m. and f.)

These pronouns are used:

—immediately after a verb for emphasis or to avoid ambiguity.

Hanno chiamato me per l'intervista, non lui.
They called me for an interview, not him.

Abbiamo visto anche lui al cinema.
We also saw him at the movies.

—after a preposition.

Matteo, vieni con me all'ufficio di collocamento, per favore!
Matthew, please come with me to the employment office!

Vengo da voi dopo che avrò preso il libretto di lavoro.
I'll come by your place after I pick up an Employment Record.

—independently of the verb.

Caro, ma io amo te! Te! Te! Solo te!
Darling, I love you! You! You! Only you!

—in exclamations.

Povero me!
    Poor me!

Fortunato te!
    Lucky you!

Beati voi!
    You lucky people!

2. *IL PRONOME NE* (THE CONJUNCTIVE PRONOUN *NE*)

The pronoun *ne* precedes the verb and is used to replace partitive structures. It therefore conveys the meaning "of it, of them."

Hai intervistato molti candidati oggi? —No, ne ho intervistati solo tre.
    Did you interview a lot of candidates today? —No, I interviewed only three of them.

Quando hai spedito la domanda di lavoro, hai allegato il tuo curriculum?
—Sì, ne ho incluso tre copie.
    When you mailed your application, did you attach your curriculum vitae? —Yes, I included three copies of it.

Note that *alcuni/alcune* (used with count nouns) and *un po' di* (used with non-count nouns) can be used in conjunction with *ne* for added emphasis.

Vuole sfogliare questi nuovi opuscoli? —Grazie, ma ne ho già visti alcuni.
    Would you like to browse through these new pamphlets? —Thanks, but I've already seen a few of them.

Ne is also used to replace phrases modified by a number or quantitative expressions. In this case, *ne* replaces the noun phrases, but the number or quantity expression remains.

Avete incontrato molti colleghi? —No, ne abbiamo incontrati pochi.
    Did you meet many colleagues? —No, we met few of them.

Quanti film di Fellini hai visto? —Ne ho visti due.
    How many movies by Fellini have you seen? —I have seen two of them.

Ne also replaces *di* + person/thing and means "of/about."

Hanno parlato dei nuovi impiegati? —Sì, ne hanno parlato.
Did they speak about the new employees? —Yes, they spoke about them.

Durante gli incontri di oggi abbiamo discusso dei programmi di riqualificazione professionale. E ne parleremo domani.
At today's seminar, we discussed retraining programs. And we'll talk about them tomorrow.

Ovunque si trovavano ne discutevano.
Wherever they were they used to speak about it.

If *ne* in its partitive meaning precedes a verb in a compound tense, then the past participle must agree with the pronoun in number and gender. However, when *ne* replaces *di* + person/thing there is no agreement.

Ma quante domande di lavoro hai preso? —Ne ho prese tre: una per Carlo, una per Marisa e una per me.
But how many job application forms did you take? —I took three of them: one for Carlo, one for Marisa, and one for me.

Gli impiegati sono arrivati tutti? —No, ne sono arrivati solo metà.
Did all the employees arrive? —No, only half of them have arrived.

Hai visto la nuova direttrice del personale? —No, ma ne ho sentito parlare molto bene.
Did you see the new director of personnel? —No, but I heard good things about her.

3. *PLURALI DEI NOMI E DEGLI AGGETTIVI: CASI PARTICOLARI* (PLURALS OF NOUNS AND ADJECTIVES: SPECIAL CASES)

a. Compound nouns

Compound nouns *(nomi composti),* as their name suggests, are made up of two parts. Although the plural formation of such nouns is sometimes complex, general guidelines do exist. The compound noun behaves like a "regular" noun (i.e., the plural form is indicated by changing the last letter) when its two parts consist of:

noun + noun:	*la madreperla* → *le madreperle* (mother of pearl), *la ferrovia* → *le ferrovie* (railway) *il manoscritto* → *i manoscritti* (manuscript)
noun + adjective:	*il palcoscenico* → *i palcoscenici* (stage)
adjective + noun:	*il gentiluomo* → *i gentiluomini* (gentleman) *il francobollo* → *i francobolli* (stamp)
verb + singular noun:	*l'asciugamano* → *gli asciugamani* (towel)

Le ferrovie italiane sono molto efficienti.
Italian railroads are very efficient.

Andrea, cambia gli asciugamani nel bagno perché sono sporchi.
Andrew, change the towels in the bathroom because they are dirty.

The compound noun remains invariable when its two parts consist of:

verb + verb:	*il viavai* → *i viavai* (coming-and-going), *il dormiveglia* → *i dormiveglia* (drowsiness).
verb + plural noun:	*il portalettere* → *i portalettere* (mail carrier), *la lavapiatti* → *le lavapiatti* (dishwasher).

C'è un annuncio nel giornale. Cercano dei portalettere.
There's an ad in the newspaper. They're looking for mail carriers.

Quel ristorante ha cambiato cinque diversi lavapiatti in un mese.
That restaurant has changed five different dishwashers in a month.

When the compound noun is made up of two nouns separated by a hyphen, only the first noun takes the plural form: *il divano-letto* → *i divani-letto* (sofabed), il vagone-letto → *i vagoni-letto* (sleeping-car).

A casa abbiamo due divani-letto.
At home we have two sofabeds.

Nei vagoni-letto si viaggia molto comodamente.
In the sleeping-cars one travels very comfortably.

b. Nouns of Greek origin

Some masculine nouns are of Greek origin. They end in *-amma, -emma, -ama, -ema, -oma, -sma, -eta*. For example: *il telegramma* (telegram), *il dilemma* (dilemma), *il diploma* (diploma), *il sistema* (system), *il fantasma* (ghost), and *il profeta* (prophet). The final *-a* of these nouns becomes *-i* in the plural: *i profeti* (prophets).

Vogliono una risposta domani, ma io devo prima risolvere quei dilemmi.
They want an answer tomorrow, but I must first solve those dilemmas.

Gli sposi hanno ricevuto molti telegrammi di auguri.
The bride and groom received many telegrams of best wishes.

c. Masculine nouns ending in *-a*

Some masculine nouns ending in *-a* are invariable. These are usually abbreviated forms.

In questo quartiere ci sono due cinema.
In this neighborhood there are two movie theatres.

d. Adjectives and nouns ending in *-ista, -cida, -ota, - eta, -asta,* and *-iatra*

Adjectives and nouns ending in *-ista, -cida, -iatra* referring to people, professions, and activities have identical masculine and feminine singular forms. In the plural, the masculine takes the characteristic *-i* ending and the feminine the characteristic *-e* ending.

La competizione è feroce. I piloti dell'Alitalia sono molto preparati.
Competition is fierce. Alitalia's pilots are well trained.

Quelle due signore sono giornaliste del Corriere della sera.
Those two ladies are journalists for the *Corriere della sera.*

Alberto Tomba e Roberto Biagio sono due degli atleti italiani più famosi.
Alberto Tomba and Roberto Biagio are two of the most famous Italian athletes.

Ragazzi, ma perché siete così pessimisti? Presto ci saranno altri impieghi!
Boys, why are you such pessimists? There will be more jobs soon!

Grazie al programma job sharing ho potuto assumere due ragazze entusiaste!
Thanks to the job sharing program I was able to hire two enthusiastic girls!

e. Feminine nouns ending in *-o*

Feminine nouns ending in *-o* are invariable in the plural. Almost all of them are abbreviated forms: *la radio (la radioricevente), l'auto (l'automobile), la foto (la fotografia), la moto (la motocicletta)*. An exception to this rule is *la mano - le mani*.

Hai portato le foto del tuo viaggio?
Did you bring the pictures of your trip?

Nel centro di Roma la circolazione delle auto è vietata.
Cars are not allowed in downtown Rome.

D. PAROLE! PAROLE! PAROLE!

As in English, animals appear in many Italian idiomatic expressions.

Sei lento come una tartaruga/lumaca.
You're as slow as a tortoise/snail.

Dino è testardo come un mulo.
Dino is as stubborn as a mule.

Tu sei un asino!
You're a fool/dunce! (lit.: an ass)

Non mangiare come un porco.
Don't eat like a pig.

Non è un'aquila.
He's no genius. (lit.: He's no eagle.)

È timido come un coniglio.
He is as timid as a hare.

Non so più che pesci prendere.
I no longer know which way to turn. (lit.: I don't know what fish to take.)

Qui mi sento come un pesce fuori d'acqua.
Here I feel like a fish out of water.

Oggi hai fatto un pesce d'aprile a qualcuno?
Today did you play an April fool's trick on anyone?

È una vecchia volpe.
He is a sly old fox.

C'erano quattro gatti alla festa.
There was hardly anyone at the party.

È coraggioso come un leone.
He's lion-hearted.

Oggi mi sento un leone.
Today I feel as strong as a lion.

È solo come un cane.
He's very lonely.

Ho una fame da lupi.
I'm as hungry as a wolf.

E. L'ANGOLO DEGLI AFFARI

LA DONNA ITALIANA NEL MONDO DEL LAVORO
(WOMEN IN THE ITALIAN WORK FORCE)

It is difficult to adequately describe the status of women in Italy. Historically, the country has held very conservative views regarding the role that women should play in society. The ideal of a patriarchal family has been pervasive in Italian culture for centuries, and although much has changed in the past fifty years in favor of women, the situation remains far from ideal. This can be explained by the pervasive belief (in society at large, not just among men) that the role of primary caregiver within the nuclear family still falls to the woman. However, such views are slowly beginning to disappear, and women have made tremendous strides towards equality in the last five decades as far as legislation is concerned.

Women did not gain the right to vote until 1945, much later than in several other industrialized countries. It was not until 1952 that women could be considered for a position in the diplomatic corps, and only in 1964 were women first allowed to become magistrates. It was not until the late sixties, when a strong feminist movement began, that women became more politically aware and active. In fact, only after the birth of Italian feminism in the sixties did laws legalizing divorce (1970) and abortion (1978) come about. Throughout the seventies and eighties, more and more women joined the work force, thanks to a healthy women's movement and many improvements in legislation. In 1977, a law was passed outlining the steps necessary to achieve the equal treatment of men and women in the workplace. Today, while many women hold positions of power and respect in both the private and public sectors, they are still in a minority, especially in the higher echelons of industry and government.

In 1985, the Italian government published the *Codice Donna* (Woman's Code), a document that outlines all existing national laws protecting women, as well as all international agreements pertaining to women. According to this document, Italy's laws protecting women in the work force are truly modern. The laws in place regarding maternity, for example, are more comprehensive than those of many industrialized nations. Women who become pregnant must retain all forms of remuneration, regular leave days, and health care benefits. They are entitled to a two-month leave prior to the birth of their child (a three-month leave if their position requires manual labor) and three months following delivery. Furthermore, no pregnant woman must be made to perform dangerous or strenuous physical tasks during the nine-month pregnancy period or seven months after the birth of her child. Following the birth, maternity leave may continue for a period of six months, and, for the first three years of the child's life, a mother is entitled to take another leave of absence if her child becomes ill (provided that a medical certificate be presented to the employer verifying the child's medical condition). Furthermore, there are guidelines outlining hours for breastfeeding (for full-time workers, two hours per day for the first year of the child's life, which may be taken consecutively or accumulated). Laws such as these have made a career outside the home a more desirable option for Italian women in the last twenty years, and consequently, female employment has increased dramatically in all sectors of business. There has been more than a doubling of women owning businesses and pursuing professional occupations. Enrollment in post-secondary institutions in the fields of science and technology is no longer predominantly male. Still, times are changing slowly, and while women may be interested in upper-level managerial positions in industry, it will take some time before the numbers of women approach those of men in the upper ranks of industry. For the moment, the sectors where one is least likely to find women in power are in managerial positions in large industries and in politics.

Despite its relatively conservative views, Italy is a modern, industrialized country, and for the most part, North American women planning to do business in Italy need not worry about differences in business etiquette between Italy and North America. Remember that Italians always appreciate professionalism and know-how combined with a relaxed attitude. While confidence is always impressive, aggressiveness and arrogance are not admired in women or men in business.

ESERCIZI

A. *Completare con il pronome oggetto diretto ed il verbo, dove necessario.* (Fill in the blanks with the direct object pronoun, and the verb when necessary.)

1. *—Volete vedere questi opuscoli? —Sì, _____ vedere.*
2. *—Dove posso ottenere un libretto di lavoro? —È possibile _____ all'ufficio anagrafe.*
3. *—Sai che dovresti anche iscriverti ad un ufficio di collocamento? —No, non _____.*
4. *—Avete visto le mie colleghe? —No, non _____ vist _____.*
5. *_____ invito tutti a casa mia stasera: siete miei ospiti.*
6. *Loredana, _____ ringrazio di tutto. Stasera, quando andiamo al cinema, pago io.*
7. *Signor Mastri, _____ ringrazio di tutte le informazioni.*
8. *—Hai visto il mio documento di identità? —No, non _____ vist _____.*

B. *Completare con il pronome indiretto ed altri elementi, se necessario.* (Fill in the blanks with the indirect object pronouns, and the verb when necessary.)

1. *—Allora cosa _____ consigli, Roberta? —Loredana, _____ consiglio innanzitutto di controllare la situazione del mercato.*
2. *Sono andata a trovare Loredana e _____ ho fatto vedere un opuscolo sulle donne e il lavoro.*

3. —Hai parlato al datore di lavoro? —Sì, _____ già.
4. —Avete dato le informazioni ai vostri genitori? —Sì, _____
   dat _____ le informazioni.
5. —Signorina, posso telefonar _____ stasera? —Sì, _____ telefoni
   stasera.
6. _____ è stato offerto un bellissimo lavoro, ma noi l'abbiamo rifiutato.

C. *Rispondere alle domande usando un pronome oggetto diretto o indiretto,
   o il pronome ne.* (Answer the following questions affirmatively using a
   direct or indirect object pronoun, or the conjunctive pronoun *ne*.)

   1. *Avete spiegato alla signorina Gentili le condizioni salariali?*
   2. *Hai fatto la domanda di assunzione?*
   3. *Carlo ha preparato i documenti per il colloquio?*
   4. *Signorina, ha consegnato la lettera d'assunzione al candidato?*
   5. *Hanno firmato il contratto?*
   6. *Avete parlato delle condizioni di lavoro?*

D. *Cambiare al plurale.* (Change the following sentences into the plural.)

   1. *La collega di mia sorella è molto pessimista.*
   2. *La mano del pianista era sicura ed agile.*
   3. *Il nuovo programma era perfetto per la neo-mamma.*
   4. *Quell'artista ha creato un vero e proprio capolavoro.*

E. *Tradurre.* (Translate.)

   1. Can you help me prepare for the interview?
   2. Mom, I want to come with you, not with him.
   3. Did he phone her friend? —Yes, he phoned her.
   4. Did you find the car keys? —No, I am still looking for them.
   5. Japanese motorcycles are the best.
   6. How many candidates did you interview today? —We interviewed
      three of them.
   7. Children, you have to give me a hand.
   8. I slept like a log!
   9. Did your employer record your duties in your Employment
      Record?
   10. What is the current job situation?

LEZIONE 5

A. DIALOGO

UN INVITO A CENA

Mentre Paola sta passeggiando per le stradine[1] di Venezia,[2] incontra la signora Elena Rossi che sta rientrando a casa dal supermercato.

S.RA ROSSI: **Ciao,[3] Paola.**

PAOLA: **Buongiorno, signora. Lasci che l'aiuti. Mi dia qualche sacchetto. Glielo porto io.[4]**

S.RA ROSSI: **Grazie.**

Paola e la signora Rossi si avviano verso casa.

S.RA ROSSI: **Come sta Andrew? Come sta andando il vostro soggiorno in Italia?**

PAOLA: **Meravigliosamente, signora. Ritornare a casa è sempre bello e poi . . . Venezia è stupenda.**

S.RA ROSSI: **Pensavo che vi fermaste soltanto qualche settimana e invece siete ancora qui.**

PAOLA: **Ci troviamo bene in Italia e non abbiamo fretta di tornare negli Stati Uniti. Io vorrei passare qualche settimana con i miei.[5] E poi Andrew non vuole perdersi il festival.[6]**

S.RA ROSSI: **Venite a cena da noi,[7] domani sera. Vi preparerò qualcosa di speciale.[8]**

PAOLA: **Signora grazie. Domani sera va benissimo. Io ed Andrew non abbiamo impegni.[9]**

S.RA ROSSI: **Allora, ci vediamo domani sera alle otto,[10] va bene? Vi aspettiamo.**

PAOLA: **A domani sera, allora. ArrivederLa e grazie, signora.**

S.RA ROSSI: **Grazie a te dell'aiuto, Paola. Arrivederci.**

Ritornata a casa, Paola informa suo[11] marito dell'invito.

PAOLA: **Andrew, la signora Rossi ci ha invitato a cena ed io ho accettato.**

ANDREW: **Per quand'è l'invito?**

PAOLA: **Per domani sera. Alle otto.**

ANDREW: **Cosa portiamo? Dei fiori? Una torta? Una bottiglia di vino?**

PAOLA: **Non so** [12] **. . . Ma tu l'anno scorso hai fatto un corso di buone maniere o no?** [13]

ANDREW: **Non prendermi in giro. L'avrò fatto,** [14] **ma forse qui in Italia si fa diversamente.**

PAOLA: **Io direi di portare dei pasticcini.** - pastries

ANDREW: **Non so se sia una cosa da fare. La signora Rossi il dessert forse lo preparerà lei. Tu la conosci benissimo. E non vorremmo costringerla a servire quello che portiamo noi.**

PAOLA: **Allora portiamo dei fiori.**

ANDREW: **Sì, hai ragione. È la cosa migliore. Ci penso io.** - I'll think about it.

PAOLA: **OK. Faglieli recapitare domani stesso, prima di cena.**

ANDREW: **Dirò al fioraio di consegnarli domani mattina . . . Ma come dobbiamo vestirci?**

PAOLA: **Io mi metto il cappello e l'abito lungo. Tu lo smoking. Sull'invito è specificato, no? Cravatta nera e . . .**

ANDREW: **Smettila! Tu pensi sempre a scherzare. Devo mettermi la cravatta, allora?**

PAOLA: **Ma sì, mettiti il blazer blu con quella bellissima cravatta che ti ho regalato a Natale. Io mi metto il tailleur di seta . . .** [15]

ANDREW: **OK.**

PAOLA: **E non farmi fare brutta figura!**

ANDREW: **Cosa vuoi dire?**

PAOLA: **Tu capisci benissimo cosa voglio dire. Devo ricordartelo allora? Beh, cominciamo . . . Fatti ricordare alcune norme basilari di comportamento a tavola. Numero uno: gli spaghetti** [16] **non si mangiano con forchetta e cucchiaio. Numero due: gli**

FORK & spoon

spaghetti vanno presi [17] in piccole quantità, senza metterne un quintale sulla forchetta.

ANDREW: E questo è tutto?

PAOLA: No, non ho ancora finito. Numero tre: il galateo non permette la scarpetta . . . In altre parole non devi raccogliere il condimento del piatto con il pane, come spesso fai a casa. Numero quattro: non metterti il tovagliolo al collo. Numero cinque: il brindisi si fa senza dire cin cin.[18] Numero sei . . .

ANDREW: E scommetto che è un sacrilegio bere il caffè con il mignolo [19] alzato.

PAOLA: Proprio così.

ANDREW: Ma finiscila! Smettila di scherzare!

A DINNER INVITATION

While Paola is walking through the narrow streets of Venice, she meets Mrs. Elena Rossi returning from the supermarket.

MRS. ROSSI: Hello, Paola.

PAOLA: Good morning. Let me help you. Give me one of the bags. I'll carry it for you.

MRS. ROSSI: Thank you.

Paola and Mrs. Rossi head for home.

MRS. ROSSI: How's Andrew? How's your stay in Italy going?

PAOLA: Wonderfully. It's nice to come home and besides . . . Venice is fantastic.

MRS. ROSSI: I thought you were going to stay for only a week but you're still here.

PAOLA: We enjoy being in Italy and we're in no hurry to go back to the United States. I'd like to spend a few weeks with my family. And plus Andrew doesn't want to miss the festival.

MRS. ROSSI: Come to our house for dinner tomorrow night. I'll make something special for you.

PAOLA: Thank you, ma'am. Tomorrow night will be fine. Andrew and I don't have any other plans.

MRS. ROSSI: Well then, we'll see one another tomorrow night at eight, okay? We will be expecting you.

PAOLA: Until tomorrow night, then. Goodbye, and thank you.

MRS. ROSSI: Thank you for your help, Paola. Goodbye.

After returning home, Paola tells her husband about the invitation.

PAOLA: Andrew, Mrs. Rossi invited us for dinner and I accepted.

ANDREW: When is the invitation for?

PAOLA: Tomorrow night. At eight.

ANDREW: What will we bring? Some flowers? A cake? A bottle of wine?

PAOLA: I don't know . . . But last year didn't you take a course in good manners?

ANDREW: Very funny. I may have taken it, but maybe things are done differently here in Italy.

PAOLA: I would say to bring some pastries.

ANDREW: I'm not sure about that. Maybe Mrs. Rossi is going to make dessert herself. You know her well enough. And we wouldn't want to force her to serve something that we bring.

PAOLA: Then we'll bring flowers.

ANDREW: Yes, you're right. It's the best thing. I'll take care of it.

PAOLA: Okay. Have them delivered tomorrow, before dinner.

ANDREW: I'll tell the florist to deliver them tomorrow morning . . . But how should we dress?

PAOLA: I'll wear my hat and my long dress. You'll wear your dinner jacket. Isn't it specified on the invitation? Black tie, and . .

ANDREW: Oh, stop it! You're always joking. Should I wear a tie then?

PAOLA: Oh, yes, put on your blue blazer with that beautiful tie I gave you for Christmas. I'll put on my silk suit.

ANDREW: Okay.

PAOLA: And don't embarrass me!

ANDREW: What do you mean?

PAOLA: You know exactly what I mean. Do I have to remind you then? Well, let's start . . . Let me remind you of some of the basic table manners . . . Number one: spaghetti is not eaten with a fork and spoon. Number two: spaghetti is taken in small quantities, without putting a ton on the fork.

ANDREW: Is that all?

PAOLA: No, I'm not done yet. Number three: proper etiquette does not permit *la scarpetta.* In other words, you can not scoop up the sauce in your plate with your bread, like you usually do at home. Number four: don't put your napkin around your neck. Number five: The toast is made without saying "cheers." Number six . . .

ANDREW: And I guess it's a sin to drink coffee with your pinky in the air.

PAOLA: Exactly.

ANDREW: Oh come on! Stop joking around!

B. IN BREVE

1. For more information on the streets of Venice, please see *Lezione 8, In Breve.*

2. Venice, the city of canals, is the capital of the Veneto region. Known as *La serenissima* ("the very serene one"), Venice has been known for centuries for its unique location and architecture. Originally built on 118 islands, the city is divided by 180 canals (measuring twenty-eight miles in length) that on average are about twelve feet in width. Its main landmarks include the *Basilica di San Marco* (St. Mark's Basilica) and *Piazza San Marco* (St. Mark square), *il Palazzo ducale* (the palace of the Doge), *il Canal Grande* (the Grand Canal), and the *Ponte dei sospiri* (the Bridge of Sighs). Venice is one of the most important tourist centers in Italy.

3. If you address a person with the polite form, you should expect the same in return. However, when there is an acknowledged differ-

ence in age or status (e.g., teacher-student relationship), it is acceptable for one person to use *Lei* and the other to use *tu*.

4. Remember that *io* is never capitalized, except at the beginning of a sentence. Note also that it is possible to place a subject after the verb for emphasis.

5. Note that the masculine plural form of the possessive pronoun (*i miei, i tuoi,* etc.) is often used to refer to one's family.

6. The Venice Film Festival, first held in 1932, was the first festival of its kind. Historically, it has been extremely influential, often dictating changes in cinematic trends on an international level. For instance, the awarding of the *Leone d'oro* ("the golden lion," the festival's highest honour) to Akira Kurosawa's *Rashomon* in 1951 brought international attention to both the director and the Japanese film industry in general, allowing this country's cinema to gain recognition and importance throughout the world. In the years following World War II, the Venice film festival caused a rebirth in the Italian film industry and helped popularize Italian neorealism.

7. The preposition *da* followed by a disjunctive pronoun (*me, te, lui, lei,* etc.), a name, or a profession is used to translate the expression "at someone's house/place." *Devo andare prima dal dottore e poi da un collega.* (First I have to go to the doctor and then to a colleague's.) For more on the use of the preposition *da,* please refer to *Lezione 2.*

8. If an adjective modifies *qualcosa* it must be introduced by the preposition *di* and be in the masculine singular form.

9. There is no translation for the negative partitive "any" in Italian. Instead, the noun is used without an article. *Mi dispiace signora, non abbiamo dolci. Abbiamo però dei pasticcini e delle torte veramente deliziose.* (I'm sorry, madame, we don't have any sweets. But we have some very delicious pastries and cakes.)

10. For breakfast Italians usually have coffee (or *un caffellate, un latte macchiato, un cappuccino*) and something light to eat *(una brioche, un cornetto, una pasta, dei biscotti)*. Italians generally enjoy a

lengthy lunch break, when stores, offices, banks, and the post office are all closed. Italians usually have dinner from seven o'clock on.

11. Remember that definite articles are not required when a possessive adjective refers to a singular, unmodified noun denoting a family relationship. For more on this grammatical rule, see *Lezione 3*.

12. Although the expressions *Non so* and *Non lo so* both mean "I don't know" and are interchangeable, the latter literally means, "I don't know it," the "it" referring to a particular fact.

13. In Italian, *no* is often used as a tag question. *È lei, no?* (It's she, isn't it?) In this context *vero* can also be used. *È lei, vero?* (It's she, isn't it?) Pay attention also to these uses of *no: Come no!* (Of course, by all means!) *Credo di no.* (I don't think so.) *Ho detto di no.* (I said no.) *Ora no!* (Not now!) *Pare di no.* (Apparently not.) *Spero di no.* (I hope not.)

14. Remember that in Italian probability in the past may be expressed with the future perfect. (See *Lezione 3*.)

15. The preposition *di* is used to describe what something is made of: *una casa di legno* (a wooden house), *una maglia di cotone* (a cotton sweater).

16. Remember that *spaghetti* is plural in Italian.

17. The verb *andare* may be used as an auxiliary. This construction renders the idea of an action that must be done. It may be used instead of *dover essere. Gli spaghetti devono essere presi in piccole quantità* or *Gli spaghetti vanno presi in piccole quantità.* (Spaghetti should be eaten in small quantitites.) *Questa pasta deve essere mangiata/va mangiata.* (This pasta should be eaten.)

18. Other expressions to make toasts are: *Salute!, Prosit!,* or simply *Auguri!*

19. The other four fingers are: *pollice* (thumb), *indice* (index), *medio* (middle finger), and *anulare* (ring finger). The toes are generally

mignolo – pinky

called *dita del piede* and only the big toe has a name: *alluce,* or colloquially, *ditone.*

C. GRAMMATICA E SUOI USI

1. *L'IMPERATIVO* (THE IMPERATIVE)

The imperative is used to express a command, an invitation, an exhortation, or a suggestion. It is formed by replacing the infinitive ending with the endings: *-a, -i, -iamo, -ate, -ino* for the first conjugation, and *-i, -a, -iamo, -ete, -ano* for the second and third conjugations. Verbs that add *-isc* in the present indicative do so in the imperative as well. Note that the *tu, noi,* and *voi* forms of the *-ere* and *-ire* verbs are identical in the present indicative and the imperative. Notice that an exclamation point normally follows an imperative in Italian.

	LAVORARE	PRENDERE	PARTIRE	FINIRE
tu	lavora	prendi	parti	finisci
Lei	lavori	prenda	parta	finisca
noi	lavoriamo	prendiamo	partiamo	finiamo
voi	lavorate	prendete	partite	finite
Loro	lavorino	prendano	partano	finiscano

Signorina Romei, finisca pure di mangiare con calma! Ritornerò fra mezz'ora.
Miss Romei, take your time eating. I'll be back in a half hour.

Carlo, per favore, prendi i tovaglioli dalla credenza!
Carlo, please take the napkins from the pantry.

Mamma, passa il sale, per favore!
Mom, please pass the salt.

The *noi* form expresses the equivalent of the English "let's + verb."

Organizziamo una cena coi fiocchi per onorare il nuovo direttore!
Let's organize a lavish dinner to honor the new director.

Usiamo le buone maniere e faremo una bella figura!
Let's use good manners and we'll make a good impression.

To form the negative imperative, simply place *non* before the verb. With the *tu* form, the infinitive form of the verb is used instead of the conjugated form.

Non mettere lo smoking per la cena dai Rinaldini!
Don't wear a tuxedo for the Rinaldini's dinner.

Non alzare il mignolo quando bevi il caffè!
Don't raise your pinky when you drink coffee.

The majority of verbs that are irregular in the present indicative are also irregular in the imperative. For the complete conjugation of irregular verbs, please refer to Appendix C, section 2.

Se vuole mangiare bene, vada al ristorante Trivelli!
If you want to eat well, go to the Trivelli restaurant.

Vieni con noi. Andiamo a farci un gelato!
Come with us. Let's go for an ice cream.

Object pronouns are attached as suffixes to the *tu, noi,* and *voi* affirmative imperative form, but they always precede the polite *Lei* and *Loro* forms.

Giovanni, sono arrivati gli ospiti. Per favore, accompagnali in cucina così possono mangiare un boccone!
Giovanni, the guests have arrived. Please escort them to the kitchen so they can have a bite to eat.

Ecco che arriva Carla. Chiediamole a che ora si cena stasera.
Here comes Carla. Let's ask her what time dinner is tonight.

Signora Crispi, Lei si sieda vicino a mio marito. Lei, signor Crispi, si sieda vicino a me.
Mrs. Crispi, sit down next to my husband. Mr. Crispi, you sit next to me.

One-syllable imperative forms, such as *da', fa', va', di',* and *sta'* drop the apostrophe and double the first consonant of the pronoun, except with *gli* in which case the first consonant is not doubled.

102

da' a + me

Per favore, dammi l'elenco degli ingredienti per gli spaghetti alla carbonara!
Please, give me the list of ingredients for spaghetti carbonara.

Facci il favore di accompagnare gli ospiti al proprio posto!
Do us a favor and accompany the guests to their seats.

Digli che è arrivato un invito per domenica prossima!
Tell him that an invitation for Sunday arrived.

Non vieni al ricevimento? —No, vacci da solo! Io ho un forte mal di testa.
Aren't you coming to the reception? —No, go by yourself. I have a bad headache.

With the negative *tu, noi,* and *voi* forms, object pronouns can either precede or follow the verb. In the latter case the pronouns are attached to the verb as a suffix. When pronouns attach to the infinitive, the verb loses its final *-e.*

La torta non è venuta bene. Non assaggiarla (non l'assaggiare) per piacere!
The cake didn't turn out well. Please, don't taste it!

Non diamole la ricetta! / Non le diamo la ricetta!
Let's not give her the recipe.

Non mi dite che devo portare lo smoking! / Non ditemi che devo portare lo smoking!
Don't tell me I have to wear a tuxedo!

The infinitive is often used to express an imperative when addressing the general public. You will notice this usage on signs, public notices, recipes, etc.

Non calpestare l'erba.
Keep off the grass.

Non fumare.
No smoking.

Cuocere dieci minuti prima di condire.
Cook for ten minutes before dressing.

Cucinare a fuoco lento e mescolare continuamente.
Cook on low heat and stir constantly.

To render a request more subtle it is common to use the present indicative or *volere/potere* + verb instead of the imperative.

Mi dai un bicchiere di vino, per favore?
Could you please give me a glass of wine?

Può/vuole passarmi quella coppa di champagne?
Could you pass me that glass of champagne?

The tone of an imperative may be rendered more subtle with the use of words such as *pure* or *un po'*.

Faccia pure con comodo! Finisca pure il suo bicchiere di champagne!
Take your time! Finish your glass of champagne!

Immaginate un po' quanta gente c'era alla festa?
Imagine how many people were at the party!

Remember that indirect imperatives, that is, imperatives expressing a command that affect a third party, use the present subjunctive.

Che mi dicano almeno il numero approssimativo degli invitati!
I wish they'd tell me the approximate number of guests!

Se il direttore vuole un ricevimento per 100 persone, che venga a darci una mano anche lui!
If the director wants a reception for 100 people, let him come and give us a hand too!

The verb *fare* followed by an infinitive renders the idea "to make/let/have someone do something." See also the section on the "causative construction" later in this lesson.

Non fatela aspettare!
Don't make her wait!

Fagli organizzare la festa come vuole lui!
Let him organize the party the way he wants!

Subject pronouns are usually left unexpressed with the imperative. They may, however, be used for emphasis. In this case, they generally follow the verb.

Porta tu il vassoio con i dolci!
You bring the tray with the sweets!

Chi accompagna la bambina al party? —Per favore, accompagnala tu!
Who is going to accompany the little girl to the party? —Please, you go with her.

The imperative forms of *volere* followed by an infinitive correspond to the English "Would you be so kind as to . . ." or "Kindly . . ."

Voglia presentarmi agli ospiti.
Kindly introduce me to the hosts.

The imperative of *sapere* (*sappi, sappia, sappiate, sappiano*), expresses the English "You should know."

Sappi che serviranno solo bevande non alcoliche!
You should know that they'll serve only non-alcoholic drinks.

Remember that rules governing the position of object pronouns with the imperative (see *Lezione 4*) also apply to the imperative of reflexive verbs.

Mettiti la cravatta prima che arrivino gli invitati!
Put on your tie before the guests arrive!

Prego, si accomodino. Il pranzo è pronto!
Please be seated. Dinner is served.

2. *I PRONOMI DOPPI* (DOUBLE PRONOUNS)

In sentences that contain both a direct and an indirect object pronoun, the indirect object pronoun always precedes the direct object pronoun. In addition, the pronouns undergo certain changes, as indicated in the following chart.

	LO	LA	LI	LE	NE
mi	me lo	me la	me li	me le	me ne
ti	te lo	te la	te li	te le	te ne
ci	ce lo	ce la	ce li	ce le	ce ne
vi	ve lo	ve la	ve li	ve le	ve ne
le/Le	glielo	gliela	glieli	gliele	gliene
gli	glielo	gliela	glieli	gliele	gliene
loro/Loro	glielo	gliela	glieli	gliele	gliene

When the indirect object pronouns *mi, ti, ci,* and *vi* are followed by the direct object pronouns *lo, la, li, le,* and *ne,* the final *-i* becomes *-e* and they change to *me, te, ce, ve* respectively.

Questi sono prodotti dolciari del luogo. —Bene, me ne dia un chilo!
These are local typical sweets. —Well then, please give me a kilo of them.

Devo ancora apparecchiare la tavola! —Non ti preoccupare, te l'apparecchio io!
I still have to set the table. —Don't worry, I'll set it for you.

The indirect object forms *gli, le,* and *Le* change to *glie* when they are followed by *lo, la, li, le,* or *ne.* The forms are combined and written as one word. The new forms are *glielo, gliela, glieli, gliele,* and *gliene* respectively.

Signor Merici, questo piatto è squisito. Glielo consiglio.
Mr. Merici, this dish is delicious. I recommend it to you.

Visto che a tuo marito piace molto l'insalata di pomodoro, gliene ho preparato un bel piatto.
Since your husband likes tomato salad so much, I've prepared a full dish of it for him.

The indirect object pronoun *loro* (to you, to them) always follows the verb and never attaches to the direct object pronouns. However, in everyday conversations *gli* commonly replaces *loro.*

Renata e Maria mi hanno invitato a cena: ricambierò loro la cortesia appena possibile.
Renata e Maria mi hanno invitato a cena: gli ricambierò la cortesia appena possibile.

Renata and Maria have invited me for supper; I will return the favor to them as soon as possible.

Double object pronouns follow the same rules as single object pronouns with regards to placement. They precede a conjugated verb and are attached to the infinitives, gerunds, and the familiar forms of the imperative as a suffix.

Carlo, ho ordinato 15 bistecche per il barbecue di domenica. Per favore, me le prendi tu dal macellaio?

Carlo, I have ordered 15 steaks for Sunday's barbecue. Could you please pick them up from the butcher?

Dino, ho dimenticato gli affettati per la festa. Potresti portarmeli tu qui?

Dino, I forgot the cold cuts for the party. Could you bring them here, please?

L'ospite stava sorbendosi il caffè, gustandoselo goccia per goccia.

The guest was sipping his coffee, savoring it drop by drop.

With modal verbs *(dovere, potere, volere)* the pronouns can either be attached to the infinitive as a suffix or precede the modal verb.

Gli spaghetti erano un po' scotti. La prossima volta potresti prepararmeli al dente, per favore?

The spaghetti was a bit overcooked. Next time could you please prepare them *al dente* for me?

Ma me lo devi dire tu come cucinare!

Who are you to tell me how to cook?

In compound tenses the past participle agrees in number and gender with the preceding direct object pronoun.

Ti ha dato la ricetta del tiramisù la tua amica? —Sì, ho insistito e me l'ha data.

Did your friend give you the tiramisù recipe? —Yes, I insisted and she gave it to me.

Ma chi ti ha mandato questi cioccolatini Perugina? —Me li ha mandati il mio ragazzo.

But who sent you these Perugina chocolates? —My boyfriend sent them to me.

Reflexive pronouns behave like indirect object pronouns when used in combination with direct object pronouns. Note that the *si* (singular and plural) changes to *se*. Agreement with compound tenses is made between the direct object pronoun (not the subject) and the past participle.

Lorenzo, dove sono i bigné? —Se li sono mangiati tutti.
Lorenzo, where are the cream puffs? —They ate all of them.

Com'è buona questa torta! Devo fare i miei complimenti alla cuoca. —Ma guarda che l'ho preparata io!

This cake is delicious! I must compliment the chef. —Actually I'm the one who prepared it!

There are also some other possible combinations with double pronouns: a) indirect object pronoun + *ne* (implying "about it"); b) *ci/vi* (implying "here, there") + direct object pronoun. Keep in mind that in compound tenses, there is no agreement between *ne* (about it) and the past participle. Furthermore, the direct object pronouns, *mi, ti, ci,* and *vi* precede pronouns of place *ci/vi* and remain unchanged.

Hai parlato loro dei preparativi per la festa del compleanno del direttore? —Sì, gliene ho già parlato questa mattina.

Did you speak to them about the plans for the manager's birthday party? —Yes, I already spoke to them about it this morning.

Quando metti le lasagne in forno? —Ce le ho messe proprio adesso.
When are you going to put the lasagna in the oven? —I just put it in right now.

Chi ti ha portato alla festa ieri sera? —Mi ci ha portato mio padre.
Who brought you to the party last night? —My father brought me (there).

3. *II FARE CAUSATIVO* (THE CAUSATIVE CONSTRUCTION WITH *FARE*)

The verb *fare* followed by an infinitive is used when the subject of the sentence does not perform the action, but causes something to be done by someone else. This construction is called the "causative construction" and conveys the following meanings: to get someone to do something, to make (to have) someone do something / to have something done by someone. Note that the "someone else" who does the action instead of the subject is expressed as an indirect object.

Il datore di lavoro mi ha fatto organizzare un ricevimento in onore del suo partner.
My employer had me organize a reception in honor of his partner.

Io non cucino mai a casa mia. Faccio sempre cucinare a mio marito.
I never cook at home. I have my husband do the cooking.

Noun objects follow the infinitive, but pronoun objects precede the form of *fare*. Object pronouns are attached to *fare* only when *fare* is in the infinitive, gerund, past participle, or the familiar forms of the imperative.

La festa la faremo preparare a Luigi. Gli faremo cucinare la sua famosa pasta alla vodka.
We'll get Luigi to organize the party. We'll have him cook his famous pasta alla vodka.

Non ti preoccupare. Ti farò invitare io al party.
Don't worry! I'll make sure you're invited to the party.

Facendolo cucinare, rischiamo di non mangiare niente.
By having him cook, we are taking a chance that we won't be eating.

When a reflexive verb follows *fare* the reflexive pronoun is omitted.

Loro mi hanno fatto divertire.
They made me enjoy myself.

Noi ti abbiamo fatto alzare presto.
We had you wake up early.

But when the subject of the sentence is *io,* the reflexive pronoun is retained.

Io mi faccio pettinare dal parrucchiere.
I'll have the hairdresser comb my hair.

Io mi sono fatta fare una bella pizza.
I had them make me a nice pizza.

The *fare causativo* may have two objects, both a direct object and the indirect object indicating the person. If they are nouns, they follow the infinitive (direct precedes indirect), and when they are pronouns they precede *fare.*

Farai preparare la ricetta a Maria?
Will you have Mary prepare the recipe?

Signor Milo, quando mi fa portare la carne che ho ordinato? —Gliela farò portare subito.
Mr. Milo, when will you have the meat that I ordered delivered to me? —I'll have it delivered to you right away.

The meaning of the indirect object in this construction may sometimes be ambiguous. For example, *Faccio preparare la cena a Giovanni* could mean "I have Giovanni prepare supper" or "I have supper prepared for Giovanni." To avoid ambiguity, replace *a* + person by *da* + person: *Faccio preparare la cena da Giovanni.*

Many common causative expressions are not normally translated by a causative in English. Here are some examples: *far costruire* (to build), *far entrare* (to let in), *far uscire* (to let out), *far osservare* (to point out), *far pagare* (to charge), *far sapere* (to inform), *far informare* (to inform), *far impazzire* (to drive someone crazy), *far vedere* (to show), *far aspettare* (to keep someone waiting), *far crescere* (to grow something).

D. PAROLE! PAROLE! PAROLE!

When Paola teased Andrew about dressing formally to go to dinner, he told her, *smettila!* The following expressions will come in handy if you want to tell someone to stop bothering you.

110

John, finiscila con queste chiacchiere! — silly talk
John, enough with this silly talk!

Roberta, è ora di finirla con questa storia!
Roberta, it's time to put an end to this matter.

Ma smettila ora!
Stop it, now! / Knock it off, now!

Non seccarmi/scocciarmi!
Don't bother me!

Lasciami stare!
Leave me alone!

Lasciami in pace! — peace
Leave me in peace!

Another idiomatic expression used in the dialog is *prendere in giro* ("to make fun of," "to pull someone's leg"). Other ways of saying the same thing are:

burlarsi di

Tutti si burlano di lui.
Everyone makes fun of him.

farsi gioco di

Loro si fanno sempre gioco di tutti.
They always make fun of everybody.

E. L'ANGOLO DEGLI AFFARI

IL GALATEO A TAVOLA (TABLE ETIQUETTE)

Food preparation and consumption are central to Italian culture, and eating etiquette is somewhat ritualized. It's important to know what to do and what not to do while dining with Italians.

If you're meeting for a prearranged business lunch, it's customary to exchange business cards at the beginning of the meeting; both women and men should shake hands when introduced. Whoever organized the luncheon normally picks up the tab. If you're paying, make sure you get a proper check, with the *partita IVA* (legal tax number allotted to all businesses) stamped on it. By law, patrons aren't supposed to leave a place of business without a receipt. The first charge on the bill will probably be the *pane e coperto* (bread and cover), which varies from establishment to establishment and region to region; the tip, between ten and 15 percent of the total, is likely to be included, too. "Business" lunches may focus on light-hearted conversation rather than on the business at hand; Italians tend to be garrulous and may choose to treat such meetings as social occasions rather than brainstorming sessions. Be flexible, since warmth may matter more to your Italian colleagues than businesslike zeal. Remember to start your meal with the words *Buon appetito,* to which the standard reply is *Altrettanto!* (likewise!).

Evening meals usually take place later in the day than in North America, around 7:00 or 8:00 p.m. Guests are expected to be punctual for dinner parties, and may wish to bring small gifts for their hosts, such as chocolates or flowers. Before dinner, an aperitif is often served—most frequently vermouth or Campari—and may be accompanied by hors d'oeuvres. Dinner, like lunch, commonly consists of a series of courses. The appetizer course is *antipasto,* which may be in the form of *affettati,* or coldcuts; *giardiniera,* vegetables in a vinaigrette; *latticini,* or dairy products such as *bocconcini* (mozzarella balls); seafood salad; *carpaccio,* thinly sliced raw meat; *crostini,* bread topped with paté or another delicacy; or *bruschetta,* toasted bread topped with chopped tomatoes, oregano, garlic, basil, olive oil, salt, and pepper. First courses, or *primi piatti,* which follow the *antipasto,* are usually pasta, risotto, or soup; entrées, or *secondi piatti,* tend to be meat, fish, or fowl, served with vegetables or potatoes. In a restaurant, you should avoid ordering just pasta; you're really expected to eat a main course.

Wine and mineral water are the drinks most regularly served with dinner; ice is not customary. Nor do Italians favor drinking hard liquor before a meal, since such liquor may numb the taste buds. Espresso and liqueurs may follow, but elaborate desserts are reserved for cafés and the local *pasticceria* (pastry shop) and not often eaten with dinner. Many Italians like to keep their recipes to themselves, so it's not normal practice to ask for a recipe after eating a good meal. Also, hosts will seldom accept an offer to help them clear the table or do the dishes at a dinner party, no matter how informal the party seems, and thank you notes are generally not sent.

ESERCIZI

A. *Sostituire le parole sottolineate con un pronome doppio.* (Substitute the underlined words with a double pronoun.)

1. *Ti compro io la carne per il pranzo?* Te la compro.
2. *Gli ospiti portano i fiori alla padrona di casa.*
3. *La signora Merlini offre il dolce agli invitati.*
4. *Noi diamo la ricetta alle nostre amiche.*
5. *Gli sposi mandano gli inviti ai loro parenti ed amici.*

B. *Rispondere in modo opportuno, usando il pronome doppio.* (Answer the following questions, using the double pronoun.)

1. *Hai già portato i fiori alla signora Rossi?*
2. *Avete dato la torta a Marco?*
3. *La mamma ti ha comprato i pasticcini?*
4. *Vuoi regalare questa bottiglia di vino a Renzo?*
5. *Hanno già mandato il regalo ai bambini?*
6. *Ci racconterai com'è andata la serata dai Rossi?*
7. *Chi ti ha regalato questa cravatta?*
8. *Hai detto a Pierino di non mettersi il tovagliolo al collo quando mangia?*

C. *Completare con il pronome opportuno ed il verbo, se necessario.* (Fill in the blanks with the appropriate pronoun, and the verb when necessary.)

1. *Signora, mi dia quel sacchetto. _____ io.*
2. *—Stasera ti metti il tailleur di seta? —Sì, _____.*
3. *—Ma tu dimentichi sempre! Devo _____ un'altra volta.*
4. *—Il dottore ti ha proibito di mangiare pasta? —Sì, _____.*
5. *—Hai chiesto a Massimo se viene a cena? —Sì, _____.*
6. *—Papà, mi compri la torta per il mio compleanno? —_____ compro, se farai il bravo.*
7. *Il caffè? _____ porterò fra un attimo, signorina.*
8. *—Avete parlato al signor Colilli della festa? —Sì, _____.*

D. *Dare i seguenti comandi.* (Give the following commands.)

1. *Chiedi a Carlo di stare più attento.*
2. *Di' alla signora Carletti di telefonare al suo dottore.*
3. *Chiedi ai tuoi impiegati di fare il lavoro più in fretta.*
4. *Ordina loro di essere più gentili con il pubblico.*
5. *Di' al tuo partner di non firmare il contratto.*

E. *Cambiare dalla forma di cortesia alla forma familiare.* (Change the following sentences from the polite to the familiar form.)

1. *Me lo dia subito.*
2. *Non ci crei problemi, per favore!*
3. *Glielo spieghino con più calma!*
4. *Ce lo dica subito e non ci faccia perdere più tempo!*
5. *Mi spedisca il contratto immediatamente!*
6. *Per favore, me ne faccia nove copie!*
7. *Gliene parlino Loro!*
8. *Mi faccia il favore di telefonare all'ufficio di collocamento!*
9. *Faccia cucinare lui!*
10. *Non glieli faccia lavare!*

F. *Tradurre.* (Translate.)

1. Stop it! Don't bother me!
2. —Why didn't you tell me! —Mom, I did tell you yesterday!
3. Fabrizio, please find my car keys and bring them to your father.
4. —Professor Veltri, could you give me a copy of your book? —Yes, Mr. Frizi, I'll bring it to you tomorrow.
5. Please send me the information as soon as possible. Send it to me by fax.
6. —Please send me some copies of the contract. —OK. I'll send you three of them.
7. Tonight we're going to the Rossi's. They've invited us for dinner.
8. Giulio, it's time to put an end to this matter!
9. Poor Pierino! Everyone makes fun of him.
10. Rino, have the secretary type this letter, check it, and have the client sign it!
11. They made us enjoy ourselves.
12. I'll let the hairdresser comb my hair.

LEGGIAMO!

MILANO: UNA CITTÀ STRATIFICATA *

In the following article that appeared in *Ulisse 2000,* Alitalia Airlines' in-flight magazine, Italian writer and journalist Guglielmo Zucconi describes Lombardia as a melting pot for almost nine million immigrants from Veneto, Emilia Romagna, and Sicily.

Nel medioevo, da Parigi a Londra, "lombardo" significava "banchiere" anche se si trattava di un toscano o di un piemontese; in Italia, fuori dalla Lombardia, "lombardo" era sinonimo di usuraio,[1] per Carlo V i "lombardi" erano i migliori armaioli[2] del suo impero, Stendhal li considerava maestri della dolcezza di vivere, Radetski li amava anche se con loro dovette usare le maniere forti,[3] Carlo Alberto ne diffidava,[4] Francesco Giuseppe II li chiamava "i miei laboriosi lombardi," Manzoni diceva che nelle donne di sangue lombardo brillava una "bellezza molle e a un tempo maestosa."[5] Il "gran lombardo" Carlo Emilio Gadda prendeva bonariamente in giro[6] i suoi conterranei per la loro mania di misurare ogni cosa: secondo lui, gli ingegneri milanesi quando si mettono in costume da bagno infilano il regolo calcolatore in un taglio della pelle,[7] all'altezza del taschino.

Ma definizioni e apprezzamenti diversi potevano andare bene, a seconda dei gusti, quando lombardi si nasceva e non lo si diventava, come adesso che la Lombardia è un "melting pot" di quasi nove milioni di veneti, emiliani, siciliani, pugliesi, campani, sardi, eccetera. Manca un censimento che identifichi i lombardi "puri," figli di lombardi, ma è probabile che essi siano ormai in minoranza. Tuttavia, questo mi pare il tratto caratteristico della "lombardità"[8] fra aborigini, meticci,[9] e immigrati, le differenze che contano sono soprattutto quelle sociali, economiche e professionali. La società lombarda, e in particolare quella milanese, è fatta a strati come le torte di nonna Papera: gli avvocati se la fanno con gli avvocati,[10] gli industriali con i loro colleghi e così tutti gli altri, ogni gruppo vive in uno strato a sé all'interno del quale non contano le diversità etniche o dialettali. Più difficili e comunque rare le comunicazioni fra un piano e l'altro. Un tempo, il "rito ambrosiano" della occasionale unificazione si svolgeva al canto di "O mia bela Madunina" (parole del milanese Bracchi e musica del pugliese Danzi), oggi al suono rit-

* Guglielmo Zucconi, "Una società stratificata," *Ulisse 2000* Anno X, n. 74 (maggio 1990), pp. 13–14.

115

mato dei clacson quando il Milan o l'Inter vincono lo scudetto[11] o una coppa internazionale. Ogni epoca coltiva la sua fede.

VOCABOLARIO

1. usurer, loan shark
2. armourers
3. even if he did have to treat them roughly
4. did not trust them
5. women with Lombard blood in their veins shone with a "soft and yet majestic beauty"
6. gently teased
7. slip a slide rule into a cut made in their skin
8. Lombardness
9. mulattoes
10. lawyers hang around with/frequent lawyers
11. soccer championship

LEZIONE 6

A. DIALOGO

GLI SPOT PUBBLICITARI

Roberto e Carla hanno appena finito di cenare e decidono di passare una serata tranquilla a casa a guardare la televisione.[1] Come si potrebbe prevedere, nasce subito una discussione.

CARLA: Roberto, ma vuoi smetterla di cambiare canale.

ROBERTO: Ma c'è la pubblicità. Non voglio vederla. Fammi vedere cosa c'è sugli altri canali.

CARLA: Dai, non cambiare! Sto guardando un film che mi piace. E poi a me non dà fastidio guardare gli spot pubblicitari.

ROBERTO: A te gli annunci piacciono? Ma scherzi!? A me invece non piacciono affatto. Non mi sono mai piaciuti! Ma come possono piacere queste stupidaggini![2] E poi alcuni sono fatti veramente male. Non c'è più limite all'indecenza di certe pubblicità.

CARLA: Tu sei sempre pronto a criticare. Io non ho detto che amo guardare gli annunci . . . Ho detto semplicemente che non mi dispiace guardarli. Dai, fammi guardare!

In televisione.

UOMO: Dolce Mara. Dolce fascino.

DONNA: Ecco un bellissimo esempio di "Dolce Mara", la nuova collezione intimo[3] che ho scelto per voi. Un dolcissimo tocco di femminilità, con tutte le novità della moda. Per noi donne.

UOMO: Solo per voi. Solo alla Upim.[4] "Dolce Mara": scelto[5] da Mara Venier.[6]

Carla e Roberto riprendono la loro discussione.

CARLA: Roberto, cosa c'è di male con questa pubblicità?

ROBERTO: Non c'è niente di male. Anzi questa, rispetto alle altre, mi piace. È fatta con gusto e Mara Venier è molto brava. Certe altre pubblicità invece . . .

CARLA: Quali?

ROBERTO: Quelle, per esempio, che pubblicizzano i jeans[7] con gli slogan "Lavare in acquasanta" e "Vi costeranno dieci Ave-marie."

CARLA: E beh!?

ROBERTO: Come "e beh"!? Non pensi che questi slogan possano turbare il senso religioso?

CARLA: Non so.

ROBERTO: Il fatto sta che questa pubblicità dei jeans sta suscitando un sacco[8] di proteste.

CARLA: Io non ci capisco proprio niente. La gente non si scandalizza a vedere deputati, cantanti, attrici, ballerine, attori nudi o quasi nudi in televisione, sui giornali, ma appena si toccano argomenti religiosi . . . E poi dov'è andata a finire la libertà di espressione!

ROBERTO: Io non sono affatto d'accordo. Credo che si dovrebbe evitare sia di offendere la dignità della gente che di fare delle pubblicità triviali.[9]

CARLA: A me invece quelle pubblicità dove è ovvia l'ironia e l'intelligenza del messaggio sono sempre piaciute.

ROBERTO: Comunque sono convinto che ora si sta veramente esagerando. Hai visto che la pubblicità è arrivata perfino sulle copertine dei quaderni di scuola?

CARLA: E come?

ROBERTO: Come? Sulle copertine dei quaderni di scuola, come in TV e nelle riviste, appaiono ora top model . . . Ma che fine hanno fatto i personaggi disneyani come Topolino e Paperino? A me sembra proprio un'istigazione alla sessualità. Ma dove siamo arrivati! Mi chiedo se sia rimasto un limite da[10] superare.

CARLA: Stai proprio esagerando!

118

ROBERTO: **Macché esagerando! Il sesso ormai non lo troviamo più soltanto nei luoghi riservati.[11] Il sesso è ormai arrivato nei nostri salotti, nelle nostre sale da[12] pranzo, perfino nelle aule scolastiche!**

CARLA: **Dai, finiscila. Fammi guardare la televisione in pace.**

TELEVISIONE: **Ogni momento felice ha il suo confetto. Confetto[13] matrimonio. Confetto battesimo. Confetto venticinquesimo. Confetto laurea. Confetto "Falqui." Se soffrite di stipsi,[14] se il vostro intestino è pigro e svogliato, affidatevi a "Falqui."**

ROBERTO: **Non so che gusto ci prendi a vederti tutte queste pubblicità. Ma non ti annoi?[15]**

CARLA: **No. Anzi tu mi fai impazzire quando con il telecomando, fra una pubblicità e l'altra, salti da un canale[16] all'altro. E poi alcuni spot pubblicizzano delle cose molto interessanti. Guarda questo, per esempio.**

TELEVISIONE: **Usa il telecomando. Usa la testa. COMPUTER BIT. Bit Genius, Bit 6 Super e Bit Junior, i giochi che fanno usare a tuo figlio la sua dote[17] migliore: l'intelligenza. Non è una cosa che si trova facilmente in giro. COMPUTER BIT. GLI ATTIVA MENTE.[18]**

COMMERCIALS

Roberto and Carla have just finished dinner and decide to spend a quiet evening at home watching TV. Predictably an argument quickly ensues.

CARLA: Roberto, could you stop changing channels, please?

ROBERTO: But the commercials are on. I don't want to watch them. Let me see what's on the other channels.

CARLA: Come on, don't change it. I'm watching a movie I like. And besides, it doesn't bother me to watch commercials.

ROBERTO: You like commercials? Are you kidding!? I don't like them at all. I've never liked them! How can anyone like such nonsense? Besides, some are very badly done. There's no longer a limit to the indecency of certain commercials.

119

CARLA: You're always quick to criticize. I didn't say I like to watch commercials . . . I simply said I don't mind watching them. Come on, let me watch.

On television . . .

MAN: Sweet Mara. Sweet fascination.

WOMAN: Here's a beautiful example of "Sweet Mara," the new intimate collection that I've chosen for you. A mild and sweet touch, feminine, with all the latest fashions. For us women.

MAN: Only for you. Only at Upim. "Sweet Mara": selected by Mara Venier.

Carla and Roberto resume their discussion.

CARLA: Roberto, what is wrong with this commercial?

ROBERTO: There's nothing wrong. Actually, compared to the others, I like this one. It's done with taste, and Mara Venier is very good. But certain other commercials . . . !

CARLA: Which ones?

ROBERTO: The ones, for example, that advertise jeans with the slogans "Wash in holy water" and "They will cost you ten Hail Mary's."

CARLA: Well?

ROBERTO: What do you mean "well"!? Don't you think that these slogans could offend someone with a religious sensibility?

CARLA: I don't know.

ROBERTO: The fact is that this advertisement for jeans is causing a wave of protests.

CARLA: I don't understand that at all. People are not shocked at seeing nude, or semi-nude members of Parliament, singers, actresses, dancers, or actors on television, in the papers, but once they touch on religious issues . . . Besides, what ever happened to freedom of expression?

ROBERTO: I don't agree at all. I think you should avoid both offending people's dignity and making vulgar commercials.

CARLA: On the contrary, I've always liked the commercials where the irony and the intelligence of the message are obvious.

ROBERTO: But I'm convinced that now they're really going too far. Have you seen that advertisements have even begun to appear on students' notebooks?

CARLA: How's that?

ROBERTO: How? On the covers of notebooks, like on TV and in magazines, there are now supermodels . . . What ever happened to Disney characters like Mickey Mouse and Donald Duck? To me it seems like encouraging sexuality. What have we come to? I wonder if there are any more lines to cross.

CARLA: You're really exaggerating!

ROBERTO: Exaggerating, not at all! Nowadays sex isn't restricted to private places. Sex is now in our living rooms, in our dining rooms, even in our classrooms!

CARLA: Come on, stop it. Let me watch TV in peace.

TELEVISION: Every happy moment has its "sugared almond." Wedding sugared almond. Baptismal sugared almond. Twenty-fifth anniversary sugared almond. Graduation sugared almond. "Falqui" sugar coated pills. If you suffer from constipation, if your bowels are sluggish, place your trust in "Falqui."

ROBERTO: I don't see what pleasure you get out of seeing all of these commercials. Don't you get bored?

CARLA: No. Actually, you drive me crazy when you jump from one channel to the next with the remote every time there's a commercial. Anyway, some commercials advertise things that are very interesting. Look at this, for example.

TELEVISION: Use the remote control. Use your head. COMPUTER BIT. Bit Genius, Bit 6 Super, and Bit Junior, the games that make your child use his best gift: his intelligence. It's not something that can be easily found. COMPUTER BIT. THE ACTIVE MIND.

B. IN BREVE

1. Remember that *la televisione* refers to television programming, while *il televisore* refers to a television set.

2. Here *stupidaggini* means stupid or ridiculous things. A *stupidaggine* can also be a *cosa da poco* (a trifle, something of little value or importance): *Ti abbiamo comprato una stupidaggine.* (We bought you something of little value, i.e. a small token.)

3. Here the adjective *intimo* is used as a noun meaning "lingerie."

4. *Upim* is a very popular department store with branches in many Italian cities.

5. Here the adjective is in the masculine singular form because it refers to *intimo*. For more on adjectives used as nouns see the grammar section of this chapter.

6. Mara Venier is an actress and a show host for the Italian state television, the RAI.

7. The English word "jeans" is commonly used in Italian. Interestingly, it is derived from the old English name ("Jene" or "Janes") for the Italian city of *Genova,* where the fabric was produced.

8. A similar expression is *un mucchio di.* Other expressions used to mean "a lot of, a great deal of, a pack of," although less popular than *un sacco di* and *un mucchio di,* are *un mare di, un'infinità di, un'ondata di.*

9. The word *triviale* is another "false friend." It means "vulgar, obscene." "Trivial" is translated as *banale, superficiale,* or *insignificante: La tua analisi del programma è superficiale.* (Your analysis of the programme is trivial.) *Il linguaggio di questo film è troppo triviale e offende la sensibilità di molti spettatori.* (The language of this movie is too vulgar and it offends the sensibilities of many spectators.)

10. The preposition *da* is equivalent here to the passive form "to be + past participle."

11. Here *riservato* does not have the meaning of "reserved" but of "private." *Riservato* is used to mean "reserved" in two cases: when speaking of a personality trait: *È una persona molto riservata.* (He is a very reserved person.); and when speaking of something pre-

assigned: *I posti sul treno sono riservati.* (The seats on the train are reserved.)

12. The preposition *da* at times indicates the purpose of something: *scarpe da tennis* (tennis shoes), *abito da sera* (evening wear).

13. Italian *confetti* are sugar-coated almonds generally distributed at weddings, baptisms, and other celebrations as party favors. The term *confetto* can also be used to mean "sugar-coated pill." The ad in the dialogue is based on the play on words with the term. The English term "confetti" is translated as *coriandoli*.

14. Remember that nouns ending in *-si (stipsi, crisi, tesi, ipotesi, analisi)* are usually feminine and are all invariable. Such nouns are of Greek origin.

15. *Annoiarsi* generally means "to get bored," not "to be annoyed." *Mi sono annoiato a morte alla riunione del marketing.* (I was really bored at the marketing meeting.) "To annoy" is *seccare* or *scocciare*. *Non mi seccare!* (Don't annoy me!)

16. The word *canale* can also be used figuratively. *Attraverso canali diplomatici.* (Through diplomatic channels.)

17. *Dote* can also mean "dowry." *La principessa aveva una dote favolosa.* (The princess had a fabulous dowry.)

18. The entire expression is a compound noun *(nome composto)* and means "mind stimulators." The compound is formed by a verb *(attiva)* + a noun *(mente)*. *Attiva mente* is invariable and masculine in gender *(l'attiva mente, gli attiva mente)*. Note, however, that generally compound nouns are written as one word and can be masculine or feminine: *arcobaleno* (rainbow), *portalettere* (letter carrier), *asciugamano* (towel), *capoufficio* (office manager), *banconota* (bank note), *ferrovia* (railroad), etc.

C. GRAMMATICA E SUOI USI

1. *IL VERBO PIACERE* (THE VERB *PIACERE*)

The Italian verb *piacere* is used differently than its English counter-part, "to like." The literal translation of *piacere* is "to appeal to/be pleasing to." *Piacere* is generally used in the third person singular (if what is liked is singular) or in the third person plural (if what is liked is plural.) That which is liked is the subject of the sentence, while the person who likes it is the indirect object.

Al signor Cabrini non piace quello spot perché offende il suo senso religioso.
Mr. Cabrini doesn't like that commercial because it offends his religious sensibility.

A Carla piacciono gli annunci pubblicitari che presentano nuovi prodotti interessanti.
Carla likes commercials that introduce new, interesting products.

The word order is relatively free. The most common structure is the following: indirect object + *piacere* + what is liked. However, if you want to emphasize a specific element (i.e., what is liked or the person to whom something is pleasing), just place it at the beginning of the sentence. For added emphasis, the stressed forms of the indirect object pronouns, such as *a me* and *a te* may be used (see *Lezione 4*).

Questa pubblicità non mi piace perché è troppo volgare.
I don't like this commercial because it is too vulgar.

A Serena non piacciono i film comici? E a te piacciono?
Serena doesn't like comedies? And you, do you like them?

When the verb *piacere* is followed by one or more infinitives, the third person singular form, *piace/piaceva* etc., should always be used.

Ci piaceva usare molto quel prodotto.
We used to like to use that product a lot.

Remember that in compound tenses *piacere* takes the auxiliary *essere* and that its past participle has to agree in gender and number with what is liked.

Dottor Insegna, Le sono piaciuti gli spot pubblicitari che abbiamo presentato al cliente?
    Dr. Insegna, did you like the commercials that we presented to the client?

Le pubblicità televisive non gli sono mai piaciute.
    He has never liked television commercials.

Even though *piacere* is usually used in the third person singular or plural, it does have other forms. The full conjugation of the present indicative is: *piaccio, piaci, piace, piacciamo, piacete, piacciono.*

Carlo, con la tua personalità accomodante, tu piaci a tutti noi.
    Carlo, we all like you because of your accomodating personality.

Voi piacete al principale perché pensate sempre ai migliori slogan.
    The boss likes you because you always think of the best slogans.

Remember that the verb *dispiacere* is not the opposite of *piacere*. It means "to be sorry" when expressing an apology or sympathy. It also expresses "not to mind." It is used and conjugated like *piacere*.

Mi dispiace, ma questo slogan non mi sembra adatto.
    I'm sorry, but this slogan does not seem suitable to me.

Non mi dispiace guardare gli spot pubblicitari.
    I don't mind watching television commercials.

Ci è dispiaciuto sentire che il messaggio non sia stato capito.
    We were sorry to hear that the message had not been understood.

2. *I VERBI MODALI* (MODAL VERBS)

The verbs *dovere* (to have to), *potere* (to be able), and *volere* (to want) are known as modal verbs because they allow you to express a modality (condition, manner, etc.). They are irregular in the present tense and are often followed by a dependent infinitive.

Non voglio vedere questa pubblicità televisiva.
I don't want to see this television ad.

Non possono evitare tutta questa pubblicità.
They can't avoid all this publicity.

Dobbiamo cancellare quell'articolo dal catalogo?
Do we have to delete that item from the catalogue?

Modal verbs have the following characteristics:

a. When they are in the present perfect and are accompanied by an infinitive, the infinitive determines which auxiliary verb should be used.

Non abbiamo voluto mettere l'annuncio sul giornale.
We didn't want to put the ad in the newspaper.

Non hanno dovuto pagare la fattura.
They didn't have to pay the invoice.

Il direttore non è potuto venire alla riunione.
The manager couldn't come to the meeting.

Loro si sono voluti divertire.
They wanted to have fun.

In current spoken Italian, however, the auxiliary *avere* may be used in all cases.

b. Pronouns and particles either precede the verb or are attached to the end of the infinitive (in which case the final *-e* is dropped).

La pubblicità? Sì, la voglio vedere. / Sì, voglio vederla.
The ad? Yes, I want to see it.

Non ci possiamo permettere di perdere questa occasione.
Non possiamo permetterci di perdere questa occasione.
We can't afford to miss this opportunity.

c. With reflexive verbs, if the pronoun comes before the verb, *dovere,* *volere,* and *potere* are conjugated with essere. If the reflexive pronoun is attached to the infinitive, then the auxiliary *avere* is used.

126

Ieri sera non mi sono potuto guardare/non ho potuto guardarmi la TV.
Last night I couldn't watch TV.

Roberto si è dovuto comprare/ha dovuto comprarsi un nuovo televisore.
Roberto had to buy a new television set.

d. The present conditional of *dovere, potere,* and *volere* is often used to make a request more polite. They are translated as: "should, could, would like" (present conditional) and "should have, could have, would have liked" (perfect conditional).

Dovrei telefonargli io.
I should phone him.

Potrei telefonargli io.
I could phone him.

Vorrei telefonargli io.
I would like to phone him.

Avrei dovuto telefonargli io.
I should have phoned him.

Avrei potuto telefonargli io.
I could have phoned him.

Avrei voluto telefonargli io.
I would have liked to phone him.

3. *USO DI AGGETTIVI E VERBI COME NOMI* (ADJECTIVES AND VERBS USED AS NOUNS)

It is not uncommon to find adjectives and verbs used as nouns. Adjectives are always masculine when used as nouns.

Il rosso è il colore che si usa più frequentemente negli spot alimentari.
Red is the color most frequently used in food advertisements.

Nell'intimo è un buon amico.
At the bottom of his heart he is a good friend.

Il suo forte è il marketing.
His forte is marketing.

Ci è voluto del bello e del buono per convincerlo a cambiare canale.
It took a lot to convince him to change the channel.

Faccio sempre più del necessario per pubblicizzare i miei prodotti.
I always do more than necessary to advertise my products.

Infinitives of verbs can also be used as nouns. Like the adjectival forms, they are always masculine and may or may not be used with an article.

(Il) cambiare sempre canale mi scoccia.
Changing channels constantly annoys me.

Some past and present participles (formed by adding *-ante* to the stem of *-are* verbs and *-ente* to *-ere* and *-ire* verbs) are also used as nouns.

Gli abitanti di quel paese hanno protestato perché lo spot pubblicitario offendeva la loro dignità.
The inhabitants of that town protested because the advertisement offended their dignity.

Il cantante ha preparato uno spot per lanciare il suo ultimo CD.
The singer prepared a commercial for his last CD.

Ben trenta neo-laureati hanno trovato lavoro nel campo pubblicitario.
No less than thirty graduates found a job in the advertisement industry.

D. PAROLE! PAROLE! PAROLE!

In the dialogue Carla, replying to Roberto, says: *"Io non ci capisco proprio niente."* (I don't understand it at all). Other expressions similar to *non capire niente* are:

Lui non capisce un'acca di russo.
He doesn't understand a word of Russian.

Quando lei parla, io non capisco un accidente.
When she speaks, I don't understand a thing.

Noi non capiamo un cavolo.
It's all Greek to us.

Accidente and *cavolo* can also be used in expressions such as *non fare/dire/importare/sapere/sentire/valere/vedere un accidente/cavolo.*

E. L'ANGOLO DEGLI AFFARI

LA PUBBLICITÀ (ADVERTISING)

Consumer spending has increased dramatically in Italy over the past twenty years, and the proliferation of advertising has been a significant contributor to this increase. While consumer spending has risen by about a third over the past decade, advertising costs have more than doubled. In Italy, in contrast to many other countries, ad time on television is relatively inexpensive, making TV a particularly lucrative medium for advertisers.

Like all industrialized countries, Italy has enacted legislation restricting the forms and content of advertisement. For instance, television advertising cannot exceed 12% of any given broadcast hour or a maximum of 4% of the broadcast week, although these regulations allow for a leeway of 2%. Despite the restrictions, Italy ranks first in Europe in terms of the number of television commercials it airs annually. In 1992, for instance, a total of one million commercials were seen on the three state-supported stations and the three private Fininvest networks (Retequattro, Canale 5, and Italia Uno)—not to mention the total from smaller, local stations. French stations aired only 252,000 in the same year, and Spain aired 375,000.

Print advertising is not nearly as ubiquitous in Italy as it has become in other European countries and in parts of North America. Magazines and newspapers are widely read in Italy, and over 9,000 different publications are produced there on a regular basis. In recent years, however, the use of print advertising has declined as a result of the development of other, newer media.

Italian advertising has a reputation among North Americans for being sexually explicit. Yet it is interesting to note that under article 565 of the Italian penal code, the printing or transmission of ideas that could potentially corrupt family values is punishable by law. Italian cultural norms and standards, in other words, are not identical to those espoused by most North Americans. For example, whereas nudity and the representation of sexual behavior are taboo in the United States, controversial depictions of religious symbols are deemed more corruptive in Italy.

Advertisement of tobacco products is banned in Italy, as is comparative advertising, in which a particular product is intentionally disparaged in favor of another. The *codice di lealtà pubblicitaria,* or code of advertising fairness, is designed to protect consumers from various types of false advertising. The code governs food labeling, restricts advertising of "miracle cure" health products, and outlines norms for the advertising of liquidation and clearance sales, among other things. In addition to the Italian law, there are norms established by the European Community that apply in Italy.

Before embarking on an advertising campaign in Italy, foreign companies should consult with an Italian market-research firm that has experience with the domestic promotion of foreign products. Local branches of the Italian consulate and Chamber of Commerce can also be helpful where rules and regulations governing such campaigns are concerned. Italy is aggressively pursuing foreign investors currently, and various government agencies are disseminating literature or investment opportunities and procedures through the World Wide Web. For more information about Italian topics on the Internet, please see *Lezione 15.*

ESERCIZI

A. *Rispondere affermativamente alle seguenti domande, seguendo l'esempio. Ricordati di usare i pronomi.* (Answer the following questions affirmatively, following the example. Remember to use the pronouns.)

ESEMPIO: A Roberto gli annunci piacciono?
          Sì, gli piacciono.

1. *A tuo figlio piace il suo nuovo lavoro?*
2. *A voi è piaciuta la pubblicità che abbiamo appena visto?*
3. *Signora Mirelli, a Lei piace guardare la televisione?*
4. *Ai tuoi genitori sono piaciuti i jeans che hai comprato?*
5. *A Melissa è piaciuto quel film?*

B. *Rispondere affermativamente alle seguenti domande, usando la forma appropriata del passato prossimo di piacere. Seguire l'esempio.* (Answer the following questions affirmatively, using the *passato prossimo* of *piacere*. Follow the example.)

1. *Il professor Di Rosa ha visto il nuovo libro di Eco?*
2. *I signori De Santis hanno visto i nuovi progetti per l'ampliamento della fabbrica?*
3. *Tu e Carla avete visto quella pubblicità dei confetti "Falqui"?*
4. *Sandra ha visto la nuova collezione intimo presentata da Mara Venier?*
5. *Hai visto le informazioni che ci hanno dato?*

C. *Formare una frase mettendo in ordine le seguenti parole* (Rearrange each group of words to form a sentence).

1. *vedere/sugli/canali/vorrei/c'è/cosa/altri/che*
2. *dobbiamo/annunci/guardare/gli/pubblicitari?*
3. *possono/accettare/non/l'/certe/pubblicità/indecenza/di/loro*
4. *sera/non/voluto/abbiamo/ieri/televisione/guardare/la/noi*
5. *Carla/appena/di/cenare/finito/ha/e/guardarsi/la/vuole/pace/in/televisione*

D. *Tradurre.* (Translate.)

1. I'll never watch this television program! I don't like it! I have never liked it! I'll never like it!
2. No one likes to go to the dentist.
3. I like to travel. My sister also likes to travel. Neither my sister nor I like to stay home.
4. I always do more than necessary.
5. When they speak, we don't understand a thing!
6. Last night I didn't want to watch television. I preferred to read the newspaper.
7. Yesterday Carla couldn't come to the meeting. She had to go to Rome.
8. We couldn't afford to miss this opportunity.
9. I would like to buy this computer for my son. I am sure he will like it.
10. Those people protested because the advertisement offended their dignity.

LEZIONE 7

A. DIALOGO

LE UNIVERSITÀ ITALIANE

Trevor Johnston è stato trasferito in Italia alla sede centrale dell'azienda con cui lavora. Sua moglie Heather e i suoi due figli gemelli di 18 anni lo hanno raggiunto in Italia. Siccome i ragazzi hanno intenzione di frequentare l'università in Italia, Trevor e Heather chiedono a Edoardo, un loro amico professore, delle informazioni sulle università italiane.

HEATHER: Edoardo, siamo un po' preoccupati perché la transizione sarà molto difficile per i ragazzi. Non solo dovranno abituarsi ad una nuova lingua e cultura, ma dovranno affrontare anche un sistema universitario completamente nuovo.

TREVOR: Edoardo, che cosa ci puoi dire delle università in Italia? Sono molto diverse da quelle negli States? [1]

EDOARDO: Beh, come in tutti i paesi, ci sono quelle buone e quelle meno buone. Dipende [2] naturalmente dall'università.

TREVOR: Ho sentito dire che c'è un problema d'affollamento. È vero?

EDOARDO: Purtroppo, sì. Uno dei problemi più seri nelle università italiane è la sproporzione tra allievi [3] e professori. Le aule sono spesso così affollate che in certi corsi è impossibile far entrare tutti gli studenti nella classe. [4]

HEATHER: Ma è impossibile seguire allora le lezioni regolarmente?

EDOARDO: Infatti. Per questo molti atenei hanno cominciato [5] ad imporre un limite al numero di studenti ammessi. Ciò ridurrebbe [6] il numero di iscrizioni e migliorerebbe la situazione.

TREVOR: Ci sono grandi differenze tra la struttura delle università italiane e di quelle americane?

EDOARDO: Beh, le università che, come La Bocconi, prendono come modello gli atenei americani non sono tanto diverse.

HEATHER: Ho sentito che la Bocconi è un'ottima università.

EDOARDO: Molti la considerano il miglior ateneo italiano. Per essere ammessi gli studenti devono superare[7] un durissimo esame di ammissione. E poi ci sono solo 2.500 posti a disposizione[8] per circa[9] 4.000 candidati.

HEATHER: Immagino che l'ottima reputazione della Bocconi sia un vantaggio per i suoi laureati in cerca di lavoro.

EDOARDO: Ovviamente. Tra i laureati della Bocconi non esiste la disoccupazione.

TREVOR: In genere, però, come sono le altre università italiane?

EDOARDO: Il sistema è molto diverso. Innanzitutto, in Italia non esiste la possibilità di sperimentare[10] con diverse discipline di specializzazione, in quanto i piani di studio sono molto più rigidi di quelli americani.

HEATHER: Vuoi dire che gli studenti devono scegliere subito la loro materia di specializzazione?

EDOARDO: Assolutamente no, ma devono scegliere subito la facoltà e il campo in cui si vogliono laureare. I corsi facoltativi sono pochi e, in molti casi, il piano di studio è prestabilito dalla facoltà a cui si iscrivono.[11]

HEATHER: Pare che stiamo parlando di due sistemi universitari completamente diversi. Almeno i metodi di valutazione sono simili, spero . . . prove in classe, saggi, partecipazione attiva ai seminari . . . ?

EDOARDO: No, anche qui ci sono delle differenze. Innanzitutto, la presenza a lezione spesso non è obbligatoria. Ogni corso si supera dando un esame, di solito orale. Per ogni esame gli studenti ricevono un voto su trenta. Per avere la sufficienza bisogna ricevere un voto minimo di 18. Alla fine di ogni esame, il voto viene registrato sul libretto universitario dello studente, un libretto che rassomiglia a un passaporto. Un'ultima cosa: gli studenti possono dare gli esami[12] quando vogliono.

HEATHER: Come sarebbe?[13]

EDOARDO: Di solito ci si prepara per un esame, massimo due, alla volta. Quando si è pronti, si dà l'esame. Ci sono tre cosiddetti appelli all'anno per gli esami. Quando uno studente è pronto, si iscrive per dare l'esame. Se supera l'esame, bene; altrimenti deve ridarlo quando si sente pronto. Un esame si può dare fin quando non si supera.

TREVOR: **Adesso tutto è molto più chiaro. Ancora una tua opinione. Roger vorrebbe studiare a Bologna,[14] mentre Paul intende iscriversi alla Normale di Pisa.[15] Cosa ne pensi di queste università?**

EDOARDO: **Entrambe scelte eccezionali. Se non sbaglio alla Normale di Pisa non si pagano tasse universitarie, ma c'è un esame di ammissione durissimo da superare. Se verrà ammesso, comunque, non dovrà pagare niente, anche l'alloggio[16] e i pasti sono gratuiti.**

TREVOR: **Che sollievo saperlo! In ogni caso qui in Italia le tasse universitarie e le altre spese sono molto basse rispetto a quelle americane.**

HEATHER: **Edoardo, approfitto della tua gentilezza per farti un'ultima domanda . . .**

EDOARDO: **Di' pure!**

HEATHER: **I ragazzi hanno tanta voglia,[17] di fare amicizia. Com'è la vita sociale del tipico studente italiano?**

EDOARDO: **Qui in Italia non abbiamo molte organizzazioni sociali come negli Stati Uniti. Non esistono, per esempio, club maschili e femminili e non ci sono neanche sport organizzati come nei vostri campus. Tuttavia, c'è sempre qualcuno nell'ambiente che organizza feste, concerti, conferenze ed altre serate culturali. Gli studenti si organizzano tra di loro: vanno magari[18] in discoteca in comitiva, preparano una spaghettata, mangiano una pizza insieme . . . Insomma, fanno quello che fanno i giovani di tutto il mondo, si divertono!**

ITALIAN UNIVERSITIES

Trevor Johnson has been transferred to the headquarters of his firm in Italy. His wife, Heather, and their two 18-year-old twin sons have joined him in Italy. Since the boys will be attending university in Italy,

Trevor and Heather ask Edoardo, a professor friend of theirs, about Italian universities.

HEATHER: Edoardo, we're a little concerned that the transition will be very difficult for the boys. Not only will they have to get used to a new language and culture, but they'll also have to deal with an entirely new university system.

TREVOR: Edoardo, what can you tell us about universities in Italy? Are they very different from the ones in the States?

EDOARDO: Well, like in all countries, there are some that are good, and some that are not so good. It depends of course on the university.

TREVOR: I've heard that there's a problem with overcrowding. Is that true?

EDOARDO: Unfortunately, yes. One of the most serious problems in Italian universities is the ratio of students to professors. The classrooms are often so crowded that in certain courses it's impossible to get all of the students into the classroom.

HEATHER: But, then, isn't it impossible to keep up with the class?

EDOARDO: Yes. Because of this many universities have begun to impose a cap on the number of students admitted. This would lower the number of enrollments and improve the situation.

TREVOR: Are there major differences between the structure of Italian universities and American ones?

EDOARDO: Well, there aren't too many universities that follow the American model, like the Bocconi.

HEATHER: I've heard that the Bocconi is a very good university.

EDOARDO: Many consider it to be the best. In order to be admitted students have to pass a very difficult entrance exam. And then there are only 2,500 spots available for about 4,000 applicants.

HEATHER: I imagine that the excellent reputation of the Bocconi must be an advantage for graduates looking for work.

EDOARDO: Oh yes. Among graduates from the Bocconi there is no unemployment.

TREVOR: In general, though, what are other Italian universities like?

EDOARDO: The system is very different. First of all, in Italy there is no possibility of experimenting with different majors, as the programs are much more rigid than those in America.

HEATHER: Do you mean that students have to choose their major right away?

EDOARDO: Absolutely not, but they do have to choose the faculty and the field in which they'll graduate right away. There aren't many electives, and, in many cases, the program is pre-established by the faculty in which a student enrolls.

HEATHER: It seems that we're talking about two completely different university systems. I hope, at least, that the methods of evaluation are similar . . . in-class tests, essays, active participation in seminars . . . ?

EDOARDO: No, there are differences here as well. First of all, attendance in class is often not mandatory. Courses are passed by taking an exam, often oral. For each exam, students receive a grade out of thirty. To pass, it's necessary to receive a minimum grade of eighteen. After each exam, the grade is recorded in the student's university record booklet, which looks like a passport. One other thing—students can take exams when they want to.

HEATHER: What do you mean?

EDOARDO: Usually students prepare for one or at most two exams at a time. When they're ready, they take the exam. There are three so-called sessions for exams throughout the year. When students are ready, they register to take the exam. If they pass, good, otherwise they must take it again when they feel ready. They can keep taking exams until they pass.

TREVOR: Now everything is much clearer. One more question. Roger wants to study in Bologna, while Paul intends to go to the Normale in Pisa. What do you think of these universities?

EDOARDO: Both excellent choices. If I'm not mistaken, there are no tuition fees at the Normale in Pisa, but there's a very difficult entrance exam. If he's admitted, he won't have to pay a thing. Even housing and meals are free.

TREVOR: What a relief to know that! In any event, here in Italy tuition fees and other expenses are very low in comparison to those in the States.

HEATHER: Edoardo, let me take advantage of your kindness by asking one last question.

EDOARDO: Go ahead!

HEATHER: The boys really want to make friends. What's the social life of the typical student like?

EDOARDO: Here in Italy we don't have many social organizations like you do in the United States. For example, there are no fraternities or sororities and no organized sports like on your campuses. Nonetheless, there's always someone around who organizes parties, concerts, conferences, and other cultural evenings. Students plan things for themselves—they might go together to clubs, prepare spaghetti dinners, go have a pizza. In short, they do what young people do all over the world—they have a good time!

B. IN BREVE

1. The abbreviation *gli States* is not uncommon in Italy.

2. Note the use of a different preposition in the translation of the phrase "to depend on." Prepositional phrases and idioms that include prepositions often differ from language to language. Often there are no rules governing the use of prepositions. It is wise, therefore, to memorize such phrases as you discover them.

3. Here *allievo* means "pupil, student." *Allievo* could also mean "cadet" (*allievo ufficiale* = cadet officer) or "apprentice."

4. Although in most cases the word "class" may be translated into Italian with its etymological equivalent, *classe,* the two terms are not direct equivalents in all contexts. "Class" meaning "rate" is translated as *classe.* For instance, "first class" is *prima classe* in Italian. A "class" in the sense of "a group of students" is also *classe.* For example, the sentence "The class was listening to the teacher" is translated as *La classe ascoltava l'insegnante.* "Class" is also rendered as *lezione* or *corso.* A "class" meaning a lecture or a lesson is *lezione.* "I am going to Italian class" would be translated into Italian as *Vado a lezione d'italiano.* On the other hand, "class" meaning a course is

corso. "I am taking an Italian class" would be translated as *Sto seguendo un corso d'italiano.*

5. *Cominciato* is the past participle of the verb *cominciare.* The form *incominciare* is also possible.

6. The verb *ridurre,* just like *tradurre* (to translate) is conjugated in the present indicative in the following way: *riduco, riduci, riduce, riduciamo, riducete, riducono.*

7. As an intransitive verb, "to pass" in an academic context can also be expressed with the expressions *ottenere/avere la sufficienza* or *essere promosso.*

8. Here, the term refers to the availability of spots. Normally, *disposizione* can be translated with "disposition." However, *essere a disposizione di qualcuno* means "to be at someone's disposal." A *disposizione* may also be an order or an instruction, as in the case of *dare disposizioni,* which means to give orders/instructions.

9. Synonyms of *circa* are *quasi, pressappoco, su per giù,* and *approssimativamente.*

10. The form *esperimentare* is also possible.

11. Note that the word for "to register" is *iscriversi* not *registrare. Registrare* is translated into English as "to record" (*Il cantante ha registrato un nuovo album.* The singer recorded a new album.), "to tape" (*Io ho registrato la nostra conversazione telefonica.* I taped our telephone conversation.), or "to enter" (*Hanno registrato la fattura nel libro delle spese.* They entered the invoice in the expense booklet.)

12. "To take" in reference to an exam can be translated with the verbs *dare or sostenere.* A written exam, *un esame scritto,* may also be referred to as *un test* or *un compito.* An oral exam, *un esame orale,* may be referred to using the term *colloquio.* Another way of translating "exam" is with the term *prova.*

13. An idiomatic expression that expresses the speaker's desire to have something explained to him/her. An equivalent in English would be "What do you mean?"

14. The *Università di Bologna* was founded in the twelfth century and is the oldest university in Europe. It has an excellent reputation for many of the programs it offers, among them medicine, *medicina,* and communications, *scienze delle comunicazioni.*

15. This university was founded by Napoleon III in the nineteenth century. It was Napoleon's intention to found an institution similar to Paris' École Normale on Italian soil. The *Normale* is famous for its theoretical disciplines: mathematical, physical, and natural sciences *(scienze matematiche, fisiche e naturali)* and Italian literature and philosophy *(lettere, filosofia).*

16. This expression may also be translated with the Italian expression *vitto e alloggio,* which is the equivalent of "room and board."

17. *Avere (tanta) voglia di* means "to (really) feel like." The same expression *avere voglia di* can mean "to feel like" or "to feel up to" such as in *Non ho voglia di venire,* "I don't feel like coming."

18. Here *magari* is equivalent to "might" or "maybe." This word, however, used in exclamatory sentences may indicate the speaker's wish to do or have something, depending on the context: *Magari potessi andare anch'io!* (I wish I could also go!) *Magari fosse vero!* (If only it were true!)

C. GRAMMATICA E SUOI USI

1. *BUONO, BELLO, GRANDE E ALTRI AGGETTIVI* (*BUONO, BELLO, GRANDE* AND OTHER ADJECTIVES)

a. *Buono*

The adjective *buono* generally precedes the noun it modifies and has regular plural forms: *buoni, buone.* Note that its singular forms are similar to the forms of the definite article: *buon, buono, buona,* and *buon'.*

Quell'università offre un buon programma d'italiano.
That university offers a good Italian program.

Il professor Minni ha una buon'assistente.
Professor Minni has a good assistant.

Dicono che sia un buono psicologo.
They say he is a good psychologist.

When *buono* follows the noun, it has the same four endings as any other adjective: *buono, buona, buoni,* and *buone.*

In Italia ci sono università buone ed università non buone.
In Italy there are good universities and not so good universities.

Le strutture di ricerca sono veramente buone.
The research facilities are really good.

b. *Bello*

When the adjective *bello* precedes the noun, it assumes forms similar to the definite article combined with *di: bel, bei, bell', bello, bella, belle, begli.*

La professoressa ha portato un bell'articolo.
The professor brought a beautiful article.

Oggi il professore mi ha dato un bel voto.
Today the professor gave me a very good grade.

È la zona con i più begli alberghi e bei ristoranti della Danimarca.
It is the area with the most beautiful hotels and restaurants in Denmark.

When *bello* follows the noun it has the regular forms: *bello, bella, belli,* and *belle.*

Questa università è molto bella.
This university is very beautiful.

I film che faranno vedere nel corso di cinema sono tutti belli.
The movies which will be shown in the cinema course are all beautiful.

c. *Grande*

When *grande* follows a noun, it has only two forms: *grande, grandi*.

I professori hanno un appartamento con due stanze grandi.
   The professors have an apartment with two large rooms.

L'aula dove ho lezione di chimica è molto grande.
   The classroom where I have chemistry class is really large.

If *grande* precedes a noun it has various forms. In the singular, the
form *grand'* may be used before a noun that begins with a vowel, and
the form *gran* may be used before singular nouns beginning with a
consonant (except masculine nouns beginning with z, s + consonant, or
ps, which are preceded by the regular form *grande*). In the plural, the
adjective is regular, having only the form *grandi*.

Hanno raccolto una gran(de) somma per la lotta all'Aids.
   They collected a large sum for the fight against AIDS.

Il grande studioso di Dante darà una conferenza alle tre.
   The great Dante scholar will hold a conference at three.

Ho sentito un gran(de) rumore in biblioteca.
   I heard a great noise in the library.

È riuscito a farne una grand' (grande) azienda.
   He succeeded in turning it into a great firm.

*Ho delle grandi notizie: ho ricevuto una borsa di studio e vado a studiare in
Italia!*
   I have some great news: I've received a scholarship and I'm going to
   study in Italy!

Notice that the forms *gran* and *grand'* are optional. The form *grande*
can be used in their place.

d. The position of adjectives

Note that in some cases the difference in position of adjectives like
buono and *grande* signals a difference in meaning.

BEFORE A NOUN	AFTER A NOUN
È un buon uomo.	*È un uomo buono.*
He's a gentle/weak/naive man.	He's a good/respectable/honest man.
È un grande uomo.	*È un uomo grande.*
He's a great man.	He is a big/tall man.

Other adjectives like *povero, caro,* and *vecchio* also acquire different meanings before and after the noun.

BEFORE A NOUN	AFTER A NOUN
È una povera ragazza.	*È una ragazza povera.*
She's a poor (not fortunate) girl.	She's a poor (not rich) girl.
È una cara ragazza.	*È un libro caro.*
She's a dear/kind girl.	It's an expensive book.
È un vecchio amico.	*È un amico vecchio.*
He's an old (of many years) friend.	He's an elderly friend.

Note finally that if the adjective is itself modified by an adverb, then both the adverb and the adjective follow the noun.

È una buona università.
È un'università molto buona.
 It's a good university.
 It's a very good university.

È un bravo studente.
È uno studente molto bravo.
 He's a good student.
 He's a very good student.

2. *GLI AVVERBI* (ADVERBS)

Adverbs modify verbs, adjectives, or other adverbs and are invariable. Some common adverbs are *bene* (well), *male* (badly), *molto* (very), *poco* (little), *tardi* (late), *spesso* (often), *insieme* (together), *così* (so), and *volentieri* (gladly).

Le lezioni di psicologia si fanno spesso nell'auditorio.
Psycology classes are often held in the auditorium.

Gli studenti hanno discusso il compito insieme.
The students discussed the assignment together.

In general, adverbs are formed by adding the suffix *-mente* (the equivalent of the English -ly) to the feminine singular of the adjective:
chiaro → chiara → chiaramente (clearly)
vero → vera → veramente (really)
felice → felice → felicemente (happily).

Some exceptions are:
leggero → leggermente (lightly)
violento → violentemente (violently)
benevolo → benevolmente (benevolently).

Le classi italiane sono veramente affollate.
Italian classes are really crowded.

La Bocconi è chiaramente una delle più prestigiose università italiane.
The Bocconi is clearly one of the most prestigious Italian universities.

Il professore ha felicemente accettato l'incarico in quest'università.
The professor happily accepted the post at this university.

Luigi ha ottenuto un voto leggermente superiore a quello di Dino.
Luigi received a slightly higher mark than Dino.

Adjectives that end in *-le* or *-re* drop the *-e* before adding *-mente:*
facile → facilmente (easily), *regolare → regolarmente* (regularly).

Noi frequentiamo i seminari regolarmente.
We attend seminars regularly.

Mio fratello ha superato l'esame facilmente.
My brother passed the exam easily.

Suffixes can be added to many adverbs to alter their meaning: *bene* (well) → *benino* (pretty well), *benone* (very well); *male* (badly) → *malissimo* (very badly), *maluccio* (pretty badly); *poco* (little, a bit, slightly) → *pochino* (a little bit), *pochettino* (a little bit). For more about suffixes, please refer to *Lezione 11.*

Lo studente ha fatto malissimo all'esame.
The student did really badly on the examination.

Alcuni studenti consideravano l'argomento del saggio un pochettino polemico.
Some students considered the topic of the essay a little bit controversial.

Some adjectives used as adverbs are: *piano* (slowly), *forte* (loudly), *chiaro* (clearly), *sodo* (hard), *svelto* (fast), *giusto* (right).

Parla più piano all'esame, altrimenti il professore non ti capisce!
Speak more slowly at the exam, otherwise the professor won't understand you!

Abbiamo lavorato sodo per finire il saggio.
We worked hard to finish the essay.

Adverbs are sometimes repeated to add emphasis. This can be translated as "very."

Ha lavorato tanto tanto per finire l'esperimento per il corso di chimica.
He worked a great deal to finish the experiment for chemistry class.

Some common adverbial expressions are: *a poco a poco* (little by little), *di solito* (usually), *ad un tratto* (all of a sudden), *per fortuna* (fortunately), *all'improvviso* (all of a sudden), *di tanto in tanto* (from time to time).

A poco a poco e col tempo imparerai l'italiano alla perfezione.
Little by little and with time you'll learn Italian to perfection.

Di solito finisco di lavorare alle cinque.
Usually I finish work at five.

Adverbs generally follow the verb. However, for emphasis, they may precede the verb or be placed between the auxiliary and the past participle.

Improvvisamente Ivo ha lasciato perdere gli studi.
All of a sudden Ivo dropped out of school.

Mai avrei pensato ad una cosa del genere!
I would have never thought of anything like that.

Mio figlio ha già finito il secondo anno al politecnico.
My son has already completed his second year at the polytechnic institute.

D. PAROLE! PAROLE! PAROLE!

The word *bello* is quite popular in Italian idioms.

Questa è una bella somma.
This is quite a sum.

Io l'ho accompagnato per un bel tratto.
I accompanied him for a fair part of the way.

Sai, sei un bel cretino!
You know, you're a real idiot!

Quell'uomo ha avuto una bella fortuna!
That man had a real stroke of luck!

Il bello della storia non è ancora arrivato (venuto)!
The best part of the story is still to come!

Ti ho presentato il mio bello?
Have I introduced you to my sweetheart?

C'è voluto del bello e del buono per convincerti!
It took heaven and earth to convince you!

È un cretino bello e buono!
He is an utter idiot!

Ieri sera me ne è capitata una bella.
Last night a strange thing happened to me.

Il bello è che poi non ha nemmeno telefonato.
The odd thing is that he didn't even phone.

Che fate di bello domani?
What are you thinking of doing tomorrow?

Che c'è di bello al cinema?
Is there anything good at the movies?

Quel ragazzo l'ha fatta bella!
That boy has really done it now!

Non abbiamo fatto una bella figura!
We did not make a good impression!

Ieri abbiamo avuto una bella nevicata!
Yesterday we had a heavy snow fall!

Non ho capito un bel niente/nulla!
I didn't understand anything at all!

Oh mio Dio! Mi sono messo in un bel pasticcio.
Oh, my God! I've gotten myself into a nice mess.

L'abbiamo scampata bella!
That was a close call!

Si è dato alla bella vita.
He has given himself over to a life a pleasure.

Non è bello quel che è bello, ma è bello quel che piace.
Beauty is in the eye of the beholder.

E. L'ANGOLO DEGLI AFFARI

L'ISTRUZIONE IN ITALIA (EDUCATION IN ITALY)

Italian school curricula are set at a national level by the *Ministero della pubblica istruzione* (public education ministry). There are eight years of education before secondary school. Five of these years are spent in elementary school, *scuola elementare*—from *prima elementare* up through *quinta elementare*—and the following three at middle school, *scuole medie.* It is compulsory for children to begin their elementary education at the age of five, and to finish *scuole medie,* or reach the age of fourteen, before they leave school. Although there have been various attempts at the reform of the school system in recent years, pedagogy is still more traditional in Italy than in North America. Oral examinations are conducted almost daily, and children are expected to write fairly intensively.

There are various categories of secondary school in Italy, geared toward different disciplines. When children complete middle school they are faced with a career decision. They may attend the *liceo classico,* or classical lyceum, which places emphasis on the humanities, including, for example, Latin and philosophy. They may also choose the *liceo scientifico,* which allows the student to concentrate on the pure sciences. Alternatively, they may opt to enroll in a school with a more technical, commercial bent, such as the *ragioneria,* which trains them for accountancy. When students graduate from an *Istituto Tecnico Commerciale (per Ragionieri),* they are qualified bookkeepers and accountants. However, in order to obtain higher, professional credentials, a *ragioniere* must attend university. Upon graduation with a *laurea in Economia e Commercio,* they may become *commercialisti* or chartered accountants.

Other kinds of secondary schools offer an eclectic combination of courses: *matematica* (mathematics), *fisica* (physics), *chimica* (chemistry), *biologia* (biology), *educazione fisica* (physical education), *italiano* (Italian), *geografia* (geography), *storia* (history), and *filosofia* (philosophy), to name a few. After five years in secondary school, students must complete a rigorous battery of oral and written final exams known as the *esami di maturità*—literally, "maturity" exams.

There are more than 60 universities in Italy. Students choose their specialization before their first year of study; there is no general or core series of courses common to all programs. Whereas admission to North American universities may be highly competitive or exclusive, few students have trouble gaining acceptance to academic programs in Italy. However, completion of most programs is not easy: significantly fewer students graduate than enroll. Programs tend to be more oriented toward independent study than their U.S. counterparts, and students frequently retake particular exams until they receive a passing grade, or a grade that signifies a certain level of mastery in the subject. Completion of a thesis, or *tesi di laurea,* is also required for the completion of a degree.

Administrative complexity is another factor that contributes to the relatively low percentage of students who graduate from post-secondary institutions in Italy. Classrooms are overcrowded; lectures, tutorials, even exams are often scheduled haphazardly. Recent efforts to improve the system, spearheaded by the *Ministero della pubblica istruzione,* have focused on streamlining programs to allow students to enter the work force sooner. The concept of the *laurea breve* or "brief degree," loosely parallel to the North American bachelor degree, is catching on; it takes three years to acquire and does not require a thesis. New programs are being developed that are more similar to technical and community college courses of study than to traditional Italian education; they emphasize practical, skills-based learning over classical liberal arts training.

ESERCIZI

A. *Riempire gli spazi vuoti con la forma corretta dell'aggettivo fra parentesi.* (Fill in the blanks with the correct form of the adjective in parentheses.)

1. *Quest'università offre un (buono, buona, buon) _____ programma di economia e commercio.*
2. *Il dottor Neri è un (buon, buono, buona) _____ psicologo.*
3. *Questa università è veramente (buon, buona, buon') _____.*
4. *Oggi ho letto un (buono, buon', buon) _____ articolo.*
5. *Che (bei, begli, belli) _____ amici che siete!*
6. *Lui è un (grande, gran, grandi) _____ amico!*
7. *Questa università è molto (grande, grand', grandi) _____.*
8. *Loro sono (grandi, grande, gran) _____ amici!*

B. *Formare delle frasi con le seguenti parole.* (Form complete sentences using the elements provided.)

1. *io / andare / spesso / Italia*
2. *aule / essere / veramente / affollate*
3. *essere / impossibile / entrare / fisicamente / studenti / aule*
4. *studente / fare / malissimo / esame*
5. *lui / lavorare / piano / ma / tanta / pazienza*
6. *solito / lui / andare / lezione / il / lunedì*

C. *Tradurre le seguenti frasi.* (Translate the following sentences.)

1. We accompanied him for a fair part of the way.
2. It took heaven and earth to convince him to go to school.
3. That student has really done it now!
4. At the seminar we did not make a good impression.
5. I attend classes regularly.
6. I didn't understand anything at all when I went to class.
7. He did really poorly at the examination.
8. I heard that the Bocconi is an excellent university.

LEZIONE 8

A. DIALOGO

I VETRI DI MURANO

Massimo e Federica hanno scelto di trascorrere la loro luna di miele[1] a Venezia. Oggi hanno deciso di visitare alcuni dei luoghi turistici di questa città meravigliosa. In albergo chiedono al portiere come andare a Murano, l'isola dove si fanno i famosi vetri.[2]

MASSIMO: **Scusi, vorremmo visitare Murano, ma non sappiamo come arrivarci. Ci potrebbe dare delle indicazioni?[3]**

PORTIERE: **Certamente. Dovete prendere il vaporetto[4] alle Fondamenta Nuove. Il numero 5 vi porterà a San Michele e poi a Murano.**

FEDERICA: **Oh, le Fondamenta[5] Nuove. Non si trovano vicino a quella chiesa domenicana che volevamo vedere, Massimo?**

MASSIMO: **SS.[6] Giovanni e Paolo?**

PORTIERE: **Sì. Il campo e la chiesa sono nella direzione delle Fondamenta Nuove. Lì vedrete anche un imponente monumento a Bartolomeo Colleoni.[7]**

FEDERICA: **Quanto è lontano Murano dalle Fondamenta Nuove?**

PORTIERE: **Ci vogliono[8] solo dieci o quindici minuti in vaporetto.**

MASSIMO: **Ancora[9] una domanda: dove dovremmo scendere a Murano?**

PORTIERE: **Scendete[10] a Murano Colonna. Da lì camminando lungo le Fondamenta dei Vetrai, dove ci sono molte delle vetrerie più famose, vedrete anche le case colorate, che una volta appartenevano ai lavoratori, e San Pietro Martire, una ricostruzione settecentesca di una più antica chiesa gotica.**

FEDERICA: **Sembra molto interessante.**

PORTIERE: **Presumo[11] che visiterete altri posti durante il vostro soggiorno a Venezia.**

MASSIMO: Certamente. Domani andiamo a Piazza San Marco[12] a visitare la basilica e la torre dell'orologio. Sono un grand'ammiratore dell'architettura bizantina, e sono molto curioso di vedere le influenze bizantine e romaniche amalgamate in una sola struttura.

PORTIERE: Anche i mosaici sono bellissimi. Non ci sono tante vetrate colorate quanto ce ne sono nelle famose cattedrali gotiche, ma i mosaici riempiono la nostra basilica di colore e di luce.

FEDERICA: Non vedo l'ora di vedere il Palazzo Ducale.[13] Voglio proprio vedere i capolavori che coprono interi muri[14] e soffitti.

PORTIERE: Oh sì. Infatti nella Sala del Consiglio c'è *Il paradiso* di Tintoretto.[15] È il quadro più grande del mondo.

FEDERICA: L'avevo letto questo. Sarà un'esperienza magnifica vederlo!

MASSIMO: Beh, dovremmo andare se vogliamo arrivare a Murano prima di mezzogiorno. È stato molto gentile. Grazie mille![16]

PORTIERE: È stato un piacere. Buona giornata.

Dopo qualche ora, Massimo e Federica arrivano a Murano. In una vetreria una guida[17] spiega ai turisti la lavorazione del vetro.

GUIDA: State assistendo alla lavorazione del vetro soffiato. Come vedete il vetraio scalda la mescola ad una temperatura altissima, fino a farla diventare quasi liquida.

MASSIMO: Che tipo di miscela è?

GUIDA: La materia prima è la sabbia di silicio. Raggiunta la temperatura necessaria per la soffiatura, come vedete, questo impasto diventa incandescente. Osservate come il vetraio mette un po' di quel materiale sulla punta di quel tubo lungo e sottile. Fra poco[18] comincerà a soffiarci dentro per ottenere la forma desiderata.

FEDERICA: Come fa il vetraio ad ottenere queste bellissime forme e questi bellissimi colori?

GUIDA: Questo metodo è un segreto secolare! Viene tramandato oralmente da una generazione di vetrai all'altra.

FEDERICA: È un processo interessantissimo. Massimo, adesso andiamo al museo a vedere tutti quei pezzi. Mi piacerebbe tanto comprare un vaso o un piatto.

MASSIMO: Ma Federica, con questi prezzi non avremo abbastanza soldi per prendere il vaporetto per tornare a Venezia! Qui costa tutto un occhio della testa!

FEDERICA: Non fa niente. Io reggo il vaso, e tu remi!

MURANO'S GLASSWARE

Massimo and Federica have chosen to spend their honeymoon in Venice. Today they've decided to visit just a few of the attractions of this marvelous city. At the hotel they ask the porter how to get to Murano, the island famous for its glassworks.

MASSIMO: Excuse me, we would like to visit Murano, but we don't know how to get there. Could you give us directions?

PORTER: Of course. You have to take a boat from Fondamenta Nuove. The number 5 will take you to San Michele and then to Murano.

FEDERICA: Oh, Fondamenta Nuove. Isn't that near that Dominican church we wanted to see, Massimo?

MASSIMO: Santi Giovanni e Paolo?

PORTER: Yes. The campo and the church are on the way to Fondamenta Nuove. You'll also see an impressive monument to Bartolomeo Colleoni there.

FEDERICA: How far is Murano from the Fondamenta Nuove?

PORTER: It's only about ten or fifteen minutes by boat.

MASSIMO: Another question: where should we get off at Murano?

PORTER: Get off at Murano Colonna. From there, walking along the Fondamenta dei Vetrai, where there are a lot of the most famous glass-works, you'll also see the colorful houses that once belonged to the workmen, as well as San Pietro Martire, a sixteenth-century recon-struction of an older Gothic church.

FEDERICA: That sounds very interesting.

151

PORTER: I assume you'll also visit some other sights during your stay in Venice.

MASSIMO: Of course. Tomorrow we'll go to the Piazza San Marco and visit the basilica and the clock tower. I'm a great admirer of Byzantine architecture, and I'm very curious to see Byzantine and Romanesque influences blended in one structure.

PORTER: The mosaics are very beautiful as well. There aren't as many stained glass windows as in famous gothic cathedrals, but the mosaics fill our basilica with color and light.

FEDERICA: I'm looking forward to visiting the Doge's Palace. I really want to see the masterpieces covering the walls and the ceilings.

PORTER: Oh yes. In fact in the Great Council Hall there's Tintoretto's *Paradise*. It's the world's largest oil painting.

FEDERICA: So I've read. I'm sure it's a magnificent experience to see it.

MASSIMO: Well, we should be on our way if we want to make it to Murano before noon. You've been very helpful. Thanks very much!

PORTER: A pleasure. Enjoy your day.

A few hours later, Massimo and Federica arrive in Murano. In one of the glassworks, a guide explains the art of glassmaking to the tourists.

GUIDE: You are now witnessing the actual manufacturing of blown glass. As you see, the glassblower heats the mixture to a very high temperature until it almost becomes a liquid.

MASSIMO: What kind of mixture is it?

GUIDE: It's mostly silicon sand. As you can see, at the temperature necessary for glass blowing, this mixture becomes incandescent. Observe how the glassblower places some of the mixture onto the end of a long, thin tube. In a moment he'll begin to blow into it, to achieve the desired form.

FEDERICA: How does the glassblower get these beautiful shapes and colors?

GUIDE: This method has been a secret for centuries! It is passed down orally from one generation of glassblowers to the next.

FEDERICA: It's an extremely interesting process. Massimo, let's go to the museum and look at all of those pieces. I'd love to buy a vase or a plate.

MASSIMO: But Federica, with these prices we won't have enough money to take the boat back to Venice! They cost an arm and a leg!

FEDERICA: That's all right. I'll hold on to the vase, and you row!

B. IN BREVE

1. A synonym is *viaggio di nozze*. The expression *luna di miele* (honeymoon) is also used metaphorically to indicate a particularly happy period in life: *Adesso che ho perso il lavoro, la nostra luna di miele è finita.* (Now that I lost my job, our good times are over.)

2. Venetian glassware is as famous as the city's gondolas, and it can be found on sale all over town. At the glass-blowing center of Murano you may watch glass being made as well as visit the showrooms. Prices for glass in Murano are much the same as in Venice itself, but the general quality will be higher.

3. There are many ways to ask for directions. Here are some examples: *Scusi, come si arriva a Murano? / Scusi, potrebbe dirmi come arrivare a Murano? / Scusi, per Murano? / Scusi, potrebbe darmi le direzioni per (arrivare a) Murano? / Scusi, potrebbe indicarmi la via per Murano?*

4. ACTV, the public transport system, runs the city's *vaporetto* service. Maps of the system are sold at newsstands. You can buy your ticket from the booths on the landing stages or on the *vaporetto* itself.

5. The word *fondamento* (foundation) has two plurals: *le fondamenta* (the foundations of a house, of a building) and *i fondamenti* (the foundations of a science, of a discipline, of a theory). *Questa casa ha delle fondamenta solide.* (This house has solid foundations.) *La libertà è uno dei fondamenti essenziali di qualsiasi società democratica.* (Freedom is one of the essential foundations of a democratic society.)

6. *SS.* is the abbreviation for *santissimi*.

7. Bartolomeo Colleoni (1400–1475) served as general-in-chief of the Venetian republic. He was renowned for his innovations in field artillery tactics.

8. The verb *volerci* is used only in the third person singular or plural, depending on the number of "what it takes." *Per andare da New York a Roma ci vogliono otto ore.* (To go from New York to Rome it takes 8 hours.) *Per finire questo lavoro ci vuole poco.* (To finish this work it won't take much.) In compound tenses *volerci* takes the auxiliary *essere.* A similar verb in structure is *mancare/mancarci: Mancano due ore alla partenza.* (There are two hours left before departure.) *Mi manca molto la mia famiglia.* (I miss my family a lot.)

9. Besides its standard meaning of "still, yet," the adverb *ancora* can take the meaning of "again, some more, another, one more." *Ancora tu?* (You again?) *Ancora un giorno e sarò in Italia.* (One more day and I'll be in Italy.)

10. When speaking about vehicles, "to get on" is translated as *salire* and "to get off" is translated as *scendere.*

11. *Assumere* and "to assume" are not always direct equivalents. When "assume" is a synonym for "imagine" or "presume" use the Italian *presumere* or *immaginare.* "I assume you know Franco" is *Immagino/Presumo che tu conosca Franco.* The cognate *assumere* is used when you mean to say "to take on," as in *assumere responsabilità,* "to assume responsibility." *Assumere* may also mean "to hire," "to employ" as in *Ho assunto tre operai.* "I hired three workers."

12. Piazza San Marco is the only *piazza* in Venice. All other squares are known as *campi,* unless they are small, in which case they're known as a *campiello* or a *corte.* A street is a *calle,* or, if it's quite large, a *calle larga,* or a *ruga,* or even sometimes a *salizzada.* A *calletta* or *ramo* is an alley, a *sottoportego* is a street that passes under buildings, and a *fondamenta* is a street flanking a canal. A street formed by a filled-in canal is known as a *rio terrà,* while a *lista* is a street that originally led to an ambassador's palace.

13. The Doge's Palace was the official residence of the leader of the Venetian Republic. This spectacular palace was built in 814. It faces St. Mark's Square.

14. Like *fondamento,* the word *muro* has two plurals, *i muri* and *le mura. I muri* are those which are found inside a structure (as the dialogue indicates), whereas *le mura* are those which are erected on the exterior as a means of protection, as in *Le mura della città sono antichissime.* (The city's walls are very old.)

15. Tintoretto (d. 1594) is considered one of the greatest Mannerist painters to come out of the Venetian school. Tintoretto was an extremely important and influential figure in the late Renaissance.

16. Here the word *mille* is used hyperbolically to mean *molte.* Study also the following examples: *Mi sembrano mille anni che non ti vedo* (It seems ages that I haven't seen you.) *Mille scuse, signor Giannini.* (I'm very sorry, Mr. Giannini.)

17. Note that *la guida* is a noun that can be used to refer both to a male and a female. *Giovanni/Anna è una bravissima guida.* (Giovanni/Anna is an excellent guide.) Similar words are *la spia* (spy) and *la guardia* (guard).

18. The prepositions *fra* and *tra* are interchangeable. Literally, *Fra/tra poco* means "between a little."

C. GRAMMATICA E SUOI USI

1. *IL PRONOME CI* (THE PRONOUN *CI*)

Ci has various functions. It can be used as a direct object pronoun ("us"), an indirect object pronoun ("to us"), or a reflexive pronoun ("ourselves"). *Ci (vi)* is also a locative particle and in this case it translates as the English "there." It can also be replaced by *vi,* which is, however, far less common. Note its position before the verb.

Ma perché dovremmo visitare questa chiesa? —Ci troverete degli affreschi di rinomati artisti.

But why should we visit this church? —You'll see frescoes by well-known artists there.

Chi avete accompagnato alla mostra? —Ci abbiamo accompagnato un gruppo di turisti.

Who did you accompany to the exhibition? —We accompanied a group of tourists there.

Ci may be used to substitute *da* + place.

Passeremo dal centro storico della città? —Certo. Ci passeremo dopo aver visitato il museo di scultura moderna.

Are we going to pass by the historical center of the city? —Of course. We will pass by after visiting the museum of modern sculpture.

Ci can be used to replace a prepositional phrase that begins with *a, su,* or *in.*

Hai mai pensato a quanto tempo c'è voluto per restaurare la Cappella Sistina? —No, non ci ho mai pensato.

Have you ever thought of how much time it took to restore the Sistine Chapel? —No, I've never given it much thought.

Ci can take the place of *a* + an infinitive phrase.

È riuscito a procurare dei libri sulle ville rinascimentali? —Sì, ci è riuscito.

Was he able to get books about Renaissance villas? —Yes, he was able to.

Some common idiomatic expressions with *ci* are:

a) *entrarci* (to have to do with something)

Lo stile gotico non c'entra affatto in questo discorso perché la basilica di San Marco è in stile bizantino e romanico.

The gothic style has nothing to do with this discussion because the Basilica of San Marco is in Byzantine and Romanesque style.

b) *caderci/cascarci* (to fall for it)

Gli ho detto che questo quadro di Raffaello è un originale e lui ci è cascato.
    I told him that this painting by Raffaello was an original and he fell for it.

c) *metterci* (to take [time])

Per completare il suo capolavoro lo scultore ci ha messo tre anni.
    It took the sculptor three years to complete his masterpiece.

d) *vederci* (to be able to see)

C'era tanta nebbia che non ci vedevo per niente: non riuscivo neanche a vedere la punta della torre.
    It was so foggy that I could not see at all: I couldn't even see the top of the tower.

e) *sentirci* (to be able to hear)

Anche se mio nonno non ci sente molto bene, è riuscito a seguire le spiegazioni della guida perché l'acustica nella cattedrale era ottima.
    Even though my grandfather cannot hear very well, he managed to follow the guide's explanations because the acoustics in the cathedral were excellent.

f) *contarci* (to count on)

Gli Uffizi erano chiusi. I turisti sono rimasti delusi perché ci contavano proprio di vederli.
    The Uffizi were closed. The tourists were disappointed because they were really counting on visiting them.

g) *volerci* (to take [time, money, . . .])

Ci vuole tanta pazienza per fare dei giri turistici con dei bambini.
    It takes a lot of patience to go sightseeing with small kids.

h) *avercela con* (to be angry at)

La guida turistica ce l'ha con me perché ho fatto molte domande.
    The tour guide is angry at me because I asked a lot of questions.

i) *mancarci* (all that is needed)

Che disastro questo giro turistico! Ci manca solo che adesso si metta a pio-
vere!
What a disastrous tour! All we need now is for it to start raining!

2. *GLI AGGETTIVI E I PRONOMI DIMOSTRATIVI* (DEMONSTRATIVE ADJECTIVES AND PRONOUNS)

The demonstrative adjective *questo* (this) and *quello* (that) agree in gender and number with the noun they precede. *Questo* has the four regular forms: *questo, questa, questi, queste.* The singular forms become *quest'* before a noun beginning with a vowel.

Questo stile architettonico è tipico di questa zona.
This style of architecture is typical of this region.

Quest'artista è vissuto durante il periodo barocco.
This artist lived during the Baroque period.

Quello has forms similar to those of the adjective *bello* (and to the definite article + *di*): *quel, quell', quello, quella, quelle, quei, quegli.*

Capisci cosa rappresenta quella pittura surrealistica?
Do you know what that surrealistic painting represents?

Quei mobili moderni occupano poco spazio.
That modern furniture occupies little space.

Questo and *quello* are also demonstrative pronouns. As pronouns they each have only four forms: *questo, questa, questi, queste; quello, quella, quelli, quelle.*

Questi mosaici non sono del periodo romano, ma quelli sì.
These mosaics are not from the Roman period, but those are.

Queste informazioni sull'artista non sono corrette; ma quelle sì.
This information about the artist is not correct; but that is.

Questo can mean "this thing" and *quello* can mean "that thing."

Sai che durante la nostra visita a Palermo abbiamo trovato molti musei chiusi? —Questo non mi sorprende affatto.
Do you know that during our trip to Palermo we found many of the museums closed? —This does not surprise me at all.

Quello and *questo* also express, respectively, "the former" and "the latter."

D. PAROLE! PAROLE! PAROLE!

In the dialogue, the word *occhio* is used metaphorically in the expression *costare un occhio* (to cost an arm and a leg, to cost a mint). *Occhio* is also used figuratively in the following expressions:

Quel ragazzo ha messo gli occhi addosso a te, non a me.
That young man has got his eyes on you, not on me.

Nessuno lo vede di buon occhio.
No one approves of him. (No one looks favorably on him.)

Sono stanco. Ieri notte non ho potuto chiudere occhio.
I'm tired. Last night I didn't sleep a wink.

Ti raccomando di non perderlo d'occhio.
Don't lose sight of him.

Povero Giuseppe, non ha più occhi per piangere.
Poor Joseph, he's cried his eyes out.

Lei è la pupilla dei suoi occhi.
She is the apple of her/his eye.

Domani devo parlarti a quattr'occhi.
Tomorrow, I have to speak to you face to face.

A Giovanni piace sempre sognare ad occhi aperti.
John likes always to daydream.

Ieri abbiamo speso un occhio della testa.
Yesterday we spent a lot of money.

The word "occhio" is also used in the following proverbs:

Lontan dagli occhi, lontan dal cuore.
Out of sight, out of mind.

Occhio per occhio, dente per dente.
An eye for an eye, a tooth for a tooth.

Occhio che non vede, cuore che non duole.
What the eye doesn't see, the heart doesn't grieve over.

E. L'ANGOLO DEGLI AFFARI

L'ARTIGIANATO IN ITALIA
(THE HANDICRAFT INDUSTRY IN ITALY)

In Italian, the term *artigianato* (handicraft) may refer to any sort of manufacturing which is handmade. Consequently, handicraft in Italy is not one sole industry, but is, indeed, the cornerstone of many industries, small and large. In addition, handicraft is not limited to what one may automatically think of when one thinks of Italian craftsmanship. Pottery and furniture-making are traditional activities that come to mind, and, while it is true that these are typical industries based on handicraft in Italy, there are many others. In fact, there are distinctions made between the various types of handicraft, according to the various sectors: *attività connesse all'agricoltura* (enterprises connected to agriculture); *alimentari* (foodstuffs); *tessili* (textiles); *vestiario* (clothing); *calzature* (footwear); *pelletterie* (leather/fur); *lavorazione legno e mobili* (woodworking and furniture-making); *edilizia* (construction); etc.

In the past, there has been a net division between handicraft and industrialism. Not only that, but craftsmen have traditionally shown an understandable hesitation towards mechanization and mass production. With the dawn of industrialization, many artisans, particularly in the food and agriculture industry, suffered great drawbacks and losses as cost-efficient methods were found in order to produce and distribute products on a mass scale. Today, however, many Italian enterprises based on the production of hand-crafted products combine the age-old tradition and savvy of the artisans who founded the craft with modern technology. This combination of technology and tradition, along with the public's re-discovery of the high quality of products produced by artisans, have allowed the handicraft industry to be successful and competitive. While handmade products produced by family and other small businesses cannot compete with large industry, many sectors of the industry have found a new niche for themselves.

In many parts of Italy the agricultural industry is favored by the contribution of handicraft. All over the peninsula small industries continue to make specialized local dairy products by hand, using processes that have been passed down from generation to generation. A famous example of this is Italian *mozzarella.* The proper form of *mozzarella* is made *artigianalmente* (in an artisan-like manner) in various parts of the region of Campania and in a very small area of Lazio. Locals boast (and justifiably so) that one has not truly tasted this now world-famous cheese unless one has tasted it as it is made in the traditional manner in the areas surrounding the provinces of Naples, Caserta, and Salerno. True *mozzarella* is made from *latte di bufala* (cow buffalo milk), and has been made in the traditional manner since the early nineteenth century. Rennet is added to cow buffalo milk that has been kept at a temperature of 102 degrees. When the milk separates into curds and whey, the curds are worked by hand until the proper consistency is reached. This complicated process has been developed into an art by farmers of Campania, and for this reason, *mozzarella* made in these regions is different than that made anywhere else in the world. In fact, the technical name for the more common version of the product, produced from cow's milk (which is made on a mass scale and is much less tasty than the traditional *mozzarella*), is *fior di latte,* and not *mozzarella.*

Although one will likely find specialty products in every region of Italy, certain regions offer a wider variety of hand-crafted goods for purchase or exportation. The region of Tuscany, for instance, has a very high concentration of small industries which specialize in hand-crafted goods in every sector, the most notable of which is the wine industry. Some parts of the region are rich in artistic production. In and around Pisa, for instance, one can find an abundance of small enterprises specializing in alabaster, ceramic, wood, glass, and leather products. Another region famous for its handicraft is Campania, mentioned above for its contribution to the agricultural sector. Here, one can also find a high concentration of small enterprises dedicated to the production of hand-crafted goods. Many of the finest leather goods (particularly gloves and footwear) are produced within the *napoletano.* As well, the Naples area is famous for its production of coral jewelry, statuettes, and cameos.

ESERCIZI

A. *Completare con la forma appropriata dell'aggettivo dimostrativo quello.* (Fill in the blanks with the correct form of the adjective *quello*.)

1. *Potrei vedere _____ opuscoli, per piacere?*
2. *_____ sinagoga è molto interessante.*
3. *Vorrei tanto vedere _____ vetrerie!*
4. *Si può andare a _____ isola in gondola?*
5. *Ancora non ho visto _____ teatro.*
6. *Chi sono _____ signori?*

B. *Completare con la forma appropriata del dimostrativo quello, aggettivo o pronome.* (Fill in the blanks, using the appropriate form of the pronoun or adjective *quello*.)

1. *Ma _____ lì è la stazione di Murano?*
2. *La prima fermata è _____ del Ponte delle Guglie?*
3. *_____ zaino costerà sicuramente un occhio della testa.*
4. *—A quale mercato andrai? —Andrò a _____ vicino alla stazione.*
5. *Le gondole si possono prendere da molti punti. _____ più consueti sono Piazza San Marco e Ponte di Rialto.*
6. *Queste lentine mi fanno male. Erano migliori _____ vecchie.*

C. *Rispondere affermativamente usando il pronome ci.* (Answer the following questions affirmatively, using the pronoun *ci*.)

1. *Siete mai stati a Venezia?*
2. *Tu vai spesso al mercato?*
3. *I tuoi genitori andranno dai Rossi stasera?*
4. *Voi avete mai pensato di fare un viaggio a Venezia?*
5. *Federica è riuscita a visitare Murano?*

D. *Tradurre.* (Translate.)

1. How long did it take you to go to Murano by boat?
2. It was so foggy that we could not see at all.
3. It takes a lot of patience in life.
4. I often think back to my trip to Venice.
5. I am very tired. Last night I didn't sleep a wink.

LEZIONE 9

A. DIALOGO

Il telegiornale della sera

CONDUTTRICE: **Buona sera dal TG2.[1] Questi i titoli principali di stasera. Il presidente[2] americano visita il Vaticano.[3] Tragedia in una miniera d'oro sudafricana. Voci sul rilevamento della Tele-mobili. Di Pietro[4] spiega come è nata operazione "Mani Pulite." Una donna veneziana viene licenziata perché non indossa la mini.**

    Oggi il presidente americano è arrivato in Italia. Da Roma il nostro Giancarlo Cecchi.

CECCHI: **Erano le dieci di questa mattina quando l'aereo della United Airlines con a bordo il presidente statunitense è atterrato all'aeroporto Leonardo da Vinci. Ad attenderlo[5] all'aeroporto c'erano numerosi esponenti politici italiani ed una folla entusiasta.[6] Nel pomeriggio il presidente e la first lady hanno visitato in Vaticano il papa. Per l'occasione il presidente statunitense ha ricevuto il cordone dell'Ordine Piano, onoreficenza vaticana. Il pontefice ha avuto parole di elogio per il suo ospite e ha benedetto tutto il popolo americano. Al commiato il papa ha salutato l'uomo più potente del mondo con un caloroso "Viva l'America."**

CONDUTTRICE: **Un fatto più triste: grave incidente in[7] SudAfrica. Questo servizio della nostra inviata speciale Carla Masini.**

INVIATA: **Più di cento persone sono morte in una miniera d'oro non lontano[8] da Johannesburg. Appena terminato il turno, i minatori stavano per risalire alla superficie quando tutto ad un tratto[9] il condotto principale è crollato. I soccorritori sono ancora impegnati a recuperare i resti dei lavoratori della miniera maledetta. Questo è tutto per ora. Passo la linea a Roma.**

CONDUTTRICE: **Per le ultime notizie sull'economia sentiamo il nostro Ernesto Conti.**

ERNESTO CONTI: **La società italiana di cellulari digitali Telemobili non ha ancora trovato un compratore. Secondo alcune indiscrezioni, sul tavolo del direttore centrale della Telemobili, Enrico Ciani, sono arrivate molte proposte per rilevare l'azienda. Ma ad una ad una sono cadute nel vuoto di fronte all'iniziale richiesta di Ciani. Giorgio Dori, amministratore delegato della Telemobili, ha detto: "La valutazione della nostra azienda mi sembra corretta, perché abbiamo superato il momento critico. Ora la situazione è migliorata. Dopo un anno e mezzo di instabilità sui mercati internazionali, i valori di borsa della ditta sono finalmente in rialzo." Sarà vero, ma qui fuori alla Borsa di Milano[10] corre voce che molti degli azionisti della società non sono soddisfatti dei tentativi di Ciani di risolvere la situazione. Tale insoddisfazione potrebbe avere degli effetti disastrosi sulla ditta. Passo la linea.**

CONDUTTRICE: **Oggi l'ex magistrato[11] e personaggio più amato dagli italiani, Antonio Di Pietro, ha spiegato com'è nato il nome della famosa inchiesta "Mani Pulite." Ascoltiamolo.**

DI PIETRO: **Io e un capitano dei carabinieri[12] dovevamo arrestare una persona e ci parlavamo con i telefonini[13] per non farci riconoscere lui si faceva chiamare Mike, io Pietro. Chi ha trascritto quelle conversazioni ha usato le iniziali M.P. e chi le ha decodificate ha pensato che fossero parole importanti. Mani pulite, come minimo.**

CONDUTTRICE: **E ora un fatto sconcertante. Una giovane donna veneziana, cameriera in un ristorante del capoluogo[14] veneto, è stata licenziata[15] perché si rifiutava di portare la minigonna durante gli orari di servizio. "La ragazza non faceva al caso nostro e, poiché era in prova, abbiamo concluso il rapporto di lavoro," ha osservato il padrone del ristorante. Vari gruppi femministi del Veneto hanno lanciato una protesta contro il ristorante, e sperano di organizzare un boicottaggio del luogo. "È veramente sconcertante," osserva Pia Rinaldi, presidente della Lega Donna, un'organizzazione femminista veneziana. "Siamo arrivati al ventunesimo secolo, e ci sono persone che hanno ancora un concetto medievale del ruolo della donna in società. Con questa nostra protesta, noi vogliamo far si che ingiustizie come questa non avvengano più."**

E per chiudere, le notizie metereologiche. Prepariamo l'om-

brello: su tutta la penisola la giornata di domani promette più nuvole e piogge che sole.[16] Un fronte freddo proveniente dal nord porterà neve sulle zone alpine. La temperatura diminuirà dappertutto di alcuni gradi,[17] mentre forti venti renderanno molto mossi tutti i mari. Per oggi abbiamo concluso. Grazie per l'ascolto. Dopo una breve pausa pubblicitaria, seguiranno le notizie sportive. Buona sera.

THE EVENING NEWS

NEWCASTER: Good evening from TG2. These are tonight's headlines. The American president visits the Vatican. Tragedy in a South African gold mine. Rumors of a take-over at Telemobili. Di Pietro explains how operation "Mani Pulite" was born. A Venetian woman is fired for not wearing a mini-skirt.

The American President arrived in Italy today. From Rome, our Giancarlo Cecchi.

CECCHI: It was ten o'clock this morning when the United Airlines plane with the American President on board landed at Leonardo da Vinci airport. Waiting for him were several Italian political representatives as well as an enthusiastic crowd. In the afternoon, the President and the First Lady visited the Pope at the Vatican. For the occasion, the American President received the *cordone dell' Ordine Piano,* a Vatican decoration. The pontiff had words of praise for his guest, and he blessed the entire American population. On taking his leave the Pope said goodbye to the most powerful man in the world with a warm "Long live America."

NEWSCASTER: On a sadder note: a serious accident in South Africa. This report from our special correspondent Attilio Masini.

CORRESPONDENT: More than one hundred people are dead in a gold mine not far from Johannesburg. The shift having just ended, the miners were about to return to the surface when suddenly the main shaft collapsed. Emergency workers are still busy recovering the remains of the workers of the unfortunate mine. That's all for now. Back to Rome.

NEWSCASTER: For the latest news on the economy, let's go to our Ernesto Conti.

ERNESTO CONTI: The Italian digital cellular firm Telemobili has not yet found a buyer. According to rumors, many take-over proposals have been put to Telemobili Chief Director, Enrico Ciani. But one by one, they failed to materialize because of Ciani's initial asking price. Giorgio Dori, Telemobili's managing director said: "Our company's estimate seems correct because we have survived a critical period. Now the situation has improved. After a year and a half of instability on the international markets, the firm's stock prices are finally going up." That may be true, but here outside the Milan Stock Exchange it is rumored that many of the firm's shareholders are not satisfied with Ciani's attempts to resolve the situation. Such dissatisfaction could have disastrous effects on the company. Back to you.

NEWSCASTER: Today, the ex-magistrate and most beloved personality among Italians, Antonio Di Pietro, explained how the name of the famous inquest "Mani Pulite" was born. Let's listen to him.

DI PIETRO: A police captain and I had to arrest a person and we spoke to one another by cellular phone: to not be recognized he made me call him Mike, and I was Pietro. Whoever transcribed those conversations used the initials M.P. and whoever decoded them thought they were important words. *Mani pulite,* at least.

NEWSCASTER: And now a disconcerting story. A young Venetian woman working in a restaurant in the Veneto capital was fired because she refused to wear a mini-skirt during working hours. "The girl was not right for us, and since she was still on probation, we terminated the working relationship," stated the restaurant owner. Various feminist groups of the Veneto region have launched a protest against the restaurant, and are hoping to organize a boycott of the establishment. "It's truly disconcerting," observes Pia Rinaldi, president of the Lega Donna, a Venetian feminist organization. "We have made it to the twenty-first century, and there are still people who have a medieval view of a woman's role in society. With our protest we want to make sure that injustices such as this one don't occur anymore."

And to conclude, the weather report. Get your umbrellas out: tomorrow promises to be another day of clouds and rain throughout the entire peninsula. A cold front moving in from the north will bring snow to the Alpine regions. Temperatures everywhere will drop by a few degrees and strong winds will make the seas very rough.

That is all for today. Thank you for tuning in. Sports will follow after these messages. Good night.

B. IN BREVE

1. *TG* is the short form of *telegiornale* (television news) which was developed by the *RAI* (*Radio Audizioni Italiane,* Italian radio television), the state institution in charge of broadcasting. Until very recently, Italians have only been able to watch the *telegiornale* on the three *RAI* stations. The *RAI* held a monopoly over national news broadcasts until Silvio Berlusconi's Fininvest corporation acquired the rights to transmit news broadcasts. The *RAI* broadcasts, TG1, TG2, and TG3, are still extremely popular among viewers.

2. The term *presidente* may also be used in the feminine *(la presidente).* It can also be used to mean "chairman" (*presidente del consiglio d'amministrazione,* chairman of the board of directors). Notice also the following: *presidente della Camera dei Deputati* (Speaker of the Chamber of Deputies, Speaker of the House of Commons, Speaker of the House of Representatives), *presidente del consiglio* (Prime Minister, Premier).

3. Situated in the heart of Rome, the Vatican is the seat of the Papacy and of the Catholic Church. With just over 108 acres and an estimated population of less than a thousand, the Vatican is the smallest state in the world. The Vatican was not formed until 1929, when the Italian state and the Church signed the *Patti lateranensi,* which settled a 60-year-long dispute between the Papacy and the Italian state.

4. The Italian magistrate Antonio Di Pietro became a celebrity of sorts when he began operation *mani pulite* (clean hands), a campaign which brought to justice many politicians who had been under investigation for having accepted bribes and taken kickbacks. The indictment of a high number of powerful figures set off the *scandalo delle tangenti* (bribes scandal), also known as *tangentopoli* (literally, city of bribes). Di Pietro personally oversaw the prosecution of many important figures in Italian politics and industry, and became a champion of justice. Di Pietro retired from the magistrature in 1995.

5. Note the different used of *attendere. L'ho atteso alla fermata dell'autobus.* (I waited for him at the bus stop.) *Chi attende a quella bambina?* (Who looks after that child?) *Attendiamo Vostra conferma.* (We await your confirmation). Do not confuse *attendere* with "to attend." *Non ho partecipato alla riunione.* (I didn't attend the meeting.) *La signorina è servita?* (Are you being attended to, Miss?)

6. *Entusiasta* can be used to describe both masculine and feminine nouns: *Marco/Maria è entusiasta del voto che ha ricevuto all'esame.* (Marco/Maria is very pleased with the mark he/she received on the exam.)

7. Normally, when the preposition *in* is followed by the name of a country, it does not require the article, unless the country is modified. *SudAfrica* could be considered a modified noun, and therefore it is also possible to say *nel SudAfrica.* For more details on the preposition *in,* refer to the *Grammatica e suoi usi* in this chapter.

8. Remember that *lontano* and *vicino* can also be considered adjectives and therefore may agree with the noun to which they refer. *La fabbrica in cui lavoro non è molto lontano/lontana dal centro.* (The factory where I work is not far from downtown.)

9. *Tutto ad un tratto* (suddenly) has several synonyms: *all'improvviso, improvvisamente, d'un tratto.*

10. The Milan stock exchange. The acronym for the exchange is MIB.

11. In Italy, the term *magistratura* refers to the judiciary or to the Bench. In Italian, the term *magistrato* may refer either to a judge (as in the case of Antonio Di Pietro), a public prosecutor, or even to an official or authority such as the mayor of a municipality.

12. The *carabinieri* are a branch of the Italian armed forces and assume what are, in essence, the duties of a police force.

13. A *telefonino* (cellular phone; literally, "little phone") is the diminutive form of *telefono.* For more information on the *telefonino,* please refer to *L'angolo degli affari* of *Lezione 3.*

14. The plural of *capoluogo* can be either *capoluoghi* or *capiluoghi*.

15. The verb *licenziare* is in the passive form. For more on the passive form refer to *Lezione 15*.

16. When one compares two qualities of the same entity, "than" is translated as *che*. For more on comparatives refer to *Lezione 11, Grammatica e suoi usi*.

17. Remember that in Italy temperature is reported in centigrade degrees (32°F = 0°C). To convert Fahrenheit into Centigrade, subtract 32 and multiply by 5/9. To convert Centigrade into Fahrenheit, multiply by 9/5 and add 32.

C. GRAMMATICA E SUOI USI

1. *L'IMPERFETTO INDICATIVO* (THE IMPERFECT INDICATIVE)

The imperfect *(imperfetto)* describes a past action or state that was in progress, but not completed, with no clearly specified beginning, end, or duration. In English it is expressed in the following ways:

I <u>was speaking</u> when the phone rang.   He <u>used to come</u> here often.

The imperfect has the same endings for all three conjugations. It is formed by dropping the *-re* of the infinitive and adding the following endings to the stem: *-vo, -vi, -va, -vamo, -vate, -vano*.

	LAVORARE	PRENDERE	DORMIRE
io	lavoravo	prendevo	dormivo
tu	lavoravi	prendevi	dormivi
lui/lei/Lei	lavorava	prendeva	dormiva
noi	lavoravamo	prendevamo	dormivamo
voi	lavoravate	prendevate	dormivate
loro/Loro	lavoravano	prendevano	dormivano

Only a few verbs are irregular in the imperfect. The following verbs have irregular stems, but regular endings: *bere,* (*beve-,* to drink), *dire,* (*dice-,* to say), *fare* (*face-,* to do, to make). Verbs in *-urre* and *-porre* also have irregular stems. For the complete conjugation of all irregular verbs refer to the Appendix. The verb *essere* is completely irregular and is conjugated as follows:

ESSERE	
io	ero
tu	eri
lui/lei/Lei	era
noi	eravamo
voi	eravate
loro/Loro	erano

Una volta il telegiornale era più informativo.
The news programs used to be more informative.

Mi ricordo che prima tu non bevevi mai.
I remember that you did not used to drink.

The imperfect is used:

a) to indicate a continued or customary action in the past.

Quando ero giovane guardavo questo programma ogni sera.
When I was young, I used to watch this program every night.

b) to indicate what was happening when something else happened.

Mentre ascoltavamo le previsioni metereologiche, si è messo a piovere.
While we were listening to the weather report, it started to rain.

c) to indicate two actions which take place simultaneously in the past.

Mentre il reporter dava le previsioni del tempo, mandavano in onda immagini dell'alluvione.
While the reporter was giving the weather forecast, they were broadcasting pictures of the flood.

170

d) to express time, age, and weather in the past.

Era l'una quando è arrivato il presidente.
It was one o'clock when the president arrived.

Quando la ginnasta ha vinto la sua prima medaglia alle olimpiadi aveva solo 12 anni.
When the gymnast won her first olympic medal she was only 12 years old.

Pioveva a dirotto e tirava un forte vento.
It was raining cats and dogs and the wind was blowing heavily.

e) to describe mental and physical states in the past.

Ero molto contento quando hanno annunciato che il regista italiano aveva vinto l'Oscar.
I was very happy when they announced that the Italian director had won the Oscar.

Gli ostaggi erano ancora in stato di shock quando sono stati liberati.
The hostages were still in shock when they were rescued.

f) to express a polite request, in place of the present conditional.

Volevamo una bottiglia di vino rosso.
We would like a bottle of red wine.

Volevo vedere le previsioni del tempo prima di partire.
I wanted to see the weather report before we leave.

g) with the verbs *dovere, potere,* and *volere* to express "should have," "could have," "would have" in place of the past conditional if the action did not take place.

Dovevo (avrei dovuto) rispettare le sue idee.
I should have respected his ideas.

I mass media dovevano (avrebbero dovuto) coprire questo evento in modo più adeguato.
The media should have covered this event more adequately.

Potevamo (saremmo potuti) partire all'una, ma Carla ha perso i bagagli.
We could have left at one o'clock, but Carla lost her luggage.

If the action did occur, then the *passato prossimo* is used.

Il giornalista voleva intervistare il ministro, ma questo si è rifiutato di rilasciare commenti.
The journalist wanted to interview the minister, but he refused to comment.

Il giornalista non ha potuto intervistare il ministro.
The journalist wasn't able to to interview the minister.

h) to indicate an action or condition which had begun in the past and continued until a certain time, similar to the past perfect progressive (had been doing) in English.

Quando ha accettato il posto come conduttore del telegiornale, Giuseppe faceva il giornalista da 10 anni.
Quando ha accettato il posto come conduttore del telegiornale, erano 10 anni che Giuseppe faceva il giornalista.
When he accepted the position as newscaster, Giuseppe had been a journalist for ten years.

Note that the meaning of *sapere* and *conoscere* depends on the tense used. The imperfect of *sapere* means "to know how," while the *passato prossimo* means "to hear about/find out."

Luisa sapeva essere molto oggettiva nel presentare i suoi servizi.
Luisa knew how to be very objective in presenting her reports.

Ho saputo che Arturo è un grande tifoso di calcio e che non si perde mai una partita alla televisione.
I found out that Arturo is a big soccer fan and never misses a televised game.

When *conoscere* is used in the imperfect, it means "to know." When it is used in the *passato prossimo,* it means "to meet."

Conoscevamo il presidente dell'azienda da molti anni quando è scoppiato lo scandalo.
We knew the president of the company for many years when the scandal broke.

Abbiamo conosciuto Michele la settimana scorsa.
We met Michael last week.

The modal verbs *dovere, potere,* and *volere* also take a different meaning if used in the *imperfetto* or in the *passato prossimo.* Compare:

Il presidente è dovuto ritornare a casa a causa di un'emergenza.
The president had to go back home for an emergency.

Mario, ma non dovevi prepararla tu la pratica?
Mario, but weren't you supposed to prepare the file?

Mi dispiace, ma non ho potuto finire il lavoro.
I'm sorry, but I didn't manage to finish the work.

Mi dispiace, ma dopo il suo ultimo commento, non potevo più stare zitto.
I'm sorry, but after his last comment, I couldn't keep quiet any more.

A pranzo la bambina non ha voluto mangiare e adesso ha fame.
At dinner the girl did not want to eat and now she is hungry.

Luigi non voleva venire con noi, ma finalmente io l'ho convinto.
Luigi did not want to come with us, but I finally convinced him.

Note that while the *imperfetto* stresses duration or repetition rather than completion, the *passato prossimo* is used with completed actions.

Ieri ho guidato un'ora per arrivare al parco nazionale.
Yesterday I drove for one hour to get to the National Park.

Ieri mentre guidavo, mia moglie ascoltava il radiogiornale.
Yesterday, while I was driving, my wife was listening to the news.

Da giovane ho visitato solo due paesi stranieri.
When I was young, I visited only two foreign countries.

Da giovane andavo spesso al parco.
When I was young, I used to go to the park a lot.

2. *LA PREPOSIZIONE IN* (THE PREPOSITION *IN*)

1. The Italian preposition *in* translates as "by" or "to go by" when it is followed by a means of transportation: *in aereo, in autobus, in barca, in bicicletta, in macchina, in treno.*

Il ministro dei trasporti ha deciso di viaggiare in treno per rendersi conto di persona delle inefficienze delle ferrovie.
The minister of transportation decided to travel by train in order to personally assess the inefficiency of the railroad system.

Questo weekend, per chi va in vacanza in macchina, sono previste lunghe code su tutte le autostrade principali.
This weekend people going on vacation by car should expect long traffic delays on all major highways.

If the means of transportation is modified, the preposition *con* is used with the appropriate form of the definite article. The contracted forms *col, coll'*, etc. are less common.

Partiamo con il treno delle diciotto.
We are leaving with the six o'clock train.

Perché non andate con la macchina che ha noleggiato Antonio?
Why don't you take the car that Antonio rented?

Note that "to go on foot, to walk (to a place)" is expressed by *andare a piedi.*

Scendi alla prima fermata e va' a piedi fino al primo semaforo.
Get off at the first stop and walk to the first set of lights.

2. The preposition *in* is also used to indicate location or motion to a place. Some examples are: *in biblioteca* (at/in the library), *in campagna* (in/to the country), *in chiesa* (in/at/to the church), *in città* (in/to the city), *in classe* (in/to the classroom), *in montagna* (in/to the mountains), *in periferia* (in/to the suburbs), *in piazza* (in/at/to the square), *in piscina* (in/to the pool), *in ufficio* (in/to the office), *in cima a* (at the top of), *in fondo a* (at the bottom of).

Il direttore delle relazioni pubbliche è stato in ufficio tutto il giorno per i colloqui.
The director of public relations was in his office all day for the interviews.

Molti operai si recano giornalmente in città.
Many workers commute daily to town.

3. *In* is also used with the names of continents, countries, states, regions, and large islands to express "to." Remember that *a* is used for cities.

La pessima reputazione della rivista è arrivata perfino in America.
   The bad reputation of the magazine is known even in America.

Andavamo in Italia tutti gli anni.
   We used to go to Italy every year.

Non sono mai stato in America.
   I have never been to America.

If the names of continents, countries, states, regions, and large islands are modified, then the definite article must also be used.

Appena arrivato negli Stati Uniti, il terrorista fu subito arrestato.
   As soon as he arrived in the United States, the terrorist was arrested right away.

Il papa ha deciso di fare un viaggio nell'Africa Centrale.
   The pope decided to travel to Central Africa.

D. PAROLE! PAROLE! PAROLE!

Let's take a look at some expressions which use the verb *perdere* (to lose).

Noi ci siamo persi di vista.
   We lost sight of each other.

Io ho perso di vista quegli amici.
   I've lost sight of those friends.

The expression *non perdere di vista qualcuno* means "not to let someone out of one's sight," "not to lose sight of someone," or "not to take one's eyes off someone."

La polizia non ha mai perso di vista il ladro.
   The police never lost sight of the robber.

Also, study the following other uses of *vista*.

Lui vuole sempre mettersi in vista.
He always wants to show off.

Quell'uomo è molto in vista dopo la pubblicità sul suo processo.
That man is very much in the public eye since the publicity surrounding his trial.

Non hanno nulla in vista per quanto riguarda nuovi investimenti.
They have nothing in view as far as further investments are concerned.

Il vostro assegno è pagabile a vista.
Your cheque is payable on demand.

Quel bambino sta crescendo a vista d'occhio.
That boy is growing quickly.

Trovo il suo punto di vista molto interessante.
I find his/her point of view very interesting.

Io la conosco solo di vista.
I know her only by sight.

E. L'ANGOLO DEGLI AFFARI

I MASS MEDIA IN ITALIA (THE ITALIAN MASS MEDIA)

Television is by far the most ubiquitous of the media in Italy, but we cannot speak of television without speaking about radio as well. Television reception is linked to radio reception. Both are simultaneously distributed by the R.A.I. *(Radio Audizioni Italiane)*. Italians pay a tax, *il canone di abbonamento alla radiotelevisione* (the radio-television license fee), in order to be able to receive both television and radio signals. This tax ensures the right of residents of a home to have radios, televisions, and, most importantly, an aerial antenna, within the home. Payment commences with the installation of an antenna. Until 1974, the R.A.I. held a monopoly over the transmission of television and radio signals. At that time, the *Corte costituzionale* (Constitutional Court) deemed that it was unconstitutional for the R.A.I. to maintain this hold.

The decision paved the way for private television stations and for local radio and television stations to begin programming.

Television has changed dramatically since the early 1970s. When R.A.I. held a monopoly over television, programming and advertising were extremely limited. The programming day would generally begin at around noon on the three stations, and it would end in the late evening. Programs were not interrupted by commercials; instead, blocks of time were set aside for advertising. Today, Italian television is much like American television (although a great deal of the programming is imported from North America, South America, and Asia, and is dubbed into Italian). There are scores of television stations from which to choose. Talk shows are becoming more and more popular, and game shows resembling their American models are abundant throughout the day and into the evening. American television shows are also very popular. In particular, Italians enjoy American soap operas. Since the genre of the soap opera has a tremendous following, Italian television moguls import soap operas from other parts of the world as well, especially from South America. Daytime programming also includes children's shows (many cartoons are imported from Japan) and American situation comedies. In the evenings, Italians usually enjoy a wide variety of films from all over the world. Also popular are variety shows and American drama series. News broadcasts are also viewed by a high percentage of the population. On the R.A.I. stations, news broadcasts are seen at lunch time, at dinner time, and in the late evening. (Times vary depending on the station.)

There are many specialty channels on Italian television. One can find stations that carry programming from the American cable networks CNN and MTV. Italians have their own specialty channels as well. VideoMusic, for instance, is the Italian equivalent of MTV. There are home-shopping networks, and recently, cable stations similar to the specialty channels seen by Americans (movie channels, sports channels, etc.) have been established. A relatively new phenomenon to Italians is the concept of the pay-per-view station.

Newspapers often play the role of the official information diffusers of any nation. In Italy, the major cities have at least one newspaper. Major newspapers serving the larger centers contain inserts for the specific areas of the *provincia* (province) to which they are distributed. The most internationally known Italian newspaper is Milan's *Corriere della sera*. It is the one most easily found abroad. Despite the fact that many newspapers exist in Italy, Italians are not avid newspaper readers. This could be in part due to the fact that many Italians tune into the detailed and politically oriented newscasts on television, and in part due to the relatively high cost of the daily papers.

For almost two decades, the Italian film industry is said to have been in crisis. Fewer directors are having their projects funded today than ever before in the past fifty years, and a substantial percentage of films being made are not considered to be "serious." A visit to any Italian center will reveal that many Italians choose to patronize theaters showing blockbuster American films. Actors such as Arnold Schwarzenegger, Sylvester Stallone, and Sharon Stone are just as popular in Italy as they are in America, and most major theaters are showing Hollywood films at any given time. Films are almost always dubbed into Italian before being distributed.

Censorship is different within the different media in Italy. The press cannot be controlled according to article 21 of the Italian constitution, which states: *tutti hanno il diritto di manifestare liberamente il proprio pensiero con la parola, lo scritto e ogni altro mezzo di diffusione* (everyone has the right to freely express their thoughts with the oral word, in writing, and with any other means of distribution). The article continues: . . . *la stampa non può essere soggetta ad autorizzazioni o censure* (the press cannot be subject to authorization or censorship). This means that there is no control over what is printed. However, if there is proof that the content of a publication in some way transgresses a law, that publication may be confiscated.

Censorship is alive and well within the cinema. According to law 21.4.1962, number 161, every film that will enter into distribution must have the approval of the *Ministero per il turismo e lo spettacolo* (Ministry of Tourism and Entertainment). A commission made up of a magistrate, a professor of law, a professor of pedagogy, a professor of psychology, and three other members who may be directors, producers, or cinema journalists, views all films which will be seen in Italy and has the right to reject a film or to cut sequences, or limit the viewing audience to those 18 and over or those 14 and over. After obtaining the approval of this commission, the film must also be approved by a second commission, and finally, by a judge.

ESERCIZI

A. *Riscrivere le seguenti frasi al passato prossimo.* (Rewrite the following sentences in the *passato prossimo*.)

1. *Il presidente americano visita il Vaticano.*
2. *Muore il pugile americano Johnny Clayson.*
3. *Una bambina diventa milionaria per aver disubbidito.*
4. *Oggi il papa arriva negli Stati Uniti.*
5. *Il papa saluta l'uomo più potente del mondo con un caloroso "Viva l'America."*

B. *Riscrivere le seguenti frasi all'imperfetto.* (Rewrite the following sentences in the *imperfetto*.)

1. *I signori Verdi fanno il vino tutti gli anni.*
2. *Andiamo al cinema tutte le settimane.*
3. *Mentre mangio, guardo il telegiornale.*
4. *Sono le due.*
5. *Voi invitate gli amici ogni weekend.*

C. *Completare in modo opportuno, scegliendo tra l'imperfetto e il passato prossimo.* (Complete each one, using either the *imperfetto* or the *passato prossimo*.)

1. _____ *mezzogiorno quando l'aereo* _____.
2. *Oggi il presidente americano* _____ *in Italia.*
3. *All'aeroporto c'*_____ *numerose persone ad attendere il presidente.*
4. *Il pontefice* _____ *parole d'elogio per il suo ospite.*
5. *Grave incidente in SudAfrica. Più di cento persone* _____ *in una miniera d'oro.*

D. *Tradurre.* (Translate.)

1. In 1980 I was 20 years old.
2. It was raining cats and dogs.
3. We met John last week.
4. Yesterday I didn't attend the meeting.
5. I know them only by sight.

LEZIONE 10

A. DIALOGO

ALLA FIERA DI MILANO[1]

Due uomini d'affari, il signor Sean Parker di Chicago e il signor Paul Dunant di Ginevra, sono arrivati all'aeroporto Malpensa di Milano. Parteciperanno alla fiera di Milano. Iniziano a parlare sullo shuttle che si dirige in città.

DUNANT: Vedo che sta leggendo un opuscolo sulla fiera di Milano. Vi parteciperà?

PARKER: Sì. Anche Lei?

DUNANT: È il quinto anno che vengo. Mi chiamo Paul Dunant. Sono di Ginevra.

PARKER: Sean Parker. Sono di Chicago. È un piacere conoscerLa. Il Suo nome è francese, ma parla italiano benissimo.

DUNANT: Beh, come sa, l'italiano[2] è una delle lingue ufficiali della Svizzera.[3] Veramente il francese è la mia madre lingua, ma in Svizzera di solito si impara a parlare più di una lingua.

PARKER: In quale campo[4] opera la Sua azienda?

DUNANT: Siamo specializzati nella produzione di strumenti di precisione. Copriamo gran parte del mercato qui in Europa, ma non siamo riusciti a guadagnare neanche una porzione del mercato in America o in Asia. Di che cosa si occupa Lei?

PARKER: Siamo nel campo delle tecnologie informatiche. Fabbrichiamo sia personal computer che modelli portatili. Sa . . . basta un'occhiata per innamorarsi dei[5] nostri computer. Oh, mi scusi. È incredibile! Non sono neanche sceso dal pulmino[6] e ho già iniziato a vendere.

DUNANT: Oh, non si preoccupi. Anzi, farò di tutto[7] per passare dal Suo stand[8] a vedere questi apparecchi eccezionali. La sua azienda è riuscita a venderne molti da quando ha cominciato a trattare con l'Italia?

PARKER: Beh, negli ultimi anni l'uso domestico dei personal computer è aumentato in modo notevole. Abbiamo lanciato una vasta campagna pubblicitaria, ma non direi che siamo ancora sulla bocca di tutti. Le cose pero cominciano a migliorare. Stiamo investendo molto nel mercato qui.

DUNANT: Oh sì. Investire[9] in Italia è una buona idea. L'Italia è il quinto potere industriale del mondo, con più di 57 milioni di consumatori con un forte potere di acquisto . . .

PARKER: Mi sembra anche che il recupero dalla recessione economica mondiale sia stato più veloce qui che in molti altri paesi. Il clima commerciale è positivo e invitante.

DUNANT: Sembra proprio così. Conosco molte persone nel mio campo qui in Italia, e loro pensano che ci sia più fiducia da parte dei consumatori. Credo che la recente tendenza alla privatizzazione di banche ed altre imprese pubbliche abbia giovato molto al paese.

PARKER: Beh, so che le cose sono molto più efficienti adesso in paragone a com'erano molti anni fa.

DUNANT: A proposito, ha scelto un buon anno per partecipare per la prima volta alla fiera. Mi dicono che la mostra, che come sa è dedicata alla tecnologia informatica, hardware e software, e telecomunicazioni, è cresciuta[10] del 40% dall'anno scorso. Sarà veramente qualcosa da vedere!

PARKER: Sì. Lo sarà certamente. Ma ciò non mi sorprende. Dopo tutto, c'è un grandissimo interesse in tecnologie del genere da parte di un pubblico sempre crescente. A proposito, dove ha sentito queste statistiche?

DUNANT: Non ha ricevuto l'opuscolo d'informazione? È tutto qui.

PARKER: No, non l'ho ricevuto. Forse perché questo è il primo anno che la mia azienda ha aderito . . .

DUNANT: Forse io ne ho un altro. Lo può tenere. Troverà delle informazioni veramente utili qui dentro: un indice merceologico dei prodotti e delle aziende, una mappa degli stand e dei padiglioni . . .

PARKER: Meraviglioso! Grazie tante.

DUNANT: **Di niente.**

PARKER: **Beh, è stato un vero piacere conoscerLa e parlarLe.
EccoLe il mio biglietto da visita.**[11] **Venga a vedere il nostro
stand.**

DUNANT: **Grazie. Farò di tutto per venirci.**

AT THE MILAN FAIR

Two businessmen, Mr. Sean Parker from Chicago and Mr. Paul Dunant
from Geneva, have arrived at Milan's Malpensa Airport. They will be
attending the Milan Fair. They strike up a conversation on the shuttle
headed into the city.

DUNANT: I see that you're reading a brochure for the Milan Fair. Will
you be attending?

PARKER: Yes. You, too?

DUNANT: This is the fifth year that I've come. My name is Paul Dunant.
I'm from Geneva.

PARKER: Sean Parker. I'm from Chicago. It's a pleasure to meet you. Your
name is French, but you speak Italian very well.

DUNANT: Well, as you know, Italian is one of the official languages in
Switzerland. French is actually my mother tongue, but in Switzerland
one usually learns to speak more than just one language.

PARKER: What sector does your firm deal with?

DUNANT: We specialize in precision instruments. We represent a good
part of the market here in Europe, but we haven't managed to gain
much of a share of the market in America or in Asia. What type of business are you in?

PARKER: We're in information technology. We manufacture both desktop
and laptop computers. You know, it only takes one look to fall in love
with our computers . . . Oh, please forgive me. It's incredible! I haven't
even gotten off the shuttle and I've already begun to sell.

DUNANT: Oh, don't worry about it. In fact, I'll certainly do my best to
stop by your stand and see these amazing machines! Has your firm
managed to sell many since you began to deal with Italy?

PARKER: Well, in the past few years the domestic use of personal computers has increased notably. We launched an extensive advertising campaign, but I wouldn't say we're a household name yet. But things are beginning to improve. We're investing a lot in the Italian market.

DUNANT: Oh, yes. Investing in Italy is a good idea. Italy is the fifth industrial power in the world, with more than 57 million consumers with strong purchasing power . . .

PARKER: And it seems to me that the recovery from the worldwide recession has been faster here than in many other countries. The business climate is positive and inviting.

DUNANT: That seems to be the case. I know many people in my field here in Italy, and they feel that there is much more confidence on the part of the consumers. I believe that the recent trend towards privatization of banks and other firms has been very beneficial to the country.

PARKER: Well, I know that things are a lot more efficient now compared to how they were some years ago.

DUNANT: Incidentally, you've picked a good year for your first visit to the fair. They tell me that the exhibition, which as you know is dedicated to computer technology, hardware and software, and telecommunications, has grown by 40% from last year. It will really be something to see!

PARKER: Yes, it certainly will. But it doesn't surprise me. After all, there's been a tremendous amount of interest in such technology from an ever increasingly diverse public. By the way, where did you hear those statistics?

DUNANT: Didn't you receive this information bulletin? It's all here.

PARKER: No, I didn't receive it. Maybe because this is the first year my firm registered . . .

DUNANT: Maybe. I have an extra one. You can have it. You'll find a lot of useful information in here: alphabetical lists of the exhibitors, an index of the merchandise and of the firms, a map of the booths and pavilions . . .

PARKER: Terrific! Thank you very much.

DUNANT: Not at all.

PARKER: Well, it was a real pleasure meeting and speaking to you. Here's my card. Come by and see our booth.

DUNANT: Thank you. I'll do everything I can to come.

B. IN BREVE

1. For more information on the SMAU, Milan's annual fair, please see this chapter, *L'angolo degli affari.*

2. Unlike English, the definite article is used with languages. *Io studio l'italiano e il francese.* (I study Italian and French.) However, the definite article is not required when the language directly follows the verb *parlare. Parliamo italiano.* (We speak Italian.)

3. Italian is one of Switzerland's four official languages, along with French, German, and Rhaeto-Romanic. Approximately ten percent of Switzerland's inhabitants have Italian as their mother tongue. Although there are pockets of Italians in various parts of Switzerland, the Ticino canton is the only canton where Italian predominates.

4. The word *campo* is used in the following expressions: *campo d'atterraggio* (landing ground), *campo delle corse* (race course), *campo di giuoco* (playground), *campo di tennis* (tennis court), *campo sportivo* (sports/athletic ground).

5. Note that "to fall in love with" is translated as *innamorarsi di.*

6. The word *pullman* derives from the American who invented it, G. M. Pullman. Note that the diminutive *pulmino* is a "minibus."

7. Other frequently used expressions include: *fare del proprio meglio* (to do one's best), *fare tutto il possibile* (to do all that is possible). *Ha fatto tutto il possibile per rendere piacevole il soggiorno dei turisti.* (He did all that was possible to make the tourists' stay a pleasurable one.)

8. The English term "stand," also used in Italian, has several Italian equivalents as well. *padiglione, chiosco, baracca,* and *bancarella.*

9. The verb also has the meaning of "to knock down, to ran over." *Un camion ha investito un uomo in bicicletta.* (The truck hit/ran over a man on a bicycle.)

10. The verb *crescere* takes the auxiliary *essere* if used intransitively and *avere* if used transitively. *La nostra produzione è cresciuta del 10 per cento.* (Our production has increased by 10 percent.) *Noi abbiamo cresciuto nostro figlio in condizioni finanziarie molto ristrette.* (We raised our son under very tight financial conditions.)

11. It is also possible to say *il biglietto/bigliettino di visita.*

C. GRAMMATICA E SUOI USI

1. *L'INFINITO, IL PARTICIPIO E IL GERUNDIO* (THE INFINITIVE, THE PARTICIPLE, AND THE GERUND)

a. *L'infinito* (The infinitive)

L'infinito is the basic, unconjugated form of the verb. It is equivalent to the English "to" form, as in "to eat" or "to think." The infinitive in Italian, as you have already seen, usually ends in *-are, -ere,* or *-ire,* as in *mangiare, potere,* and *dormire.* This form is known as the *infinito presente* (present infinitive) and has the following uses:
It is used after many verbs, sometimes with the preposition *a,* sometimes with the preposition *di,* and sometimes with no preposition at all. For a list of verbs which are followed by certain prepositions, see Appendix C.

Tutte le aziende desiderano partecipare alla fiera estiva.
All the firms want to participate in the summer fair.

Avranno dimenticato di prendere il telefonino.
They must have forgotten to take the cellular phone with them.

Lei vuole venire in ufficio e parlare con il signor Andreini?
Do you want to come into the office and speak with Mr. Andreini?

The infinitive is also used after adjectives to complete the meaning of the adjective.

È importante dare delle informazioni dettagliate ai commessi.
It's important to give detailed information to the sales representatives.

Era difficile sentire il discorso perché c'era molto rumore.
It was difficult to hear the speech because there was a lot of noise.

The infinitive may also be used as a noun.

Fare un sondaggio internazionale è un'ottima idea.
Taking an international survey is a great idea.

Lavorare nel dipartimento di relazioni pubbliche può essere molto stressante.
Working in the public relations department can be very stressful.

Dirigere un dipartimento così grande non è stato facile.
Directing such a large department wasn't easy.

Where English uses the "-ing" form after certain prepositions, Italian uses the infinitive.

Prima di valutare il costo del nuovo progetto, il gruppo ha analizzato il mercato.
Before estimating the cost of the new project, the team analyzed the market.

Prima di andare alla fiera il signor Rossi non conosceva i competitori.
Before going to the fair, Mr. Rossi did not know his competitors.

There is also a past form of the infinitive. It is formed with the infinitive of the appropriate auxiliary verb (*essere* or *avere*) and the past participle of the main verb. It is used when the action in the dependent clause (or past infinitive) takes place before the action of the main clause. Remember that the final *-e* of *avere* may be dropped.

Credevo di aver(e) dato l'opuscolo all'espositore della compagnia di software.
I thought I had given the brochure to the exhibitor from the software company.

Speravano di essere entrati prima del direttore.
They hoped they had entered before the director.

186

Dopo essersi vestito, il signor Martini è uscito.
After getting dressed, Mr. Martini went out.

Object pronouns, reflexive pronouns, *ci (vi),* and *ne* may be attached to the infinitive. In this case, the final *-e* of the infinitive is dropped. If the infinitive ends is *-rre,* the final *-re* is eliminated.

—Può darmi notizie sui consumatori italiani? —Pensavo di avergliele già date.
—Can you give me some information on Italian consumers?
—I thought I had already given it to you.

Dopo avergli mostrato il nuovo prodotto, l'espositore gli ha offerto dei campioni.
After having shown the new product to him, the exhibitor offered him samples.

Dopo averci parlato del mercato europeo, ci ha mostrato i prodotti più richiesti.
After having spoken to us about the European market, he showed us the products most in demand.

Le fiere? Dopo averne visitate alcune ha deciso di contattare il direttore.
The fairs? After having visited some of them he decided to contact his director.

b. *Il participio* (The participle)

The present participle is a verb form that is used as a noun or as an adjective. To form the present participle, for first conjugation verbs remove the *-are* and add *-ante,* and for second and third conjugation verbs remove the *-ere* or *-ire* and add *-ente.* Note that not all verbs have a present participial form. When the present participle is used as an adjective, it must agree with the noun that it modifies.

C'è ancora un buon posto vacante.
There is still a good job open.

Il crescente interesse nei computer ha creato un mercato molto più esteso.
The increasing level of interest in computers has created a much larger market.

La parte più interessante della presentazione è stata la dimostrazione del prodotto.
The most interesting part of the presentation was the demonstration of the product.

Questi sono solo tre dei fattori contribuenti alla decisione presa dalla mia ditta.
These are only three of the factors contributing to my firm's decision.

The present participle can also be used as a noun.

La nostra ditta ha assunto un assistente del personale.
Our firm has hired a staff assistant.

Dovete reclamare presso il vostro rappresentante per la qualità scadente della merce che vi hanno mandato.
You must complain to your representative about the poor quality of the goods they've sent you.

Sometimes the present participle replaces a relative clause beginning with conjunctions such as *che* ("who" or "that").

Ho un bel quadro raffigurante (che raffigura) il Palazzo Municipale.
I have a beautiful picture showing the Town Hall.

Hanno comprato dei quadri rappresentanti (che rappresentano) scene pastorali.
They bought pictures depicting pastoral scenes.

The *participio passato* (the past participle) is regularly formed by removing the *-are, -ere,* or *-ire* of the infinitive and adding *-ato, -uto,* and *ito* respectively to the stem. The past participle is most commonly used in the formation of compound tenses.

Ha confermato la notizia.
He confirmed the information.

Avranno visto oltre 50 esposizioni di vari settori del commercio.
They must have seen over 50 expositions of various sectors of the business.

The past participle can also be used as an adjective or as a noun.

La nostra fabbrica è divisa in dieci reparti.
Our factory is divided into ten departments.

Dov'è l'uscita?
Where is the gate?

Prima di esprimere un'opinione vorrei avere tutti i fatti.
Before expressing an opinion I would like to have all the facts.

The *participio passato,* like the *participio presente,* may replace a secondary clause.

Vinte le elezioni il sindaco fece un discorso di ringraziamento.
After having won the elections, the mayor gave a thank you speech.

The phrase *vinte le elezioni* could also be rendered in the following ways:
dopo che ebbe vinto le elezioni / dopo aver vinto le elezioni / avendo vinto le elezioni.

All pronouns (direct, indirect, reflexive, etc.) are attached to the *participio passato.* (See *Lezione 4.*)

Messosi il cappello e i guanti, uscì per andare alla Fiera di Milano.
Having put on his hat and gloves he headed for Milan's Fair.

c. *Il gerundio* (The gerund)

The *gerundio* is formed by adding *-ando* to the stem of first-conjugation verbs and *-endo* to the stem of second-and third-conjugation verbs. Its form is invariable, so it never changes to agree with the word it modifies. The *gerundio* is another verb form which corresponds to the English "-ing" form, but its functions are different from those of participles or infinitives.

The gerund can express an action which is happening at the same time as the action of the main clause of the sentence. In English, this may be translated as "by doing something," "while doing something," or "upon doing something."

Parlando coi rappresentanti ho imparato molto su quei prodotti.
By speaking with the representatives I learned a great deal about those products.

189

Preparando lo stand, gli espositori parlavano della loro presentazione.
While preparing the booth, the exhibitors discussed their presentation.

Sentendo parlare del prelevamento dell'azienda, gli azionisti si sono innervositi.
Upon hearing about the business take-over, the shareholders became very nervous.

The *gerundio* also has a past form, which is made by using the gerund of the appropriate auxiliary plus the past participle of the main verb. The past gerund is used to express an action that precedes the action of the main verb.

Avendo analizzato il mercato, la ditta ha deciso di investire nella regione.
Having analysed the market, the firm decided to invest in the region.

Essendo stati all'esposizione parecchie volte, hanno riconosciuto molti degli espositori.
Having gone to the exhibition several times, they recognized many of the exhibitors.

Note that the above examples may also be expressed with *dopo* + an infinitive:

Dopo aver analizzato il mercato, la ditta ha deciso di investire nella regione.
After analyzing the market, the firm decided to invest in the region.

Object pronouns, reflexive pronouns, *ci(vi)*, and *ne* are all attached to the gerund. *Loro* is not attached, but follows the gerund.

Essendosi informato bene, ha comprato delle azioni.
Having informed himself well, he bought some shares.

Parlandogli, ho capito che andava anche lui alla mostra dell'arte orafa.
By speaking to him I understood that he was going to the gold exhibition too.

Avendo parlato loro, ho capito che la loro clientela è molto vasta.
Upon speaking to them I understood that their clientele is very wide.

2. *I TEMPI PROGRESSIVI* (THE PROGRESSIVE TENSES)

An action in progress in the present may be expressed with the present of *stare* + the gerund. This translates as the English "to be doing something,"

Io sto pensando all'annuncio che ho letto sul giornale di oggi.
I'm thinking about the ad I read in today's paper.

To express an action in progress in the past, the imperfect form of *stare* + the gerund is used.

Il negoziante stava vendendo programmi per i computer.
The dealer was selling computer programs.

3. *CONOSCERE E SAPERE (CONOSCERE* VS. *SAPERE)*

While both *conoscere* and *sapere* mean "to know," they are not used interchangeably. *Conoscere* means "to know" or "to be acquainted with" a person, place, or thing. It can also signify "to meet." It is always used with a direct object.

La mia ditta conosce il mercato molto bene.
My firm knows the market very well.

Renato ha conosciuto sua moglie a Roma.
Renato met his wife in Rome.

Sapere means "to know a fact" or "to know how to do something."

Sapevo che i nostri competitori volevano fare un'offerta per quel progetto.
I knew that our competitors wanted to put in an offer for that project.

Sapevo che la nostra offerta non era stata ancora discussa in consiglio d'amministrazione.
I knew that our tender had not yet been submitted to the board of directors.

Sai usare la carta telefonica in Italia?
Do you know how to use a telephone card in Italy?

4. NUMERI (NUMBERS)

a. *Numeri cardinali* (Cardinal numbers)

For a complete table on both ordinal and cardinal numbers, please refer to Appendix B, section 21. Here are a few notes you should remember when dealing with numbers.

Note that *venti, trenta, quaranta, cinquanta, sessanta, settanta, ottanta,* and *novanta* drop the final vowel when they are followed by *uno* or *otto*. When *tre* is added to *venti, trenta,* etc., . . . it requires the accent.

One hundred is expressed by *cento* and one thousand by *mille;* the English "one" is not translated.

Note that the plural form of *mille* is *mila*.

Note the use of a period instead of a comma.

Alla fiera di Milano ci sono espositori di cento ventitrè nazioni diverse.
   At the Milan Fair there are exhibitors from one hundred twenty-three different nations.

Quanto costa questo prodotto esposto in vetrina? —Tremila dollari.
   How much does this product in the display window cost? —Three thousand dollars.

Milione, milioni, miliardo, miliardi require the preposition *di*, unless they are followed by another number.

Ha fatto stampare un milione di opuscoli per la fiera.
   He had one million brochures printed for the fair.

Quella città ha un milione duecento mila abitanti.
   That city has one million two hundred thousand inhabitants.

b. *Numeri ordinali* (Ordinal numbers)

Here is a list of ordinal numbers from 1 to 10.

primo	first
secondo	second
terzo	third
quarto	fourth
quinto	fifth
sesto	sixth

settimo	seventh
ottavo	eighth
nono	ninth
decimo	tenth

After *decimo,* ordinal numbers can be formed by dropping the last vowel of the cardinal number and adding *-esimo.* If the cardinal number ends in *-tre* the final *-e* is retained in the ordinal number. Ordinal numbers are adjectives and must therefore agree in gender and number with the noun they modify. The ordinal number is preceded by the definite article

Questa è la terza volta che la nostra ditta partecipa a questa esposizione.
This is the third time that our firm is participating in this exhibition.

When the ordinal number follows the name of a dignitary, the definite article is not required.

Papa Giovanni Paolo Secondo ha dato la benedizione pasquale.
Pope John Paul the Second gave his Easter blessing.

D. PAROLE! PAROLE! PAROLE!

Numbers appear in many Italian idiomatic expressions and proverbs.

Fu licenziato su due piedi.
He was fired on the spot.

Ti racconterò tutto in due parole.
I will tell you the whole story in a nutshell.

E andata a fare due (quattro) passi.
She went for a short walk.

Non c'è due senza tre.
All things come in threes.

Lui lavora per tre.
He does the work of three men.

Ieri sera finalmente gliene ho dette quattro.
Last night I finally told him a thing or two.

Si è fatto in quattro per finire quel lavoro.
He did his very best to finish that job.

È arrivato in quattro e quattr'otto.
He arrived in a flash.

Mi hanno fatto sudare sette camicie.
They made me sweat bullets.

Lui trova sempre cento scuse per non venire.
He always finds a million excuses not to come.

Sono sicuro al cento per cento.
I'm 100% sure.

Cento di questi giorni!
Many happy returns!

Mille grazie!
Many thanks!

Mi sembrano mille anni!
It seems ages!

Chi ha fatto trenta, può fare trentuno.
Now that you've gone that far you might as well finish.

Avrà detto questo almeno un milione di volte.
She must have said this at least a hundred times.

E. L'ANGOLO DEGLI AFFARI

LE FIERE E I MERCATI IN ITALIA
(TRADE SHOWS AND MERCHANT FAIRS IN ITALY)

The merchant fair has existed for thousands of years. In Italy, numerous fairs are held throughout the year, many of which are well established and of worldwide importance. According to Article 117 of the Italian Constitution, the administration of all trade shows and fairs is handled by the region in which the fair is held. If you wish to inquire about the kinds of shows that may be in progress during your stay in Italy, you should contact the region you are visiting. Your chamber of commerce may have some information as well. It is useful to be aware of certain shows if one is planning a trip to Italy, because it may prove profitable not only to visit one such fair, but also perhaps to be an exhibitor. Below are descriptions of some specialized annual trade fairs that take place in Italy.

Those interested in computers should be aware that one of the largest annual trade shows of this industry in Europe is held on Italian soil. The Milan Fair, SMAU, is an annual fair held every fall. It is an international exposition of information and communications technology. In 1995, it was held in a venue of over 67,000 sq. mt., and welcomed almost 300,000 visitors. It had delegations from the United States, Canada, Japan, Russia, Spain, the United Kingdom, and Australia, to name a few. Not only did over 6,000 participants have expositions at the SMAU, but over 1,600 members of the world press covered the event as well. The price in 1995 for the renting of space at the SMAU was approximately 244,000 lira per square meter.

One of the attractions of SMAU, especially in recent years, has been the exhibitions devoted to the Internet. These enable a visitor to learn a great deal regarding the information superhighway and about the tools in existence in order to aid one's access to the vast amount of information available on the World Wide Web. Corporations and government agencies release new technology at the SMAU, making this fair a desirable one to attend. In 1995, for instance, the RAI introduced its interactive news forecast at this fair.

Finally, while at the SMAU, one can also listen to a wide variety of seminars regarding different facets of the computer and communications industry, technology and architecture, desktop publishing, etc. Needless to say, one can easily establish important business contacts in such an environment, as well as learn about the industry.

For more information regarding this annual fair, contact:

Ufficio Stampa e Relazioni Esterne SMAU
Corso Venezia 47/49
20121 Milano
Tel. (02) 7606752
fax (02) 784407

If you are interested in design and home decoration, you should consider attending the SAIEDUE annual fair in Bologna. It is held in the early spring, usually in March. Over 1,200 exhibitors from 104 nations exhibited their merchandise in 1995. The sectors represented included: interior decor; marble and fireplaces; tiles and other coverings; draperies and accessories; doors and windows and accessories (including technological accessories such as alarm systems); and construction materials for the upkeep and restoration of structures. The high quality of Italian products in the field of construction and design make this trade show a very desirable one to attend.

For more information contact:

SAIEDUE
via Moscova 7
Milano
Tel (02) 29017144
fax (02) 29005279

Remember that at most international trade shows one can find assistance with everything from interpreting to travel arrangements. Because trade shows are a long-standing tradition in Italy, they are generally extremely well organized events. Everything is done to ensure that visitors will have a positive experience.

One could go on at length describing the countless fairs and trade shows that go on in Italy throughout the year. There are the spring and fall fashion collections in October and March; there are international fairs dedicated to footwear, toys, jewelry, antiques, and medical equipment, just to name a few. In addition, there are various general trade shows such as the Fiera Milano, at which one can find a wide variety of products. Italy is a strategic place to exhibit one's products and to search for new partnerships. Its trade shows attract merchants from all over the world. The country itself has a large internal market, and the standard of living is high, which means that consumers have a great deal of buying power. Finally, the exchange rate is favorable in comparison to the dollar. For all of these reasons, attending and being involved in a trade show in Italy can prove quite profitable.

ESERCIZI

A. *Completare con l'infinito o il gerundio.* (Fill in the blanks with the infinitive or gerund.)

1. _____ *computer non è una cosa facile, perché c'è molta concorrenza.*
2. *Questa fiera è molto importante. La mia azienda non poteva* _____.

3. *Abbiamo fatto di tutto per _____ in questo paese. L'Italia è infatti il quinto potere industriale nel mondo e ultimamente sta _____ un forte recupero dalla recessione economica mondiale.*
4. *Il signor Dunant non è capace di _____ dal francese all'inglese.*
5. *_____ con lui, ho capito che è a Milano per affari.*
6. *_____ diverse volte alla Fiera, conosceva Milano molto bene.*

B. *Completare con il participio presente. Scegliere tra i seguenti verbi.* (Fill in the blanks with the present participle. Choose from the list below.)

rappresentare   assistere   amare   cantare   crescere

1. *Il signor Dunant fa il _____ di strumenti di precisione.*
2. *L'economia italiana sta godendo di un business climate positivo e dinamico, con una _____ fiducia da parte delle imprese e dei consumatori.*
3. *L' _____ di volo disse ai passeggeri di allacciarsi le cinture di sicurezza.*
4. *—In albergo ho visto Giovanni con la moglie. —Ma quella non era la moglie. Era l' _____.*
5. *Ieri sera sono stato a vedere lo spettacolo di Claudio Baglioni, un bravissimo _____ italiano.*

C. *Trascrivere in lettere i seguenti numeri.* (Write out the following numbers.)

1. 17	2. 38	3. 63	4. 515	5. 1000
6. 91	7. 3400	8. 55.430	9. 1.000.000	10. 454.329

D. *Tradurre.* (Translate.)

1. I still do not know French very well. I am learning it now.
2. Mr. Parker, as you know, this is one of the most important exhibitions in the world.
3. I do not know Milan, but I know Rome very well.
4. —Do you know that Italian products are well known all over the world for their style and design? —Yes, I know.
5. I would like to cash this check, please.
6. This is the fifth time that I've come to Italy.
7. Pope John Paul the Second visited the United States.
8. Many happy returns, my dear!
9. They were fired on the spot.
10 Last night I finally told her a thing or two.

PRIMO RIPASSO (FIRST REVIEW)

A. *Completare dove necessario.*

1. _____ spos _____ hanno ricevuto molt _____ telegramm _____
   _____ augur _____.
2. *Ecco a Lei,* _____ bigliett _____ e _____ nuov _____ cart
   _____ d'imbarc _____. _____ imbarc _____ è previst _____
   _____ qualche minut _____.
3. _____ articoli elencat _____ sono _____ vendita solo su _____
   vol _____ internazional _____.
4. *Siete pregati* _____ allacciare _____ cintur _____ _____
   sicurezz _____, di mettere _____ bagagl _____ _____ man
   _____ sotto _____ poltron _____ davanti _____ voi e _____
   porre _____ schienal _____ in posizion _____ vertical _____.
5. *"Signora Pozzi, sono Max Creech,* _____ amico _____ figlio
   Andrea."
6. *Mark, sono a* _____ disposizion _____. _____ mio ufficio offr
   _____ diversi supporti informativ _____ e assistenzial _____.
   Quando _____ vediamo ti porto de _____ opuscoli informativ
   _____.
7. *Quest* _____ è un messaggi _____ automatic _____. _____ quest
   _____ moment _____ non sono _____ casa. Lasciate il _____
   nom _____ e numer _____ _____ telefon _____ e _____
   richiamer _____ il _____ presto possibile.
8. *Antonio, cambi* _____ _____ asciugamani nel bagn _____ perché
   sono sporc _____!
9. *Quell* _____ aut _____ giappones _____ sono molt _____ bell
   _____.
10. *Oggi il professor* _____ Rossi mi ha dato un bel _____ vot _____.

B. *Completare con il pronome ed altri elementi mancanti.*

1. —*Vuoi vedere questo opuscolo?*
   —*Certo,* _____ ved _____ volentieri.
2. *Gianni, chi* _____ ha dat _____ questi documenti?
3. —*Hai riempito tutti i moduli per la domanda di lavoro?*
   —*Sì,* _____ ho riempit _____.
4. *Ho perso la mia borsa. Dobbiamo trovar* _____ subito.
5. —*Hai spiegato le condizioni di lavoro a Linda?*
   —*Sì,* _____ ho spiegat _____.

6. *Dottor Valesi, la settimana scorsa _____ ho spedit _____ la mia domanda di lavoro. _____ ha ricevut _____?*
7. *—Hai intervistato molti candidati oggi?*
   —No, _____ ho intervistat _____ solo due.
8. *—Quando mi dai quei libri?*
   —_____ do domani. Va bene?
9. *—Domani arriva il dottor Neri.*
   —Davvero? Ma chi _____ dett _____, signora?
10. *—Passerete anche dal centro storico della città?*
    —Certo. _____ passeremo più tardi.

C. *Completare i seguenti comandi.*

1. *Ragazzi, _____ a cena da noi stasera. Vi preparerò qualcosa di speciale.*
2. *Renzo, non _____ in giro. Tu pensi sempre a scherzare.*
3. *Teresa, _____ un po' di pazienza!*
4. *—Domani sera devo mettermi la cravatta?*
   —Sì, _____ la cravatta con quel bellissimo blazer blu che ti ho regalato a Natale.
5. *Gabriella, _____ ottimista. Vedrai che tutto andrà bene.*
6. *Signorina, _____ di mangiare. Poi venga a vedermi.*
7. *Dottor Rossi, non si dimentichi. Domani _____ presto in ufficio. Dobbiamo finire quel lavoro.*
8. *—Non vieni al ricevimento?*
   —No, _____ da solo. Io ho un forte mal di testa.
9. *—Chi accompagna la bambina alla festa?*
   —Per favore, _____ tu!
10. *—Avvocato, c'è un signore che vuole parlarLe.*
    —Beh, ora non posso parlargli. Sono occupato. Gli _____ che non ci sono.

D. *Completare le seguenti frasi con i verbi dati, scegliendo tra imperfetto, presente, passato prossimo, futuro, infinito e gerundio.*

organizzarsi dormire fare avere dare stare potere arrivare durare partire farsi essere (x2) dimenticarsi preferire volere

1. *Lei, signorina, _____ un posto vicino al finestrino o al corridoio?*
2. *Paolo: Diana, _____ un bel viaggio? Diana: Sì. Fortunatamente il volo _____ in orario ed _____ in orario. A bordo _____ il programma per la settimana e poi _____ una bella dormitina.*

3. *Noi _____ sempre di telefonarti.*
4. *Ieri Carla non _____ venire al bar perché la riunione _____ tutto il giorno.*
5. *—Dove ha lo studio il signor Triolo?*
   —Non lo so. L' _____ fuori città, vicino all'aeroporto.
6. *—Roberta, dov' _____ il bambino?*
   —Nella culla. Sta _____.
7. *Quel film? Sì, _____ vederlo.*
8. *_____ le dieci di questa mattina quando l'aereo dell'Alitalia è atterrato a Roma con a bordo il papa.*
9. *Appena terminato il turno, i minatori _____ per risalire alla superficie quando tutto ad un tratto il condotto principale è crollato.*
10. *È importante _____ informazioni dettagliate ai clienti.*

E. *Tradurre.*

1. Tonight we'll come to see you and have a chat. Will you be at home?
2. —Did you know that my wife is expecting a baby?
   —No, I didn't know. Is this your first child?
3. —Mr. Roppa, when will you have the furniture that I ordered delivered to me?
   —I will have it delivered to you right away.
4. Michael, it's time to put an end to this matter! Do you understand?
5. Franco doesn't like those commercials. Do you like them?
6. —Did you like those cars?
   —No, I didn't like them.
7. When they speak English, I don't understand a thing.
8. We worked hard to finish the work before the due date.
9. They didn't travel alone. I accompanied them for a fair part of the way.
10. —Do you know those men?
    —No, I know them only by sight.

LEGGIAMO!

LE DONNE ITALIANE E LA POLITICA [*]

In the following article, journalist Miriam Mafai explains why Italian women are not numerous in the Italian Parliament, although many of them have been extremely successful in other male-dominated fields (e.g., magistrature, journalism, business, sciences, advanced technology).

Dobbiamo chiederci perché le donne italiane sono così poche in Parlamento, mentre sono tanto numerose e qualificate in tutte le attività e professioni, anche in quelle più impegnative, moderne e fino a ieri monopolio dei maschi, dalla magistratura all'imprenditoria, al giornalismo, alla scienza e alla tecnologia avanzata. La prima risposta possibile è questa: la politica, cioè l'arte di governare gli uomini, è il luogo del potere per eccellenza. E qui le resistenze ai "new comers," ai nuovi venuti, è fortissima: non a caso, la stessa composizione sociale del Parlamento è sostanzialmente la stessa da cinquant'anni ad oggi, con una netta[1] prevalenza di avvocati, dipendenti pubblici,[2] anche giornalisti, eccetera, e totale esclusione di altre categorie (un operaio alle Camere[3] viene considerato, ed è effettivamente,[4] una rarità, una mosca bianca;[5] e questo la dice lunga sull'effettiva[6] rappresentatività del nostro Parlamento, alla vigilia[7] dell'anno Duemila, in riferimento alla composizione sociale ed economica del Paese). Più si sale nella scala del potere, dunque, e maggiori si fanno le difficoltà di accesso per coloro che il potere non l'hanno mai avuto. E dunque le donne sono vittime anche di questa antichissima esclusione.

Ma c'è una seconda risposta che attiene invece a noi stesse. Poche sono le donne che amano partecipare, da protagoniste, al gioco della nostra politica che, essendo gioco per il potere (invece che, essenzialmente, per un'accorta gestione[8] della cosa pubblica), risulta molto duro, un gioco nel corso del quale si danno e si ricevono colpi[9] molto pesanti, non solo dagli avversari ma anche dagli "amici."

E, per finire, coloro che amano partecipare a questo gioco non conoscono il cosiddetto[10] "gioco di squadra," indispensabile per il successo in politica. In altre professioni e attività si può ottenere successo anche correndo da sole, fidando[11] sulla propria capacità. In politica, no. In politica è indispensabile il

[*] Miriam Mafai, *"Pe quale motivo sono così poche le donne nel nuovo Parlamento?"* Oggi. Anno LII, n. 21 (22 maggio 1996), p. 8.

gioco di squadra, appunto, quella forma di solidarietà per cui un gruppo sostiene [12] un leader, per anni, fino a quando questo arriva alla cima, [13] riconoscendone di fatto l'autorità e le capacità. Tra le donne questo non accade. Ognuna corre da sola, per questo è più raro che qualcuna arrivi all'obiettivo.

VOCABOLARIO

1. clear
2. civil servants
3. two Houses
4. indeed
5. a rare bird
6. actual
7. eve
8. management
9. blows
10. so-called
11. relying
12. supports
13. top

LEZIONE 11

A. DIALOGO

UNA CASA IN SARDEGNA

Norman e Theresa Roberts, una coppia di coniugi americana che trascorre solitamente l'estate in Italia, hanno deciso di investire in beni immobili in Sardegna.[1] Un agente immobiliare gli sta facendo visitare una casa in vendita sulla baia di Palau,[2] non lontano da Olbia.[3]

AGENTE: **Ottima idea quella di investire in beni immobiliari. Il mercato al momento è favorevole agli acquisti e perciò i prezzi sono abbastanza bassi.**

THERESA: **È sicuramente una decisione importante. Veniamo qui ormai da molti anni e abbiamo finalmente deciso di comprare.**

NORMAN: **Dopo aver preso per tanto tempo una casa in affitto, ci è sembrato finalmente ora di acquistarne una. E non potevamo che comprarla qui, in Sardegna.**

AGENTE: **Beh, non c'è scelta più buona del complesso residenziale Miramar. È veramente il miglior complesso della zona che io conosca.[4] L'avrei suggerito io stesso, se voi non avreste chiesto.[5]**

THERESA: **Mi fa piacere. E che bellezza tutte queste ville che si affacciano sulla costa. Norman, guarda un po' dalla finestra. Dà sul mare.[6]**

AGENTE: **Sì, da tutte queste ville si gode la vista della baia. Come potete vedere, queste case sono a due piani,[7] sono rifinite in[8] marmo,[9] hanno un bell'ingresso, un salone doppio,[10] il giardino, il posto auto,[11] il terrazzo, la cantina . . .**

NORMAN: **Le pareti delle stanze sono rivestite?**

AGENTE: **Alcune sì, altre invece sono semplicemente verniciate. Comunque va da sé che i proprietari possono decorarsele come vogliono.**

THERESA: **Queste mattonelle sono molto belle. Ci sono in tutte le stanze?**

AGENTE: **Soltanto nell'ingresso, nel salotto, in cucina, in sala da pranzo e nel bagno. Sopra, le camere da letto hanno il parquet. Allora, andiamo in cucina . . . Come vedete, la cucina è molto spaziosa. Il piano di lavoro è molto ampio. Il frigo,[12] la cucina[13] e la lavastoviglie hanno meno di due anni, mentre il forno microonde è nuovissimo.**

NORMAN: **La venatura degli armadi è molto bella. Ma di che legno sono?**

AGENTE: **È legno di noce. Un legno molto pregiato. Le maniglie sono in ottone . . . Se non avete domande sulla cucina, andiamo sopra a vedere le camere da letto . . . Le scale sono di qua . . .**

THERESA: **Ma qui sotto il tetto d'estate farà un bel caldo!**

AGENTE: **Beh, grazie alle finestre, qua sopra le stanze sono ben ventilate. E poi c'è una bella brezza marina. Comunque non dimenticate che c'è anche l'aria condizionata.**

NORMAN: **E il balcone?**

AGENTE: **Il balcone è qui, in camera da letto. Un attimo che apro la finestra. Eccoci. Guardate che bel panorama . . . La stanza degli ospiti è abbastanza grande per due letti matrimoniali. Ogni camera viene pure con degli armadi a muro abbastanza grandi . . .**

THERESA: **Sarebbe bello di tanto in tanto ospitare qui i nostri amici americani. Vero, Norman? Ora avremmo sicuramente più spazio.**

NORMAN: **Infatti. Avrei un'altra domanda. La casa ha il riscaldamento autonomo?**

AGENTE: **Si, ogni villetta ha il riscaldamento e l'acqua calda autonomi[14] a metano.**

NORMAN: **Sia l'impianto elettrico che idrico saranno sicuramente in buone condizioni. Queste case non mi sembrano molto vecchie.**

AGENTE: **Infatti. Tutto è in ottime condizioni. Comunque, se desiderate, potremmo sempre far controllare gli impianti.**

THERESA: **Beh, c'è molto da considerare. Io e mio marito dobbiamo pur prendere una decisione. Tra non molto Le faremo sapere.**

AGENTE: **Benissimo. Se avete altre domande, sono a vostra disposizione.**

A HOUSE IN SARDINIA

Norman and Theresa Roberts, an American couple who spend their summers in Italy, have decided to invest in real estate in Sardinia. They are with an agent visiting a house for sale on the bay of Palau, not far from Olbia.

AGENT: You have definitely made a wise decision in investing in real estate. The market is a bit flooded now, so prices are rather low.

THERESA: It's a big decision, but we've been coming here for so many years we decided that it was finally time to buy.

NORMAN: After renting for so long, we thought it would be nice to own a house. And we couldn't buy it anywhere else but in Sardinia.

AGENT: Well, you'll not find a better choice than this residential complex Miramar. It's the best complex that I know in the area. I would have suggested it myself, if you hadn't asked.

THERESA: That's good to hear. And it's so beautiful, with the villas that overlook the bay. Norman, take a look through this window! It overlooks the sea.

AGENT: Yes, all of the villas have a view of the bay. As you can see, they all have two floors and are finished in marble. There have a nice entrance, a double sitting room, garden, garage, terrace, cellar.

NORMAN: Are the walls papered?

AGENT: Some of the rooms have papered walls and some are painted, but naturally the owners may decorate as they wish.

THERESA: These tiled floors are beautiful. Are they in every room?

AGENT: Only in the foyer, the living room, the kitchen, the dining room, and the bathroom. The bedrooms upstairs have hardwood floors. Now if you'll follow me to the kitchen . . . As you can see, the kitchen is very roomy, with a lot of counter space. The refrigerator, the stove, the oven, and the dishwasher are all less than two years old, and the microwave is brand new.

NORMAN: The wood grain on those cabinets is beautiful. What kind of wood is it?

AGENT: It's walnut and its quality is very high. The fixtures are all brass. If you don't have any questions about the kitchen, let's go upstairs and see the bedrooms. The staircase is this way . . .

THERESA: It must get pretty hot up here right under the roof.

AGENT: Well, the windows give the upstairs rooms very good ventilation, and there is usually a breeze off of the sea. And of course, the house comes equipped with air conditioning.

NORMAN: And the balcony?

AGENT: Yes. The balcony is here, off of the master bedroom. Let me open the window. Look what a beautiful view! The guest bedroom is large enough for two double beds. In each room there's a large closet.

THERESA: It really would be lovely to have guests from the States stay with us from time to time. We certainly would have the room now.

NORMAN: That's right. I just have one question. Is there an independent heating system?

AGENT: Yes, each villa has an independent gas heat and hot water system.

NORMAN: I suppose the electricity and plumbing are in good condition. The villas don't seem very old.

AGENT: Oh yes, everything is in very good condition. But we could always have someone take a look if that makes you feel more comfortable.

THERESA: Well, we have a lot to consider. My husband and I have to make a decision sooner or later. We'll let you know soon.

AGENT: Please do. And don't hesitate to call me if you have any questions at all.

B. IN BREVE

1. Sardinia is the second largest island (23,813 sq. km / 9,301 square miles) in the Mediterranean Sea. Its surface is generally mountainous and its territory also includes the smaller islands around it (Sant'Antioco, San Pietro, Asinara, La Maddalena, Caprera, etc.). Its population is just over 1.6 million inhabitants. The region's capital is Cagliari. Other major cities include: Nuoro, Oristano, and Sassari. One of the region's main resources is tourism. The tourist season goes from April to October, with the highest peak in August. The tourist zone which is more developed and organized is *Costa Smeralda* (northeast), where Palau, La Maddalena, and Olbia are located.

2. Palau, in the northern part of Sardinia, facing the islands of La Maddalena and Caprera, and part of the famous resort *Costa Smeralda,* is one of Sardinia's busiest ports to the mainland.

3. Olbia is a gateway to the *Costa Smeralda* and a port of call to the mainland. The city's airport is also one of the busiest in the region.

4. For the uses of the subjunctive, please refer to *Lezione 16.*

5. The if-clause construction is introduced in this chapter (see grammar section on the conditional) and is fully discussed in *Lezione 20.*

6. Note the idiomatic use of *dare* with the preposition *su:* it means "to face something." A synonym is *affacciarsi su,* as can be seen in the previous dialogue sentence.

7. In Italy, one starts counting floors after the *pianterreno* (main floor).

8. Here the preposition *in* indicates the material of which something is made.

9. Italy is a leader in marble production and therefore marble is one of the main elements in the construction of houses.

10. *Salone doppio* is a combination of living room and family room. It is far less common to have such a combination in Italian houses.

11. Synonyms are *autorimessa, rimessa,* and *garage.* The latter is more used.

12. *Frigo* is a short form of *frigorifero.*

13. In Italian the word *cucina* indicates both the kitchen and the stove. The word *stufa* is a false friend and could mean both a wood-burning stove *(stufa a legno)* and an electrical or gas heater *(stufa elettrica or stufa a gas).*

14. The adjective is in the masculine plural form because it refers to both *acqua* and *riscaldamento.*

C. GRAMMATICA E SUOI USI

1. *IL CONDIZIONALE PRESENTE E PASSASTO* (THE PRESENT AND PAST CONDITIONAL)

The conditional mood conveys possibility. Actions expressed in the conditional have the potential to occur or to become a reality, but they are conditioned by outside circumstances and are therefore hypothetical. Generally, the Italian conditional translates to the English construction " 'would' + verb."

a. *Il condizionale presente* (The present conditional)

To form the present conditional, the conditional endings are added to the infinitive after dropping the final *-e.* As in the formation of the simple future indicative, the *a* of *-are* verbs becomes an *e.* The endings are the same for all three conjugations, and *-ire* verbs all follow the same pattern.

	LAVORARE	PRENDERE	DORMIRE
io	lavorerei	prenderei	dormirei
tu	lavoreresti	prenderesti	dormiresti
lui/lei/Lei	lavorerebbe	prenderebbe	dormirebbe
noi	lavoreremmo	prenderemmo	dormiremmo
voi	lavorereste	prendereste	dormireste
loro/Loro	lavorerebbero	prenderebbero	dormirebbero

Affitterei volentieri quella casa che dà sul mare, ma non ho i soldi.
> I would gladly rent that house which overlooks the ocean, but I don't have the money.

È il tipo di investimento che non le interesserebbe.
> It is the type of investment that would not interest her.

Vorremmo vedere la casa ma non possiamo fissare un appuntamento con l'agente.
> We would like to visit the house but we can't make an appointment with the agent.

I coniugi Smith non si trasferirebbero in Italia per motivi di lavoro.
> Mr. and Mrs. Smith would not move to Italy for work reasons.

Verbs ending in *-sciare, -ciare, -giare, -care,* and *-gare* undergo the same orthographical changes as in the future tense. Also, all verbs with irregular stems in the future use the same stem in the conditional. Please refer to *Grammatica e suoi usi* in *Lezione 3.*

Vorremmo investire un milione di dollari in proprietà immobiliari.
> We'd like to invest a million dollars in real estate.

Sapresti consigliarmi una buona agenzia immobiliare?
> Could you recommend a good real estate agency?

The present conditional is used to express:

a) actions that would occur in the present or in the future, were it not for some uncertainty or for conditions preventing them from occurring.

Comprerei quella casa ma ha bisogno di troppo lavoro.
I would buy that house but it needs too much work.

Vorrei arredare il salone ma non riesco ancora a trovare i mobili adatti.
I would like to furnish the living room but I still can't find the right furniture.

    b) polite wishes or requests.

Ci permetteresti di vedere la cantina?
Would you allow (permit) us to see the cellar?

Vorrei sapere di più riguardo alla formula di multiproprietà.
I would like to know more about time-share program.

Potrebbero seguirmi in sala da pranzo?
Could you follow me into the dining room?

    c) unconfirmed news or pieces of information. This use of the conditional is most typically used in journalism when the information given has not been confirmed.

Il ministro sarebbe sotto indagine.
The minister is allegedly under investigation.

L'attrice sarebbe in vacanza in Sardegna.
The actress is said to be vacationing in Sardinia.

    d) the consequences of a hypothetical situation. The hypothesis is expressed with the imperfect verb in the subjunctive following "if" *(se)*.

Se potessi, investirei i miei soldi in un appartamento in questo quartiere.
If I could, I would invest my money in an apartment in this neighborhood.

Se avessero delle informazioni, ci direbbero qualcosa.
If they had any information, they would tell us something.

    b. *Il condizionale passato* (The past conditional)

The past conditional is a compound tense. It is formed with the present conditional of the appropriate auxiliary verb *(avere, essere)* and the past participle of the verb. It is translated as the English "would have" + past participle.

	LAVORARE	*ANDARE*
io	avrei lavorato	sarei andato/a
tu	avresti lavorato	saresti andato/a
lui/lei/Lei	avrebbe lavorato	sarebbe andato/a
noi	avremmo lavorato	saremmo andati/e
voi	avreste lavorato	sareste andati/e
loro/Loro	avrebbero lavorato	sarebbero andati/e

Si sarebbero trasferiti nella casa nuova prima, ma i carpentieri hanno sospeso il lavoro.
> They would have moved into their new home sooner, but the carpenters stopped working.

Se avessimo avuto tempo, saremmo andati al cinema.
> If we had had time, we would have gone to the movies.

The conditional perfect is used in circumstances similar to those in which the present conditional is used. However, it refers to a past time. The conditional perfect is used to express:

a) actions that would have occurred in the past, had certain conditions not prevented them from occurring.

Noi avremmo comprato quella carta da parati, ma avevamo deciso di imbiancare la stanza.
> We would have bought the wallpaper, but we had decided to paint the room instead.

Avrei preferito una villetta sul Lago di Como, ma non ce ne era una disponibile.
> I would have preferred a villa on Lake Como, but there were none available.

b) unconfirmed news or pieces of information that allegedly occurred in the past.

L'attore avrebbe comprato una casa sull'isola di Capri.
The actor is said to have bought a house in Capri.

Il presidente sarebbe svenuto durante un incontro con la regina.
The president allegedly fainted during a meeting with the queen.

c) the consequences of a hypothetical situation. The past conditional expresses actions which *would have* occurred if certain circumstances had been different. The hypothesis is expressed in the imperfect or past perfect subjunctive.

Se sapessi dove abita, sarei già andata a trovarlo.
If I knew where he lived, I would have already gone to visit him.

Se fossimo arrivati in tempo, avremmo visto l'inizio dello spettacolo.
If we had arrived on time, we would have seen the beginning of the show.

d) A future action in a past time, in a sentence introduced by a verb of telling, saying, informing, or knowing. This use of the conditional perfect is quite different from English; generally, such actions are expressed with the present conditional in English.

Pensavo che l'agente ci avrebbe mostrato una splendida casa nuova, invece abbiamo visto un tugurio.
I thought the agent would show us a splendid new house; instead we saw a shack!

Ieri la signora Rossi mi ha detto che mi avrebbe telefonato alle tre.
Yesterday Mrs. Rossi told me that she would telephone me at three.

Pensavamo che non sarebbe piovuto, invece ha diluviato.
We thought it would not rain; instead; it poured.

Sapevo che il tappeto non sarebbe arrivato in tempo.
I knew that the carpet would not arrive on time.

2. I COMPARATIVI E I SUPERLATIVI (COMPARATIVES AND SUPERLATIVES)

a. *I comparativi* (Comparatives)

In Italian, as in English, comparisons can be of equality (as/so . . . as, as much/as many . . . as) or of inequality (more/less . . . than).

a) The comparisons of equality are: *così . . . come* and *tanto . . . quanto*. The first part of the comparison can be omitted, unless it is required for emphasis.

La camera degli ospiti è (tanto) grande quanto la camera principale.
La camera degli ospiti è (così) grande come la camera principale.
　The guest room is as large as the master bedroom.

Il salotto è (tanto) illuminato dal sole quanto la sala da pranzo.
Il salotto è (così) illuminato dal sole come la sala da pranzo.
　The living room is as sunny as the dining room.

Arredare l'ingresso è stato (tanto) difficile quanto rifare il bagno.
Arredare l'ingresso è stato (così) difficile come rifare il bagno.
　Furnishing the entrance was as difficult as redoing the bathroom.

When a comparison of equality is made between nouns, the form *tanto . . . quanto* must be used, and appropriate agreements must be made.

Tanti uomini quante donne lavorano in questa ditta.
　As many women as men work at this firm.

Quell'agenzia vende tante case quanti appartamenti.
　That agency sells as many houses as it does apartments.

Tanto quanto can also make an equal comparison between two agents performing the same action. In this case, they follow the verb, are inseparable, and do not agree.

Mio marito guadagna (tanto) quanto me.
　My husband earns as much as I do.

Questo agente lavora (tanto) quanto me.
　This agent works as much as I do.

b) The comparisons of inequality can be either of superiority *più* (more . . . than, -er than) or of inferiority *meno* (less . . . than, fewer . . . than).

"Than" is translated as *di* when the elements being compared are numerals or when two entities are compared in terms of the same quality or action.

Il latino è più complicato dell'italiano.
Latin is more complicated than Italian.

Col cambio 20 dollari sono più di 20 mila lire.
With the exchange 20 dollars are more than 20 thousand lire.

La terrazza è più ampia del balcone.
The terrace is more spacious than the balcony.

L'aria condizionata e più efficiente del ventilatore.
Air conditioning is more efficient than a fan.

"Than" is translated with *che* when two qualities (expressed by nouns, adjectives, verbs, or adverbs) of the same entity are being compared.

Io mangio più frutta che verdura.
I eat more fruit than vegetables.

È più comodo sedersi che rimanere in piedi.
It is more comfortable to sit than to remain standing.

Ci sono meno donne che uomini in questa ditta.
There are fewer women than men at this firm.

Questo lavoro è meno interessante che faticoso.
This job is less interesting than tiring.

"Than" is translated with *di quel(lo) che* or *di quanto* before a conjugated verb.

Ti amo più di quel(lo) che credi.
I love you more than you think.

Hanno pagato questa villa meno di quanto tu pensi.
They paid less for this villa than you think.

b. *I superlativi* (Superlatives)

There are two types of superlatives in Italian: the relative superlative ("the most talented") and the absolute superlative ("very talented"). The relative superlative is formed by placing the appropriate definite article before the comparatives *più* or *meno*.

La vendita di quella proprietà è il più riuscito degli affari che l'agenzia abbia fatto quest'anno.
　The sale of that property is the most successful of deals for the agency this year.

Pavarotti è considerato il più famoso fra tutti i tenori.
　Pavarotti is considered to be the most famous of all tenors.

When the superlative follows the noun, the article is not repeated before *più* or *meno*.

La balena è il mammifero più grande.
　The whale is the largest mammal.

Il salotto è la stanza più grande della casa.
　The living room is the largest room in the house.

The English "in" or "of" of superlative constructions may be translated with the prepositions *di* or *fra/tra*.

Fra (Di) tutti i quartieri della città, questo è il più rinomato.
　This neighborhood is the most renowned in the city.

Tra (Di) tutti i quadri che abbiamo visto, questo è il più adatto per lo studio.
　Among all the paintings we have seen, this is the most suitable for the study.

Relative superlatives may be formed with adverbs as well as adjectives. In such cases, the definite article is omitted before *più* or *meno* unless the word *possibile* follows the adverb.

Il presidente ha parlato più chiaramente di tutti.
　The president spoke the most clearly of everyone.

Abbiamo pensato all'investimento il più attentamente possibile.
　We considered the investment as carefully as possible.

The absolute superlative is formed by adding the appropriate form of
the suffix *-issimo (-issima, -issimi, -issime)* to the masculine plural form
of the adjective. The final vowel must be dropped before adding the
suffix: e.g., *breve-brevi-brevissimo (-a, -i, -e); lungo-lunghi-lunghissimo
(-a, -i, -e); bianco-bianchi-bianchissimo (-a, -i, -e); nero-neri-nerissimo
(-a, -i, -e)*

La discussione è stata interessantissima
The discussion was extremely interesting.

Dalla terrazza il panorama è bellissimo.
The view from the terrace is very beautiful.

To make an absolute superlative of an adverb, simply drop the final
vowel of the adverb before adding *-issimo (presto-prestissimo; bene-
benissimo)*. As is the case with all adverbs, this form is invariable.

Era tardissimo quando i nuovi compratori sono venuti a vedere la casa.
It was very late when the new buyers came to see the house.

If the adverb ends in *-mente,* then simply add *-mente* to the feminine
form of the absolute superlative form of the adjective *(raramente-rara
(f.)-rarissimamente; velocemente-veloce (f.)-velocissimamente.)*

Ho dovuto portare velocissimamente il contratto d'affitto dall'avvocato.
I had to bring the lease to the lawyer right away.

Lo vediamo rarissimamente.
We very rarely see him.

As alternatives to using the suffix *-issimo,* one can use adverbs such as
molto, assai, and *estremamente,* or prefixes such as *ultra-* or *stra-* to
construct an absolute superlative.

Sono molto contento di abitare in quest'appartamento.
I am very happy to live in this apartment.

Erano estremamente stanche dopo il lungo viaggio.
They were extremely tired after their long trip.

Questo quartiere residenziale è ultramoderno.
This residential area is ultra-modern.

Il mio bicchiere è strapieno.
My glass is extremely full.

In addition to their regular forms, certain adjectives have irregular comparatives and superlatives.

	COMPARATIVE	RELATIVE SUPERLATIVE	ABSOLUTE SUPERLATIVE
piccolo (small)	*più piccolo* *minor(e)* (smaller)	*il più piccolo* *il minor(e)* (the smallest)	*piccolissimo* *minimo* (very small)
grande (big, great)	*più grande* *maggior(e)* (bigger, greater)	*il più grande* *il maggior(e)* (the biggest)	*grandissimo* *massimo* (very big)
alto (tall, high)	*più alto* *superiore* (taller, higher)	*il più alto* *il supremo* (the tallest, highest)	*altissimo* *supremo* (very high)
basso (short, low)	*più basso* *inferiore* (shorter, lower)	*il più basso* *l'infimo* (the shortest, lower)	*bassissimo* *infimo* (very short, low)
buono (good)	*più buono* *miglior(e)* (better)	*il più buono* *il miglior(e)* (the best)	*buonissimo* *ottimo* (very good)
cattivo (bad)	*più cattivo* *peggior(e)* (worse)	*il più cattivo* *il peggior(e)* (the worst)	*cattivissimo* *pessimo* (very bad)

In general, the irregular forms of these adjectives are used to indicate figurative qualities, whereas the regular forms signify literal qualities.

Il mio appartamento è più grande del tuo.
My apartment is bigger than yours.

Questa marca di macchina è la più buona.
This brand of car is the best.

L'irresponsabilità è il suo maggior * difetto.
Irresponsibility is his/her greatest flaw.

La tua è la migliore idea.
Yours is the best idea.

In reference to people, *maggiore* and *minore* can mean "older" and "younger." In a similar fashion *il maggiore* and *il minore* mean "the oldest" and "the youngest." The terms are usually used when describing the members of a family.

Chi è maggiore, lui o sua sorella?
Who is older, he or his sister?

La mia sorella minore è avvocato.
My younger sister is a lawyer.

Io sono la minore della famiglia.
I am the youngest in the family.

In spoken Italian, the expressions *più grande* (or *più vecchio*) and *più piccolo (più giovane)* may express age as well as physical size.

Chi è più grande (più vecchio), lui o sua sorella?
Who is older, he or his sister?

Io sono la più piccola (la più giovane) della famiglia.
I am the youngest in the family.

Often the regular and irregular forms can be used interchangeably, especially when literal or material qualities are compared.

Questa proposta è più buona (migliore) di quella.
This proposal is better than that one.

La qualità di questo materiale edile è più alta (superiore).
The quality of this building material is higher.

---

* *Migliore, peggiore, maggiore,* and *minore* drop the final *-e* before all singular nouns except those beginning with *s* + consonant, *z, ps,* etc.

Certain adverbs have irregular comparatives and superlatives as well.

	COMPARATIVE	RELATIVE SUPERLATIVE	ABSOLUTE SUPERLATIVE
poco (little)	*meno, di meno* (less)	*il meno* (the least)	*pochissimo* (very little)
molto (a lot)	*più, di più* (more)	*il più* (the most)	*moltissimo* (very much)
bene (well)	*meglio* (better)	*il meglio* (the best)	*benissimo* *ottimamente* (very well)
male (badly)	*peggio* (worse)	*il peggio* (the worst)	*malissimo* *pessimamente* (very badly)

—*Come sta, signor Farfalla?* —*Benissimo, grazie.*
   —How are you, Mr. Farfalla? —Very well, thank you.

La cucina era pessimamente arredata.
   The kitchen was very badly finished.

Quando si lavora di più ci si riposa di meno.
   When one works more one rests less.

L'estate scorsa abbiamo cercato di andare in montagna il più possibile.
   Last summer we tried to go to the mountains as much as possible.

3. *I SUFFISSI* (SUFFIXES)

In Italian, the meaning of a noun can be altered by the addition of a suffix. These suffixes refer to size or quality and often express the speaker's feelings toward the person or object. There are no rules governing the choice of suffixes, so it is advisable to learn to recognize the suffixes before using them.

To render the idea of smallness or cuteness, or to express affection, the following suffixes can be used: *-ino, -etto, -ello, -icino, -uccio, -olino, -ellino.* These are referred to as diminutives. Note that the majority of nouns keep their original gender, and that the final vowel is dropped before the suffix is added.

A nessuno è piaciuta quella casuccia che l'agente ci ha mostrato.
None of us liked the small house the agent showed us.

Nel 1950 i miei nonni comprarono una casetta in Canada.
In 1950 my grandparents bought a small house in Canada.

Durante il mio soggiorno in Italia ho affittato per una settimana una casina al mare.
During my stay in Italy I rented a small house by the sea for a week.

The suffixes *-one* and *-ona* are used to express largeness. Note that feminine nouns often become masculine when the suffix *-one* is added:

Quell'appartamento ha un finestrone che dà sul mare.
That apartment has a large window which looks onto the ocean.

Ma quanti cassettini e cassettoni ci sono in questo armadio?
But how many different size drawers are there in this dresser?

The suffixes *-accio, -astro, -ucolo,* convey roughness or a negative quality.

Carlo, ma perché devi dire sempre le parolacce?
Carlo, why do you always have to use obscene words?

Che tempaccio!
What lousy weather!

Note that a suffix cannot be used with all nouns. Sometimes, the addition of a suffix can change the meaning of a word: e.g., *la porta* (the door); *il portone* (the large front door to a building).

Nello stanzino della terrazza abbiamo la lavatrice.
In the little room on the terrace we have the dishwasher.

Il finestrino della macchina non funziona.
The car window doesn't work properly.

Suffixes can also be added to adjectives and proper nouns.

L'agenzia mi ha indicato un appartamento bellino.
    The agency pointed out a cute apartment.

L'agente che mi ha promesso una casa in Sardegna si chiama Antonello.
    The agent who promised me a house in Sardinia is named Antonello.

D. PAROLE! PAROLE! PAROLE!

The verbs *dare* and *fare* are found in numerous idiomatic expressions. For example, in the dialogue, Theresa points out that *tutte le ville danno sul mare* (all the houses overlook the beach). Study the following idiomatic uses of *dare* and *fare*.

A. *DARE*

Claudio, non dargli ascolto!
    Claudio, don't listen to him.

Chi deve dare le carte, io o tu?
    Who has to deal the cards. You or I?

Lei si è data molto da fare per ottenere quel lavoro.
    She did all she could to get that job.

Lui dà tutto per scontato.
    He takes everything for granted.

Ti ha dato di volta il cervello?
    Have you gone out of your mind?

Loro si sono dati alla compra-vendita di immobili.
    They went into real estate.

Loro si danno del tu.
    They are on familiar terms.

B. *FARE*

Ogni mattina faccio ginnastica.
   I exercise every morning.

Giovanni, non fare lo stupido!
   John, don't be a fool.

Io ti facevo più intelligente.
   I thought you were more intelligent.

Un soggiorno in campagna mi farà bene.
   A stay in the country will do me good.

Fa' attenzione a quello che dico!
   Pay attention to what I am saying.

Questa città non fa per me.
   This city is not for me.

Non mi fa né caldo né freddo.
   It's all the same to me.

Lei fa l'agente immobiliare.
   She is a land broker/real estate agent.

E. L'ANGOLO DEGLI AFFARI

GLI INVESTIMENTI (INVESTMENTS)

The Italian market is quite open to foreign investment. In May 1990, foreign exchange restrictions were abolished in accordance with EC regulation regarding the free movement of funds. Furthermore, the Italian government offers many of the same incentives to foreign investors that it makes available to Italian residents, including cash grants and subsidised loans. To find out what kinds of incentives exist, it is best to contact the region, province, or municipality in which one intends to invest.

While the Italian government does not impose limitations on foreign ownership of domestic entities, special laws are in place that limit investment in sectors such as shipping and air transportation. For investment in sectors that may affect the national interest (insurance, banking, etc.), foreign investment is permitted, but only after special permits have been acquired. Finally, the Italian government holds a monopoly on some sectors, including electricity production and distribution and telecommunications (although there is increasing demand for the hold to be lifted on the latter). Relatively speaking, therefore, the restrictions on foreign investment are few.

The incentives offered by the Italian government are far more generous if one intends to invest in the country's southern regions. Because of the economic disparities between North and South, it has been the tendency of Italian governments to find feasible ways to build up the economy of the *Mezzogiorno* (literally, "noon," this term is used to refer to the regions of Italy south of Lazio). One of the ways to do this is to aid foreign investors as much as possible in the creation of new business initiatives. Funds have been allocated to create cash grants and subsidised loans in order to assist in such large-scale enterprises as the development of abandoned factories, the modernisation and/or enlargement of outdated forges and plants, as well as major research initiatives. In addition to providing capital for business ventures, the Italian government offers a variety of tax breaks for foreign investors interested in the *Mezzogiorno*. Investors are exempt from paying registration and mortgage taxes and stamp duties on subsidized loans and on related liens and mortgages. Furthermore, there is a ten-year period of exemption from several taxes, as well as from contribution to the INPS, the social-security tax fund that each business is required to pay into for every employee it hires (a sum that equals approximately 30% of each employee's salary).

It is possible to receive credits and incentives for ventures begun in northern Italy as well. Generally speaking, however, incentives for the northern regions are geared towards aiding small and medium business ventures as opposed to large-scale ventures. Bear in mind, also, that as well as applying for incentives from the Italian government, one can always request aid from the EC. Financing for loans is not generally handled by commercial banks in Italy, but rather by special credit institutions. Commercial banks tend to specialize in providing working capital rather than supplying a business with a start-up loan. Remember that within the EC low-interest loans may be acquired through the European Investment Bank.

ESERCIZI

A. *Indovinando il verbo dal contesto, completare con la forma del condizionale.* (Fill in the blanks with the appropriate form of the verb in the conditional, guessing the verb from the context.)

1. *Io _____ volentieri una casa in Sardegna, ma non ho i soldi.*
2. *Noi _____ in vacanza in Italia, ma purtroppo dobbiamo lavorare.*
3. *Mio padre _____ dei soldi in Italia, ma non sa a chi rivolgersi.*
4. *Ci _____ una bellissima casa in Calabria, ma purtroppo non fa per noi.*
5. *Signorina, per favore, mi _____ dare un consiglio?*

B. *Rispondere alle seguenti domande, come nell'esempio. Usare i pronomi.* (Answer the following questions, following the example. Use the pronouns.)

ESEMPIO: *Perché non hai comprato quella casa?*
   Io l'avrei comprata, ma non ho potuto.

1. *Perché non sei andato in Sardegna?*
2. *Perché non avete investito quei soldi?*
3. *Perché loro non sono rimasti in Italia?*
4. *Perché Lei quest'anno non ha scambiato la Sua multiproprietà?*
5. *Perché non ci avete telefonato?*

C. *Completare in modo opportuno.* (Fill in the blanks appropriately.)

1. *Preferisco comprare più una casa _____ un appartamento.*
2. *Questa casa mi piace moltissimo. È _____ bella _____ quanto immaginassi.*
3. *La mia casa in Sardegna è tanto grande _____ la tua.*
4. *Quell'appartamento costa _____ _____ quella casa.*
5. *Questa casa mi piace _____ _____ appartamento.*
6. *Questa villetta costa _____ _____ quel che si crede.*
7. *Quello è _____ _____ grande palazzo _____ città.*
8. *Dovresti rivolgerti a quest'agenzia immobiliare. È tra le _____ (best) della zona.*

224

9. *Per un appartamento in questa zona si può spendere da un* _____ *di 50 ad un* _____ *di 150 milioni.*
10. *Questo complesso residenziale è stupendo. È il* _____ (best) *che io conosca.*

D. *Tradurre.* (Translate.)

1. We would like to invest some money in Italy. We would like to buy a house or an apartment.
2. I earn as much as my parents.
3. I paid less than you think for that house.
4. That house is ultra-modern. I don't like it.
5. They take everything for granted.
6. He has gone out of his mind. He paid more than a million dollars for that house.
7. We exercise every day.
8. Children, pay attention to what the teacher is saying.

LEZIONE 12

A. DIALOGO

VITA SANA: IL PROGRAMMA RADIO DELLA SALUTE

CONDUTTORE: **Benvenuti al programma settimanale "Vita Sana,"
il programma radio della salute che mira ad aiutare i radioascoltatori a capire i sintomi e le cause delle malattie e a
conoscere meglio le medicine che vengono[1] prescritte dai
medici. Oggi abbiamo come ospite[2] il dottor Francesco Perna,
primario[3] presso[4] l'ospedale San Carlo di Milano. Buon giorno,
dottore!**

DOTTORE: **Buon giorno a Lei e a tutti i Suoi ascoltatori.**

CONDUTTORE: **Abbiamo in linea la nostra prima ascoltatrice.
Pronto! È in onda con il dottor Perna.**

ASCOLTATRICE: **Buon giorno, sono la signora Borsetti e ho una
domanda[5] per il dottore.**

DOTTORE: **Prego, la faccia pure.**

ASCOLTATRICE: **Beh, di recente ho molti problemi di respiro. In
un primo momento credevo che fossero delle allergie, ma, a
quanto ne sappia, io non sono allergica a niente.**

DOTTORE: **Magari ha sviluppato un'allergia.**

ASCOLTATRICE: **Immagino che sia possibile, ma non sembra che
ci sia nessuna spiegazione logica a questo problema. All'improvviso il petto mi si restringe e ho la sensazione di non poter
far entrare abbastanza aria nei polmoni per respirare.**

DOTTORE: **A me sembra che si potrebbe trattare di asma. È
andata dal medico per un controllo?**

ASCOLTATRICE: **No, non ancora.**

DOTTORE: **Beh, dovrebbe proprio andarci. L'asma può essere una
condizione molto seria. Ma dovrebbe anche scoprire se si tratta
di una reazione allergica che ha sviluppato recentemente.**

ASCOLTATRICE: **Grazie, dottore. Lo farò.**

CONDUTTORE: **Allora chi abbiamo sull'altra linea?**

ASCOLTATRICE: **Pronto, Mi chiamo Carla e sono una studentessa universitaria. Circa un mese fa mi è venuta l'influenza e ho fatto tutto il necessario per ricuperare. Mi sono riposata molto, ho bevuto molto, ecc. Dopo qualche giorno mi sembrava di migliorare, ma poi penso di aver subito una ricaduta. Da allora non mi sento affatto bene e non riesco a migliorare.**

DOTTORE: **Mmm . . . Quanto tempo fa ha subito la ricaduta?**

ASCOLTATRICE: **Circa tre settimane fa.**

DOTTORE: **E che sintomi ha?**

ASCOLTATRICE: **Ho una tosse continua che porta molto muco, sono sempre un po' febbricitante, ho bisogno di dormire molto più del solito, e non mi sembra di avere le forze che ho normalmente.**

DOTTORE: **Si sveglia mai di notte tutta sudata?**

ASCOLTATRICE: **Qualche volta, ma non sempre.**

DOTTORE: **Beh, le possibilità sono diverse. Una cosa è certa, deve andare dal dottore. Può darsi che stia combattendo un'infezione o che è stata esposta a un virus che non è stato curato bene. In ogni caso, deve andare dal medico al più presto. Vi ricordo ancora una volta che è estremamente importante non trascurare nessuna malattia, anche se può sembrare una cosa da niente. Questo è un consiglio essenziale per tutti gli ascoltatori!**

ASCOLTATRICE: **Grazie, dottore. Ascolterò senz'altro il Suo consiglio. Spero che non sia una cosa seria.**

DOTTORE: **Lo spero anch'io. Buona fortuna, Carla.**

CONDUTTORE: **Sì, buona fortuna a Carla, e buona fortuna a tutti i nostri asoltatori. Ricordate il consiglio[6] che ha dato il dottor Perna: se avete un malanno, andate dal medico prima che diventi un problema serio. Abbiamo tempo ancora per un'altra telefonata, ma diamo prima la parola ad un altro nostro sponsor.[7]**

ANNUNCIO: **Ti cadono i capelli? Chiedi aiuto alla natura. Prova TRICOVITAL, il trattamento completo capace di risolvere i problemi che stress, trascuratezza e un uso eccessivo di prodotti aggressivi, provocano sui capelli. TRICOVITAL, in vendita[8] nelle migliori erboristerie e farmacie con settore erboristico.**

VITA SANA: THE RADIO HEALTH PROGRAM

BROADCASTER: Welcome to the weekly program "Vita Sana," the radio health program that aims to help listeners understand the symptoms and the causes of illnesses and be better acquainted with the medicines that are prescribed by doctors. Today we have as our guest Dr. Francesco Perna, who is Chief Physician at San Carlo's Hospital in Milan. Good morning, doctor!

DOCTOR: Good morning to you and to all of the listeners.

BROADCASTER: We have our first caller on the line. Hello! You're on the air with Dr. Perna.

LISTENER: Good morning, my name is Mrs. Borsetti and I have a question for the doctor.

BROADCASTER: Please, go ahead.

LISTENER: Well, lately I've been having a lot of trouble breathing. I thought at first that it might be allergies, but I'm not allergic to anything that I know of.

DOCTOR: You may have developed an allergy.

LISTENER: I suppose it's possible, but there doesn't seem to be any logical pattern to this problem. All of a sudden my chest becomes tight and I feel that I can't get enough air into my lungs to breathe.

DOCTOR: It seems to me that there's a real possibility that it could be asthma. Have you gone to your doctor for a check-up?

LISTENER: No, not yet.

DOCTOR: Well, you really should go. Asthma can be a very serious condition. But you should also find out if it's an allergic reaction that you've developed recently.

LISTENER: Thank you, doctor. I'll do that.

BROADCASTER: So who do we have on the other line?

LISTENER: Hello. My name is Carla, and I'm a university student. About a month or so ago, I came down with the flu, and I took all of the necessary steps to recover. I rested a lot, I drank a lot of fluids, and so on. I seemed to get better after a few days, but then I think I may have had a relapse. Ever since then, I haven't felt well at all, and I haven't seemed to get better.

DOCTOR: Hmm . . . How long ago was your relapse?

LISTENER: About three weeks.

DOCTOR: And what are your symptoms?

LISTENER: I've had a chronic cough which brings up a lot of phlegm, I've been running a low grade fever, I need much more sleep than usual, and I never seem to have the energy that I normally have.

DOCTOR: Do you ever wake up in the middle of the night in a sweat?

LISTENER: Once or twice, but not all the time.

DOCTOR: Well, it could be a number of things. One thing is certain, you definitely have to go to your doctor. You could be fighting off an infection, or you could have been exposed to a virus that has not been treated properly. In any event, you must go to see a doctor as soon as possible. I cannot stress enough the importance of not neglecting any illness, no matter how insignificant it may seem. This is essential advice for all of the listeners!

LISTENER: Thank you, doctor. I will definitely take your advice. I hope it's not serious.

DOCTOR: I hope so too. Best of luck, Carla.

BROADCASTER: Yes, best of luck to Carla, and best of luck to all of our listeners. Remember the advice that the doctor gave—if you have an illness, go to your doctor before it becomes a serious problem. We have time for one more caller, but first, a word from another one of our sponsors.

ADVERTISEMENT: Is your hair falling out? Ask nature for help. Try TRI-COVITAL, the complete treatment that can resolve the problems that stress, neglect, and an excessive use of harsh products can have on your hair. TRICOVITAL, on sale in better herbal stores and in pharmacies with an herb department.

B. IN BREVE

1. The verb is in the passive form. In Italian it is possible, in simple passive tenses, to substitute the normal auxiliary with the verb *venire*.

2. Note that *ospite* can mean both "host/hostess" or "guest." *Spero che sarete miei ospiti a Firenze.* (I hope you'll be my guests in Florence.)

3. The title *primario* is given to the doctor in charge of a hospital ward.

4. *Presso* can be used in addresses to mean "care of": *Sig. Gianni Mancini, presso Dario Cecchin* (Mr. Gianni Mancini, c/o Dario Cecchin).

5. Note that *domanda* is equivalent to "question," not "demand." *Domanda* is "demand" only when talking of "supply and demand" *(la domanda e l'offerta)*. *Domanda* can also mean "application" or "request": *domanda di fondi* (application for funds), *domanda d'impiego* (application for a job), *fare domanda di impiego* (to apply for a job), *domanda di denaro* (request for money), *su domanda* (by request). "Demand" is rendered as *richiesta* or sometimes *esigenza*.

6. In Italian "advice" is translated as *consiglio*. The Italian word *avviso* means "announcement, piece of information."

7. Another less frequently used term is *patrocinatore*.

8. Study the following expressions with *vendita: essere in vendita* (to be for sale), *vendite a bordo d'aerei* (sales on aircrafts), *vendita a contanti* (cash sale), *vendita a credito* (credit sale), *vendita a domicilio* (door-to-door sale), *vendita a rate* (sale by instalments), *vendita al dettaglio* (sale by retail, over-the-counter sale), *vendita al minuto* (sale by retail), *vendita all'ingrosso* (wholesale), *vendita all'asta* (auction sale), *vendita al miglior offerente* (sale to the highest bidder), *vendita condizionata* (conditional sale), *vendita di liquidazione* (clearance sale), *vendita di rimanenze* (bargain sale), *vendita di seconda mano* (second-hand sale, resale), *vendita giornaliere* (daily

sales), *vendita immobiliare* (a sale of real property), *vendite nette* (net sales), *vendita privata* (sale by private treaty), *vendita sotto costo* (underselling), *in vendita* (on sale, for sale), *non in vendita* (out of stock, unavailable, not for sale).

C. GRAMMATICA E SUOI USI

1. *I PRONOMI RELATIVI* (RELATIVE PRONOUNS)

A *pronome relativo* (relative pronoun) links a noun or a pronoun to a dependent clause.

La dieta che ha raccomandato è ricca di vitamine e proteine.
The diet that he recommended is rich in vitamins and proteins.

In the above sentence *che* links the noun *la dieta* to the clause *ha raccomandato*. The relative pronouns are *che* (that, which, who, whom), *cui* (which, whom), *il quale (la quale, i quali, le quali)* (who, whom, that, which), and *chi* (he/she who, the one who, whoever).

1. *Che* (that, which, who, whom) is invariable and is never used with prepositions. Note that in English, it is possible to omit "that," but in Italian *che* must always be expressed.

La pomata che il dottore mi prescrive contiene l'aloe.
The ointment which the doctor prescribes for me contains aloe vera.

Vedo che il prezzo della rivista medica è aumentato.
I see that the cost of the medical magazine went up.

2. *Cui* (which, whom) is always accompanied by a preposition and is invariable.

La nuova cura di cui ho letto è ancora nella fase sperimentale.
The new treatment which I read about is still in the experimental stage.

Il chirurgo di cui ti ho parlato è molto conosciuto nel campo della cardiologia.

The surgeon about whom I spoke to you is well-known in the field of cardiology.

3. The definite article + *quale/quali* (who, whom, that, which) can be used to replace *che* and *cui,* primarily to avoid ambiguity since this form agrees in number and gender with the noun it refers to. Note that when *il quale* (and its forms) is preceded by a preposition, the article and preposition may be contracted.

L'infermiera alla quale (a cui) ho parlato mi dirà dove si trova il paziente.

The nurse with whom I spoke will tell me where the patient is.

L'ospedale nel quale (in cui) è stato operato è conosciuto in tutto il mondo.

The hospital in which he was operated on is world renowned.

La donna alla quale (a cui) ho parlato ha organizzato una festa di beneficenza per l'Unicef.

The woman to whom I spoke has organized a charity event for Unicef.

4. *Chi* (he who, the one who, whoever) is invariable and is only used for people. *Chi* is often found in proverbs and popular sayings. It is also an interrogative pronoun.

Chi è causa del suo male pianga se stesso.

For your problems you can only blame yourself.

Chi dorme non piglia pesci.

The early bird gets the worm.

5. *Quello che, quel che, ciò che* (that which) usually refer to things.

Quello che dicono i dottori non mi convince.

What (That which) the doctors say does not convince me.

Ciò che ha raccomandato il dietologo non sarà facile da seguire.

That which the dietician recommended will not be easy to follow.

6. The definite article + *cui* (whose, of which) denotes possession. The article agrees with the noun it refers to.

Il paziente il cui intervento chirurgico è andato a perfezione è ancora in sala operatoria.
    The patient whose surgery went perfectly is still in the operating room.

È lui il medico interno le cui procedure sono così controverse?
    Is that the internist whose procedures are so controversial?

2. *IL PARTITIVO* (THE PARTITIVE)

The *partitivo* (the partitive) expresses indefinite quantities and translates the English "some," "any," or "a few." There are several ways of expressing these concepts in Italian.

1. The partitive is usually expressed by the contracted form of *di* + the definite article *(del, della, etc.)*

Delle persone saranno allergiche a questa crema per la pelle.
    Some people will be allergic to this skin cream.

Delle diete richiedono una drastica riduzione di grassi e aumento di cibi integrali.
    Some diets require a drastic reduction in fat and an increase in whole grain products.

2. *Alcuni/alcune* can only be used with a plural noun.

Alcuni prodotti senza grassi non sono sani perché hanno un contenuto superiore di sodio.
    Some fat-free products are not healthy because they are high in sodium.

Alcune allergie sono provocate dal cibo.
    Some allergies are caused by food.

Alcuni/e are also the only partitives that can be used as a pronoun.

Hai trovato le lozioni e le pillole di cui avevi bisogno in farmacia? Sì, alcune.
Did you find the lotions and pills you needed at the pharmacy? Yes, some of them.

3. *Qualche* must be accompanied by a singular noun, but remains plural in meaning.

La dieta gli ha causato qualche problema gastrointestinale.
His diet caused him some gastrointestinal problems.

Dopo l'operazione c'è stata qualche complicazione.
Some complications arose after the operation.

4. *Un po' di/un poco di* (a bit of, a little) is used with noncount nouns (nouns that normally do not have a plural form, abstract qualities, things that can be measured but not counted). This concept can also be expressed by *di* + a singular definite article.

Della/un po' di vitamina A ti farà passare il mal di testa.
Some vitamin A will help your headache.

La vittima dell'incidente ha perso solo un po' di sangue.
The accident victim lost only a little blood.

5. In Italian, the partitive is frequently either not expressed in negative statements or replaced by *non . . . nessun / nessuno / nessuna / nessun'* + a singular noun.

Non conosco erboristerie in questa città.
Non conosco nessun'erboristeria in questa città.
I don't know any herbalist shops in this city.

6. The partitive is frequently omitted in interrogative sentences and in sentences with a series of items.

Ci sono dermatologhi buoni in quella clinica?
Are there any good dermatologists in that clinic?

Durante la convalescenza avrà bisogno di riposo, liquidi e tanta attenzione.
During her recovery she will require rest, liquids, and a lot of attention.

234

7. The following words can also be used to express quantitative concepts: *abbastanza* (enough), *assai* (quite, enough), *molto* (a lot, many, much), *parecchio* (a lot, several), *poco* (a little, a bit), *tanto* (a lot, much, many), *troppo* (too many/too much), *tutto* (all, everything).

Tante persone soffrono di stress.
Many people suffer from stress.

Il dottore non ha prescritto abbastanza antidolorifici.
The doctor did not prescribe enough painkillers.

Parecchi passeggeri hanno avuto dolori addominali dopo aver mangiato il pesce.
Several passengers had abdominal pains after eating the fish.

D. PAROLE! PAROLE! PAROLE!

In the dialogue we saw the expression *sentirsi in forma* (= *essere in forma* = to be in shape).

Oggi non mi sento in buona forma.
Today I am not in good shape.

Come ti senti oggi?
How do you feel today?

Sentirsi can also be used to mean "to feel like" (or "to feel up to"):

Non mi sento di andare al lavoro.
I don't feel like going to work.

Ti senti di venire al cinema?
Do you feel up to coming to the movies?

Also in the dialogue the verb *tenere* is used idiomatically in the expression *tenere ad una persona* (to care about a person). Study the following examples.

Io tengo molto a quei bambini.
I care a lot about those children.

Loro tengono molto al vestiario.
They care a lot about clothes.

Tenere is also used figuratively in the following expressions:

Le tiene il sacco in tutte le sue imprese.
He is her accomplice in all her undertakings.

Pierino, non toccare! Tieni le mani a posto.
Pierino, don't touch. Keep your hands to yourself.

A lui piace tenere le distanze.
He likes to keep his distances.

Tieni duro. Sono certo che ce la farai.
Hold out. I'm sure you'll make it.

Devi imparare a tenere testa alla gente.
You must learn to stand up to people.

E. L'ANGOLO DEGLI AFFARI

IL SISTEMA SANITARIO IN ITALIA
(THE ITALIAN HEALTH CARE SYSTEM)

In Italy, many basic medical needs are covered by the health care system. According to article 32 of the Italian Constitution, *La Repubblica tutela la salute come fondamentale diritto dell'individuo e interesse della collettività.* (The Republic protects health as a fundamental right of the individual and as a concern of the collective.) Medical, pharmaceutical, specialist, and some hospital services are under the jurisdiction of the various units of the *Unità Sanitaria Locale* or *USL* (local health unit). These local units are funded by the *Servizio Sanitario Nazionale* or *SSN* (National Health Service). The *SSN* is the entity responsible for the gathering of contributions that are to be made by all Italian residents in order to keep the system functioning. From the moment a child is born, it must be registered at the local *USL* so that it may be entitled to health care in Italy. Individuals and families are able to choose a general practitioner, but this choice must be made from a limited list of doctors practicing in their area. Health care coverage does not allow patients to choose a doctor outside their geographical area.

Although basic medical necessities are free of charge and covered by the *SSN,* most diagnostic tests and all visits to specialists must be paid for, unless they are performed on an in-patient basis. Italians pay a *ticket* (user fee) for such extra services, unless the patient happens to fall under one of the categories of individuals who are exempt from paying the fees. Different categories of individuals are exempt from paying for pharmaceuticals and user fees in Italy. These are: children under the age of twelve; seniors over the age of sixty-five who earn an annual income of under 70 million lire; the unemployed; and those deemed to have an illness or medical condition which would require an ongoing expense.

There are three categories of medications: the first is covered fully by the *SSN* and consists of pharmaceuticals labeled as *necessari* (necessary). Insulin, for instance, falls under this category. The second category is comprised of pharmaceuticals which are considered *non insostituibili* (essentially, able to be substituted), which are subsidized up to 50%. The final category must be paid for in full and is made up of medications which are considered *non indispensabili* (not indispensable). Apart from the expense of the pharmaceutical itself, a basic ticket is charged for the dispensing of the medication. Although persons falling under the categories described above are not required to pay for medications, no one is exempt from the paying of this user fee.

For those interested in alternative forms of medicine, it is becoming easier and easier to find chiropractic services, homeopathic practitioners and pharmacies, acupuncture specialists, and other specialized professionals and services, especially in larger Italian centers. If you require specific methods of alternative medicine, it is best to check well in advance of your trip to Italy.

If you are travelling to Italy, be advised that you should make arrangements in the United States to take out an insurance policy for visitors. No vaccinations are required to enter Italy, nor to re-enter the U.S. from Italy. Note that if you will be in Italy for an extended period of time and will be earning taxable income, you are eligible for health care coverage, however, you are required to make the same contribution to the *SSN* that residents must make.

ESERCIZI

A. *Completare con il pronome relativo appropriato.* (Complete with the appropriate relative pronoun.)

1. *"Vita Sana" è il programma radio sulla salute _____ vuole aiutare i nostri radioascoltatori a capire i sintomi e le cause delle nostre malattie.*
2. *Il motivo per _____ ti telefono è il seguente.*
3. *Loro sono delle persone a _____ teniamo molto.*
4. *È una festa alla _____ sono state invitate molte persone.*
5. *_____ vorrei farLe notare è questo: se lo stato d'ansia è tale da procurare serie difficoltà, chiami il medico.*
6. *Allora _____ abbiamo sull'altra linea?*
7. *Ho dei puntini neri sul viso, i _____ mi danno molto fastidio.*
8. *Non sappiamo più _____ dobbiamo fare.*
9. *_____ io ti consiglio è di farti dei lavaggi con acqua e sapone.*
10. *_____ nota che il brufoletto è accompagnato da infezione, deve consultare il dermatologo.*

B. *Scrivere sei frasi usando le seguenti parole. Seguire il modello.* (Write six sentences using the following words. Follow the example.)

MODELLO: *Oggi ho comprato delle medicine.*

	delle	*latte*
	del	*carne*
Oggi ho comprato	*della*	*zucchero*
	alcuni	*medicine*
	qualche	*libri*
	dello	*pomodoro*

C. *Completare le seguenti frasi usando la parola appropriata. Tre delle parole non saranno usate.* (Complete the following sentences with the appropriate words below. Four of the words will not be used.)

qualche	nessun	chi	quale	abbastanza
qualche	nessun'	poco	alcuni	un po'
qualche	nessuna	ciò che	alcune	

1. *Oggi non ho mangiato _____. Ora ho fame.*
2. *_____ dorme non piglia pesci.*
3. *Avrei _____ domande da fare al dottore.*
4. *La dieta gli ha causato _____ problema gastrointestinale.*
5. *Stamattina ho preso dei cereali con _____ di latte.*
6. *Non ha _____ amico in Italia.*
7. *Non conosco _____ crema allo zolfo.*
8. *_____ dubbio sulla salute, ogni tanto, lo abbiamo tutti.*
9. *Ho fame. Stamattina ho mangiato _____.*
10. *_____ ora prima di un appuntamento importante sono sempre molto nervoso.*

D. *Tradurre.* (Translate.)

1. Doctor, I would like to ask you a question.
2. Our products are on sale in all pharmacies.
3. Today I am not in good shape.
4. I care a lot about those children.
5. What he says does not convince me.
6. Today our guest is Doctor Francesco Perna.

LEZIONE 13

A. DIALOGO

UN INCONTRO D'AFFARI

La signora Monika Wilkinson è in visita alla ditta Lineatre di Poggibonsi[1] (Siena),[2] con cui vorrebbe intrattenere rapporti d'affari. L'industria della Lineatre è considerata una delle firme[3] più prestigiose nell'arredamento del bagno.

WILKINSON: **Sono Monika Wilkinson della Bath Tech Canada Inc. Ho un appuntamento con il dottor[4] Di Mauro alle dieci.**

SEGRETARIA: **Sì, L'attendevamo.[5] Un attimo che glielo chiamo subito.**

WILKINSON: **Grazie.**

Il dottor Di Mauro, direttore generale dell'impresa, viene ad incontrare la signora Wilkinson.

DI MAURO: **Buongiorno. La signora Wilkinson?**

WILKINSON: **Sì, sono io. Buongiorno.** *(stretta di mano)*

DI MAURO: **Finalmente riusciamo ad incontrarci. Ho ricevuto il Suo fax qualche settimana fa. Ma c'eravamo già sentiti al telefono, vero?[6]**

WILKINSON: **Sì, infatti. È un piacere conoscerLa finalmente di persona.**

DI MAURO: **Le è stato difficile trovare lo stabilimento?**

WILKINSON: **No, non è stato affatto difficile. Non è la prima volta che vengo da queste parti. C'ero già stata qualche anno fa. In quell'occasione ero venuta però in vacanza. Ora invece sono qui[7] per affari.**

DI MAURO: **Possiamo offrirLe un caffè, un cappuccino?[8]**

WILKINSON: **Sì, grazie.**

DI MAURO: *(chiama la segretaria)* Signorina, può farci portare due caffè, delle brioche e una bottiglia di acqua minerale?

SEGRETARIA: Sì, provvederò immediatamente.

DI MAURO: Allora iniziamo la riunione?[9]

WILKINSON: Sì, benissimo.

DI MAURO: Signora, come Lei sa, la nostra impresa è tra le più grandi del nostro paese.

WILKINSON: Sì, lo so. La vostra è una delle firme italiane più importanti.

DI MAURO: Noi ci distinguiamo per raffinatezza di design, practicità e versatilità nella scelta dei materiali[10] e delle tipologie di arredo, unitamente ad una attenta politica di qualità e di prezzo. E va da sé che per i nostri prodotti non scegliamo un materiale qualsiasi.

WILKINSON: Beh, sappiamo che la vostra azienda non si è imposta solo sul mercato italiano . . .

DI MAURO: Sì, ci troverete anche in diversi ambiti internazionali quali: Europa, Stati Uniti, Giappone, Australia, ecc. Non ci dispiacerebbe vendere i nostri prodotti anche in Canada.

WILKINSON: Sì, la Bath Tech Canada è molto interessata al Suo prodotto.

DI MAURO: Se legge riviste e giornali italiani, avrà sicuramente visto la nostra pubblicità.

WILKINSON: Sì, infatti l'ho vista in *Epoca*.[11] Ma l'avevo già vista altrove.[12] E poi nel nostro settore tutti conoscono questo nome.

DI MAURO: Vorrei comunque farLe vedere alcune nostre collezioni per darLe un'idea migliore[13] della nostra compagnia. Abbiamo un gruppo preparatissimo[14] che è responsabile dell'ideazione dei pezzi e operai e tecnici specializzati che provvedono alla loro realizzazione.[15] Con un fatturato[16] annuo di numerosi miliardi.

WILKINSON: Straordinario!

DI MAURO: La nostra tecnologia è sicuramente d'avanguardia, ma non ha perduto i pregi della manualità insostituibile dei vecchi tempi. Insomma alla Lineatre facciamo di tutto per conciliare modernità e tradizione.

WILKINSON: Bene.

DI MAURO: Ecco, questa è la collezione "Tuscania": la struttura è in legno massello invecchiato e trattato con cera d'api. Le voglio far notare i cassetti con alzatina in marmo.

WILKINSON: Anche il piano con lavabo è in marmo?

DI MAURO: Sì, il piano con lavabo è in marmo Bianco di Carrara.[17]

WILKINSON: Avete dei modelli veramente eccezionali. Avevo già sentito parlare della bellezza e della qualità dei vostri prodotti, ma devo dire che dopo averli visti sono convinta che la mia ditta sarà molto interessata nell'esplorare la possibilità di un accordo con la Lineatre.

DI MAURO: Beh, intanto, in attesa di risentirci presto, se desidera potremmo farLe avere dei cataloghi e qualche campione.

WILKINSON: Ottima idea. La ringrazio.

A BUSINESS MEETING

Mrs. Monika Wilkinson is visiting the firm Lineatre in Poggibonsi (Siena), with which she would like to have a business relationship. Lineatre is considered one of the most prestigious names in bathroom furnishing.

WILKINSON: I'm Monika Wilkinson from Bath Tech Canada Inc. I have an appointment with Dr. Di Mauro at ten.

SECRETARY: Yes, we were expecting you. One moment, I'll call him for you right away.

WILKINSON: Thank you.

Dr. Di Mauro, general manager of the firm, comes to meet Mrs. Wilkinson.

DI MAURO: Good morning. Mrs. Wilkinson?

WILKINSON: Yes. Good morning. (handshake)

DI MAURO: We finally meet. I got your fax a few weeks ago. But we had already spoken on the phone, right?

WILKINSON: Yes, that's correct. It's a pleasure to finally meet you.

DI MAURO: Was the plant hard to find?

WILKINSON: No, it wasn't hard at all. It's not my first time in the area. I had been here a few years ago. At that time, however, I had come on vacation. Now, instead, I am here on business.

DI MAURO: Can we offer you a coffee, a cappuccino?

WILKINSON: Yes, thank you.

DI MAURO: (calls the secretary) Miss, could you have two coffees, some croissants, and a bottle of mineral water brought to us?

SECRETARY: Yes, I will see to it right away.

DI MAURO: Well, should we start the meeting?

WILKINSON: Yes, fine.

DI MAURO: Ma'am, as you know, our firm is among the largest in our country.

WILKINSON: Yes, I know. Yours is one of the most important Italian names.

DI MAURO: We distinguish ourselves by refinement of design, practicality and versatility in selection of materials, the types of furnishings, combined with an attention to quality and price. Naturally, we don't choose just any sort of materials either.

WILKINSON: Well, we know that your firm has not only established itself on the Italian market . . .

DI MAURO: Yes, you will also find us in several international locations such as: Europe, the United States, Japan, Australia, etc. We wouldn't mind selling our products in Canada as well.

WILKINSON: Yes, Bath Tech Canada is very interested in your product.

DI MAURO: If you read Italian magazines and newspapers, you surely must have seen our advertisements.

WILKINSON: Yes, in fact, I saw it in *Epoca*. Of course, I had already heard of Lineatre before I saw the ad. Everyone in the industry knows the name.

DI MAURO: However, I would like to show you a few of our collections to give you a better idea of our company. We have a well-qualified group responsible for coming up with the concept for the pieces, and workers and specialized technicians that see to their completion. And with a yearly turnover of many billions.

WILKINSON: Impressive.

DI MAURO: Our technology is clearly avant-garde, but it doesn't lose sight of the value of the handicraft of the old days. In short, at Lineatre we do everything to reconcile the modern with the traditional.

WILKINSON: Fine.

DI MAURO: Here, this is the "Tuscania" collection: the structure is in solid wood aged and treated with beeswax. I want you to take note of the drawers with the raised marble strip.

WILKINSON: Are the counter and washbasin made of marble as well?

DI MAURO: Yes, the counter with washbasin is made of White Carrara marble.

WILKINSON: It's a very impressive line, and very unique. Of course I had heard about the quality and beauty of your products, but after seeing them I'm sure my firm will be quite interested in exploring the possibility of an agreement with Lineatre.

DI MAURO: We look forward to discussing this further as well. In the meantime, I'll gladly arrange to have catalogues and samples sent if you'd like.

WILKINSON: Great idea. Thank you.

B. IN BREVE

1. This small town (pop. approximately 18,000) is located in the Siena province. It is an agricultural and commercial center. Principal products produced in Poggibonsi include chemicals, metals, and furniture.

2. The parentheses are used to indicate the *provincia* in which Poggibonsi is located.

3. Note that here *firma* means "name," not "firm." A *firma* is also a "signature." *La firma del dottor Vitti è illegibile.* (Doctor Vitti's signature is illegible.)

4. The definite article is required before a title except in direct address. Note also that masculine titles ending in *-re (signore, professore, ingegnere . . .)* drop the final *-e* before a proper name.

5. Here *attendere* means "to wait for," not "to attend." "To attend" is rendered as: 1. *intervenire a: Non è intervenuto alla riunione.* (He didn't attend the meeting.); 2. *frequentare/andare a: Loro vanno a scuola tutti i giorni.* (They attend school every day.); 3. *assistere/avere cura di/accudire a: Noi assistiamo sempre i malati.* (We always attend to the sick.)

6. You can also say *non è vero?*

7. *Qui* and *qua* are used interchangeably. Preference is given to the form which avoids any cacophony.

8. A *cappuccino* is also a Capuchin friar. Note that the expression *fare una vita da cappuccino* means "to live a life of poverty."

9. Note that "a meeting of the board of directors" is translated as *una riunione del consiglio d'amministrazione;* "an informal meeting" as *una riunione non ufficiale,* and "to postpone a meeting" as *rinviare una riunione.*

10. *Materiale* is translated as "materials/material" or "equipment": *materiali aeronautici* (aeronautical equipment), *materiale d'archivio* (file material), *materiale grezzo* (raw material), *materiale da costruzione* (building materials). Note that the English word "material" (fabric, cloth) is rendered as *tessuto* or *stoffa. Ho comprato un bel tessuto per tende.* (I bought beautiful curtain material.) *Questo è un bellissimo tessuto di seta.* (This is beautiful silk material.)

11. *Epoca* was founded in 1950, and has been one of the more widely read Italian periodicals throughout the decades. It is roughly the equivalent of *Life* Magazine.

12. The word *altrove* can also be used figuratively with the expression *essere altrove col pensiero,* and *avere la testa altrove* to mean "to be elsewhere in thought, distracted."

13. Note that *migliore* is an adjective and has two forms *(migliore, migliori)*. *Meglio* is the adverb and as such is invariable.

14. Remember that the suffix *-issimo* means "very," "a lot" and can be used with most adjectives and some adverbs *(bene, male, tanto, molto, poco)*. The ending changes with adjectives but remains invariable with adverbs: *È una collezione bellissima.* (It is a very beautiful collection.) *Quel lavabo sta benissimo con l'arredamento.* (That sink goes very well with the furnishings.)

15. *Realizzazione* is not always the direct equivalent of the English "realization." Study the following examples: *la realizzazione di un ambizione* (the realization of an ambition), *l'ottenimento di un utile* (the realization of a profit), *il realizzo della proprietà di un fallito* (the realization of an estate in bankruptcy), *bilancio di liquidazione* (realization and liquidation account). A "realization" as in "a moment of comprehension" is translated into Italian as *percezione, comprensione,* or *consapevolezza.*

16. "Our firm's yearly turnover has hit a record high" is translated as *Il fatturato annuo della nostra azienda ha raggiunto cifre da primato.*

17. Carrara marble is famous all over the world, and is sought after for its variety of colors and for its high quality. The marble caves of Carrara are actually located outside the city of Carrara, in the province of Massa-Carrara. The caves have been well-known since Roman times, well before the actual founding of the city of Carrara in the year 963. Consequently, the marble industry has been the most important industry of the province for centuries.

C. GRAMMATICA E SUOI USI

1. *IL TRAPASSATO PROSSIMO* (THE PLUPERFECT INDICATIVE)

The *trapassato prossimo* (the pluperfect) is used to express an action which happened before another action in the past. It corresponds to the English "had + past participle" and it is formed with the imperfect of the auxiliary verb (*avere* or *essere*) and the past participle of the main verb. The rules for agreement are identical to those for the *passato prossimo* and other compound tenses. The *trapassato prossimo* is often introduced by temporal expressions such as *già, prima, l'anno scorso*, etc.

	LAVORARE	*ANDARE*
io	*avevo lavorato*	*ero andato/a*
tu	*avevi lavorato*	*eri andato/a*
lui/lei/Lei	*aveva lavorato*	*era andato/a*
noi	*avevamo lavorato*	*eravamo andati/e*
voi	*avevate lavorato*	*eravate andati/e*
loro/Loro	*avevano lavorato*	*erano andati/e*

Quando è arrivato il rappresentante della ditta, la riunione era già iniziata.
When the firm's representative arrived, the meeting had already started.

Siccome il cliente era già arrivato, la segretaria ha informato il direttore.
Since the client had already arrived, the secretary informed the director.

Le trattative con la ditta italiana sono state affidate a Wilkinson, perché aveva già portato a termini altri accordi simili.
The negotiations with the Italian firm were entrusted to Wilkinson because she had already brought similar agreements to conclusion.

Remember that if the *trapassato prossimo* is used in independent clauses, often the subsequent action is implied.

Hai dovuto riempire il modulo per l'assicurazione? —No, l'avevo già riempito.

Did you have to fill in the application for the insurance? —No, I had already filled it in.

Che bella macchina! È tua? —Come!? Non l'avevi vista prima?

What a beautiful car! Is it yours? —What!? Hadn't you seen it before?

2. *AGGETTIVI E PRONOMI INDEFINITI* (INDEFINITE ADJECTIVES AND PRONOUNS)

There are three categories of *aggettivi* and *pronomi indefiniti* in Italian: those that are used strictly as adjectives, those that are used strictly as pronouns, and those that are used as both adjectives and pronouns.

a. *Aggettivi indefiniti* (Indefinite adjectives)

The words *ogni* (each), *qualche* (some), and *qualsiasi/qualunque* (any, any kind of) are used only as adjectives. They are invariable, and they can only modify singular nouns.

Ogni comunicazione va rivolta al direttore.
All communications are to be addressed to the manager.

Abbiamo suggerito qualche provvedimento per combattere la stagflazione.
We suggested some measures to combat stagflation.

Dobbiamo riuscire a vendere questo prodotto a qualsiasi costo.
We must succeed in selling this product at any cost.

b. *Pronomi indefiniti* (Indefinite pronouns)

Chiunque (anyone), *niente, nulla* (nothing), *ognuno/ognuna* (everyone), *qualcosa* (something, anything), and *qualcuno* (someone, anyone) are all singular indefinite pronouns.

In questa fabbrica ognuno è obbligato dalla legge a portare occhiali di protezione.
In this plant everyone is obliged by law to wear goggles.

Non sappiamo niente delle loro tecniche di programmazione e pianificazione.
We know nothing about their programming and planning techniques.

Se dovesse telefonare qualcuno, gli dica che non ci sono.
If anyone should call, please tell him I'm not in.

Note that when there is a question of agreement, *qualcosa, niente,* and *nulla* are all masculine.

Niente è perso se dobbiamo elaborare un nuovo programma operativo per la fabbrica.
Nothing is lost if we have to plan a new schedule of operations for the factory.

È successo qualcosa oggi in fabbrica?
Did anything happen at the factory today?

If an adjective follows *qualcosa* or *niente,* the adjective is preceded by *di.* If an infinitive follows *qualcosa* or *niente,* it is preceded by *da.*

Venite a visitare la nostra fabbrica: troverete certamente qualcosa di interessante.
Come and visit our factory: you'll certainly find something of interest.

Non c'è niente da fare fino a quando non riceviamo la spedizione dal deposito.
There is nothing to do until we receive the shipment from the warehouse.

c. *Aggettivi e pronomi indefiniti*

The following may be used either as adjectives or as pronouns:
alcuni/alcune (some, a few), *certo/-a/-i/-e* (certain), *ciascuno/ciascuna* (each, each one), *molto/-a/-i/-e* (much, many, a lot), *nessuno/nessuna* (no, none, no one), *parecchio/parecchia/parecchi/parecchie* (a lot, several), *poco/poca/pochi/poche* (little, few), *quanto/-a/-i/-e* (how much, how many), *tanto/-a/-i/-e* (so much, so many), *troppo/-a/-i/-e* (too much, too many).

Molte attività non sono più produttive a causa dell'assenteismo degli operai.
Many activities are no longer productive owing to workers' absenteeism.

La nuova direzione ha preso alcuni provvedimenti che contribuiranno alla redditività dell'impresa.
> The new management has taken some steps that will contribute to the profitability of the company.

I nostri clienti sono pochi, ma molto affezionati.
> Our customers are few but very devoted.

Abbiamo pagato troppo, non Le pare?
> We paid too much, don't you think?

Quanto avete lavorato oggi?
> How much did you work today?

Ci hanno promesso un tanto per cento sul fatturato.
> They promised us so much percent on the proceeds of sales.

Altro (other) may be used as an adjective, and it follows the regular pattern of agreement. As a pronoun, the invariable form *altro* means "something/anything else" and the plural forms *altri/altre* mean "others."

Gli altri produttori possono scegliere fra diversi sbocchi per le loro merci. Noi invece no.
> Other producers have a choice of several outlets for their goods. We, instead, don't.

Gli altri hanno rifiutato le proposte salariali della società?
> Have the others refused the company's wage proposals?

Tutto (all, whole, every) when used as an adjective also follows the regular pattern of agreement. As an adjective *tutto* and its forms are followed by an article. The invariable form *tutto* means "everything" and the plural forms *tutti/tutte* mean "everyone."

La nostra società sta trasferendo tutto in una sede più centrale.
> Our company is transferring everything to a more central location.

Si comunica con la presente che tutti gli stipendi verranno pagati con due giorni di ritardo.
> Notice is hereby given that all wages will be paid with a two-day delay.

Tutto il processo produttivo fu turbato dagli scioperi.
> The whole production process was disturbed by the strike.

Tutti amano il nostro prodotto. È l'ultima novità in fatto d'attrezzature per uffici.

Everyone loves our product. It is the latest in office equipment.

D. PAROLE! PAROLE! PAROLE!

The verb *dormire* is popular in Italian idioms.

Quell'hotel dà da dormire a 800 persone.
That hotel accommodates 800 people.

Sta dormendo come un ghiro.
He's sleeping like a log.

Cerchiamo di dormirci su!
Let's try to sleep on it!

Stasera dormo in piedi!
Tonight I can't keep my eyes open!

Questo è un film che fa dormire.
This film puts me to sleep.

Sto dormendo a occhi aperti.
I am very sleepy.

Puoi finalmente dormire tra due guanciali.
You can finally put your mind to rest.

Chi dorme non piglia pesci.
The early bird catches the worm.

Invece di investirli, abbiamo lasciato dormire i nostri capitali.
Instead of investing we left our capital dormant (inactive).

Finalmente possiamo dormire sonni tranquilli.
We can finally sleep peacefully.

In questo ufficio le pratiche dormono per sempre.
In this office files are shelved forever.

Non fa altro che dormire sugli allori.
He does nothing but rest on his laurels.

Non dormire!
Get a move on! Get going!

E. L'ANGOLO DEGLI AFFARI

L'INDUSTRIA IN ITALIA (ITALIAN INDUSTRY)

Italian industry is comprised of a relatively small number of large enterprises, and a large portion of very specialized, small- to medium-size companies in a large variety of sectors. Service industries have accounted for between 45–49% of the total industry throughout the nineties, with manufacturing wavering between 30–35%, and a combination of agriculture, forestry, and fishing making up between 3% and 4%. Services which have shown the most growth into the nineties include communications, real estate rental, insurance, and banking. As for manufacturing, the major industries include textiles and fashion, construction, machinery and transportation vehicles, chemicals, pharmaceuticals, and non-metal minerals. While certain regions of the country such as Lombardy, Emilia-Romagna, and Tuscany have been very dynamic in this decade, other regions, particularly those of the South, have not contributed a great deal to the Gross Domestic Product.

Italy's natural resources include mercury, potash, marble, sulfur, natural gas and crude oil reserves, fish, and coal. However, many of these resources, particularly the gas and oil reserves, are dwindling.

The majority of Italy's exports are within the European Economic Community, although Italian products are exported throughout the world. Germany, France, the United Kingdom, and the Netherlands count themselves among the major importers of products bearing the "Made in Italy" label within the EU. The United States falls closely behind the Netherlands. Among other major importers of Italian goods are Switzerland, Austria, and many republics of the former Soviet Union. Italy's primary exports are furniture, machinery and transportation vehicles, textiles and garments, rubber and plastic products, chemicals, ferrous and non-ferrous metals, non-metallic minerals, and foodstuffs and produce. There are no quantitative limitations placed on exports in Italy, with the exception of those which fall under international agreements. For instance, at the present time, arms and nuclear materials ordered by any country require advance authorization prior to export. It could be said that Italy's economy depends in large part on its exports. In 1994, the country was pulled out of a deep recession that had begun in 1991, and this was due to the demand placed on enterprises with a strong export orientation. In the past three years, exports have continued to increase. In 1993, Italy exported a total of 169.6 billion dollars; in 1994, this number increased to 179.2 billion, and in 1995, to 199.2 billion.

Italy's primary import is energy. Most electric power is produced from coal, hydroelectric power, or oil, but the country's resources are not enough to keep up with its needs. Italy's need to import a large percentage of electric power also arises from the fact that the use of nuclear energy has been banned following a nationwide referendum. Italy's other significant imports include chemicals, and ferrous and non-ferrous metals. In order to protect Italian industries, certain imports are subject to quantitative restrictions. For example, at the present time, quotas are in place for the importing of motor vehicles, television monitors, and video equipment. The figures for total Italian imports over the past three years are: 1993: 147.8 billion dollars; 1994: 148.6 billion dollars; and 1995: 160.5 billion dollars.

For those investigating Italian industry in order to research exporting prospects to Italy from the U.S., the following have been deemed to be the goods and services most in demand in recent years: 1) aircrafts and parts; 2) industrial chemicals; 3) airport and ground support equipment; 4) computer services; 5) telecommunications equipment; 6) electronic components; 7) process controls: industrial; 8) franchising; 9) computer software; 10) computers and peripherals; 11) laboratory scientific instruments; 12) insurance services; 13) paper and paperboard; 14) films and videos; 15) electrical power systems; 16) pollution control equipment and services; 17) sporting goods and recreational equipment; 18) printing and graphic arts equipment; 19) apparel; 20) medical equipment; 21) building products; 22) automotive parts and service equipment; 23) air-conditioning and refrigeration equipment; 24) security and safety equipment; 25) drugs and pharmaceuticals.

ESERCIZI

A. *Rispondere negativamente alle sequenti domande, usando il trapassato prossimo. Usare i pronomi se necessario.* (Answer each question negatively by using the *trapassato prossimo*. Use the pronoun when necessary.)

ESEMPIO: *Quando la signorina Wilkinson ti ha chiamato, tu dovevi ancora scrivere la lettera?*
—No, l'avevo già scritta.

1. *Quando la signorina Wilkinson ti ha telefonato, tu dovevi ancora spedire il fax?*
2. *Quando è venuto Luigi, tu dovevi ancora iniziare la riunione?*
3. *Quando l'hai conosciuto, tu dovevi ancora sposarti?*
4. *Quando ti hanno chiamato, tu dovevi ancora parlare con il dottor Di Mauro?*
5. *Quando ti hanno telefonato, tu dovevi ancora vedere la collezione?*
6. *Quando sono arrivati gli amici, tu dovevi ancora andare a dormire?*

B. *Completare in modo opportuno. Scegliere tra i seguenti verbi.* (Fill in the blanks appropriately. Choose from the list below.)

promettere   uscire   sentirsi   parlare   essere   vedere

1. *Ieri ho visto degli accessori di bagno che non _____ mai _____ prima.*
2. *Quando sono arrivato in ufficio tu _____ già _____.*
3. *Finalmente siamo stati a Siena. Non c' _____ mai _____.*
4. *Ieri ho comprato ai ragazzi un mobile che gli _____ da tanto tempo!*
5. *Ieri mattina la signorina Wilkinson non è andata all'appuntamento, perché la sera prima non _____ molto bene.*
6. *Quando gli hai telefonato, loro _____ già _____ con il dottor Di Mauro.*

C. *Dal seguente annuncio pubblicitario mancano le seguenti parole. Inseritele negli spazi vuoti.* (Fill in the blanks, choosing from the following words.)

arredamento	tempi	versatilità	tradizione	avanguardia
internazionali	pregi	materiali	prezzo	qualità
bagno	firme			

LINEATRE: UN SERVIZIO COMPLETO

LINEATRE è una delle _____ più prestigiose nell' _____ del _____. Raffinatezza di design, praticità e _____ nella scelta dei _____ e delle tipologie di arredo, unitamente ad una attenta politica di _____ e di _____, hanno portato l'Azienda ad imporsi non solo sul mercato italiano, ma anche in ambiti _____. La tecnologia, prettamente d' _____, senza perdere i _____ della manualità insostituibile dei vecchi _____, concilia modernità e _____ in un rassicurante rapporto dialettico tra l'uomo e gli oggetti che lo circondano.

D. *Tradurre.* (Translate.)

1. That sink goes very well with the furnishings.
2. The movie I watched last night put me to sleep.
3. —Where is Peter? —Can't you see? He's sleeping. He always sleeps like a log.
4. Tonight I'm so tired! I can't keep my eyes open!
5. Do you know the proverb "The early bird catches the worm?"
6. They do nothing but rest on their laurels.
7. They have suggested a few measures to combat inflation.
8. You must sell this article at any cost.
9. Here everyone must wear goggles.
10. We haven't paid much, don't you agree?
11. They have promised us much more on the proceeds of sales.
12. Come and see our new products; you'll certainly find something beautiful.

LEZIONE 14

A. DIALOGO

Tra i vigneti del Chianti:
intervista a Francesco Ricasoli

INTERVISTATRICE: **Allora è possibile affittare[1] una di queste tenute?**

RICASOLI: **Certamente. Nei Castelli qui attorno[2] non si produce soltanto il celebre Chianti classico . . . ma offriamo al visitatore esperienze di agriturismo uniche. Chi, per esempio, viene a Firenze, dopo aver visitato la città, potrà venire a cercare rifugio tra questi meravigliosi colli, fare un tuffo[3] in piscina e poi degustare un bel bicchiere di pregiatissimo Chianti.**

INTERVISTATRICE: **Signor Ricasoli, potrebbe darci qualche informazione storica su questi castelli?**

RICASOLI: **La storia del Castello di Brolio è legata alla mia famiglia, i Ricasoli. Già nel 1141 la famiglia Ricasoli diventò proprietaria del castello. Nel 1530 il castello divenne una lussuosissima villa[4] padronale.**

INTERVISTATRICE: **Il Suo antenato più famoso è . . . come si chiama . . . il nome ce l'ho proprio sulla punta della lingua . . . Sì, ora ricordo . . . è Bettino Ricasoli, che se non erro, succedette[5] a Camillo Benso di Cavour.[6]**

RICASOLI: **Precisamente. E fu proprio questo Bettino l'ideatore della ricetta[7] originale del Chianti Classico: dopo che ebbe provato e riprovato per vent'anni, finalmente riuscì a raggiungere la mescolanza giusta.**

INTERVISTATRICE: **La formula del Chianti è un segreto?**

RICASOLI: **No. Il Chianti odierno si ottiene con un uvaggio tra i rossi (Sangiovese e Canaiolo) e i bianchi (Malvasia e Trebbiano).**

INTERVISTATRICE: **Una mescita uguale dei vini?[8]**

RICASOLI: No. I vitigni Sangiovese costituiscono la percentuale più alta della miscela (dal 75 al 90%), mentre il restante 10–25% della miscela viene in ugual misura dagli altri tre vini. Il Sangiovese dà corpo, profumo e gradazione al vino, mentre il Canaiolo ne diminuisce la forza alcolica. Infine i vitigni Trebbiano e Malvasia ne alleggeriscono e intensificano l'aroma.[9]

INTERVISTATRICE: Ma il processo sembra molto semplice!

RICASOLI: "Sembra" è la parola chiave[10] della Sua frase. Non bisogna dimenticare che le precise proporzioni del Chianti sono il frutto di secoli di esperienza. Inoltre, bisogna seguire delle tecniche ben precise in tutte le fasi della produzione.

INTERVISTATRICE: Potrebbe elaborare ulteriormente?

RICASOLI: Per esempio, i vigneti situati oltre i 550 metri dal livello del mare non sono considerati adatti. Gli stessi terreni su cui impiantare i vigneti devono possedere delle caratteristiche molto particolari.

INTERVISTATRICE: Ci sono delle regole d'oro nella produzione del Chianti?

RICASOLI: Di regole ne esistono tante e ogni coltivatore ha il suo decalogo personale. Comunque, senza tema di smentita, tre sono le regole seguite da tutti: 1) bassa produzione per ogni ettaro[11] di vitigni, 2) controllo dell'uva durante la crescita e la vendemmia,[12] 3) costante controllo dei metodi di fermentazione, vinificazione e maturazione del vino.

INTERVISTATRICE: Qual è la gradazione alcolica del Chianti?

RICASOLI: Anche questa varia a seconda del vino, ma va dal 10 al 14%.

INTERVISTATRICE: Ma oggi la qualità del vino è diversa da quella di una volta?

RICASOLI: Beh, devo dirLe che i cambiamenti nell'impianto dei vigneti ad un certo punto hanno influito[13] pure sulla qualità dei vini . . .

INTERVISTATRICE: Cioè?

RICASOLI: Durante la mezzadria[14] i vini erano molto buoni. La vite non era reimpiantata spesso e di conseguenza essa poteva

avere diversi anni di vita. Si sa che una vite vecchia non produce molta uva, ma l'uva che produce è di ottima qualità. Per
di più ai tempi della mezzadria i vini venivano conservati in
botti in legno, botti[15] che contribuivano alla longevità del
vino . . .

INTERVISTATRICE: **Dunque negli anni sessanta, con la fine della
mezzadria e in pieno boom economico, è scesa anche la qualità
del vino?**

RICASOLI: **Sì. Siccome l'enfasi era in quel periodo sulla produzione, i vecchi vigneti furono eliminati e rimpiazzati[16] con
vigneti moderni e più specializzati. Inoltre, le botti in legno
furono messe da parte e sostituite con vasche in cemento . . .**

INTERVISTATRICE: **Oggi, comunque, le cose sono decisamente
cambiate.**

RICASOLI: **Sì, oggi abbiamo eliminato gli errori fatti in passato. Per
esempio, si dà nuovamente molta importanza all'uso del legno.
Si utilizzano non solo le botti, ma anche le piccole botti in
rovere francese, le cosiddette "barriques" . . .**

INTERVISTATRICE: **Tutto questo è molto interessante. Comunque,
siamo qui per parlare di agriturismo . . .**

IN CHIANTI'S VINEYARDS:
INTERVIEW WITH FRANCESCO RICASOLI

INTERVIEWER: Is it possible, then, to rent one of these estates?

RICASOLI: Certainly. Not only is the famous Chianti Classico produced at
the Castelli in the vicinity . . . but we also offer visitors unique agricultural tourism experiences. Those who, for example, come to Florence,
after having visited the city, can come to seek refuge in these marvelous hills, take a dive in the pool, and then taste a lovely glass of very
precious Chianti.

INTERVIEWER: Mr. Ricasoli, could you give us some historical information on these castles?

RICASOLI: The history of the Brolio castle is linked to my family, the Rica-
solis. Back in 1141 the Ricasoli family became the owners of the castle.
In 1530 the castle became the epitome of a luxury country villa.

INTERVIEWER: Your most famous ancestor is . . . what's his name . . . I have his name right on the tip of my tongue . . . Yes, now I remember . . . Bettino Ricasoli, who, if I am not mistaken, succeeded Camillo Benso di Cavour.

RICASOLI: Precisely. And it was this Bettino who was the creator of the original recipe of the Chianti Classico. After having tried and tried again for twenty years, he finally succeeded in reaching the proper composition.

INTERVIEWER: Is the Chianti formula a secret?

RICASOLI: No. The modern Chianti is made with a mixture of red (Sangiovese and Canaiolo) and white grapes (Malvasia and Trebbiano).

INTERVIEWER: An equal mixture of wines?

RICASOLI: No. The Sangiovese species of grape constitutes a higher percentage of the mixture, between 75 and 90%, while the remaining 10–25% of the mixture comes from the other three types of grape, in equal parts. The Sangiovese gives body, bouquet, and alcoholic content, while the Canaiolo decreases the alcoholic strength. Finally, the Trebbiano and Malvasia species make it light and intensify the bouquet.

INTERVIEWER: But the process seems very simple!

RICASOLI: "Seems" is the key word in your statement. One must not forget that the precise proportions of Chianti are the product of centuries of experience. In addition, one must follow some very precise techniques in every phase of production.

INTERVIEWER: Could you elaborate further?

RICASOLI: For example, vineyards located 550m above sea level are not considered suitable. Even the land on which the vineyards are planted must have some very particular characteristics.

INTERVIEWER: There are some golden rules in the production of Chianti?

RICASOLI: Many rules do exist and every grower has his or her own personal Ten Commandments. In any case, without fear of contradiction, three rules are followed by everyone: 1) low production for every hectare of grapes; 2) inspection of the grapes during the growing and harvesting phases; and 3) constant inspection of the methods of fermentation, wine-making, and aging of the wine.

INTERVIEWER: What is the alcoholic content of Chianti?

RICASOLI: This, too, varies, with different wines, but it runs between 10 and 14%.

INTERVIEWER: But is the quality of the wine different today than it was in the past?

RICASOLI: Well, I must tell you that the changes in the implantation of the grapes did influence the quality of the wines at a certain point . . .

INTERVIEWER: Meaning?

RICASOLI: When there was sharecropping the wines were very good. The vines were not reimplanted often and as a result they could have a long life span. It is known that an old vine does not produce many grapes, but the grapes it does produce are of a superb quality. In addition, at the time of sharecropping wines were preserved in wooden barrels, barrels that contributed to the longevity of the wine . . .

INTERVIEWER: In the sixties, then, with the end of sharecropping and in the midst of the economic boom, the quality of the wine declined?

RICASOLI: Yes, since the emphasis was on production during that time, the old vineyards were eliminated and replaced with modern, more specialized vineyards. Also, the wooden barrels were set aside and substituted with cement tanks . . .

INTERVIEWER: Today, in any case, things have definitely changed.

RICASOLI: Yes, today we have eliminated past errors. For example, a great deal of importance is placed on the use of wood again. Not only are wooden barrels used, but even the small French barrels, the so-called barriques . . .

INTERVIEWER: All of this is very interesting. However, we're here to speak about agricultural tourism . . .

B. IN BREVE

1. Study these uses of *affittare: Io preferisco affittare una casa piuttosto che comprarla.* (I prefer renting a house rather than buying it.)

Questa casa è da affittare. (This house is for rent.) *A quanto s'affitta quest'appartamento?* (How much does this apartment rent for?) *Quest'appartamento è affittato ad un milione di lire al mese.* (This apartment rents for one million lire a month.) *Affittasi* (For rent.)

2. A synonym of *attorno* is *intorno* (*qua intorno* = "around here," *là intorno* = "around there," *stare intorno a qualcuno* = "to hang around someone").

3. *Tuffo* (dip, plunge, dive, jump) can also be used figuratively: *Quando l'ho vista ho provato un tuffo al cuore* (When I saw her my heart missed a beat.) Study these other uses of *tuffo: gara di tuffo* (diving contest), *tuffo indietro* (back dive), *tuffo con doppio salto mortale* (double somersault dive), *tuffo di testa* (straight header).

4. A *villa* is usually a small suburban house with its own garden, or a holiday house, especially by the sea or in the mountains. It can also be a luxurious residence, with extensive grounds and often with an agricultural estate attached.

5. The form *successe* can be used instead of *succedette. Bettino Ricasoli successe a Cavour.* (Bettino Ricasoli succeeded Cavour.)

6. Count Camillo Benso di Cavour (1810–61) was a Piedmontese statesman who made the union of modern Italy a reality. He formed an alliance with Napoleon III of France, and obtained annexation of southern Italian states in the new kingdom of Italy (1861).

7. A *ricetta* is also a medical prescription.

8. Study the following: *vino in bottiglia* (bottled wine), *vino da dessert* (dessert wine), *vino dolce* (sweet wine), *vino frizzante* (sparkling wine), *intenditore di vino* (wine connoisseur), *vino invecchiato* (aged wine), *vino leggero* (light wine), *lista dei vini* (wine list), *vino da pasto* (table wine), *portare bene il vino* (to hold one's wine well), *vino pregiato* (vintage wine), *vino rosato* (rosé), *vino secco* (dry wine), *tagliare il vino* (to mix wine). The Italian proverb *buon vino fa buon sangue* means that "good wine engenders good blood."

9. Note that *aroma* is masculine. *Questo vino ha un aroma bellissimo.* (This wine has a very beautiful aroma.)

10. Note that when *chiave* is an adjective, it is invariable: *Chi sono i personaggi chiave del romanzo?* (Who are the key characters of the novel?)

11. A hectare equals 2.471 acres.

12. Note that "to harvest the grapes" is rendered as *fare la vendemmia.* A *festa della vendemmia* is a "grape-harvest festival." The verb is *vendemmiare* ("to harvest grapes"); a *vendemmiatore* is a "grape harvester."

13. *Hanno inciso (inciso* from *incidere)* can be used instead of *hanno influito.*

14. "To hold land as a share cropper" is rendered in Italian as *condurre un podere a mezzadria.*

15. *Botte* is used figuratively in *essere in una botte di ferro* (to be safe on all sides). Note also the proverb *volere la botte piena e la moglie ubriaca* (to want to have one's cake and eat it too).

16. A synonym of *rimpiazzare* is *sostituire.*

C. GRAMMATICA E SUOI USI

1. *IL PASSATO REMOTO* (THE PAST ABSOLUTE)

The *passato remoto* (past absolute) is a simple tense. It is used to indicate, as its name suggests, events in the remote past. It is used when the events have no continuing effect on or reference to the present. Remember that, in contrast, the *passato prossimo* is used for past actions in a time period that continues to have an effect on the present. The *passato remoto* is formed by adding the *passato remoto* endings to the stem of the verb. The following chart illustrates the endings of regular verbs in the three conjugations. Note that verbs of the second conjugation may have an alternate set of endings for the first and third person singular and for third person plural.

	LAVORARE	RIPETERE	PARTIRE
io	lavorai	ripetei/ripetetti	partii
tu	lavorasti	ripetesti	partisti
lui/lei/Lei	lavorò	ripetè/ripetette	partì
noi	lavorammo	ripetemmo	partimmo
voi	lavoraste	ripeteste	partiste
loro/Loro	lavorarono	ripeterono/ripetettero	partirono

L'industriale trasformò il palazzo in una bellissima enoteca.
The industrialist changed the building to a beautiful wine-tasting shop.

Gli agricoltori finirono la costruzione della cantina sociale nel 1970.
The farmers finished the construction of the wine growers' cooperative in 1970.

L'enologo ripetette l'esperimento fino a quando non riuscì a trovare una miscela perfetta.
The vintner repeated the experiment until he found the right blend.

Most of the verbs which are irregular in the *passato remoto* belong to the second conjugation (*-ere* verbs). The majority of these verbs follow the 1-3-3 pattern, that is, they are irregular only in the first and third person singular and in the third person plural; *-i, -e,* and *-ero* are the respective endings. Verbs that follow the 1-3-3 pattern can be found in Appendix C.

L'enologo scelse i vini di questi vigneti.
The vintner chose the wines of these vineyards.

Videro dei terreni situati oltre i 550 metri dal livello del mare.
They saw land 550 meters above sea level.

The verbs *essere, dare,* and *stare* do not follow a pattern and must be memorized. The verbs *bere, dire,* and *fare* and any verbs formed from them maintain the original Latin stems (*bev-, dic-,* and *fac-*). For their complete conjugations refer to Appendix C.

Il 1978 fu un'annata cattiva per la produzione del vino perché un temporale distrusse molti vigneti.
1978 was a bad year for wine production because a storm destroyed many vineyards.

Per il compleanno, il principale diede in regalo alla segretaria una pregiatis-
sima bottiglia di vino.
For her birthday, the boss gave the secretary a bottle of wine of excellent vintage.

Bevemmo tutti alla sua salute!
We all drank to his health!

The *imperfetto* can be used with the *passato remoto* just as it can be
used with the *passato prossimo*.

Era tempo di vendemmia, ma lasciammo la campagna lo stesso.
It was grape-harvest time but we left the country anyway.

A giugno andavano sempre in campagna per la mietitura del grano, ma
quell'anno non vi andarono.
In June they would always go the country for the wheat harvest, but
that year they didn't go.

2. *THE TRAPASSATO REMOTO* (THE PAST PERFECT)

The *trapassato remoto* is formed with the *passato remoto* of the auxiliary (*avere* or *essere*) + the past participle.

	LAVORARE	ANDARE
io	ebbi lavorato	fui andato/a
tu	avesti lavorato	fosti andato/a
lui/lei/Lei	ebbe lavorato	fu andato/a
noi	avemmo lavorato	fummo andati/e
voi	aveste lavorato	foste andati/e
loro/Loro	ebbero lavorato	furono andati/e

The *trapassato remoto* is used only when the verb of the main clause is
in the *passato remoto* and only in subordinate clauses introduced by
conjunctions of time such as *allorchè* (when), *quando* (when), *dopo che*
(after), *(non) appena* (as soon as), *come* (as soon as, just as), *finché*
(until) . . .

Dopo che ebbero finito la raccolta del grano, gli agricoltori incominciarono la raccolta del granturco.
   Having finished the wheat harvest, the farmers started to harvest the corn.

Non appena ebbe finito la raccolta, portò le olive nel frantoio.
   As soon as he finished harvesting, he brought the olives to the oil mill.

The *trapassato remoto* can be rendered in the following ways. Study the examples and note that there is no difference in meaning or usage:

Dopo che ebbe finito di fare la semina, l'agricoltore ritornò a casa.
Dopo aver finito di fare la semina, l'agricoltore ritornò a casa.
Finita la semina, l'agricoltore tornò a casa.
   Having finished the seeding, the farmer went back home.

D. PAROLE! PAROLE! PAROLE!

In the dialogue you saw the idiomatic expression *avere qualcosa sulla punta della lingua* (to have something on the tip of one's tongue.) Similar expressions are:

La parola non mi viene in mente.
   The word doesn't come to mind.

Non ricordo la parola.
   I do not remember the word.

In questo momento mi sfugge la parola.
   At this moment I don't recall the word.

The following are more expressions with *lingua:*

Quell'uomo ha la lingua lunga/tagliente.
   That man has a sharp tongue.

Che lingua lunga che hai!
   Don't you ever stop talking?

Sei una malalingua!
   You're a backstabber!

Glielo dico io! Io non ho peli sulla lingua.
I'll tell him. I do not mince words.

Mauro, di' qualcosa. Hai perso la lingua?
Mauro, say something. Has the cat got your tongue?

Il vino scioglie la lingua.
Wine loosens one's tongue.

Che gli secchi la lingua!
May his tongue rot!

Che lingua!
What a chatterbox!

Quella donna ha il cuore sulla lingua.
That woman is open-hearted.

Study also these two proverbs with *lingua.*

La lingua batte dove il dente duole.
The tongue ever turns to the aching tooth. (We always go back to what is bothering us.)

Uccide più la lingua che la spada.
The tongue is sharper than the sword.

E. L'ANGOLO DEGLI AFFARI

L'AGRICOLTURA IN ITALIA (AGRICULTURE IN ITALY)

Because of the difference in climate between the northern and southern regions of the Italian peninsula, Italy's major agricultural products are rather diverse. The north primarily produces rice and other grains, potatoes, sugar beets, soybeans, and meat and dairy products. The south's principal agricultural products are grapes and wine, olives and olive oil, vegetables, fruits, and durum wheat. Italy's agriculture accounts for about 4% of the Gross Domestic Product and approximately 9.8% of the work force. Most Italian farms are relatively small, averaging seven hectares.

The origins of present agricultural policy may be found at the beginning of the twentieth century. At this time, the Italian government favored free trade, and consequently allowed international trade to flourish. The southern regions contributed much of the foodstuffs for export as well as for domestic consumption. In fact, wine and citrus fruits were the main exports during the first three decades of the century, and cereals, meat, and dairy products were the main imports.

Under Fascism (1922–1943) free trade policies for agriculture continued. Although Italy suffered hostility on the international market for its political policies in Africa, it continued to flourish. For instance, in 1935, Italian wheat was sold for almost two and a half times the world market price. Other northern crops were also in demand, and northern agricultural products became more in demand. However, the success of crops grown in the north led the government to take a protectionist stance in favor of northern farmers. Southern farms were excluded from government aid, and the southern economy began to suffer as a result.

The fifties and sixties saw many changes in Italian agriculture. The *riforma agraria* (agricultural reform) put into practice in the years following World War II saw thousands of large land owners dispossessed of portions of their property and allowed small land owners to expand their properties. This action made more Italian farmers competitive, and as a result, the industry prospered once again. Also beneficial was the fact that Italy went through a period of phenomenal economic growth between the late fifties and late sixties, during the period that is commonly referred to as the *miracolo economico* (economic miracle). In 1962, the Common Agricultural Policy or CAP was created in order to integrate the agricultural industries of Europe. This policy helped to stabilize the Italian agricultural industry.

The seventies were a black period for the agricultural industry. During the early seventies poor crop yields forced prices to skyrocket. Furthermore, international monetary crises caused the Italian economy to precipitate into a deep recession, and the industry lost many forms of subsidy. Still, measures were taken at the European level to aid the industry, and by the end of the decade, the EC was the second largest exporter of agricultural products, thanks in part to Italy's contribution.

Between the early seventies and the mid eighties the Italian government did little in the way of agricultural planning. Beginning in 1986 and continuing into the nineties, however, Italian governments both at the regional and national levels have increased funding on a yearly basis. This has caused a rejuvenation in the industry, especially in the nineties. Despite this, tensions continue to exist between governments and the industry, as defenders of the industry point out that more should be done in order to insure Italy's competitiveness on the international market. Considering the high quality of Italian agricultural products for export, it is felt that perhaps it is in the best interest of governments to ensure that the industry continue to flourish.

The governing body which prevails over the agriculture industry in Italy is the A.I.M.A. or *Azienda (di Stato) per gli Interventi nel Mercato Agricolo* (the (state) agency for exchanges in the agricultural market). This agency oversees transactions within the agricultural industry in accordance with the objectives of the C.I.P.A.A. or *Comitato Internazionale per la Politica Agricola e Alimentare* (International committee for agricultural and nutritional politics). The A.I.M.A. consists of a national council, but also gives individual regions the right to institute regional councils in order to decide on matters concerning only these smaller political units.

ESERCIZI

A. *Completare con il passato remoto dei verbi dati.* (Fill in the blanks with the past absolute of the verbs given.)

ESEMPIO: avere   *lui* _____ *loro* _____
RISPOSTA: *lui ebbe*   *loro ebbero*

1. *essere*   *lui* _____ *loro* _____
2. *chiudere*   *lui* _____ *loro* _____
3. *conoscere*   *lui* _____ *loro* _____
4. *decidere*   *lui* _____ *loro* _____
5. *leggere*   *lui* _____ *loro* _____
6. *capire*   *lui* _____ *loro* _____
7. *andare*   *lui* _____ *loro* _____
8. *prendere*   *lui* _____ *loro* _____
9. *vedere*   *lui* _____ *loro* _____
10. *venire*   *lui* _____ *loro* _____

B. *Completare le frasi usando il passato remoto di un verbo appropriato, scegliendo fra i seguenti.* (Choosing from the verbs listed below, complete each sentence using the past absolute.)

fare	*venire*	*cercare*	*passare*
degustare	*essere*	*succedere*	*diventare*

1. *Chi _____ a Firenze, _____ rifugio tra questi meravigliosi colli.*
2. *Loro _____ un tuffo in piscina e poi _____ un bel bicchiere di pregiatissimo Chianti.*
3. *Nel 1141 la famiglia Ricasoli _____ proprietaria del castello.*
4. *Bettino Ricasoli _____ a Camillo Benso di Cavour.*
5. *L'ideatore della ricetta originale del Chianti Classico _____ Bettino Ricasoli.*
6. *Nel 1500 questa villa _____ da costruzione medievale a villa con corte, orto, frantoio e cantine scavate nella roccia.*

C. *Completare le frasi usando il trapassato remoto.* (Complete each sentence, using the *trapassato remoto.*)

1. *Mi portò il vino, appena l' _____ (comprare).*
2. *Bettino Ricasoli riuscì a raggiungere la mescolanza giusta del Chianti, dopo che _____ (provare) e riprovato per tantissimi anni.*
3. *Quando _____ (finire) di fare il vino, entrarono in casa.*
4. *Dopo che loro _____ (eliminare) i vecchi vigneti, li rimpiazzarono con vigneti moderni e più specializzati.*
5. *Dopo che la famiglia Sonnino _____ (acquistare) la villa, la cedette ai Tognana, industriali di porcellana da tavola.*

D. *Tradurre.* (Translate.)

1. My ancestor, Bettino Ricasoli, was the creator of the original recipe of the Chianti Classico.
2. Is the quality of the wine different today than it was in the past?
3. It is known that an old vine does not produce many grapes, but the grapes it does produce are of a superb quality.
4. I'll tell them. I do not mince words.
5. I have that person's name on the tip of my tongue.
6. This villa rents for two million lire a month.
7. Wines were preserved in wooden barrels.
8. Could you give me some historical information on these castles?
9. He finally succeeded in unveiling the secret.
10. We took refuge in these marvelous hills.

LEZIONE 15

A. DIALOGO

IL FASCINO DI INTERNET

Il signor Liberman è stato invitato per un caffè dai signori Martelli.

ANTONIO: **Marisa, ma Carlo dov'è?**

MARISA: **Sta montando il computer appena comprato. Va' a chiamarlo e digli che c'è il signor Liberman così viene a salutarlo.**

LIBERMAN: **No, lasciatelo stare! . . . Anzi, vado io nello studio e vedo se posso aiutarlo in qualche modo.**

ANTONIO: **Ottima idea, ma prima godiamoci il nostro caffè!**

Dopo il caffè, il signor Liberman va nello studio di Carlo.

LIBERMAN: **Allora, come va questo computer? Tua madre mi ha detto che stai avendo dei problemi con l'installazione.**

CARLO: **Sì, ma finalmente sono riuscito a farlo funzionare.[1] Prima non riuscivo a collegare lo schermo con il disco rigido . . . poi nell'installare il programma di videoscrittura ho dimenticato di creare una nuova directory e di trasferirvi dei file.**

LIBERMAN: **Vedo che dopo tutto non hai bisogno[2] del mio aiuto.**

CARLO: **Grazie lo stesso. Le piace? Mi è stato regalato dalla nonna.**

LIBERMAN: **Lo so che te l'ha regalato la nonna. Come mai hai deciso di comprare un PC compatibile?**

CARLO: **Beh, qui in Italia il mercato è dominato dalla Olivetti[3] e dai PC. Per gli altri computer si trova poco supporto[4] e pochi programmi.**

LIBERMAN: **Che programmi hai installato?**

CARLO: **Pochi per adesso: DOS, Windows, Word per Windows, qualche gioco. Come vede, c'è anche un CD e una stampante.**

LIBERMAN: **Ha il modem?**

CARLO: Sì, è un vero computer multimediale. Infatti ho intenzione di andare su Internet. Anzi, so che Lei è un esperto in questa materia e vorrei che mi spiegasse come accedere al Web.[5]

LIBERMAN: Senz'altro. Perché non vieni a trovarmi in ufficio e così ti do una breve dimostrazione.

Diversi giorni dopo nell'ufficio del signor Liberman.

LIBERMAN: Prima di tutto, per accedere a Internet ci si deve collegare via modem o tramite ethernet a un sistema che offre tali possibilità.

CARLO: Sì, io spero di collegarmi al sistema universitario.

LIBERMAN: Devi anche ottenere una copia di un programma che ti dia accesso a Internet. Io, per esempio, uso Netscape. Guarda come è semplice! Dopo il collegamento, si fa doppio clic su Netscape e si arriva alla Homepage della compagnia che ti offre il servizio di collegamento. Ecco.

CARLO: Facilissimo.

LIBERMAN: Eccoci su Internet! Il resto è facile. Per navigare, si devono premere[6] i vari pulsanti sullo schermo: questo per fare una ricerca; questo per andare avanti; questo per andare indietro; questo per andare ad un'altra Homepage.

CARLO: Fantastico.

LIBERMAN: Io ho una riunione fra qualche minuto, ma se vuoi, puoi restare e fare un po' di surfing.

Diverse ore dopo, ancora nell'ufficio del signor Liberman.

LIBERMAN: Vedo che sei ancora qui . . . Dimmi quali siti hai visitato.

CARLO: Mi sono collegato con la Homepage del *Corriere della sera* e della *Gazzetta dello Sport,*[7] ho visitato le rovine di Pompei,[8] ho visto un video[9] pubblicitario sulla Sardegna.[10]

LIBERMAN: Prima[11] di partire vorrei fare un ultimo collegamento con la pagina della ABC[12] per ascoltare le ultime notizie.

Dopo il collegamento, i due sono pronti per andare.

CARLO: Grazie mille, signor Liberman. Grazie per avermi introdotto[13] al mondo della realtà virtuale.

LIBERMAN: **Di niente!**[14] **La prossima volta si fa insieme una visita virtuale della Scala di Milano.**[15] **Va bene?**

FASCINATION WITH THE INTERNET

Mr. Liberman has been invited for coffee at the Martelli's.

ANTONIO: Marisa, where is Carlo?

MARISA: He is putting together the computer he just bought. Go call him and tell him that Mr. Liberman is here so he can come and say hello.

LIBERMAN: No, leave him alone . . . In fact, I'll go in his study and see if I can help him in any way.

ANTONIO: Great idea, but first let's enjoy our coffee!

After coffee, Mr. Liberman goes into Carlo's study.

LIBERMAN: Well then, how's everything with the computer? Your mother told me that you were having some problems with the installation.

CARLO: Yes, but I've finally managed to make it work. First, I couldn't hook up the monitor to the hard drive . . . then in installing the word-processing program I forgot to create a new directory and to transfer the files to it.

LIBERMAN: I see that you don't need my help after all.

CARLO: Thanks, anyway. Do you like it? It was given to me by my grand-mother.

LIBERMAN: I know that your grandmother gave it to you. Why did you decide to buy a PC compatible?

CARLO: Well, here in Italy the market is dominated by Olivetti and by PCs. For other computers very little support and few programs are found.

LIBERMAN: What programs have you installed?

CARLO: Just a few for now: DOS, Windows, Word for Windows, some games. As you can see, I've also got a CD-ROM drive and a printer.

LIBERMAN: Does it have a modem?

CARLO: Yes, it's a real multimedia computer. In fact, I am planning on getting on the Internet. Actually, I know that you are an expert on the subject and I'd like you to tell me how to access the WWW.

LIBERMAN: Of course. Why don't you come by the office and that way I'll give you a brief demonstration.

A few days later in Liberman's office.

LIBERMAN: First of all, to access the Internet, you have to link by modem or by ethernet to a system that offers internet access.

CARLO: Yes, I hope to hook into the university system.

LIBERMAN: You've also got to get a copy of the program that lets you navigate the Internet. I, for example, use Netscape. Look how simple it is! After the connection, you double click on Netscape and you arrive at the Home Page of the company that offers you the service link. Here.

CARLO: Very easy.

LIBERMAN: Here we are on Internet! The rest is simple. To navigate, you click the buttons on the screen: this to do a search; this to go ahead; this to go back; this to go to another Home Page.

CARLO: Fantastic.

LIBERMAN: I have a meeting in a few minutes, but if you want, you can stay and do a little surfing.

A few hours later, still in Mr. Liberman's office.

LIBERMAN: I see you're still here . . . Tell me which sites you've visited.

CARLO: I've gotten on to the Home Page of *Corriere della sera* and of *Gazzetta dello Sport;* I visited the ruins of Pompei; I visited a video advertisement on Sardinia.

LIBERMAN: Before we leave I would like to get on to the ABC page to hear the latest news.

After the link, the two are ready to leave.

CARLO: Thanks a lot, Mr. Liberman. Thank you for introducing me to the world of virtual reality!

LIBERMAN: It was nothing! The next time we'll both take a virtual visit to La Scala in Milan. Okay?

B. IN BREVE

1. The verb "to work" may be translated in Italian in more than one way. If one wishes to express that an object "works," meaning that it functions properly, then the verb *funzionare* must be used. On the other hand, if one wishes to translate to work as in "to perform a task or duty," then one must use the verb *lavorare*. *L'orologio funziona.* (The watch works.) *L'insegnante lavora.* (The teacher works.)

2. Unlike the English verb "to need," the Italian *avere bisogno di* is not transitive; it cannot take a direct object. "I need time" is translated as *Ho bisogno di tempo.* The verb *bisognare* cannot be used as a direct equivalent of "to need." It is used in impersonal expressions, and means "to be necessary." For instance, "It is necessary that you arrive on time" would be translated as *Bisogna che tu arrivi in orario.* (Notice that *bisogna che,* like many impersonal expressions, takes the subjunctive. Please see *Lezione 16* for an explanation of impersonal expressions that take the subjunctive.)

3. Olivetti is a multinational corporation specializing in a wide variety of computer and telecommunications products, including PCs and notebook computers, printers, office products, computer systems and services, and cellular phones. For more information on Olivetti, see the company's web page at: http://www.olivetti.it.

4. Remember that the verb *sopportare* is a false friend and has the meaning of "to stand, to tolerate, to put up with." *Non lo riesco più a sopportare!* (I cannot stand him anymore.) *Io ho una moglie e due figli da mantenere.* (I have a wife and two kids to support.)

5. The Web is also known as the Internet (same in English and Italian) or the information superhighway.

6. A synonym for *premere* is *pigiare. Mauro, pigia il pulsante, per favore.* (Mauro, push the button, please.)

7. This daily paper was founded in Milan in 1895. It focuses on sports stories and information from all over the world, although it does tend to focus on Italy's more popular sports. It is an extremely popular newspaper among Italians. At the *edicola* (news stand) *La*

Gazzetta is extremely easy to spot, because it is printed entirely on pink newsprint. For the location of *Corriere della sera/Gazzetta dello sport* on the Internet, refer to the *Angolo degli affari* at the end of this chapter.

8. Under the Campania home page: http://194.20.24.33/tci.sdp/html/0400101.htm click on *Località* (places) and look for Pompeii. There are some images of structures and frescoes of the ancient city of Pompeii, as well as a description of the ancient city.

9. The word "video" is invariable in the plural *(il video > i video)*.

10. There is a great deal of information on the region of Sardinia on the Internet. The Center for Advanced Studies, Research, and Development in Sardinia *(Centri di Ricerca, Sviluppo e Studi Superiori in Sardegna)* has an excellent web page that includes historical information, as well as a 37-minute tourism video. The web page is located at "http://www.crs4.it".

11. If followed by an infinitive, *prima* always requires the preposition *di. Dopo,* however, does not require a preposition and is always followed by the past infinitive or the past participle. *Dopo aver mangiato (Dopo mangiato) siamo usciti.* (After having eaten we went out.)

12. This network's page contains up-to-the-minute news, sports, and entertainment coverage, among other items. One can even hear sound news reports from World News Tonight and ABC radio. The address is "http://www.abcradio.ccabc com".

13. *Introdotto* is the past participle of *introdurre.* The word *introdurre* can also mean "to put/to insert" *(introdurre la chiave nel buco della serratura* = "to put/insert the key in the keyhole").

14. The expression is equivalent to *Prego.* (You're welcome.)

15. If you are interested in opera and will be travelling to Milan, do not forget to consult La Scala's web page. In addition to a program of the current season, other items included are a virtual tour of the theater and news and information. This page is located at "http://lascala.milan.it".

C. GRAMMATICA E SUOI USI

1. *IL PASSIVO* (THE PASSIVE VOICE)

In Italian, as in English, verbs have both an active and a passive voice. When the subject of a sentence performs the action, it is called the active voice. In the passive voice, this is reversed, and the subject receives the action. Study the following examples:

Active voice	*Il signore*	*trasmette*	*il messaggio.*
	The man	transmits	the message.
Passive voice	*Il messaggio*	*è trasmesso*	*dal signore.*
	The message	is transmitted	by the man.

The passive construction is formed with the appropriate tense of the auxiliary *essere* + the past participle. The agent (the performer of the action) is preceded by the preposition da (by). A verb can be passive in any tense or mood. Remember that the past participle always agrees in gender and number with the subject of the passive construction.

Una copia del programma è stata ottenuta da me.
A copy of the program has been obtained by me.

I computer multimediali erano usati dagli impiegati della ditta.
Multimedia computers were used by the employees of the firm.

The passive is generally used to emphasize the object of the action. It is often used in print media and in scientific writing when a more objective style is required.

Venire and *andare* can also be used as auxiliaries in the passive voice. *Venire* can only be used in simple tenses in passive constructions. *Andare* conveys the meaning of an act that must be done, and it is parallel to *dover essere.*

Il modem viene usato per accedere all'Internet.
The modem is used to access the Internet.

Quel programma va installato con cautela.
That program must be installed carefully.

The passive voice can also be expressed by placing *si* before the third person singular or plural form of the verb in any simple tense, or by attaching *si* to the end of the infinitive or gerund. The passive can be formed with *si* only if the agent is not expressed.

Oggigiorno non si usa più tanto la macchina da scrivere perché è stata rimpiazzata dal computer.
Nowadays the typewriter is not used very often because it has been replaced by the computer.

I programmi di videoscrittura si apprendono meglio se usati costantemente.
Wordprocessing programs are better learned if used constantly.

To form the passive with *si* in a compound tense, place *si* before the appropriate form of the auxiliary *essere*. The past participle agrees in gender and number with the subject.

Ieri si sono comprate tre stampante laser.
Yesterday three laser printers were bought.

Non si sono installati i programmi perché non c'era abbastanza spazio nel disco rigido.
The programs were not installed because there was not enough hard drive space.

2. *IL SI IMPERSONALE* (THE IMPERSONAL *SI*)

The pronoun *si* is often used in impersonal constructions, that is, when there is no expressed subject. This construction is equivalent to the English "one," "they," or "people" when making general statements.

Se si avesse un computer in tutte le case!
If only people had a computer in every house!

A Internet si accede tramite il modem o con un cavo ethernet.
One accesses the internet through a modem or with an ethernet connection.

In compound tenses, the auxiliary is always *essere*. If the auxiliary of the verb is normally *avere* when it is not used in an impersonal construction, then the past participle agrees in number and gender with the direct object or will end in *-o* if there is no direct object.

Si è parlato del prezzo di una nuova stampante alla riunione.
People discussed the cost of a new printer at the meeting.

Si sono persi tutti i documenti del disco rigido.
One lost all of the files on the hard drive.

If the auxiliary of the verb is normally *essere* when it is not used in an impersonal construction, then the past participle will end in either *-i* or *-e,* depending on the gender of the impersonal element.

Marco e Paolo hanno detto: Dopo la riunione, si è andati a prendere un caffè.
Marco and Paolo said: After the meeting, we went for a coffee.

Luisa e Alessandra hanno detto: Dopo la riunione, si è tornate a lavorare.
Luisa and Alessandra said: After the meeting, we went back to work.

If a reflexive verb is used in an impersonal construction *ci si* takes the place of *si si* (the impersonal *si* and the reflexive *si*).

In ufficio ci si è divertiti tutto il giorno facendo del surfing sull'Internet.
At the office we had fun all day surfing the net.

Ci si è impegnati a creare subito una Homepage per la nostra compagnia.
We've begun the task of creating a Home Page for our company right away.

Note that even if the verb is in the singular, all adjectives, nouns, and all other reference words related to the object will be in the masculine or feminine plural form.

Dopo aver lavorato al computer una giornata intera, ci si sente stanchi.
After having worked at the computer for a whole day, one feels tired.

Grazie alla realtà virtuale, ci si crede lontani e in luoghi remoti.
Thanks to virtual reality, we believe ourselves to be in far away places.

In ads or other public notices or signs, the impersonal *si* may be attached as a suffix to the verb. If the verb is in the plural, drop the final *-o* before adding *-si.*

Cercasi segretaria. Buona conoscenza WP.
   Secretary wanted. Good knowledge WP.

Affittasi spazio per uffici.
   Office space for rent.

Cercansi programmatori esperti. Creazione Homepage.
   Expert programmers wanted to create a Home Page.

Offronsi servizi traduzione inglese-italiano.
   Translation services English-Italian available.

D. PAROLE! PAROLE! PAROLE!

The word *mano* is used metaphorically in many idiomatic expressions.
The following examples show more idiomatic uses of the word *mano*.

John ha le mani bucate.
   John spends money like it grows on trees.

Si è messa le mani nei capelli per la disperazione.
   She tore out her hair in despair.

Quella macchina andava contromano.
   That car was driving on the wrong side of the road.

Sono talmente sicuro che metterei la mano sul fuoco.
   I am so certain that I would swear on it.

Lui ha le mani lunghe. Gli piace rubare.
   He has sticky fingers. He likes to steal.

Dopo quello che è successo, volevo mordermi le mani.
   After what happened, I wanted to kick myself.

Lui ha le mani di ricotta.
   He has butter-fingers.

Non aiuta mai. Sta sempre con le mani in mano.
   He never helps. He never lifts a finger.

Io ci credo solo se lo tocco con mano.
   I'll believe it only if I see it with my own eyes.

I due ragazzi sono venuti alle mani.
   The two boys got into a fight.

Non mettermi le mani addosso!
Do not lay your hands on me!

Gli italiani quando si incontrano si danno la mano.
When Italians meet, they shake hands.

Giù le mani!
Hands off!

E. L'ANGOLO DEGLI AFFARI

L'INTERNET IN ITALIA (THE INTERNET IN ITALY)*

In Italy, as in the U.S., the information superhighway has become the new frontier to discover and conquer. Searching the net for web sites originating in Italy will lead to countless personal, commercial, cultural, and educational sites. In fact, as the twenty-first century approaches, perhaps the most immediate way to become acquainted with Italy, short of living in the country, is to search for Italian sites on the Internet.

For instance, if you are interested in reading about current events from an Italian point of view, several newspapers and periodicals are now available on the World Wide Web. For general information on Italian newspapers available on WWW, check "http://www.citinv.it" and then follow the link to *Edicola.* The most prominent Italian dailies available on the Internet are: *La Stampa* (http://www.lastampa.it), *La Repubblica* (http://www.repubblica.it), *Il Corriere della Sera,* and its sports equivalent, *La Gazzetta dello Sport* (http://rcs.it). *Panorama,* the weekly news periodical, is available on-line at "http://www.mondadori.com/panorama".

If you are planning to travel to Italy and wish to find information about the city where you'll be staying, it's interesting to note that many *comuni* (municipal administrations) have set up Web pages. Rome's Web page, for instance, is located at "www.comune.roma.it/". On this web page you'll find a wealth of information on a variety of topics, such as links to the Vatican's on-line information service, entertainment listings and other tourist information, photographs of many of Rome's

---

* Although every effort has been made to ensure that the links mentioned here are active, please keep in mind that the Internet is constantly changing.

sites, as well as political and administrative information. In fact, there's even an interactive page, *Chiedi al sindaco* (Ask the mayor), which offers the possibility of communicating with Rome's administrative leader. The Rome Web page can be read in a variety of languages, including English.

For other up-to-date information about Italy in English, one can find information at the following ANSA news agency: see Windows on Italy, http://www.mi.cnr.it/WOI/.

Other sites filled with information about Italy are Maurizio Oliva's Italia (http://italia.hum.utah.edu/, or Lucio Picci's gopher at the University of Bologna. This site, entitled "Virtual Italy," is dedicated mostly to Italian politics (gopher://spfo.unibo.it). It is possible to contribute to Virtual Italy by writing to gopher@spfo.unibo.it.

If you will be living in Italy for an extended period of time and wish to have Internet access, there are several options available. Most network providers offer a wide variety of technologically advanced services. Generally speaking, you will be able to find all of the services to which you have access in the United States, including ftp, talk, telnet, bitnet, usenet, etc. However, be prepared to spend the equivalent of hundreds of dollars or more per year for SLIP connections and full services. Remember that the telephone is an expensive service in Italy, and the use of the phone will add substantially to your bill.

If you will be involved with a university in any capacity while in Italy, keep in mind that some Italian universities offer Internet access. For the most part, access is limited to students, researchers, and staff. The universities of Padova, Trento, Milan, Pisa, and Venice (among others) offer a wide variety of Internet services to the university community. CINECA, an interuniversity consortium, has a service called NETTuno which offers internet access to industries and the public at large. Their web page is located at "http://www.cineca.it/.

If you will be staying for an extended period in the Bologna area and wish to set up an e-mail account, it is interesting to note that Bologna's *comune* (municipal administration) has set up a project, *progetto Iperbole,* which offers e-mail service and access to newsgroups and other local information through NETTuno. This service is free to all citizens of Bologna. For more information on this, you can find *progetto Iperbole's* web page at http://www.nettuno.it/bologna. For further information on NETTuno, contact "CINECA—Servizio consulenza 051-6599423 (consulenza@nettuno.it)".

Outside the univerity setting it is possible to use e-mail and other services through private networks. A list of providers of network services in Italy is maintained in Pisa at the following gopher: gopher.nis.garr.it/. Other service providers include MC-link, Agorà, CompuServe (based in Milan), Galactica, ITALIA ON LINE, Sublink, and IUnet.

One final word about Italy and the Internet. If you are worried about having to communicate with Italians about the Internet or computers in general, do not be. The majority of computer terms and expressions come directly from English, and consequently, it will be easy for you to understand terminology and to communicate. It is not difficult to guess what Italian terms such as *downloadare* or *uploadare* might mean, much less terms like *"mouse"* or *"on-line."* The following diagram and list of terms include the most common vocabulary associated with computers.

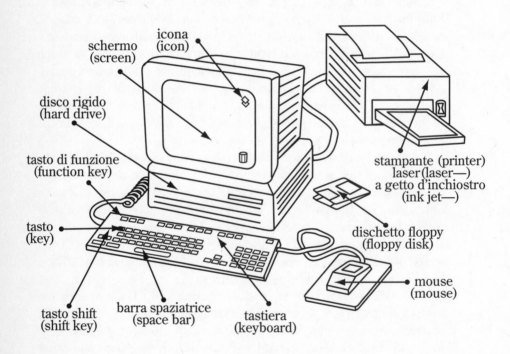

schermo (screen)

icona (icon)

disco rigido (hard drive)

tasto di funzione (function key)

tasto (key)

stampante (printer) laser (laser—) a getto d'inchiostro (ink jet—)

dischetto floppy (floppy disk)

mouse (mouse)

tasto shift (shift key)

barra spaziatrice (space bar)

tastiera (keyboard)

VOCABULARY

select (to)	*selezionare*
bold	*grassetto*
button	*pulsante*
CD ROM	*CD-ROM*
CD ROM drive	*unità CD-ROM*
click (to) the file menu	*fare click sul menu file*
cursor	*puntatore*
cut and paste	*taglia e incolla*
data	*dati*
disk drive	*unità a disco*
e-mail	*e-mail, posta elettronica*
error	*errore*
file	*un documento*
backup (to)	*fare il backup*
close (to)	*chiudere*
open (to)	*aprire*
print (to)	*stampare*
save (to)	*salvare*
save as (to)	*salvare con nome*
font	*carattere*
help	*guida*
input (to)	*immettere*
interface	*interfaccia*
italic	*corsivo*
laptop	*portatile, computer portatile*
memory	*memoria*
modem	*modem*
periferals	*periferiche*
program	*programma*
RAM	*RAM*
ROM	*ROM*
software	*software*
toolbar	*barra degli strumenti*
underline	*sottolineare*
word processor	*programma di videoscrittura*

ESERCIZI

A. *Trasformare le seguenti frasi dalla forma attiva a quella passiva*
(Rewrite the following sentences in the passive form.)

ESEMPIO: *Molte persone usano il World Wide Web.*
Il World Wide Web è usato da molte persone.

1. *Gli esploratori hanno portato il caffè in Europa.*
2. *Mia nonna mi ha regalato il computer.*
3. *Gli studenti visiteranno le rovine di Pompei tramite l'Internet.*
4. *L'Olivetti domina in Italia il mercato dei computer.*
5. *Il signor Liberman aiuterà Antonio con l'installazione di alcuni programmi.*
6. *Tutti ammiravano il suo computer.*

B. *Trasformare le frasi usando il pronome impersonale si.* (Rewrite the following sentences using the impersonal pronoun *si*.)

ESEMPIO: *Tutti sanno che in Italia i computer costano ancora molto.*
Si sa che in Italia i computer costano ancora molto.

1. *Andiamo all'università alle nove ogni mattina.*
2. *Non abbiamo bisogno del loro aiuto.*
3. *Ci colleghiamo all'Internet via modem.*
4. *Speriamo di riuscire a fare una visita virtuale della Scala di Milano.*
5. *Compriamo computer usati.*
6. *Quando uno è troppo stanco, non deve guidare.*

C. *Tradurre.* (Translate.)

1. Today one cannot live without a computer.
2. From the window one can see Pompeii.
3. One cannot always be happy.
4. This computer doesn't work very well.
5. With what we earn today, we cannot support a family.
6. They never help. They never lift a finger.
7. After what happened, I wanted to kick myself.
8. When Mr. Jones and Professor Mastri met, they shook hands.

LEGGIAMO!

LA NEVE DI VENEZIA *

In the following reading, writer Nantas Salvalaggio, a native of Venice, tells us that when it is snowing on the lagoon, the city of the doges is an enchantment.

Ci sono cose che un uomo deve vedere almeno una volta: la baia di New York all'alba,[1] dalla tolda[2] di una nave; il "raggio verde" che fende[3] le acque del Bosforo[4] al tramonto;[5] e infine Venezia d'inverno, sotto la neve. La neve veneziana è stata la prima meraviglia della mia infanzia. L'ho vista cadere per due giorni e due notti di seguito, più di mezzo secolo fa, dalla finestrina della mia camera da letto che buttava[6] sul Canal Grande. Ne cadde tanta che i metorologi la misurarono in due metri e più. Era il 1929, l'anno del "grande gelo." Io avevo quattro anni e per una settimana non andai all'asilo. Mia madre racconta che d'un tratto mi misi a saltare e a battere le mani: "Guarda che bello, piove zucchero!"

Agli occhi di un bambino, che non aveva mai visto la neve prima d'allora, pareva un diluvio universale di zucchero filato.[7] Quella che non cadeva in acqua, sciogliendosi e sprecandosi immediatamente, si accumulava senza posa sui tetti delle case e sui davanzali, sui campielli[8] e sulle fondamenta.[9] La cupola di rame[10] di San Simeone era diventata tutta bianca, simile a un panettone alla vaniglia. Bianchi erano i cappotti della gente che camminava per strada; bianchi i felzi[11] delle gondole e i tetti delle lance,[12] i fili della luce e i comignoli,[13] sui quali si posava intirizzito qualche nero colombo.

Ma come tutte le gioie dell'infanzia, anche quelle della prima neve durò poco, meno di quel che durano le rose, lo spazio di un sospiro.[14] Saggia, pratica, razionale, mia madre affondò un cucchiaino nella neve del davanzale e me la fece assaggiare: "Hai visto che non è zucchero?" disse in un tono di mezzo rimprovero: "Tutta questa neve è un disastro. Moriranno gli uccellini, e le mucche in campagna. E i bambini che non hanno una casa si ammaleranno . . . Altro che zucchero!"

* Nantas Salvalaggio, "La neve di Venezia," *Ulisse 2000* Anno VII, n. 45 (dicembre 1987), p. 8.

VOCABOLARIO

1. at dawn
2. from the deck
3. that cleaves
4. Bosphorus
5. at sunset
6. that opened onto
7. candy floss
8. on the squares
9. on the streets
10. copper dome
11. the cabins
12. motor launches
13. chimneys
14. the mere moment of a sigh

LEZIONE 16

A. DIALOGO

SFILATA DI MODA A MILANO

Federica e la madre sono al Teatro[1] Nuovo di Milano per assistere ad una sfilata di moda[2] che presenta la collezione[3] primavera-estate dell'anno prossimo.

FEDERICA: **Mamma, allora cosa sarà *in*[4] la prossima estate?**

MADRE: **Non lo so. Spero comunque che si ritorni al buon gusto[5] di un tempo.**

FEDERICA: **Ho sentito dire che ci vestiremo come facevano Brigitte Bardot e Audrey Hepburn molti anni fa . . .**

MADRE: **Come ai miei tempi, allora. Il nudo esagerato quindi non sarà più di moda.[6] Meno male!**

FEDERICA: **Sono sicura però che nessuno[7] rinuncerà a un po' di pelle[8] nuda. È importante essere raffinati e allo stesso tempo sexy.[9]**

MADRE: **Ecco . . . la sfilata sta per cominciare.**

Mentre Federica e la madre parlano, le modelle[10] cominciano[11] una dopo l'altra a sfilare. Una voce descrive i modelli.[12]

VOCE: **Alda Vestibene indossa uno splendido modello da[13] sera di Giorgio Armani. Abito di paillettes rosso, schiena scoperta . . .**

FEDERICA: **Ho l'impressione che gli abiti da sera siano intramontabili. Il taglio è così elegante.**

VOCE: **Modello di Valentino. Shorts[14] a fiorellini, giacchino baby[15] a roselline, guantino di pizzo. Sandali con tacchi a spillo . . .[16]**

MADRE: **Quei tacchi mi sembrano dei grattacieli.**

VOCE: **Fausta San Giovanni indossa uno spettacolare completo di Missoni. Ampia gonna "glossy" in un tessuto di cellophane. Borsetta a forma di cuore.**

FEDERICA: **Bellissimi!**

MADRE: **Ma che cosa vuol dire "glossy?"**

FEDERICA: **È una parola inglese. Vuol dire "lucente," "brillante," "lucido."**

VOCE: **Il prossimo modello è di Chiara Boni . . . Completino giallo sole[17] con hot pants e giacchina . . .**

FEDERICA: **Mamma, mi pare che questa modella nella cintura abbia una pistola.**

MADRE: **Sì, è strano che porti proprio una pistola. Chissà quale sarà il messaggio. È chiaro che la pistola è di plastica.**

FEDERICA: **Sembra che i colori per la prossima primavera-estate siano per lo più, soffici: rosa nuvola, bianco aurora . . . Sono i miei colori preferiti.**

MADRE: **Ed è anche sin[18] troppo evidente che molti degli abiti sono tagliati sotto il seno. Tutto è striminzito. Questi abiti paiono di una taglia[19] in meno di quella che ci vorrebbe.**

FEDERICA: **Mamma, non esagerare . . . Guarda come sta bene quell'abito a Mina Hirsch.**

MADRE: **Si, ma anche quell'abito è molto ridotto.**

FEDERICA: **Si dice che Mina negli ultimi tempi stia uscendo con un ragazzo italiano.**

MADRE: **Sì, è probabile che sia vero. Anch'io l'ho letto. Ho anche letto[20] che guadagna un sacco con questo lavoro.**

FEDERICA: **Eh sì . . . Sembra che guadagni circa trentadue milioni a sfilata. Si dice che negli ultimi giorni soltanto abbia partecipato ad una decina di défilé.**

MADRE: **I conti si fanno presto.**

VOCE: **Camicia Ferrè di organza bianca con pantaloni a campana verdi . . . Linea giovane Dolce & Gabbana: Renata Calzon porta una magliettina attillata sotto un meraviglioso giubbettino di plastica trasparente, gonna lunga di camoscio, sandali con megazeppa, borsettina con frange . . . Ed ora è la volta di questi bellissimi tailleur pantalone di maglia, con giacca doppiopetto su pantaloni a zampa d'elefante . . .**

MADRE: È ovvio che con questi modelli ritorniamo al passato, agli anni Sessanta e Settanta . . . Da quello che vedo sembra che dobbiamo anche cominciare a cotonarci i capelli.

FEDERICA: Anche tu, mamma, ti cotonavi i capelli?

MADRE: Sì, certamente. E li tenevo anch'io a posto come quella modella lì: con cerchietti del colore degli abiti.

VOCE: Terminiamo questa nostra sfilata primavera-estate con i costumi da bagno di Gianni Versace . . .

FEDERICA: Stupendi!

Fashion show in Milan

Federica and her mother are at the Teatro Nuovo in Milan to see the fashion show that will be presenting next year's spring-summer collection.

FEDERICA: Mother, so what will be "in" next summer?

MOTHER: I don't know. But I hope we return to the good taste of the olden days.

FEDERICA: I heard that we'll dress just as Brigitte Bardot and Audrey Hepburn did many years ago . . .

MOTHER: Like in my times, then. Exaggerated nudity will no longer be in style. Thank heavens!

FEDERICA: I'm sure, though, that no one will give up showing some bare skin. It's important to be refined and sexy at the same time.

MOTHER: Here . . . the fashion show is about to begin.

While Federica and her mother talk, the models begin to walk down the runway one after another. A voice describes the models.

VOICE: Alda Vestibene is wearing a splendid evening gown by Giorgio Armani. Sequined red suit, bare back . . .

FEDERICA: I get the feeling that evening gowns are timeless. The cut is so elegant.

VOICE: Fashion by Valentino. Flowery shorts, rose bolero jacket, lace gloves. High-heeled sandals . . .

MOTHER: Those heels seem like skyscrapers to me.

VOICE: Fausta San Giovanni is wearing a spectacular suit by Missoni. Wide "glossy" skirt in cellophane texture. Heart-shaped purse.

FEDERICA: Very beautiful!

MOTHER: What does "glossy" mean?

FEDERICA: It's an English word. It means "shiny," "brilliant," "bright."

VOICE: The next piece is by Chiara Boni . . . Suit in sun yellow with hot pants and bolero jacket . . .

FEDERICA: Mother, it looks like this model has a gun in her belt.

MOTHER: Yes, it is strange that she would be carrying a gun. I wonder what the message is. It's obvious it's a plastic gun.

FEDERICA: It seems that the colors for next spring-summer are more or less softer: pink cloud, white dawn . . . They are my favorite colors.

MOTHER: And it is evident that many of the suits are cut beneath the breast. Everything is so skimpy. These suits seem like they're one size too small.

FEDERICA: Mother, don't exaggerate . . . Look how nice that suit looks on Mina Hirsch!

MOTHER: Yes, but even that suit is very tight.

FEDERICA: They say that lately Mina has been going out with an Italian guy.

MOTHER: Yes, it is probably true. I read it too. I even read that she earns a bundle with this job.

FEDERICA: Yes . . . It seems that she earns about thirty-two million per fashion show. They say that within just the past few days she's appeared in about ten shows.

MOTHER: It's easy to do the math.

VOICE: Ferrè white organza shirt with green bell-bottom pants . . . Dolce & Gabbana junior line: Renata Calzon is wearing a small sweater tucked under a marvelous transparent plastic jacket, long suede skirt, big platform sandals, small purse with fringes . . . And next these beautiful tailored knit pants, with double-breasted jacket and palazzo pants.

MOTHER: It is obvious that with these models we are returning to years past, the sixties and seventies . . . From what I see it seems that we should also start to tease our hair.

FEDERICA: Did you tease your hair too, mother?

MOTHER: Yes, certainly. And I had it done like that model: with headbands the color of the suits.

VOICE: Our spring-summer fashion show ends here with bathing suits by Gianni Versace . . .

FEDERICA: Stupendous!

B. IN BREVE

1. Note that "to go to the theater" is rendered as *andare a teatro*.

2. A *sfilata di moda* is often referred to as *défilé*.

3. The word *collezione* is also used, for example, in *collezione di fran-cobolli* (stamp collection), *esemplare da collezione* (collector's piece), *una collezione di giornali* (a file of newspapers), *fare collezione di qualcosa* (to collect something).

4. *In* is used as an abbreviated form of *in voga* (in style).

5. *Gusto* is also used to signify "flavour." *Mi dia un gelato al gusto di fragola.* (I would like a strawberry ice cream.)

6. Some common expressions with *di moda* include *essere di moda* (to be in style), *andare di moda* (to be in style), *tornare di moda* (to come back in style), *uscire di moda, passare di moda* (to go out of style).

7. In this sentence note the placement of *nessuno*. When negative words precede the verb for emphasis, *non* is not needed.

8. The word *pelle* is also used for "leather."

9. The English words "sex-appeal" (in Italian also *fascino sessuale*), "sex movie" (also *film a luce rossa* or *film pornografico*), and "sex-symbol" (also *simbolo sessuale*) are also used in Italian.

10. A synonym is *indossatrice*.

11. All verbs indicating the beginning of an action, like *cominciare, incominciare, iniziare,* etc., require the preposition *a* when followed by an infinitive. *Il pubblico ha incominciato ad applaudire le modelle.* (The public started to applaud the models.) All verbs indicating the end of an action, like *finire, smettere, terminare,* etc., require the preposition *di* when followed by an infinitive. *Le modelle hanno finito di prepararsi per la sfilata.* (The models finished getting ready for the fashion show.)

12. Note these other uses of *modello: I modelli che ci avete inviati non ci piacciono.* (We don't like the samples you sent us.) *Questo vestito è un modello.* (This dress is an original.) *Lui è un modello di impiegato.* (He's a model employee.)

13. *Modello da sera* is the equivalent of *abito da sera. Abito da mezza sera* is used for "cocktail dress." When used before a noun the preposition *da* expresses purpose or manner. Some common expressions include *cane da caccia* (hunting dog), *macchina da scrivere* (typewriter), *costume da bagno* (bathing suit). For more information on the preposition *da* and its uses, refer to *Lezione 2.*

14. Together with the Italian *pantaloncini (corti)* or *calzoncini (corti),* the English counterpart "shorts" is also often used.

15. You may hear Italians also say "baby-food" *(cibo preparato per bambini)* and "baby-sitter" (*bambinaia* or *bambinaio).*

16. The preposition *a* is used to describe the noun. *La signora portava una giacca a quadri e il marito una cravatta a palline.* (The lady was wearing a plaid skirt and her husband a polka-dotted tie.)

17. Different shades of colors are often expressed by the color and a noun. For example, *verde prato, giallo limone, rosso fuoco, verde bandiera, verde bottiglia, verde pisello.* These "compound" colors do

not change in the plural. *Vorrei vedere quei due abiti verde pisello.* (I would like to see those two pea green outfits.)

18. *Sin (sino)* is interchangeable with *fin (fino)*. One may be preferred over the other to avoid cacophony.

19. Remember that when referring to "shoe size," *numero* is used. *Che numero di scarpe porti?* What's your shoe size?

20. Note that placing the subject immediately after *anche* puts emphasis on the subject.

C. GRAMMATICA E SUOI USI

1. *L'USO DEL CONGIUNTIVO* (THE USE OF THE SUBJUNCTIVE)

While the indicative mood is used to express certainty, and factual reality, the subjunctive mood allows you to add a personal perspective to the message. The subjunctive is primarily used in dependent clauses and is connected by *che* to an independent clause. When the verb or expression in the independent clause expresses opinion, doubt, uncertainty, emotion, advice, or volition, the subjunctive is used in the dependent clause.

Here is a list of verbs which require the subjunctive in a dependent clause: *aspettare* (to wait for), *avere paura* (to be afraid), *comandare* (to command), *credere* (to believe), *dubitare* (to doubt), *essere contento* (to be happy), *lasciare* (to allow), *ordinare* (to order), *pensare* (to think), *permettere* (to permit), *preferire* (to prefer), *proibire* (to prohibit), *proporre* (to propose), *sperare* (to hope), *suggerire* (to suggest), *volere* (to want).

Credo che questo vestito sia più adatto per l'occasione.
I believe that this suit is more appropriate for the occasion.

Dubito che tu senta più caldo in un vestito di cotone che in un vestito di lana.
I doubt that you'll be hotter in a cotton suit than in a wool suit.

Penso che in questo negozio di abbigliamento facciano lo sconto.
    I think that in this clothing store they offer discounts.

    Impersonal expressions implying doubt, necessity, desire, or emotion
    require the subjunctive: *è necessario che* (it is necessary that), *è possi-*
    bile che (it is possible that), *è probabile che* (it is probable that), *è meglio*
    che (it is better that), *è strano che* (it is strange that).

È probabile che quest'abito sia di velluto ricamato.
    It's probable that this dress is made of embroidered velvet.

È possibile che lei stia meglio con un abito confezionato su misura.
    It's possibile that she'll look better with a dress made to measure.

    Positive assertions do not require the subjunctive.

È vero che preferisco la linea Dolce & Gabbana.
    It's true that I prefer Dolce & Gabbana.

È ovvio che i modelli in quella boutique sono più costosi.
    It's obvious that clothes in that boutique are more expensive.

    The subjunctive is used after the following conjunctions: *affinché* (in
    order that, so that), *a meno che . . . non* (unless), *benché* (although), *a*
    condizione che/a patto che/purché (provided that), *prima che* (before),
    senza che (without).

Se vuoi, puoi venire al lavoro anche senza cravatta, purché sia vestito elegan-
temente.
    If you want, you can come to work without a tie, provided that you are
    elegantly dressed.

Sbrigati a togliere i panni dall'asciugatrice prima che si sgualciscano!
    Hurry to take the laundry out of the dryer before it wrinkles!

    If the verb in the dependent clause expresses a future action, the
    future tense may be used instead of the subjunctive, except for verbs
    expressing wish or command.

Credo che troverà quell'abito nella rivista di moda di questo mese.
    I think you will find that dress in this month's fashion magazine.

Spero che scelga quel maglione a lana d'angora.
I hope she'll choose that angora sweater.

When the subject of both verbs is the same, the infinitive is used instead of the subjunctive.

È tardi. Ho paura di arrivare in retardo alla sfilata.
It is late. I am afraid I'll be late for the fashion show.

2. *IL CONGIUNTIVO PRESENTE* (THE PRESENT SUBJUNCTIVE)

The present subjunctive is formed by adding the appropriate endings to the stem of the infinitive. Note that third conjugation verbs that take *-isc-* (like *capire*) in the present indicative also keep it in the present subjunctive. Also note that the ending of the first, second, and third person singular forms are identical and therefore the subject must be expressed if ambiguity arises.

	LAVORARE	VEDERE	PARTIRE	FINIRE
io	lavori	veda	parta	finisca
tu	lavori	veda	parta	finisca
lui/lei/Lei	lavori	veda	parta	finisca
noi	lavoriamo	vediamo	partiamo	finiamo
voi	lavoriate	vediate	partiate	finiate
loro/Loro	lavorino	vedano	partano	finiscano

È necessario che tu porti questi pantaloni di lino in lavanderia.
It is necessary that you bring these linen pants to the laundry.

Credo che sia importante portare giacca e cravatta se si lavora a contatto con il pubblico.
I believe it is important to dress in a jacket and tie if working in contact with the public.

Verbs that end in *-care* or *-gare* insert an *h* between the stem and the endings. Verbs that end in *-ciare, -giare,* or *-gliare* drop the *-i* of the stem before adding the subjunctive endings, unless the *-i* is stressed (like *inviare*).

Credo che lei cerchi una giacca a doppiopetto.
I believe she is looking for a double-breasted jacket.

Credo che Loretta consigli di portare delle scarpe di lustrino con quel vestito di sera.
I believe Loretta recommends wearing patent leather shoes with that evening dress.

Some irregular verbs are: *avere, essere, dare, sapere, stare, andare, dovere, uscire, bere, dire, fare, potere, volere.* For their conjugations see Appendix C.

D. PAROLE! PAROLE! PAROLE!

The word "sacco" appears in many Italian idiomatic expressions.

Loro hanno un sacco di soldi.
They have a lot of money.

Roberta mi ha detto un sacco di bugie.
Roberta told me a pack of lies.

Hanno colto il ladro con le mani nel sacco.
They caught the thief red-handed.

Quei loschi individui volevano mettermi nel sacco.
Those shady characters wanted to cheat me.

Ce ne tornammo con le pive nel sacco dalla svendita.
We returned empty-handed from the sale.

Quei due se ne dissero un sacco e una sporta.
Those two called each other all sorts of names.

Gino fa tutto con la testa nel sacco.
Gino does everything thoughtlessly.

È stato lui a vuotare il sacco.
It was he who spilled the beans.

Pierino, questa non è farina del tuo sacco.
Pierino, this is not your own work.

296

E. L'ANGOLO DEGLI AFFARI

LA MODA IN ITALIA (FASHION IN ITALY)

The "Made in Italy" label on clothing and accessories is a symbol of quality and status in countries throughout the world. Since the world-wide recession of the seventies, Italy has managed to make a name for itself on an international level. In fact, although Italians are great supporters of Italian designers, the eighties and nineties have been especially lucrative for the Italian fashion industry in large part due to exports. The industry's various sectors are almost single-handedly responsible for the economic prosperity of the country. While many industries seem to be on the wane or maintaining a steady pace, the fashion industry seems to be constantly expanding. Second only to the production of office machinery and precision instruments, the combination of leather, footwear and clothing, and textile industries are the most lucrative in Italy. During the 1990s, Versace, Gucci, Dolce & Gabbana, Fendi, and Armani, to name just a few, have become household names on just about every continent.

Milan is the fashion capital of Italy. Although a small percentage of design houses are based in Rome, most prefer Milan. This is in large part due to the fact that Milan is the focus of international attention for its spring and fall runway shows, which take place in March and October. Milan's reputation as a fashion capital is not limited to Italy. Many of the world's finest designers are based there. In recent years, even designers originating from other countries, such as Rifat Ozbek, have spent time in Milan. Furthermore, the house of Byblos has made this cosmopolitan city their permanent base.

Italy is widely known for its knitwear. Thanks to houses such as Missoni, whose quality and innovation have brought Italian knits to the forefront of the market, discriminating consumers have come to appreciate this product. And of course, when one speaks of knitwear one must mention Treviso's Benetton. This multinational corporation has proven that Italian creativity and know-how in this sector can be tremendously successful. Although Benetton's main factory is in Treviso, its main operational centers are spread throughout Italy, France, and Spain. Benetton products can be purchased in 120 countries at 7,000 outlets. This strong presence outside of Europe is largely responsible for its success. Throughout the past decade, it has exported over

70 percent of its production, and has consolidated a net income of 210 billion lire.

In order to be more competitive on the international as well as domestic markets several Italian designers have expanded their base by introducing lower-priced lines. Versace's Versus line and Armani's Emporio Armani are but two of the lines now competing on international markets with comparable lines of other designers such as America's Calvin Klein and France's Jean-Paul Gaultier. Such shrewd business ventures have brought the highly sought-out Italian prêt-à-porter (ready-to-wear) to a greater number of people around the world.

ESERCIZI

A. *Completare le frasi usando il congiuntivo presente. Scegliere fra i seguenti verbi.* (Fill in the blanks with the present subjunctive of the appropriate verb. Choose from among the following verbs.)

essere   ritornare   avere   venire
stare   andare   cominciare

1. *Io spero che con la moda si _____ al buon gusto di un tempo.*
2. *Mi pare che questa modella _____ una pistola nella cintura.*
3. *Si dice che Linda _____ uscendo con un ragazzo italiano.*
4. *Mi sembra che anche loro _____ con noi alla sfilata di moda.*
5. *Prima che tu _____ al cinema, vorrei parlarti un momento.*
6. *Voglio che voi _____ subito a studiare.*
7. *Sebbene noi _____ ricchi, non spendiamo molto.*

B. *Completare le seguenti frasi usando il congiuntivo o l'indicativo. Indovinare il verbo dal contesto della frase.* (Fill in the blanks with the appropriate form of the subjunctive or the indicative. Choose a verb which makes sense according to the context of each sentence.)

1. *È strano che quella modella _____ in tasca proprio una pistola.*
2. *Tutti sanno che quest'estate noi ci _____ come Brigitte Bardot e Audrey Hepburn.*
3. *È evidente che questi vestiti non _____ più di moda.*
4. *Mi dispiace che tu non _____ venire con noi a teatro.*
5. *Sono sicurissimo che quello _____ un modello di Valentino.*

6. *Lo faccio io, a meno che non* _____ *farlo tu.*
7. *Anche se a te non* _____, *quell'abito è molto bello.*

C. *Formare delle frasi con le seguenti parole.* (Form complete sentences using the elements provided.)

1. *io/avere/impressione che/abiti da sera/essere/intramontabili*
2. *noi/essere/contenti/che/loro/stare/bene*
3. *io/preferire che/tu/comprare/questa/borsetta*
4. *miei/genitori/volere che/io/non/mi/cotonare/capelli*
5. *io/sapere che/questa/modella/guadagnare/dieci/milioni/ dollari/a/sfilata*
6. *tu/pensare che/questo/modello/Valentino/ispirarsi/film/Amy Hickering?*
7. *benché/questi/pantaloni/zampa/elefante/costare/molto/io li comprare/lo stesso*

D. *Tradurre.* (Translate.)

1. It's obvious that she doesn't like these sandals.
2. Although that sweater is beautiful, I will not buy it.
3. I hope I can go to the fashion show tonight.
4. She's wearing a sweater, a long suede skirt, and a beautiful pair of brown sandals.
5. We caught the thieves red-handed.
6. They told me a pack of lies. I don't want to see them anymore.
7. It was John who spilled the beans.
8. I believe she is wearing a white organza skirt.
9. That linen suit looks very nice on you.
10. I think a suit and a tie would be more appropriate.

LEZIONE 17

A. DIALOGO

UN COLLOQUIO D'ASSUNZIONE

Michael O'Connor ha inviato una domanda d'impiego[1] e il suo curriculum vitae alla ditta Rossi S.p.A.[2] di Milano, che cerca un direttore delle vendite[3] con esperienza commerciale e amministrativa. Il dottor[4] Neri, direttore del personale della ditta, lo ha convocato per un colloquio selettivo.

NERI: **Il dottor O'Connor?**

O'CONNOR: **Sì, piacere.**

NERI: **Prego, si accomodi.**

O'CONNOR: **Grazie. Molto gentile.**

NERI: **Nel curriculum[5] vedo che Lei è italo-canadese.[6] Quando Le ho parlato al telefono non avrei mai immaginato che Lei fosse di origine italiana.**

O'CONNOR: **Mia madre è italiana. Mio padre è irlandese.**

NERI: **Abita in Canada?**

O'CONNOR: **Sì. Abito a Toronto.**

NERI: **Nell'annuncio del posto ha notato che richiediamo la residenza in zona?[7]**

O'CONNOR: **Sì. Va benissimo. Infatti ho intenzione di trasferirmi[8] a Milano.**

NERI: **Bene. Allora dal suo curriculum risulta che è laureato in economia e commercio.**

O'CONNOR: **Sì, esattamente. Mi sono laureato in economia e commercio presso[9] l'Università di Toronto nel 1987.[10]**

NERI: **Lei sembra avere i requisiti[11] da noi richiesti. Come sa, cerchiamo un direttore delle vendite con una vasta esperienza commerciale e amministrativa . . . È importante avere una buona conoscenza dell'inglese e del tedesco . . . Deve essere** disponibile a viaggiare . . . Dovrà occuparsi più che altro della Lombardia e delle regioni limitrofe . . . Come Le dicevo prima richiediamo anche la residenza in zona . . . Desidereremmo infine che il candidato avesse un'esperienza consolidata di almeno cinque anni nell'industria alimentare. E negli ultimi dieci anni la Sua attività professionale si è svolta proprio in questo settore.[12]

O'CONNOR: Sì, dal 1987 al 1990 ho lavorato presso la Bertolli U.S.A. come agente[13] di vendita. Attualmente[14] lavoro come direttore delle vendite presso la National Cheese Company Limited di Toronto, una delle più grandi aziende produttrici di formaggio del Canada, ma il mio incarico[15] termina alla fine di dicembre. Penso di avere un'ottima conoscenza dell'amministrazione aziendale e delle vendite.

NERI: Come mai il Suo impiego con la National Cheese termina alla fine di dicembre?

O'CONNOR: Beh . . . mi sono dimesso in quanto, come Le dicevo, intendo seriamente trasferirmi in Italia. Per di più questa nuova esperienza mi permetterebbe di crescere sia intellettualmente che dal punto di vista professionale.

NERI: Benissimo. Lei ha lavorato anche all'estero?

O'CONNOR: Sì, infatti la mia esperienza si è esplicata in gran parte anche fuori del Canada. Come Le ho già accennato, ho lavorato negli Stati Uniti.

NERI: Lei parla molto bene l'italiano.

O'CONNOR: Beh, parlo correntemente sia l'italiano che l'inglese e il tedesco.

NERI: È coniugato?

O'CONNOR: Sì, sono sposato.

NERI: Con prole?

O'CONNOR: No, non abbiamo ancora bambini.

NERI: Sua moglie verrebbe dunque anche a vivere in Italia?

O'CONNOR: Certamente. Non vede l'ora!

NERI: Suppongo che Lei sappia lavorare con i computer?

O'CONNOR: Sì . . . Ho seguito diversi corsi di informatica e ho lavorato non poco con i computer.

NERI: È disposto a viaggiare?

O'CONNOR: Sì, certamente. Mi piace molto viaggiare.

NERI: Come ha letto nell'annuncio, questo posto Le offrirà grandi opportunità di sviluppo professionale, una retribuzione decisamente incentivante, l'auto aziendale, i rimborsi spese ed un ottimo pacchetto assicurativo. Cosa gliene pare?

O'CONNOR: La cosa mi interessa molto. Come Le ho detto ho intenzione di dimettermi dal mio impiego attuale. E fortunatamente a mia moglie non dispiace affatto l'idea di venire ad abitare a Milano.

NERI: Se l'assumessimo,[16] potrebbe iniziare a lavorare a gennaio?

O'CONNOR: Sì, potrei sicuramente farcela.

NERI: Vorrei allora ricordarLe ciò che Le si offre: opportunità di sviluppo professionale, l'auto aziendale, i rimborsi spese, un pacchetto assicurativo molto incentivante . . . Prima di farLa andare, vorrei anche darLe un'idea dello stipendio [17] che percepirà nel caso dovessimo offrirLe il posto. Infine, in un modo o nell'altro, ci faremo presto sentire telefonicamente. E Lei ha qualche domanda da porci?

A JOB INTERVIEW

Michael O'Connor has sent a job application and his resumé to the firm Rossi S.p.A. in Milan, which is looking for a sales manager with commercial and administrative experience. Doctor Neri, personnel director of the firm, has called him for a meeting.

NERI: Mr. O'Connor?

O'CONNOR: Yes. I'm pleased to meet you.

NERI: Please, make yourself comfortable.

O'CONNOR: Thank you. Very kind.

NERI: In your resumé I see that you are Italian-Canadian. When I first spoke to you on the phone, I didn't know that you were of Italian origin.

O'CONNOR: My mother is Italian. My father is Irish.

NERI: Do you live in Canada?

O'CONNOR: Yes. I live in Toronto.

NERI: In the ad posted, did you notice that we are looking for a resident of the area?

O'CONNOR: Yes. In fact I intend to move to Milan. That wouldn't be a problem at all.

NERI: Very good. Now, from your resumé I see that you graduated with a degree in Commerce.

O'CONNOR: Yes, exactly. I graduated in Commerce from the University of Toronto in 1987.

NERI: You seem to have all the qualifications that we are looking for. As you know, we're looking for a sales manager with commercial and administrative experience . . . Knowledge of both English and German is essential . . . The candidate must be willing to travel . . . and will be responsible mainly for Lombardy and adjoining regions. We would also prefer the candidate to have at least five years of consolidated experience in the food industry. And in the last ten years your professional activities have been right in that area.

O'CONNOR: Yes, from 1987 to 1990 I worked at Bertolli U.S.A. as a sales representative. At the moment I work as a sales manager at the National Cheese Company Limited in Toronto, one of the largest cheese manufacturers in Canada, but my position ends at the end of December. I think I have an excellent understanding of both administration and sales.

NERI: Why will your position with National Cheese be terminated at the end of December?

O'CONNOR: Well . . . I resigned because, as I told you, I seriously intend to move to Italy. Also, I feel that a new position like this one will offer me the opportunity to grow intellectually and professionally.

NERI: I see. You have worked abroad?

O'CONNOR: Yes, in fact a lot of my experience has been gained outside of Canada, too. As I said, I have worked in the United States.

NERI: You speak Italian very well.

O'CONNOR: Well, I speak Italian fluently, as well as English and German.

NERI: Are you married?

O'CONNOR: Yes, I am married.

NERI: With children?

O'CONNOR: No, we don't have any children yet.

NERI: Your wife would also come to live in Italy?

O'CONNOR: Certainly. She's looking forward to it.

NERI: I assume you know how to work with computers.

O'CONNOR: Yes . . . I took a few computer science courses, and of course I've worked rather extensively with computers.

NERI: Are you willing to travel?

O'CONNOR: Yes, certainly. I like traveling very much.

NERI: As you read in the ad, this position will offer you many opportunities to develop professionally, a decidedly competitive salary, a company car, an expense account, and a benefits package. How does it sound to you?

O'CONNOR: I'm most certainly interested. As I said, I'm planning on leaving my current position in December, and luckily my wife likes very much the idea of living in Milan.

NERI: If we hire you, would you be able to start in January?

O'CONNOR: I don't see any problem with that.

NERI: Well then, I would like to remind you what it is we offer: an opportunity to grow professionally, a company car, allowances, a benefits plan which is unequaled . . . Before I let you go, I would also like to give you an idea of the salary you would receive in the event that we were to offer you the position. Whatever our decision, we will contact you by phone shortly. Do you have any questions you would like to ask us?

B. IN BREVE

1. Note that "an application for employment" is rendered in Italian as *una domanda d'impiego*. The word "application" is translated also as *applicazione*. *Questo lavoro richiede una grande applicazione.* (This work requires close application.)

2. Società per Azioni (S.p.A.): a joint-stock company. Just as in English, in Italian there are different terms for different kinds of firms, partnerships, and corporations. Some of these include a *società in nome collettivo* (a general partnership, either a general or unlimited partnership); a *società per azioni a proprietario unico* (a sole corporation). A *società di persone* is a partnership or a non-stock corporation; a *società in compartecipazione* is a joint venture; a *società a responsabilità limitata* is a limited company, whereas a *società a responsabilità illimitata* is an unlimited company; a *società a partecipazione statale* is a government-controlled company; a *società multinazionale* is a corporation or a multinational company; a *società controllata* is a controlled company, whereas a *società di controllo* is a controlling company. A *società madre* or *società capogruppo* is a parent company, and a *società consociata* is a subsidiary or sister company. A *società autorizzata* is an incorporated association, and finally, a *società non registrata* is an unincorporated association.

3. Also *direttore vendite*. Study the following: *direttore alle vendite di zona* (area sales manager), *direttore dei lavori* (works manager), *direttore del marketing* (marketing director), *direttore del personale* (personnel manager), *direttore della produzione* (production manager), *direttore di banca* (bank manager), *direttore di stabilimento* (plant manager), *direttore generale alle vendite* (general sales manager).

4. The title of Dr. is given to any individual that has completed a university degree.

5. In English *curriculum* is also rendered as "record." (*Il signor Centuori ha un eccellente curriculum come dirigente.* (Mr. Centuori has an excellent record as an executive.)

6. Compound nouns and adjectives of nationality change only the second part in the plural formation. *Negli Stati Uniti molti italo-americani sono presidenti di ditte prestigiose.* (In the United States many Italian-Americans are presidents of prestigious firms.)

7. Note that the definite article is omitted just as in expressions such as *in città, in biblioteca, in paese.* If the place is modified then the definite article is used. *Vuole che io mi trasferisca nella zona periferica della città.* (He wants me to move to the suburban area of the city.)

8. *Trasferirsi* is "to move." Remember the Italian verb *muovere* cannot be used with the meaning of "to relocate, to change job, to change house."

9. *Presso* can also mean "with" and "for." *Lavoro presso una ditta tedesca.* (I work with a German firm.) *Sono ragioniere presso il signor Bartolomei.* (I am a bookeeper for Mr. Bartolomei.) *Presso* can also mean "nearby, near, close at hand." *Abito presso il lago.* (I live close to the lake.) Often it translates "among." *Era comune bere del vino presso i popoli antichi.* (It was common to drink wine among the ancient people.)

10. Note that the year is always accompanied by the defininte article. When making reference to an action occurring in a certain year, we use the compound preposition *nel. Nel 1996 ho iniziato un nuovo impiego presso un'azienda francese.* (In 1996 I started a new job with a French firm.) When referring to the year (without using the preposition *in*), the definite article precedes the year. *Il 1986 è stato un anno con tanta disoccupazione.* (1986 was a year with a lot of unemployment.)

11. "Qualification" can also be translated as *qualifica* or *titolo* (*qualifiche personali* = personal qualifications) *Lei non ha i titoli per quella carica.* (You don't have the qualifications for that office.) "Prerequisite" is rendered in Italian as *prerequisito indispensabile.*

12. Study these other words with *settore: il settore degli affari immobiliari* (the real estate sector), *il settore dei trasporti* (the transport industry), *il settore dela distribuzione/il settore terziario* (the services sector), *il settore economico* (product sector), *il settore edilizio*

(the building sector), *il settore privato* (the private sector), *il settore pubblico* (the public sector).

13. Study these other words with *agente: agente d'assicurazione* (insurance agent), *agente di cambio* (stock broker), *agente di pubblicità* (advertising agent), *agente doganale* (customs agent), *agente immobiliare* (real estate agent), *agente per gli acquisti* (purchasing agent), *agente pubblicitario* (press agent/advertising agent).

14. The cognate English word "actually" is translated as *in realtà, in verità, veramente, realmente. Ti trasferisci veramente a Milano?* (Are you actually moving to Milan?)

15. *Incarico* can also be used to mean "duty," "task," "charge," "commission." *Ho l'incarico di rispondere a coloro che hanno inviato un curriculum vitae.* (I am in charge of answering all those who sent in a resumé.) *Mi è stato dato un incarico di fiducia.* (I have been entrusted with a delicate task.)

16. Note that here *assumere* means "to hire," not "to assume." In Italian "to assume" is translated as *assumere* when saying, for example, "He assumed the direction of that business." (*Ha assunto la direzione di quell'azienda.*) "To assume" is also rendered as *presumere* or *supporre.* (Let us assume that . . . = *Supponiamo che . . .*)

17. A *stipendio* (salary/pay) can be *base* (*stipendio base* = base salary), *iniziale* (*stipendio iniziale* = commencing salary), *netto* (*stipendio netto* = take-home pay), *pensionabile* (*stipendio pensionabile* = pensionable salary).

C. GRAMMATICA E SUOI USI

1. *IL CONGIUNTIVO IMPERFETTO* (THE IMPERFECT SUBJUNCTIVE)

The *imperfetto del congiuntivo* (imperfect subjunctive) is formed by adding the appropriate endings to the stem of the infinitive. Note that except for the characteristic vowel of the conjugation (*-are, -ere, -ire*), the endings are the same for all three conjugations. Also notice that there is an -*ss* in all the endings except for the second person plural -*ste*. Few verbs are irregular in the imperfect subjunctive. The most common are *essere, dare, stare,* and *fare* (For their conjugations refer to Appendix C.)

	LAVORARE	VEDERE	PARTIRE
io	lavorassi	vedessi	partissi
tu	lavorassi	vedessi	partissi
lui/lei/Lei	lavorasse	vedesse	partisse
noi	lavorassimo	vedessimo	partissimo
voi	lavoraste	vedeste	partiste
loro/Loro	lavorassero	vedessero	partissero

Avevo paura che assumessero qualcuno senza le qualifiche necessarie.
I was afraid they would hire someone without the necessary qualifications.

Ero contento che il direttore gli offrisse quel posto.
I was happy that the director offered him that position.

The imperfect subjunctive expresses uncertainty, doubt, emotion, possibility, or opinion when the verb in the independent clause is in a past tense. It conveys an action that is simultaneous to the action of the independent clause, or which takes place after the action of the independent clause. In essence, it is the subjunctive counterpart of the imperfect of the indicative mood.

Pensavo che richiedessero almeno tre anni di esperienza nell'industria tessile.
I thought they required at least three years' experience in the textile industry.

Non era sicura se offrissero opportunità di sviluppo professionale.
She was not sure if they offered professional growth opportunities.

If the verb of the independent clause is in the conditional, the imperfect subjunctive is also required. (See *Lezione 11* for a review of the conditional.)

Preferirei che tu non presentassi domanda per questo posto.
I would prefer that you not apply for this position.

Mi trasferirei a Roma, se mi offrissero i rimborsi spese.
If they offered to reimburse my expenses, I would move to Rome.

Se Paolo mandasse il curriculum vitae, lo convocherebbero per un colloquio d'assunzione.
If Paolo were to send in his resumé, they would call him in for a job interview.

2. *I DOPPI NEGATIVI* (DOUBLE NEGATIVES)

A simple negative statement is made by placing *non* before the verb. If there are object pronouns, they are placed between *non* and the verb.

Non abbiamo ricevuto il suo curriculum.
We didn't receive his resumé.

L'inglese? No, non lo parla correntemente.
English? No, he does not speak it fluently.

Other negative words may be used in conjunction with *non* for more specific negation. Here are the most common:

non . . . niente, non . . . nulla	nothing
non . . . nessuno	no one, not . . . anyone
non . . . nessun/nessuno/nessuna/nessun'	not . . . any
non . . . più	no longer, no more
non . . . affatto	not at all
non . . . ancora	not yet
non . . . né . . . né	neither . . . nor
non . . . mai	never
non . . . mica (familar)	not at all, not in the least
non . . . che	only
non . . . neanche, non . . . nemmeno, non . . . neppure	not even, not either

Il direttore del personale non ha ancora convocato nessuno per un colloquio selettivo.
The personnel director still has not called anyone for an interview.

Il nuovo amministratore non ha neanche esperienza commerciale e amministrativa.
The new director doesn't even have commercial or administrative experience.

Questo tipo di lavoro non mi interessa affatto.
This kind of work doesn't interest me at all.

Come mai non avete ancora assunto nessuno per il nuovo posto?
Why on earth haven't you hired anybody for the new position?

Non ho nemmeno la più pallida idea di che salario potrebbero offrire.
I haven't even the faintest idea of the salary they could offer.

When these negative words precede the verb, *non* is omitted. This structure is used for emphasis, when negating the subject, or when the negative word itself is the subject.

Nessuno riuscirà mai a convincermi che non ha seguito dei corsi d'informatica.
No one will ever convince me that he did not take any computer courses.

Nemmeno lui ha capito che Mario è stato licenziato.
Not even he understood that Mario has been fired.

With compound tenses, *ancora, mai, mica, affatto,* and *più* are usually placed between the auxiliary and the past participle.

Non abbiamo mai sentito parlare di questa ditta.
We never heard of this firm.

Il datore di lavoro non ha affatto offerto un salario così competivo.
The employer did not at all offer such a competitive salary.

The adjective *nessun/nessuno/nessuna/nessun'* is always used before a singular noun and has the same forms as the indefinite article *un/uno/una/un'*. Its form depends on the gender and first letter of the noun it is modifying.

Nessun candidato aveva un'esperienza consolidata da almeno cinque anni.
No (not one) candidate had at least five years of consolidated experience.

As a pronoun *nessuno* (no one, not . . . anyone) is invariable.

Nessuno vede l'importanza di avere un direttore delle vendite che si occupi di questa regione.
No one sees the importance of having a sales manager for these regions.

When *niente, nulla,* and *nessuno* are used in questions the *non* is omitted.

Hanno annunciato niente ai candidati?
Did they announce anything to the candidates?

Hanno deciso nulla per quanto riguarda il salario?
Did they decide anything with regards to the salary?

Hanno trovato nessuno che voglia fare del volontariato per quell'agenzia?
Did they find anyone who wants to volunteer for that agency?

Certain negative expressions *(nessuno, niente, nulla, mai)* can be used on their own as one word answers.

Chi assumerebbe qualcuno che non abbia conoscenza del settore? —Nessuno.
Who would hire someone who doesn't have any experience in the field? —No one.

Ha lavorato come direttore delle vendite? —Mai!
Have you ever worked as sales manager? —Never!

The English "not . . . any" is expressed by *non* + verb + plural noun or by *non* + verb + singular noun preceded by the suitable form of *nessuno*. This latter form emphasizes "not a single."

Non assumo persone delle quali non mi fido.
I don't hire people I don't trust.

Non assunse nessuna persona senza aver prima guardato il curriculum.
He didn't hire a single person without having first looked at his curriculum vitae.

D. PAROLE! PAROLE! PAROLE!

The word *mai* (never, ever) appears in many expressions. Note, however, that it isn't always translated as "never" or "ever".

Come mai non sei venuto alla festa?
Why on earth didn't you come to the party?

Caso mai telefonasse, puoi dirgli che l'appuntamento è alle due?
If he should phone, could you tell him that the appointment is for two o'clock?

Ora più che mai abbiamo bisogno di risparmiare.
Now more than ever we need to save.

Mai più telefonerò a quella persona.
Never again will I phone that person.

Mai e poi mai ti porterò con me.
I'll never ever take you with me.

Non si sa mai!
You never can tell!

Non sia mai!
May it never happen! (Let that never be!)

Non lo vediamo quasi mai!
We hardly ever see him!

Che mai avrà fatto?
What on earth has he done?

Io farei tutto. Questo mai!
I would be prepared to do anything but that!

Sono quanto mai soddisfatto!
I have never been so satisfied!

Quanto è mai sciocco!
He's so silly!

Meglio tardi che mai!
Better late than never!

E. L'ANGOLO DEGLI AFFARI

1) *ANNUNCI DI LAVORO* (JOB ADS)

DIRETTORE AMMINISTRATIVO E FINANZIARIO

assume multinazionale leader settore.
Richiesta esperienza almeno quinquennale analoga posizione.
Gradita provenienza settore industriale,
tematiche reporting e controllo gestione.
Indispensabile buona conoscenza
lingua inglese e francese.
Inquadramento, retribuzione,
sviluppo carriera di sicuro interesse.

Leading multinational corporation seeks
ADMINISTRATION AND FINANCE MANAGER.

At least five years' experience required.
Industrial sector and management experience preferred.
Competent knowledge of English and French essential.
Competitive placement, remuneration,
possibility of advancement.

Ingegnere elettronico

*con qualificata esperienza
nel settore brevettuale.*

Electrical engineer

with relevent experience
in the field of patents.

*Redattori specialisti programmazione Pc/Lan, database,
Networking, As/400 cerca editore riviste informatica.*

Editorial staff specializing in PC/Lan, database, Networking,
As/400 programming sought by publisher of periodicals.

AZIENDA LEADER

settore alimentare, zona ovest Milano, cerca direttore delle vendite dinamico con vasta esperienza commerciale ed amministrativa.

Si richiede:

> *Età: 30\40 anni*
> *Titolo di studio: diploma o laurea*
> *buona conoscenza inglese e tedesco*
> *uso Pc e gestionali*
> *residenza in zona*
> *esperienza consolidata da almeno 5 anni*
> *massima serietà*
> *spiccato orientamento al conseguimento di risultati ambiziosi*
> *disponibilità a viaggiare*

Si offre:

> *opportunità di sviluppo professionale*
> *retribuzione incentivante*
> *auto aziendale*
> *rimborsi spese*
> *un pacchetto assicurativo di sicuro interesse*

Inutile rispondere se non in possesso dei requisiti richiesti.

Si prega di inviare dettagliato curriculum, citando il Rif. 919 sul cv e sulla busta, per espresso (o fax: 02\8695555) al ns. indirizzo:

Rossi S.p.A.
Ufficio del Personale
Corso Mazzini, 50
20100 Milano

314

LEADING FIRM

Food sector, area of west Milan, seeks dynamic sales manager with vast commercial and administrative experience.

Qualifications sought:

Age: 30–40 years

Education: secondary school diploma or university degree

Good knowledge of English and German

Knowledge of PC and systems management

Residence in area

minimum 5 years' relevant experience

very serious

goal-oriented and ambitious

willing to travel

We offer:

opportunity for professional growth

motivating salary

company car

expense account

excellent benefits package

Only qualified applicants need apply.

Send detailed resumé by Special delivery (or fax: 02\8695555) to:

Rossi S.p.A.

Personnel Office

Corso Mazzini, 50

20100 Milano

Mark resumé and envelope with reference number 919.

2. LETTERA DI RICHIESTA DI IMPIEGO (COVER LETTER)

Michael O'Connor
1530 Bloor Street
Toronto, Ontario
Canada M9S 1A1

Toronto, 28 novembre 1998

Spettabile Direzione Rossi S.p.A.
Ufficio del Personale
Corso Mazzini, 50
20100 Milano

Spettabile Ufficio,

in riferimento al Vostro annuncio sul Corriere della Sera del 25 novembre (Rif. 919), mi permetto di presentare domanda per il posto in questione.

Ho 35 anni, sono italo-canadese e mi sono laureato in economia e commercio presso l'Università di Toronto nel 1987. Come potrete constatare dal curriculum allegato, la mia attività professionale si svolge da oltre 10 anni nell'industria alimentare. La mia esperienza si è esplicata per lo più fuori d'Italia, prima negli Stati Uniti e poi in Canada.

Ora, avendo seriamente intenzione di trasferirmi in Italia, in base all'esperienza accumulata e alle mie competenze ritengo di possedere un'ottima conoscenza del Vostro settore.

Faccio presente di parlare correntemente sia l'inglese che l'italiano e il tedesco. Attualmente lavoro presso la National Cheese Company di Toronto, ma il mio incarico termina alla fine di dicembre.

Ho in programma, per il prossimo gennaio, un viaggio in Italia e se lo ritenete opportuno, sarei felice di incontrarVi. Nel frattempo, voglio comunque ringraziarVi per l'attenzione accordatami e, in attesa di un Vostro cortese cenno di riscontro, Vi prego di gradire i miei più distinti saluti.

Michael O'Connor

dott. Michael O'Connor

Allegato: curriculum vitae

Michael O'Connor
1530 Bloor Street
Toronto, Ontario
Canada M9S 1A1

Toronto, November 28, 1998

Rossi S.p.A.
Personnel Office
Corso Mazzini, 50
20100 Milano

To Whom It May Concern:

In reference to your ad in the November 25 edition of the *Corriere della Sera* (ref. no. 919), I would like to submit my application for the position in question.

I am a 35-year-old Italian-Canadian with a degree in Commerce and Economics from the University of Toronto (1987). As you can see from my resumé (attached), I have over ten years' professional experience in the food industry. I have acquired experience mainly outside of Italy, first in the United States and then in Canada.

I am now seriously considering moving to Italy. Based on the experience I have accumulated and on my qualifications, I believe I possess an excellent knowledge of your sector.

I speak English, Italian, and German fluently. I am presently employed by National Cheese Company in Toronto, but my contract terminates at the end of December.

I intend to travel to Italy this January. If you are interested, I would be pleased to meet with you. In the meantime, I wish to thank you for your time and extend my best regards to you.

Sincerely,

Michael O'Connor

Michael O'Connor
resumé attached

3. CURRICULUM VITAE (RESUMÉ)

CURRICULUM VITAE

Michael O'Connor

Data di nascita:	*11 luglio 1963*
Nazionalità:	*canadese e italiana*
Stato civile:	*coniugato*
Attività professionali:	*1987–1990* *Agente di vendita* *Bertolli U.S.A.* *201 East 50th Street* *New York, New York 10022*
	1990–1998 *Direttore delle vendite* *National Cheese Co. Ltd.* *111 Rivermede Rd.* *Toronto, Ontario* *Canada M9L 2G2*
Lingue conosciute:	*inglese (lingua madre)* *italiano (ottima conoscenza)* *tedesco (buono scritto e parlato)*
Studi:	*1987* *Laurea in economia e commercio* *Università di Toronto, Canada*
Referenze:	*disponibili su richiesta*
Indirizzo:	*1530 Bloor Street* *Toronto, Ontario* *Canada M9S 1A1*
Telefono:	*416-978-3313*
Fax:	*416-978-3314*
E-mail:	*oconnor@leader.com*

RESUMÉ

Michael O'Connor

Date of Birth: July 11, 1963

Nationality: Canadian and Italian

Marital Status: Married

Job Experience: 1987–1990
Sales Agent
Bertolli U.S.A.
201 East 50th Street
New York, New York 10022

1990–1998
Sales Manager
National Cheese Co. Ltd.
111 Rivermede Rd.
Toronto, Ontario
Canada M9L 2G2

Languages: English (mother tongue)
Italian (excellent knowledge)
German (good writing and speaking skills)

Education: 1987
B.Com.
University of Toronto, Canada

References: Available upon request

Address: 1530 Bloor Street
Toronto, Ontario
Canada M9S 1A1

Telephone: (416) 978-3313

Fax: (416) 978-3314

E-mail: oconnor@leader.com

A. *Completare le frasi con un verbo al congiuntivo imperfetto.* (Complete each sentence with the correct form of the imperfect subjunctive.)

1. *Dove lavorava il signor O'Connor prima di lavorare in Italia?*
   —*Penso che* _____ *in Canada.*
2. *Cosa faceva il dottor Neri quando tu hai telefonato?* —*Credo che*
   _____ *parlando con la segretaria.*
3. *C'erano molte persone in ufficio?* —*No. Mi pare che ci* _____
   soltanto il direttore.
4. *A quel tempo loro andavano all'università o lavoravano?* —*Mi sembra che* _____ *all'università.*
5. *Che tempo faceva quel giorno?* —*Penso che* _____ *molto caldo.*
6. *Si dice che lei* _____ *soltanto ventun anni quando si laureò.*

B. *Rispondere iniziando con* Pensavo che, *come nell'esempio.* (Answer the following questions using *Pensavo che.* Follow the example.)

ESEMPIO: Loro sono canadesi. (americani)
   Oh, io pensavo che fossero americani.

1. *A Toronto il* Corriere della Sera *esce lo stesso giorno che esce in Italia. (il giorno dopo)*
2. *Io studio legge. (economia e commercio)*
3. *Noi viviamo a Milano. (Torino)*
4. *Il signor O'Connor parla correntemente sia l'italiano che l'inglese e il tedesco. (anche il francese)*
5. *Il direttore parte oggi. (domani)*
6. *La riunione finisce alle undici. (a mezzogiorno)*
7. *Il cognato di Maria è medico. (ingegnere)*

C. *Formare delle frasi con le seguenti parole.* (Form complete sentences using the elements provided.)

1. *desidereremmo che/candidato/avere/esperienza/industria alimentare*
2. *vorrei che/Lei/cominciare/lavorare/inizio/mese*
3. *miei genitori/vorrebbero che/io/studiare/italiano*
4. *io/preferirei che/tu/trasferirsi/a Milano*
5. *vorrei che/voi/seguire/corso/informatica*
6. *desidererei che/Lei/inviare/subito/suo curriculum vitae*

D. *Rispondere negativamente alle seguenti domande usando* nessuno, niente, più, né . . . né, affatto, ancora, mai, nemmeno. (Answer each question negatively using *nessuno, niente, più, né . . . né, affatto, ancora, mai, nemmeno.*)

1. *Ti piace ancora questo lavoro?*
2. *Tu vuoi fare il direttore delle vendite o il direttore del personale?*
3. *Tu hai mai lavorato a tempo pieno?*
4. *Chi c'è oggi in ufficio?*
5. *Il salario che offrono è competitivo?*
6. *Che cosa fai domani?*
7. *Signorina, il direttore è già arrivato?*
8. *Neanche tu farai domanda per quel posto?*

E. *Tradurre.* (Translate.)

1. I thought you were a sales manager.
2. —You'll get an adequate remuneration for your work. —Will I also get reimbursement of expenses?
3. I would like to give you an idea of the salary you would receive in the event that we would offer you the position.
4. If they should call, could you tell them that I went out?
5. I finally found the job I like. Better late than never!
6. —Are you actually moving to Milan? —Yes, I would like to work in Italy.
7. I never heard of this firm.
8. For this job we haven't hired any men.
9. Did you ever work abroad? —No. Never.
10. Nobody made us a more reasonable offer.

LEZIONE 18

A. DIALOGO

IN GIRO PER FIRENZE

John e Lisa, due ragazzi australiani e studenti di storia dell'arte, sono in visita in Italia. Oggi sono con Marco, un ragazzo italiano che hanno conosciuto qualche giorno fa in una discoteca di Firenze.[1] Marco sta facendo fare a John e Lisa il giro della città.

MARCO: Eccoci a piazza del Duomo. Siamo nel cuore della città.[2]

LISA: La culla del Rinascimento! È meravigliosa . . . proprio come l'avevo immaginata!

JOHN: Sì, è una città meravigliosa, ma devo ammettere che l'architettura che ho visto finora mi lascia un po' perplesso. Mi aspettavo di vedere molto di più dell'esuberanza barocca o della grazia ed eleganza tipiche dell'alto Rinascimento.

MARCO: A molti sorprendono le facciate dei palazzi di questa città. In effetti esse appartengono allo stile del primo Rinascimento. Nel Medioevo i padroni di questi palazzi erano chiaramente più interessati a tenere lontano i loro nemici che all'estetica delle loro abitazioni.

LISA: Sì . . . e non gli do torto. Ecco il Battistero.[3] Ho sentito dire che all'origine era un tempio[4] romano dedicato a Marte.

MARCO: È uno dei più vecchi monumenti di Firenze, ma dubito che fosse stato mai un tempio romano.

JOHN: Marco ha ragione. Gli scavi hanno rivelato che le fondamenta furono gettate nel sesto o settimo secolo. Le decorazioni romaniche della parte esterna sono dell'undicesimo e dodicesimo secolo.

LISA: Credo che qui siano ora conservate le opere di Donatello.[5] Le porte di bronzo di Ghiberti sono veramente da vedere!

MARCO: Sì, le sculture di Donatello sono conservate proprio qua dentro. Le porte comunque sono soltanto una riproduzione.

Alcuni dei pannelli delle porte originali sono stati restaurati e sono ora conservati nel Museo dell'Opera del Duomo. Purtroppo è necessario prendere questi provvedimenti per salvare tutto questo patrimonio artistico dalla pioggia acida e da altre forme di inquinamento.

JOHN: La facciata della cattedrale non è comunque tanto vecchia. È di stile neogotico e fu costruita nel diciannovesimo secolo.

LISA: Guardate un po' come la facciata si addice bene all'originale stile gotico del campanile di Giotto.[6]

MARCO: Penso che la parte più imponente della cattedrale sia la cupola. Fu disegnata da Brunelleschi. Per chiudere uno spazio interiore così grande le tecniche architettoniche del periodo erano inadeguate e Brunelleschi fu costretto ad inventare i macchinari e congegni necessari.

LISA: Penso infatti che abbia inventato la gru.[7]

MARCO: Sì, hai ragione. I lavori ebbero inizio ai primi del 400.[8] Se non erro proprio nel 1420. La cattedrale fu poi consacrata nel 1436. Nel campo dell'ingegneria questo fu sicuramente uno dei più importanti passi avanti di tutti i tempi. Se queste tecniche non fossero state sviluppate e messe in pratica qui a Firenze, non sarebbero mai state costruite molte delle più grandi cupole europee.

JOHN: È veramente magnifica. Non mi sorprende il fatto che tutti i fiorentini ne siano fieri.

MARCO: Sì! Quando ci allontaniamo da qui per molto tempo, noi ne sentiamo la mancanza.

LISA: Quello sarà il Museo dell'Opera del Duomo.

MARCO: Sì. E io che credevo che voi non aveste mai visto queste cose.

JOHN: Beh, le abbiamo viste nei libri e nelle cartoline.[9]

LISA: Ma nel Museo dell'Opera del Duomo non è conservata la Maria Maddalena di Donatello?

MARCO: Sì. E vi è conservata anche la Pietà[10] di Michelangelo.

LISA: **Davvero!? Credevo che la Pietà fosse nella Basilica di San Pietro**[11] **a Roma.**

MARCO: **Hai ragione, ma non dimenticare che Michelangelo ha scolpito tre Pietà.**

LISA: **Entriamo nel museo?**

MARCO: **Pensavo che voleste andare a Ponte Vecchio. Andiamo di qua.**[12] **Passeremo da Piazza della Signoria. Lì c'è ancora tantissimo da vedere. Dobbiamo ancora visitare il Palazzo Medici, il Palazzo Vecchio, la Galleria dell'Accademia, il palazzo degli Uffizi . . .**

JOHN: **Fermiamoci a prendere un boccone.**[13] **Ho una fame**[14] **da lupi!**

AROUND FLORENCE

John and Lisa are two Australian art history students visiting Italy. Today, they are with Marco, a young Italian whom they met a few days earlier at a discotheque. Marco is showing John and Lisa around the city.

MARCO: Here we are in the Duomo Square. This is the heart of the city.

LISA: The cradle of the Renaissance! It's as astounding as I had imagined.

JOHN: I agree, but I also have to admit that I was a little shocked to see a lot of the architecture on the way here. I thought we would have seen far more of the grace and elegance of the High Renaissance or the exuberance of Baroque.

MARCO: Many people are surprised by the facades of the buildings in this city. They're actually mostly Early Renaissance in style, and you can really see that in the Middle Ages the owners of these palazzi were not nearly as interested in aesthetics as they were concerned with keeping intruders out of their homes!

LISA: I can understand that. Oh, look! There's the Baptistery! I once heard that it was originally a Roman temple to the god Mars.

MARCO: It's one of the oldest buildings in Florence, but I doubt that it was ever a Roman temple.

JOHN: Marco's right. I read that excavations have proven that its foundation was constructed in the sixth or seventh century. The Romanesque decoration on the exterior is from the eleventh or twelfth century.

LISA: Now it houses Donatello's work, I believe. And the bronze doors by Ghiberti are certainly a sight to see.

MARCO: Yes, Donatello's sculptures are housed inside. And the doors are actually copies, but some of the panels of the original doors have been restored and are in the Museo dell'Opera del Duomo. Unfortunately, such steps have to be taken to save some of the art treasures from the effects of acid rain and other forms of pollution.

JOHN: The facade of the cathedral itself is not actually so old. It's neo-Gothic in style and it was constructed in the nineteenth century.

LISA: Look how wonderfully the facade fits in with Giotto's original gothic belltower.

MARCO: I think the most impressive part of the cathedral is the dome. It was designed by Brunelleschi to enclose an interior space so large that all of the engineering techniques of the day were useless. Brunelleschi even had to invent equipment on his own.

LISA: I think he invented the crane.

MARCO: Yes, that's right. Construction began at the beginning of the 1400s; if I'm not mistaken precisely in 1420, and the cathedral was finally consecrated in 1436. This was certainly one of the most important engineering breakthroughs of all time. If these techniques hadn't been developed and implemented here in Florence, many of Europe's greatest domes would never have been built.

JOHN: It really is magnificent. I see why Florentines are so proud of it!

MARCO: Yes! When we're away for too long, we feel homesick for the dome!

LISA: That must be the Museo dell'Opera del Duomo.

MARCO: Yes. I thought you had never seen these monuments.

JOHN: Well, we have seen them in books and on postcards.

LISA: Isn't Donatello's Mary Magdalen in this museum?

MARCO: Yes. And there's also Michelangelo's Pietà.

JOHN: Really? I thought that the Pietà was in St. Peter's Basilica in Rome.

MARCO: You're right, but don't forget that Michelangelo sculpted three Pietàs.

LISA: Are we going into the museum?

MARCO: I thought you wanted to go to the Ponte Vecchio. Let's go this way. We'll pass through the Piazza della Signoria. And there's still so much for you to see there. We still have to visit the Medici Palace, the Palazzo Vecchio, the Academy, the Uffizi . . .

JOHN: Let's get some lunch first! I'm starving!

B. IN BREVE

1. This city of approximately half a million inhabitants is the principal center of the Tuscany region. It lies in a plain on the banks of the river Arno, and extends into the hills that surround it in all directions. Florence's past is glorious and illustrious. Florence is considered the birthplace of the Renaissance, and indeed, the birthplace of the Italian language itself.

2. Other common expressions include *cuore della notte* (heart of the night) and *cuore dell'estate* (heart of the summer). Take note also of the following expressions with the word *cuore: stare a cuore* (to take to heart, to be of great concern), *col cuore in mano* (with sincerity), *con tutto il cuore* (gladly), *dar cuore* (to encourage). *Proteggere l'ambiente gli sta a cuore.* (He takes protecting the environment to heart.) *Ci ha parlato col cuore in mano.* (He spoke to us with sincerity.) *Vi aiuterà con tutto il cuore.* (He will gladly help you out.) *Vedere tanto interesse per i nostri prodotti mi ha dato cuore.* (Seeing so much interest in our products encouraged me.)

3. The Baptistry date of origin is unknown. It dates back anywhere between the fifth and tenth centuries, and is among the most ancient Florentine monuments. Besides housing the works of Donatello, the Baptistry boasts numerous other works of art, including some golden mosaics in its cupola.

4. The plural of *tempio* is *templi. La Valle dei Templi si trova ad Agrigento.* (The Valley of the Temples is in Agrigento.)

5. Donatello lived most of his life in Florence, although he spent time in Rome, Siena, and Padua. His art was strongly influenced by Humanist theory. His sculptures portray the human body in a way that had not been seen since antiquity. His figures are strong and seem endowed with power, dignity, and worth. His rendition of the David (completed 1435) is the first freestanding nude of the Renaissance.

6. Giotto di Bondone (1266–1337), painter, architect, and sculptor, was already a renowned figure when he was commissioned to head a project to build a Gothic bell tower in Florence. This tower would eventually bear his name, although he himself did not see the project to its fruition. The bell tower, which is one of the most recognizable structures in Florence, was completed by Francesco Talenti.

7. The word *gru* is invariable in the plural.

8. This is a short form of *Millequattrocento*. In Italian, one can say *Duecento, Trecento, Quattrocento,* etc. up to *Novecento* in order to signify the names of the thirteenth to twentieth centuries.

9. It is very common for Italians to send picture postcards when they travel. In Italy, postcards are readily available and generally very inexpensive to buy.

10. Depictions of the *Pietà* (Mary holding the dead body of Christ in her arms) are copious in art, but Michelangelo's renditions are probably the most well-known. The Florentine Pietà was begun in 1550 and, after Michelangelo's death in 1564, was to have been completed by Tiberio Calcagni, who died in 1565 before its completion. This version of the Pietà includes Mary Magdalene and Nicodemus.

11. Built on the site of old St. Peter's (ca. 326–356), the present Basilica was begun under Pope Julius II in 1506 and completed in 1615 under Paul V. Plans for the basilica were altered numerous times by illustrious figures such as Donato Bramante, Michelangelo, and Pirro Ligorio. The basilica houses countless masterpieces of Renaissance and Baroque art and is one of the major pilgrimage sites for Catholics around the world.

12. *Andare di qua* is frequently used, as is *andare di là*. Expressions with the verb *andare* are many. To mention a few, *andare bene/male* (to go well/badly), *andare a fondo di una questione* (to examine a problem thoroughly), *andare a ruba* (to sell like hot cakes), *andare a monte* (to fail).

13. Also widely used is *fare uno spuntino*. Common is the expression *Non è un boccone per i vostri denti.* (It is out of your reach.)

14. *Morire di fame* is also used. The expression *essere brutto come la fame* expresses the English "to be ugly as sin."

C. GRAMMATICA E SUOI USI

1. *IL PASSATO CONGIUNTIVO* (THE PAST SUBJUNCTIVE)

The *passato congiuntivo* is the subjunctive equivalent to the *passato prossimo*. It is used to express past actions when the verb of the main clause is in the present tense, the future, or the imperative, and it requires a subjunctive tense. The *passato congiuntivo* is formed with the present subjunctive of the auxiliary verb (*avere* or *essere*) + the past participle.

	LAVORARE	ANDARE
io	abbia lavorato	sia andato/a
tu	abbia lavorato	sia andato/a
lui/lei/Lei	abbia lavorato	sia andato/a
noi	abbiamo lavorato	siamo andati/e
voi	abbiate lavorato	siate andati/e
loro/Loro	abbiano lavorato	siano andati/e

Penso che abbiano posteggiato accanto a quel monumento.
I think they parked next to that monument.

Dubito che i signori siano saliti sino alla terrazza per godersi il panorama.
I doubt that the gentlemen climbed to the terrace to enjoy the panorama.

Credete che il gruppo abbia già visitato le rovine?
Do you think the group already visited the ruins?

2. *IL TRAPASSATO CONGIUNTIVO* (THE PAST PERFECT SUBJUNCTIVE)

The *trapassato congiuntivo,* like the *passato congiuntivo,* expresses an action that occurs before the action of the main clause. It is used, however, when the verb in the main clause is in a past tense or in the conditional and requires the subjunctive. The *trapassato congiuntivo* is formed with the imperfect subjunctive of the auxiliary verb (*avere* or *essere*) + the past participle.

	LAVORARE	*ANDARE*
io	*avessi lavorato*	*fossi andato/a*
tu	*avessi lavorato*	*fossi andato/a*
lui/lei/Lei	*avesse lavorato*	*fosse andato/a*
noi	*avessimo lavorato*	*fossimo andati/e*
voi	*aveste lavorato*	*foste andati/e*
loro/Loro	*avessero lavorato*	*fossero andati/e*

Era contento che io avessi visitato il palazzo.
He was happy that I had visited the palace.

Pensavo che voi vi foste avviati a piedi fino alle vicinanze della cattedrale.
I thought that you had started walking to the vicinity of the cathedral.

I nostri amici temevano che il cattivo tempo ci avesse impedito di vedere molto della città.
Our friends were afraid that the bad weather had prevented us from seeing much of the city.

3. *NOMI CON DOPPI PLURALI* (NOUNS WITH TWO PLURAL FORMS)

Some masculine nouns have two plurals: one is a regular masculine plural, while the other is an irregular feminine plural ending in *-a.* In general, one of the plurals keeps the original meaning and the other takes on a different (often metaphorical) meaning. Some of these nouns (many of which refer to parts of the body) include:

il braccio   i bracci (di una lampada, una croce)
le braccia (del corpo umano)

I bracci della lampada sono molto belli.
The lamp brackets are very beautiful.

Quando l'ho vista, mi sono gettato fra le sue braccia.
When I saw her, I threw myself into her arms.

il ciglio   i cigli (di una strada, un fosso)
le ciglia (degli occhi)

Gli piace camminare sui cigli della strada.
He likes to walk along the edges of the road.

Ha delle ciglia molto belle.
She has very beautiful eyelashes.

il fondamento   i fondamenti (di una scienza)
le fondamenta (di un palazzo)

Non ho ancora scoperto i fondamenti di questa scienza.
I haven't yet discoverd the fundamentals of this science

Le fondamenta di questo palazzo furono gettate nel sesto secolo.
The foundations of this building were laid in the sixth century.

il membro   i membri (di un comitato, una famiglia)
le membra (del corpo umano)

I membri del comitato dovranno essere convocati per posta.
The members of the committee shall be summoned by mail.

Le membra di quel bambino sono gracili.
That child's limbs are frail.

l'osso   gli ossi (per il cane)
        le ossa (del corpo umano)

Questi ossi sono per il cane?
    Are these bones for the dog?

È una persona dalle ossa grosse.
    He is a big-boned person.

Le sue ossa riposano in questa chiesa.
    His bones are resting in this church.

il muro   i muri (di una casa)
        le mura (della città)

I muri hanno orecchie.
    Walls have ears.

Questi muri sono di mattone?
    Are these brick walls?

Queste sono le mura di Firenze.
    These are Florence's town walls.

il labbro   i labbri (di una ferita, un vaso)
        le labbra (della bocca)

Ha rotto i labbri del vaso.
    He broke the rim of the vase.

Ha labbra sottili.
    She has thin lips.

D. PAROLE! PAROLE! PAROLE!

The word *pieno* is used in many idiomatic expressions which may
come in handy.

È un ragazzo pieno di vita.
    He is a boy full of life.

Ho mangiato troppo. Mi sento pieno.
    I ate too much. I feel full.

Ho colto in pieno il bersaglio.
I hit it on the nose.

Siamo già in piena stagione turistica.
We are already at the height of the tourist season.

Faccia il pieno, per favore!
Fill it up, please.

Era giorno pieno quando sono uscito.
It was broad daylight when I went out.

Povero Gino! È pieno di guai.
Poor Gino! He has more than his share of troubles.

Hai sbagliato in pieno.
You were completely wrong.

Sono pieno di lavoro.
I am up to my eyes in work.

Sono pieno fino agli occhi di musei!
I am thoroughly fed up with museums!

Tutto è in piena regola.
Everything is in perfect order.

Gianni è pieno di sé.
John is full of himself.

Ho le tasche piene di quell'uomo.
I am fed up with that man.

Sono stati tutti promossi a pieni voti.
They all passed with full marks.

La piazza è piena zeppa di gente.
The square is packed with people.

E. L'ANGOLO DEGLI AFFARI

L'INDUSTRIA DEL TURISMO IN ITALIA
(TOURISM IN ITALY)

Tourists have been attracted to Italy for centuries, and have made this country one of the most frequently visited throughout the world. Italy has been a favorite vacation spot for countless tourists, and has also attracted artists, poets, and philosophers seeking inspiration. Because of its marvelous natural beauty and remarkable cultural and artistic treasures, Italy has developed an extremely lucrative tourism industry. Tourism is by far the top-grossing service industry in Italy.

The industry's infrastructure is very well developed. Travel offices have been set up by all levels of government, and are an important resource for those considering traveling to the Italian peninsula. The Italian Government travel office (ENIT) may be a good place to start if one is considering a trip to Italy. While in the country, provincial tourist offices (EPT) and local information offices (AAST) are easily found and offer a wealth of information to travelers. They provide sightseeing information, opening hours of shops and museums, accommodations listings, and other information. Remember, though, that these offices do not make reservations.

Most commercial airlines with international travel routes provide service to Italy, and consequently, traveling to Italy by air is very convenient. Italy's two largest airports are Rome's Fiumicino airport and Milan's Malpensa airport, but the country has several other international airports, including Venice, Naples, Genoa, Palermo, Cagliari, Rome's Ciampino, and Milan's Linate airports. Fares to Italy can vary from one carrier to another, therefore, it is wise to keep an eye open for any promotions, and to consult with a trusted travel agent who can suggest the best route to take. Often fares can be reduced drastically if one is willing to travel to Italy via another country.

Within Italy, air travel is rather expensive. The lack of competition in the industry allows Alitalia, the national airline, to keep fares relatively high. Many tourists prefer to travel throughout the peninsula by using the efficient and relatively inexpensive rail system. Although Italy can be an unpredictable and expensive place to visit, these characteristic traits of the country do not apply to the rail system. The *FS* or *Ferrovia statale* (National Railway) is probably one of the most tourist-friendly institutions in Italy, offering many different types of tourist passes, including the *Turistico Circolazione* pass, allowing a tourist to travel throughout the mainland and even to Sicily on its train ferry. The pass offers first-class or second-class travel, and travel periods of 8, 15, 21, or 30 days. The pass allows one to travel even on the very rapid EuroCity and *rapidi** (rapid) trains. As well as offering a variety of ticket options for tourists, *FS* trains are efficient and generally on-schedule and make traveling relatively hassle-free.

If one wishes a more economical means of travel within Italy, another option is the bus system. Italian buses offer an affordable alternative, and are also fairly speedy and comfortable. This means of transportation may, in certain cases, be more convenient than train travel, because one can travel to some locales that may not be reachable by train. Of course, if one wishes a maximum amount of independence while traveling in Italy, one may opt to rent an automobile. This option has many advantages, but can also be very expensive (see *Lezione 19* for more details).

There are approximately 38,000 hotels in Italy. They range from five-star, luxury hotels and resorts, to modest *pensioni* (pensions or bed-and-breakfast) and youth hostels. While hostels and *pensioni* in smaller centers are fairly economical, for the most part accommodations in Italy are very expensive, particularly in cities such as Rome, where one can spend up to L100.000 for rather modest accommodations.

Although it is comparatively slow in the winter months, the tourism industry is an all-season industry. This is in part due to the fact that Italy is known not only for its physical assets, natural as well as artistic, but also for its year-round festivals and other events. Top seasonal events in Italy include Epiphany celebrations in January (such as the Epiphany Fair at Piazza Navona in Rome); carnival celebrations in February (see *Lezione 20*); Easter celebrations in Rome and Florence; the Florence May Music Festival (the oldest and most prestigious festival of the performing arts); Siena's *Palio,* a colorful horse race held in the medieval Piazza del Campo in July and in August; the Maritime

---

* Because the *FS* is so extensive and covers much of Italy's hinterland, many trains are much slower than others and are used by commuters. It is useful, therefore, to learn the names of the different kinds of trains: the *locali* (local trains) stop at every town on FS routes and are best avoided if one has limited time in Italy. The *espressi* (express trains) make far fewer stops, but still tend to stop at smaller centers. *Rapidi* stop only at major centers. The *EuroCity* and *InterCity* trains make very few stops. For instance, the *InterCity* between Naples and Venice stops only in Rome. They travel at very high speeds and offer a variety of services such as dining cars and air conditioning, making them a viable and convenient alternative to air travel.

Republics' Regatta in June, held in turn in Venice, Genoa, Amalfi, and Pisa; and the Venice Film Festival in late summer. Of course, if one also wishes to enjoy Italy's natural beauty, one can do so throughout the year. Whether one is interested in skiing and hiking, or fishing and sailing, Italy's terrain provides ample opportunity for outdoor activities throughout the year.

ESERCIZI

A. *Completare usando il congiuntivo passato. Usare i pronomi dove necessario.* (Fill in the blanks using the past subjunctive. Use pronouns when necessary.)

1. —*John e Lisa hanno conosciuto Marco in discoteca? —Sì, credo che _____ in discoteca.*
2. —*Marco li ha invitati a fare un giro della città? —Sì, penso che Marco _____ a fare un giro della città e che loro _____ volentieri.*
3. —*Sono andati a piedi in centro? —Non sono sicuro, ma mi sembra che _____ in macchina.*
4. —*Lisa e John hanno visitato il Battistero? —Sì, è probabile che _____ perché tutti e due sono amanti delle opere di Donatello.*
5. —*Che bella questa chiesa! La facciata è meravigliosa! Ma chi l'ha disegnata? —Dicono che _____ Leon Battista Alberti.*
6. —*Questo non è il Palazzo degli Uffizi? —Sì, mi pare che questo palazzo _____ sede degli uffici amministrativi del ducato dei Medici.*
7. —*Ma è qui che lui ha comprato quella scultura? —Non so con precisione, ma immagino che _____ proprio qui.*
8. *Marco ci ha fatto fare il giro della città. Peccato che tu _____ venire con noi.*

B. *Formare delle nuove frasi usando il congiuntivo o l'indicativo. Seguire l'esempio.* (Form new sentences using either the indicative or the subjunctive. Follow the example.)

ESEMPIO: Sono andati in Italia. (Credo che)
   Credo che siano andati in Italia.
   Sono andati in Italia. (Sono sicuro)
   Sono sicuro che sono andati in Italia.

1. *Hanno seguito l'itinerario. (Credo che)*
2. *Rosalba ha voluto conoscere la storia del David di Michelangelo. (Mi hanno detto che)*
3. *Non avete avuto molto tempo a vostra disposizione. (Mi dispiace che)*
4. *La mostra dei capolavori del Botticelli è stata inagurutata l'8 maggio. (Tutti sanno che)*
5. *Ha voluto visitare anche gli uffici amministrativi. (Non capisco perché)*
6. *Michelangelo è nato a Caprese. (Sembra che)*
7. *L'hanno studiato a scuola. (Sono convinto che)*
8. *Queste cose tu le hai lette nei libri. (È ovvio che)*

C. *Completare con la forma corretta del trapassato del congiuntivo.* (Fill in the blanks with the appropriate form of the past perfect subjunctive.)

1. —*È la prima volta che veniamo in Italia.* —*Io pensavo che voi ci* _____ *già* _____ *prima.*
2. —*Loro avevano già visitato Firenze?* —*No, non credo che l'*_____ *prima di ieri.*
3. —*Michelangelo ha scolpito tre Pietà.* —*Veramente?! Io pensavo che ne* _____ *solo una.*
4. —*Erano già andati in centro?* —*Sì, mi sembra che* _____ *già in centro.*
5. —*Quando siete arrivati al Duomo, avevate già visto il Ponte Vecchio?* —*Sì, mi pare che l'*_____ *già* _____ .

D. *Tradurre.* (Translate.)

1. We stopped to get a bite. I ate too much and now I feel full.
2. Is this the Baptistry? Is this where the works of Donatello are kept?
3. Behind that monument there is a palace that dates back to the Renaissance.
4. I think this is the most important art gallery in Italy.
5. It was broad daylight when we went out.
6. Yesterday we went to visit one of the most famous churches in Florence. It was packed with people.
7. She has very long eyelashes.
8. The foundations of this building were laid in the sixteenth century.
9. The members of the committee held a meeting yesterday.
10. Be careful; walls have ears.

LEZIONE 19

A. DIALOGO

Una gita in macchina

I signori Miceli desiderano noleggiare una macchina per un viaggio a Siena con dei loro familiari.

AMEDEO: **Ma questo autonoleggio dov'è?**

ALIDA: **Il signore che mi ha dato le informazioni mi ha detto che è proprio[1] qui vicino. Ah, eccolo lì.**

AMEDEO: **Buona sera. Vorremmo noleggiare una Lancia Y 1200.**

IMPIEGATA: **Mi dispiace, ma le 1200 sono tutte esaurite.[2]**

AMEDEO: **Ma questa mattina al telefono mi hanno detto che ce n'era ancora una libera e che potevo venire a firmare il contratto.**

IMPIEGATA: **Scusi, non avevo capito che Lei aveva già fatto la prenotazione. Come si chiama?**

AMEDEO: **Miceli. Amedeo Miceli.**

IMPIEGATA: **Oh, sì. Ecco qui il Suo modulo di prenotazione. Dunque, Lei ha detto che voleva una Lancia Y 1200.**

AMEDEO: **Sì, mi hanno detto che è un'ottima macchina.**

IMPIEGATA: **Le diamo la 1200 con 5 marce,[3] OK?**

AMEDEO: **Sì, va bene. C'è l'aria condizionata?**

IMPIEGATA: **Sì, viene con aria condizionata, airbag per guidatore e passeggero. Non consuma molta benzina e l'interno è abbastanza comodo.**

AMEDEO: **Posso lasciare la macchina in un'altra città?**

IMPIEGATA: **Sì, ma dovrà pagare un supplemento.**

AMEDEO: **Va bene. E l'assicurazione[4] per il furto e contro i danni?**

IMPIEGATA: L'assicurazione è inclusa nella tariffa di noleggio. Dunque, la macchina Le serve solo[5] per il weekend?

AMEDEO: Sì.

IMPIEGATA: Potrei vedere la patente?[6]

AMEDEO: Eccola.

IMPIEGATA: Il veicolo glielo consegniamo con il serbatoio pieno[7] e abbiamo bisogno di un deposito a titolo di garanzia . . .

AMEDEO: Sì, certamente. Ecco la mia carta di credito.

Sbrigate le pratiche, i signori Miceli si mettono in macchina.

AMEDEO: Allora, che cosa ti ha detto tuo fratello al telefono?

ALIDA: Ma te l'ho detto che non ho potuto parlare con lui. Ho parlato con Sandra. Lui era uscito per farsi controllare la macchina. Sandra comunque mi ha detto che il marito le ha lasciato detto di riferirmi che ci avrebbero incontrato sulla A1,[8] alla prima stazione di servizio dopo Montepulciano.[9]

AMEDEO: Ti ha detto a che ora partivano?

ALIDA: Ha detto che sarebbero partiti subito e che dovrebbero arrivare alla stazione di servizio verso le otto e mezzo.

AMEDEO: Tutto a posto allora. Abbiamo tempo per fare tutto con calma.

ALIDA: Caro, visto che abbiamo tempo, potresti fermarti davanti a quel tabacchino?[10] Solo un attimino[11] per prendere le sigarette. Sai, non vedo l'ora di arrivare a Siena. Finalmente potrò vedere il Palio![12]

Il signor Miceli si ferma davanti al tabacchino. Mentre aspetta, un vigile[13] si avvicina allo sportello della macchina.

VIGILE: Signore, non ha visto che qui non si può sostare?

AMEDEO: No. Mi dispiace. Non ho trovato parcheggio e sto aspettando mia moglie che è dal tabacchaio . . .

VIGILE: Mi dispiace, se non si sposta subito sono costretto a farLe la multa.

AMEDEO: Va bene, mi sposto subito.

La signora Miceli ritorna e non trova più la macchina. Dopo due minuti il marito ritorna e lei sale in macchina.

ALIDA: **Ma dove sei andato?**

AMEDEO: **Ho dovuto fare un giro qui intorno. Quasi quasi mi beccavo[14] una multa per sosta vietata. È arrivato un vigile e mi ha detto che non potevo parcheggiare qui. Io gli ho spiegato che ti stavo aspettando e che tu saresti ritornata subito. Non ha voluto sentire ragioni e mi ha detto che se non mi spostavo era costretto a farmi una multa.**

ALIDA: **Meno male[15] che l'hai scampata[16] bella. Mi raccomando ora . . . guida piano e con calma, perché sicuramente arriveremo alla stazione di servizio[17] di Montepulciano prima di mio fratello.**

A CAR TRIP

The Micelis are planning to rent a car for a trip they'll be taking with relatives to Siena.

AMEDEO: Where is this car rental place?

ALIDA: The man who gave me the information said it's near here. Ah, here it is.

AMEDEO: Good evening. We would like to rent a Lancia Y 1200.

EMPLOYEE: I am sorry, but all of the 1200s are sold out.

AMEDEO: But this morning on the phone they told me that there was one available and that I could come to sign the contract.

EMPLOYEE: I am sorry, I didn't think that you had already booked it. What is your name?

AMEDEO: Miceli. Amedeo Miceli.

EMPLOYEE: Oh, yes. Here is your reservation form. Now then, you said that you wanted a Lancia Y 1200.

AMEDEO: Yes, they told me that it is an excellent car.

EMPLOYEE: Shall we give you the 5-speed 1200, is that OK?

AMEDEO: Yes, that is fine. Does it have air conditioning?

EMPLOYEE: Yes, it comes with air conditioning, passenger and driver side airbag . . . It gets excellent mileage, and the interior is rather comfortable.

AMEDEO: May I drop off the car in another city?

EMPLOYEE: Yes, but you'll have to pay an additional charge.

AMEDEO: That's fine. And theft and liability insurance?

EMPLOYEE: The insurance is included in the cost of the rental. So, you'll be needing the car only for the weekend?

AMEDEO: Yes.

EMPLOYEE: May I see your license?

AMEDEO: Here it is.

EMPLOYEE: The car will be given to you with a full tank of gas and a deposit is required as a guarantee . . .

AMEDEO: Yes . . . Absolutely. Here is my credit card.

Having completed the forms, the Micelis get into the car.

AMEDEO: So, what did your brother say to you on the phone?

ALIDA: I told you I couldn't speak to him. I spoke with Sandra. He had gone out to get his car checked out. Sandra said that her husband had told her that they would meet us on the A1, at the first service station after Montepulciano.

AMEDEO: Did she tell you what time they would be leaving?

ALIDA: She said that they would be leaving right away, and that they should be arriving at the service station by about eight-thirty.

AMEDEO: Everything's okay, then. We have time to take it easy.

ALIDA: Dear, since we have time, could you stop in front of that smoke shop? Just a second so that I can get some cigarettes. You know, I can't wait to arrive in Siena. I will finally be able to see the Palio.

Mr. Miceli stops in front of the smoke shop. While he is waiting, a policeman approaches the car door.

POLICEMAN: Sir, didn't you see that this is a no parking zone?

AMEDEO: No. I am sorry. I couldn't find any parking and I am waiting for my wife, who is in the smoke shop . . .

POLICEMAN: I'm sorry, if you don't move right away, I'll have to give you a ticket.

AMEDEO: Fine, I will move right away.

Mrs. Miceli returns and doesn't find the car. After a few minutes, her husband pulls up, and she gets in the car.

ALIDA: Where did you go?

AMEDEO: I had to go around. I almost got a fine for illegal parking. A policeman came and told me that I couldn't park here. I explained to him that I was waiting for you and that you would return right away. He didn't want to listen to my explanation and he told me that if I didn't move he would be forced to give me a ticket.

ALIDA: You're lucky that you got away with it. Be careful now . . . drive slowly and calmly, because we will surely arrive at the Montepulciano service station before my brother.

B. IN BREVE

1. *Proprio* also expresses the English "really," "quite." *Non avevo proprio capito.* (I really had not understood.) As an adjective *proprio* can also indicate or emphasize possession and translates the English "own," "one's own." *L'ha sentito con le sue proprie orecchie.* (He heard it with his own ears.)

2. *Esaurito* also expresses "worn out," "exhausted," "weary."

3. Note that the singular of *marce* is *marcia.* A second meaning of *marcia* is "march" as in *marcia nuziale/trionfale* (wedding, triumphal march).

4. *Assicurazione* also expresses "assurance." *Mi ha dato assicurazione della verità del fatto.* (He gave me assurance of the truthfulness of the fact.) The verb *assicurare* can be used with the following meanings: "to register," "to fasten," "to secure," "to assure." *Preferirei assicurare il pacco.* (I would prefer registering the package.) *Mi ha assicurato una vacanza senza preoccupazioni.* (He assured me a vacation without worries.)

5. *Solo* can be used to express the English "sole." *È il solo rappresentante della nostra ditta che non abbia accettato il contratto.* (He is the sole agent of our firm who did not accept the contract.)

6. Note the "false friends" *licenza* and "license." A "car license" is a *patente. Licenza* is used to express "leave" (*Il direttore gli ha concesso una licenza di tre giorni.* The director granted him a three-day leave.), and "permit" as in *licenza di caccia, di pesca. Non rischiate di andare a caccia senza la licenza.* (Don't risk going hunting without a hunting license.)

7. The expression *fare il pieno* is used for "to fill up (with gas)." As a noun *pieno* also means "at the height of," *nel pieno dell'estate* (at the height of the summer.)

8. This Italian superhighway, called *autostrada del sole,* stretches the length of the Italian peninsula, from Milan in the northwest, to Reggio Calabria, at the southern tip of Italy.

9. This small Tuscan center falls under the jurisdiction of Siena. It has approximately 16,000 residents, and is world-famous for its wines.

10. Smoke shops are easily recognizable in Italy. Their shopfronts bear a black-and-white sign with a large "T." *Tabacchini* are state-licensed shops, selling products on which the Italian government has a monopoly. This includes stamps as well as tobacco products. Other items traditionally carried by *tabacchini* are newspapers, magazines, and postcards.

11. *Un attimino* can be used to emphasize that it will be a short moment.

12. In the Middle Ages, the term *palio* was used to identify a particular type of cloth or drape which was used as a prize in races, particularly during equestrian competitions. Later, the term came to be used as the name of this type of race itself. Siena's *Palio,* begun in 1275, takes place on July 2 and August 16 of every year, and is a huge festival. The races are held in the main square, and the riders are dressed in Medieval costumes which represent the various districts of the city. At one time, different families ruled the different districts of Siena.

13. The tasks of this core of law enforcement officials include directing traffic and distributing violations to pedestrians and motor vehicles in urban centers. In Italy, policing is divided among several groups. The *carabinieri* are part of the Italian military. The *polizia* (police) are a distinct group, roughly the equivalent of North American police forces. At times, the functions of these groups may overlap. For instance, the *carabinieri* and the *polizia* may both conduct investigations and apprehend criminals. The *carabinieri,* under certain circumstances, may also deal with certain, more serious traffic violations such as excessive speeding and dangerous driving on highways and freeways.

14. *Beccarsi* is used to express the English "to catch, to get." *Mi sono beccato un raffredore.* (I caught a cold.) *Beccarsi* can also mean "to walk away with." *Lei si è beccato il primo premio.* (She walked away with first prize.)

15. The expression is equivalent to *per fortuna.* Other expressions with *meno* include, *farne a meno* (to do without), *del più e del meno* (more or less), *per lo meno* (at least), *venir meno* (to faint), *venir meno alla propria parola* (to break one's word).

16. Note also *Dio me ne scampi!* (God forbid!)

17. When entering an Italian *autostrada* one must take a ticket which is issued at an automated *casello.* Upon exiting the highway, a *pedaggio,* a toll for use of the highway, must be paid. The toll is calculated according to the distance travelled (based on the point of entrance) as well as the type of car. Luxury cars pay higher fees on Italian highways. Tolls may be paid in cash, or at selected automated *caselli,* with a prepaid card.

C. GRAMMATICA E SUOI USI

1. *IL DISCORSO INDIRETTO* (THE INDIRECT DISCOURSE)

While direct discourse reports a person's speech word for word, indirect discourse reports speech indirectly by using verbs such as *dire* (to say), *domandare* (to ask), *affermare* (to affirm), *dichiarare* (to declare), *esclamare* (to exclaim), *chiedere* (to ask), and *rispondere* (to answer), etc.

DIRECT DISCOURSE	INDIRECT DISCOURSE
Aldo dice: "Desidero noleggiare una macchina."	*Aldo dice che desidera noleggiare una macchina.*
Aldo says: "I wish to rent a car."	Aldo says he wishes to rent a car

When changing from direct to indirect discourse, no change of tense occurs if the verb introducing the indirect discourse is in the present or future.

L'impiegato dice: "Le macchine con il cambio automatico sono esaurite."
The employee says: "Cars with automatic transmission are not available."

L'impiegato dice che le macchine con il cambio automatico sono esaurite.
The employee says that cars with automatic transmission are not available.

When the verb introducing the indirect discourse is in a past tense *(passato prossimo, passato remoto, imperfetto, trapassato)*, the verbs of the discourse change in the transition from direct to indirect discourse. The following chart summarizes the changes that govern the transition.

DISCORSO DIRETTO	DISCORSO INDIRETTO
presente (indicativo or *congiuntivo)*	*imperfetto (indicativo* or *congiuntivo)*
imperfetto (indicativo or *congiuntivo)*	*imperfetto (indicativo* or *congiuntivo)*
passato prossimo, passato remoto	*trapassato indicativo*
trapassato (indicativo or *congiuntivo)*	*trapassato (indicativo* or *congiuntivo)*
futuro semplice, futuro anteriore	*condizionale passato*
condizionale (presente or *passato)*	*condizionale passato*
imperativo	*di + infinito*
	che + congiuntivo imperfetto
passato congiuntivo	*trapassato congiuntivo*

344

L'impiegato disse: "Può venire a firmare il contratto alle due del pomeriggio."
The clerk said: "You can come to sign the contract at 2 o'clock in the afternoon."

L'impiegato disse che potevo venire a firmare il contratto alle due del pomeriggio.
The clerk said that I could come to sign the contract at 2 o'clock in the afternoon.

Enrico ha detto: "Abbiamo deciso di fermarci alla prima stazione di servizio."
Enrico said: "We decided to stop at the first service station."

Enrico ha detto che avevano deciso di fermarsi alla prima stazione di servizio.
Enrico said that they had decided to stop at the first service station.

Roberto ha chiesto: "Avete sentito quello strano rumore che viene dal motore?"
Robert asked: "Did you hear that strange noise coming from the engine?"

Roberto ha chiesto se avevamo sentito quello strano rumore che veniva dal motore?
Robert asked if we had heard that strange sound coming from the motor.

In hypothetical sentences of all types (please refer to *Lezione 20*) the change from direct discourse to indirect discourse calls for the use of the *congiuntivo trapassato* in the *se* clause and the *condizionale passato* in the main clause.

Ha detto: "Se gli faranno la multa, non la pagherà."
He said: "If they give him a fine he will not pay it."

Ha detto che se gli avessero fatto la multa non l'avrebbe pagata.
He said that if they were to fine him he would not pay.

As in English, in the change from direct discourse to indirect discourse first and second person subject pronouns and possessive adjectives change to the third person.

DISCORSO DIRETTO	DISCORSO INDIRETTO
io, tu	*lui/lei*
noi, voi	*loro*
mi, ti (direct object)	*lo/la*
mi, ti (indirect object)	*gli/le*
ci, vi (direct object)	*li/le*
ci, vi (indirect object)	*gli/loro*
mio, tuo	*suo*
nostro, vostro	*loro*

Ha esclamato: "Il commesso che mi ha venduto la macchina mi ha fatto una bidonata!"
He exclaimed: "The car salesman sold me a lemon!"

Ha esclamato che il commesso che gli aveva venduto la macchina gli aveva fatto una bidonata.
He exclaimed that the car salesman sold him a lemon.

Other changes which occur include the following:

DISCORSO DIRETTO	DISCORSO INDIRETTO
questo	*quello*
qui (qua)	*lì (là)*
oggi	*quel giorno*
ieri	*il giorno prima*
	il giorno avanti
domani	*il giorno dopo*
domani mattina	*l'indomani mattina*
poco fa	*poco prima*
l'anno scorso	*l'anno precedente*
l'anno prossimo	*l'anno seguente/dopo*
sabato scorso	*il sabato prima*
sabato prossimo	*il sabato seguente/dopo*
fra	*dopo*
fra poco, tra poco	*poco dopo*

Ci ha detto che aveva già noleggiato una macchina la settimana precedente.
He told us that the week before he had already rented a car.

Le hanno spiegato che quella sera volevano prendere una strada panoramica.
They told her that they wanted to take a scenic route that night.

D. PAROLE! PAROLE! PAROLE!

The word "forte" appears in many Italian expressions:

Lui è forte in matematica.
He is good at mathematics.

Lei nutre una forte antipatia per quella gente.
She has a strong dislike of those people.

Abbiamo forti motivi per sospettare di John.
We have sound motives for suspecting John.

Gli ho prestato una forte somma di denaro per le riparazioni dopo l'incidente.
I lent him a large sum of money to get the repairs done after his accident.

Quando guido troppo a lungo, mi viene spesso una forte emicrania.
When I drive for a long time, I usually get a splitting headache.

Tieni forte il volante.
Hold the steering wheel tight.

Stamattina è piovuto forte e pertanto le strade sono pericolose.
This morning it rained heavily so the roads are dangerous.

Dubito forte che lui venga alla festa.
I greatly doubt whether he will come to the party.

Non parlate troppo forte!
Don't talk too loudly!

Quel ragazzo corre veramente forte.
That boy runs very hard.

L'italiano è il suo forte.
Italian is his strong point.

Questo vino sa di forte.
This wine has a sour taste.

Dai, vai più forte!
Come on, speed up.

Quell'uomo è un forte bevitore/fumatore.
That man is a heavy drinker/smoker.

Lei si dimostra sempre forte nelle avversità della vita.
    She always displays strength in the adversities of life.

Lo puoi dire forte!
    You can say that again!

Abbiamo forti dubbi su di lui.
    We have grave doubts about him.

Si fa forte del suo diritto.
    She avails herself of her right.

È più forte di noi!
    We can't help it!

Quell'uomo è forte come un toro.
    That man is as strong as an ox.

L'ho fatto per un forte motivo.
    I have done it for a very good reason.

Tieniti forte perché a causa della strada ghiacciata possiamo slittare facil-mente.
    Hold tightly as we can easily skid because of the icy road.

E. L'ANGOLO DEGLI AFFARI

NOLEGGIARE UNA MACCHINA E GUIDARE IN ITALIA (RENTING A CAR AND DRIVING IN ITALY)

When planning to rent a car in a foreign country, it is always wise to book the car from home, well in advance of the trip. Often one can save up to 50% if one reserves a rental car from the States. The most substantial savings come on weekly rentals. Often weekly packages include unlimited mileage. Further reductions may be granted if one rents for more than three weeks. Whatever your needs, be sure to shop around before deciding on a rental car, because prices and packages may vary. In order to rent a car in Italy, one must present a driver's license and a major credit card with enough credit to cover the cost of rental. Try to deal with a major rental agency such as Europcar, Hertz, Avis, Budget, or Maggiore. Branches of these dealers may be found at airports and train stations, and at various other locations in major cities.

An international license may be used to drive in Italy. A U.S. license is also valid, but it must be accompanied by an official translation of the document in Italian. One cannot drive in Italy without obtaining a visitor's insurance card known as a *Carta Verde* (Green Card). The *Carta Verde* is issued for a period of 15, 30, or 45 days. If you intend to utilize a vehicle for more than 45 days, you must obtain a regular Italian insurance policy. Consult the car rental agency with which you will be dealing for more information.

If you intend to drive a motorcycle in Italy, note that there is a helmet *(casco)* law in place. One may drive a motorcycle over 49 cc with a driver's license or with a motorcycle license. Traveling around Italy by car is a pleasure.

The system of *autostrade* (superhighways) is excellent, and car travel allows one to see the beautiful scenery for which Italy is famous. Superhighways are recognizable in that their names consist of the letter "A" followed by a number, and they are marked with green signs. Remember that tolls must be paid on the *autostrade*. These are calculated according to the distance covered as well as the size of the vehicle. A ticket is issued at the entrance of the highway, and it is returned when the toll is paid at the exit. If you are planning a very long trip, do not forget to factor in a sum of cash for the tolls, as well as for the gas, *benzina,* which is at least three times as expensive as it is in the United States. When traveling on superhighways, remember that no U-turns are permitted, and that stopping is allowed only in specified emergency parking areas. One must drive on the right, and pass in the left lane. The speed limit is 110 km (68.74 miles) per hour for all motor vehicles up to 1099 cc and 130 km (81.25 miles) per hour for vehicles over 1100 cc. If you are hesitant about traveling on Italy's superhighways because of the expense, or if you prefer to travel more picturesque roads at a slower pace, you can opt for state roads. These are indicated by the letters "SS" followed by a number, and are labeled by blue road signs. For the most part, these state roads may be followed up and down Italy's coasts, as well as through the interior of the country.

Italy uses international road signs, and directions are generally marked very clearly. Even in cities and towns, one will find signs indicating directions and distances towards highways and neighboring towns and cities. The speed limit within cities and towns is 50 km (31.25 miles) per hour, and it is 90 km (56.25 miles) per hour on main roads and highways.

The driving age in Italy is eighteen. Seat belts are compulsory for the driver and front-seat passenger. At unmarked intersections, right of way is given to the vehicle approaching from the right, and to streetcars and trains. Pedestrians have the right of way on *strisce pedonali* (pedestrian stripes), which are the equivalent of American crosswalks. Also, many urban centers have *zone pedonali* (pedestrian zones), entire areas where cars cannot travel. In major centers such as Rome, Naples, and Milan, traffic may be rather chaotic, and parking rather difficult. Remember to always obey traffic signals so as to avoid being stopped by the *carabinieri* (military police) or *vigili urbani,* and to avoid an unpleasant experience such as having your car towed away.

ESERCIZI

A. *Cambiare le seguenti frasi dal discorso diretto al discorso indiretto.* (Change the following sentences from the direct to the indirect discourse.)

1. *Enzo ha detto: "Domani mattina uscirò presto."*
2. *Amedeo ha detto: "Abbiamo tempo per fare tutto con calma."*
3. *Teresa dice sempre: "Io non voglio noleggiare un'auto troppo grande."*
4. *Il vigile disse ad Amedeo: "Lei non può posteggiare qui."*
5. *Mio padre disse al vigile: "Mia moglie è andata al tabacchino."*
6. *Mio padre ha detto al vigile: "Sto aspettando mia moglie. Ritornerà subito."*
7. *Il vigile mi ha risposto: "Se Lei non si sposta, Le faccio la multa."*
8. *Amedeo ha detto: "Ho paura che oggi non vada niente per il verso giusto."*

B. *Trasformare il seguente dialogo usando il discorso indiretto.* (Change the following dialogue using the indirect discourse.)

Un carabiniere fa segno ad Amedeo di fermarsi.

Carabiniere: Patente di guida e carta di circolazione.
Amedeo: C'è qualcosa che non va?
Carabiniere: Sì, Lei ha i faretti antinebbia accesi.
Amedeo: Allora sono in contravvenzione?
Carabiniere: Sì. Lei è il proprietario della macchina?

Amedeo: No, l'ho appena noleggiata. Devo ancora familiarizzarmi con tutti questi bottoni. Potrebbe evitarmi questa multa?
Carabiniere: Mi dispiace, non si può far nulla. La prossima volta faccia più attenzione.

C. *Completare il seguente dialogo in modo opportuno.* (Complete the following dialogue appropriately.)

Alida: Ma dove sei andato?
Amedeo: Ho dovuto fare un _____ qui intorno. Quasi _____ mi beccavo una _____ per sosta vietata. È arrivato un _____ e mi ha detto _____ non potevo _____ qui. Io gli ho spiegato che ti _____ aspettando e che tu saresti ritornata subito. Non ha voluto sentire _____ e mi ha detto che se non mi spostavo era costretto a farmi una _____.
Alida: Meno _____ che l'hai scampata _____. Mi raccomando ora ... _____ piano e con calma, perché arriveremo alla _____ di Montepulciano prima _____ mio fratello.

D. *Tradurre.* (Translate.)

1. My manager granted me a three-day leave.
2. Here is your reservation form, Miss. This car also comes with air conditioning. The insurance for theft and damages is included in the cost of the rental.
3. They have a strong dislike of those people.
4. I greatly doubt that he will like that car.
5. He always displays strength in the adversities of life.
6. You can say that again! Today nothing seems to be going right

LEZIONE 20

A. DIALOGO

A CARNEVALE OGNI SCHERZO VALE

Siamo ad Acireale,[1] vicino Catania,[2] in Sicilia[3] alla fine del Carnevale. Barbara e Domenico sono venuti da Bolzano[4] a trovare i loro amici Salvatore ed Alessandra e a partecipare alle festività carnevalesche. Le due coppie si fermano in un bar della città per prendere qualcosa da bere e per festeggiare l'ultima serata insieme in Sicilia.

SALVATORE: **Domenico, dato che domani mattina ritorni a casa, sei sicuro che non vuoi portarti uno dei miei maglioni?**

DOMENICO: **Come sei spiritoso! È vero comunque che sentirò la mancanza di questo bellissimo clima. Ah, se potessimo fermarci ancora qualche altro giorno!**

BARBARA: **Sì, è stato meraviglioso! Ora capisco perché questo Carnevale è uno dei migliori d'Italia e perché tanta gente ne parla.**

DOMENICO: **I carri allegorici[5] erano veramente magnifici!**

ALESSANDRA: **Sì, sono veramente unici. Secondo me, nessun altro Carnevale ha carri allegorici così interessanti e così pittoreschi.**

BARBARA: **E poi tutti così illuminati da migliaia[6] di fiaccole . . . e tutta quella gente travestita, che suonava trombette e che buttava coriandioli[7] dappertutto . . . Che baldoria! Veramente indimenticabile! Comunque se alla fine dovessi pulire tutto io, non sarei così contenta.**

DOMENICO: **Beh, se io dovessi ripetere questa esperienza, la ripeterei subito.**

SALVATORE: **Mimì,[8] l'avevamo capito. Infatti per poco non sei salito[9] anche tu su uno di quei carri. Un bel modo per festeggiare il Martedì Grasso[10] con gli acesi.[11]**

ALESSANDRA: **Salvatore, ma tu hai sempre voglia di scherzare!**

DOMENICO: È vero. Totò[12] non saprebbe cosa fare, se non sfottesse un po' . . .

SALVATORE: Ma non siamo a Carnevale? Come si dice: "A Carnevale ogni scherzo vale!" E poi il Carnevale non è forse la festa delle ultime gioie prima di affrontare la Quaresima, tempo di penitenza e di astinenza?

BARBARA: Salvatore, ma non avevi una barzelletta[13] da raccontarci?

ALESSANDRA: Oh no! Ma dovevi proprio ricordarglielo? Se ne sarebbe sicuramente dimenticato, se tu non glielo avessi ricordato.

SALVATORE: Sì! Hai ragione! Me n'ero quasi dimenticato. Beh, allora lasciatemi raccontarvi l'ultima.[14]

ALESSANDRA: E spero che non sia fredda.[15]

DOMENICO: Né troppo lunga.

BARBARA: Dai,[16] Salvatore, racconta!

SALVATORE: Allora . . . Sapete qual è la migliore definizione del paradiso?

BARBARA: Boh![17]

SALVATORE: In paradiso, gli inglesi ti danno i benvenuto, i francesi cucinano, i tedeschi organizzano tutto e gli italiani programmano tutte le attività ricreative. Adesso, qual è la migliore definizione dell'inferno?

BARBARA: Qual è?

SALVATORE: In inferno, i francesi ti danno il benvenuto, gli inglesi cucinano, i tedeschi programmano tutte le attività ricreative e gli italiani organizzano tutto.

DOMENICO: Ah, ah, ah . . . Bellissima!

BARBARA: Ah, ah, ah . . . Sì, è bellissima. Immaginate un po' cosa succederebbe se gli italiani fossero gli organizzatori! Povero Paradiso! Che Dio ce ne liberi!

ALESSANDRA: È carina, ma, secondo me, non fa altro che rinforzare certi stereotipi.

SALVATORE: **Ma le barzellette spesso sono fatte proprio così. Se non fosse così, che razza[19] di barzellete sarebbero? E poi la gente dovrebbe poter ridere di sé, no?**

DOMENICO: **Beh, mentre voi due discutete la natura e i limiti dell'umorismo, io vi interrompo per ringraziarvi dell'invito e della squisita ospitalità.**

BARBARA: **Ed io vi invito a venire a sciare a Bolzano l'anno prossimo . . . Sarete nostri graditissimi ospiti!**

SALVATORE: **Grazie dell'invito. Se veniamo, io non dimenticherò di portarmi maglione, cappotto, scarponi, passamontagna . . .[20]**

AT CARNIVAL TIME ANY PRANK GOES

We are in Acireale, near Catania in Sicily, at the end of Carnival. Barbara and Domenico have come from Bolzano to visit their friends Salvatore and Alessandra and to take part in the festivities. To celebrate their last evening together in Sicily, the two couples are having drinks at a bar.

SALVATORE: Domenico, since you're returning home tomorrow morning, are you sure you don't want to borrow one of my sweaters?

DOMENICO: Very funny. But it's true that I will miss the lovely weather! If only we were staying a few more days!

BARBARA: Yes. It's been splendid. And I now understand why this Carnival is considered one of the best in Italy and why so many people speak about it.

DOMENICO: Those floats were magnificent!

ALESSANDRA: It's true that they're unique. In my opinion, no other carnival has such interesting and colorful floats.

BARBARA: They were all so beautifully lit by those torches. And all of the people dressed in costumes, blowing horns and throwing confetti everywhere. What a party! Unforgettable! Of course I wouldn't be so happy about it if I were the one who had to clean up!

DOMENICO: Well, if I had to repeat this experience, I would repeat it right away.

SALVATORE: Mimì, we had already realized it. In fact, you almost climbed up on one of the floats. A great way of celebrating Mardi Gras with the Acesi.

ALESSANDRA: Salvatore, you always feel like joking!

DOMENICO: It's true. Totò wouldn't know what to do if he didn't joke around.

SALVATORE: Well, aren't we at Carnival? As the saying goes, "At Carnival time any prank goes." Isn't Carnival a time for the last delights before lent, time of penance and abstinence?

BARBARA: Salvatore, didn't you have a joke to tell us?

ALESSANDRA: Oh no! Did you have to remind him? He would surely have forgotten if you hadn't said anything!

SALVATORE: Yes! You're right! I almost forgot. Well . . . let me tell you the latest.

ALESSANDRA: It better be funny!

DOMENICO: And not too long!

BARBARA: Come on, Salvatore. Start.

SALVATORE: As I was saying . . . Do you know what's the best definition of heaven?

BARBARA: I give up.

SALVATORE: In heaven, the British greet you when you arrive, the French do all of the cooking, the Germans organize everything, and the Italians plan all the fun. Now, what is the best definition of hell?

BARBARA: What is it?

SALVATORE: In hell, the French greet you when you arrive, the British do all of the cooking, the Germans plan all of the fun, and the Italians organize everything.

DOMENICO: Ha, ha, ha . . . Great!

BARBARA: Ha, ha, ha! Yes, it's very funny. Just imagine what would happen if the Italians were the organizers! Good heavens! God forbid!

ALESSANDRA: It is funny, but as far I'm concerned it just reinforces certain stereotypes.

SALVATORE: But this is usually the way jokes are! If this were not the case, what kind of jokes would they be? And besides, people should be able to laugh at themselves!

DOMENICO: Well, while you two debate the nature and limits of good humor, I want to thank you for your invitation and for your exquisite hospitality.

BARBARA: And I'm inviting you two for skiing in Bolzano next year! It will be a pleasure to have you with us.

SALVATORE: Thank you for your invitation. If we come, I will not forget to bring my sweater, my coat, my boots, and my ski mask . . .

B. IN BREVE

1. This Sicilian town is located in the province of Catania, on the Ionian sea, at the foot of Mount Etna. The most famous Sicilian Carnival is held in Acireale.

2. Catania (population approx. 350,000) is a *comune* of Sicily, located at the foot of Mount Etna. Historically, this beautiful city has been dominated by Greek, Roman, Ostrogoth, and Arab conquerors, among others. It became part of the kingdom of Italy in 1861. It was almost completely destroyed in World War II, but flourished again soon after. Catania's main industries are agriculture, fishing, and minerals. The city has been the birthplace of many illustrious figures, most notably the writers Luigi Capuana and Giovanni Verga, and the composer Vincenzo Bellini.

3. *Sicilia* (Sicily) is one of Italy's two island regions, the other being *Sardegna* (Sardinia). Sicily is a beautiful region, rich in culture and tradition. It has the most temperate climate in Italy and is the largest island in the Mediterranean. It is separated from the rest of Italy by the strait of Messina.

4. Bolzano (population approx. 100,000) is one of the northernmost *comuni* (municipalities) of Italy, and is one of the two *capoluoghi di provincia* (provincial capitals) of the mountainous Trentino-Alto Adige region. Its principal industries include marble and agriculture. Throughout history, Bolzano has been under the rule of Ger-

man-speaking peoples on more than one occasion. In fact, the city did not become definitively Italian until the end of World War I (in 1918), when it was acquired from Austria. Because of the influence of German, many inhabitants of the province of Bolzano have German as their mother tongue.

5. Generally these floats are used to satirize public figures (often, those satirized are politicians). People wearing masks of the target figures may re-enact situations for which the figures have become notorious. All of this is staged on the floats.

6. The plural of *il migliaio* (about a thousand) is *le migliaia*. Remember to place the preposition *di* before the noun. *Sembrava che nella piazza ci fossero migliaia di persone che buttavano coriandoli.* (It seemed as if there were thousands of people in the square throwing confetti.)

7. *Coriandoli* (confetti) is used in particular for *Carnevale*. The Italian word *confetti* indicates almond candies, which are used as a party favor at weddings.

8. In Sicilian *Mimì* is a short form of Domenico.

9. *Salire* requires *essere* when it is used intransitively (*Sono salito sul carro allegorico.* I got on the float.) and *avere* when used transitively (*Ha salito le scale.* He went up the stairs.)

10. The English equivalent of *Martedì Grasso* is Fat Tuesday, also known as Mardi Gras or Pancake Tuesday. It is the last Tuesday of *Carnevale* and precedes Ash Wednesday *(mercoledì delle ceneri)*.

11. The *acesi* are the inhabitants of Acireale. Normally, to indicate the inhabitants of a town or city you add *-ani* or *-esi* to the name of the town, e.g., *i milanesi, i romani, i baresi, i veneziani, i napoletani,* etc.

12. In Sicilian *Totò* is a short form of Salvatore.

13. *Barzelletta* is the term used for "joke" in Italian. A riddle is an *indovinello,* and a punch-line or one-liner is referred to as a *battuta.*

14. The noun *barzelletta* or *notizia* is understood. The adjective is here used as a noun to indicate "the latest joke."

15. The adjective *freddo* is here used methaphorically to indicate "lack in humour" in the jokes. Common expressions containing *freddo* include *fare il freddo* "to act indifferently," *sangue freddo* "cold blooded," *testa fredda* "not ruled by passions," *tavola fredda* "cold buffet."

16. From the verb *dare,* this can be translated by the English "come on". Similar expressions are *Forza! Su! Coraggio!* or in this context *Sbrigati!*

17. *Boh!* is an interjection commonly used to express uncertainty and incredulity.

18. *Il tutto* signifies "the whole," "the entire thing."

19. The expression *che razza di . . .* expresses "what kind of . . . " *Razza* can also be used to express "type," "kind," as in the expressions *che razza di educazione ha?* (What kind of manners does he have?), *Se ne vedono di tutte le razze.* (One sees all kinds.)

20. The compound word *passamontagna* is masculine and is invariable in the plural.

C. GRAMMATICA E SUOI USI

1. *USI PARTICOLARI DEL CONGIUNTIVO* (SPECIAL USES OF THE SUBJUNCTIVE)

The present subjunctive may be used alone in an independent clause to express an exhortation or a strong wish or desire.

Dio vi benedica!
Che Dio vi benedica!
    May God bless you.

Che sia una barzelletta pulita!
Make sure it's a clean joke!

The imperfect subjunctive in independent clauses is used to express regret or wishes which are contrary to reality.

Magari fosse vero!
If only it were true!

Venisse a trovarci oggi!
If only he would come and visit us today!

Almeno le sapesse raccontare le barzellette!
If only he knew how to tell jokes!

2. *LA FRASE IPOTETICA* (THE "IF" CLAUSE)

The *frase ipotetica* (the "if" clause) is used to communicate hypotheses and their consequences. It is made up of two parts: the dependent clause introduced by *se* (if), which expresses the condition, and the independent clause, which states the consequence.

Se assisteranno alla sfilata del Carnevale, si divertiranno.
If they attend the Carnival parade, they will have fun.

Se leggessero quella tragedia, capirebbero l'autore.
If they read that tragedy, they would understand the author.

Se avessero raccontato un'altra barzelletta, avremmo perso la sfilata.
If they had told another joke, we would have missed the parade.

The tense and the mood of the verbs in hypothetical sentences depends on whether the situation is 1) real or likely to occur *(il periodo ipotetico della realtà)*, 2) possible *(il periodo ipotetico della possibilità)*, or 3) contrary to fact *(il periodo ipotetico dell'irrealtà)*.

a. Real or likely to occur situations

When real or plausible situations are described, the *se* clause is always in the *indicativo* and the result clause is in the *indicativo* or the *imperativo*.

CONDITION ("IF" CLAUSE)	CONSEQUENCE
se + presente	*presente*
	futuro
	imperativo
se + futuro	*futuro*
	imperativo
se + passato prossimo	*presente*
passato remoto	*futuro*
imperfetto	*imperfetto*
	passato prossimo
	passato remoto
	imperativo

Note that after "if," Italian uses the future tense when the action will occur in the future. In English, the present tense is used, and the future is only implied.

Se ritornano ora, andremo alla festa.
   If they're returning now, we will go to the party.

Se andrai al Carnevale vedrai i carri allegorici.
   If you go to the Carnival you will see the allegorical floats.

Se hanno incontrato gli amici solo un'ora fa, sono ancora al bar.
   If they met their friends only an hour ago, they are still at the bar.

   b. Possible situations

   When the *se* clause describes situations that are probable (likely or not likely to happen), the *congiuntivo imperfetto* is used in the *se* clause and the *condizionale* in the result clause.

CONDITION (IF-CLAUSE)	CONSEQUENCE
se + congiuntivo imperfetto	*condizionale presente*
	condizionale passato

Se avessi il coraggio, gli direi tutta la verità.
   If I had the courage I would tell him the whole truth.

Se fosse informata, non ti avrebbe chiesto delle informazioni.
   If she were informed she would not have asked you for information.

Se oggi non lavorassimo, potremmo prenderci il sole alla spiaggia.
If we were not working today, we could be sunbathing at the beach.

c. Contrary to fact situations

To express a contrary to fact situation, use *se* + *congiuntivo trapassato* and the *condizionale presente* or *passato*

CONDITIONAL ("IF" CLAUSE)	CONSEQUENCE
se + *congiuntivo trapassato*	*condizionale presente*
	condizionale passato

Se avesse organizzato la festa lui, non avrebbe invitato quei signori.
If he had organized the party, he would not have invited those gentlemen.

Se Carla e Bianca non fossero venute a incontrarci, noi saremmo rimasti a lavorare fino a tardi.
If Carla and Bianca had not come to meet us, we would have worked till late.

Non parlerebbe l'italiano così bene, se non avesse studiato tanto.
He would not speak Italian so well if he hadn't studied so much.

Unlike in English, *se* can be omitted in Italian.

Fosse veramente comica la barzelletta, ve la racconterei.
If the joke were really funny, I would tell it to you.

Note that the order of the clauses is interchangeable. However, when the "if" clause is stated first, *se* is required.

Se avessi avuto una maschera, avrei partecipato anch'io.
Avrei partecipato anch'io, se avessi avuto una maschera.
If I had had a mask, I would have participated, too.

In present day Italian, and especially in conversation, the *imperfetto indicativo* replaces both the *congiuntivo trapassato* in the *se* clause, and the *condizionale passato* in the result clause.

Se avessi avuto i coriandoli, li avrei buttati.
Se avevo i coriandoli, li buttavo.
   If I had had the confetti, I would have thrown it.

   d. Other uses of *se*

   Se can also mean "whether."

Non sono sicura se si vestirà da Arlecchino.
   I am not sure whether he will dress as Harlequin.

   Se + congiuntivo imperfetto can also be used to make a suggestion. This
   construction expresses the English "What if . . ." or "How about . . ."

Se affittassimo dei costumi?
   What if we rented some costumes?

Se organizzassimo un ballo in maschera questo sabato?
   What about organizing a costume party this Saturday?

   Se used with the *congiuntivo imperfetto* or *trapassato* expresses regret
   ("if only").

Se potessero tacere!
   If only they could keep quiet!

Se non fossi arrivato in ritardo!
   If only I hadn't been late!

3. *LA CONCORDANZA DEI TEMPI DEL CONGIUNTIVO* (THE SEQUENCE OF TENSES IN THE SUBJUNCTIVE)

The tense of the subjunctive is determined by the tense of the main
verb. If the verb in the principal clause is in the present or future tense
or in the imperative, the present subjunctive is used in the independent
clause to express a simultaneous or future action. If the action has
already taken place, then the present perfect subjunctive is used.

Non credo che scherzi adesso.
   I don't think he is joking now.

Vorrà che Sandro paghi l'entrata.
   He will want Sandro to pay the entrance fee.

Dubito che abbia sospettato qualcosa.
   I doubt that he suspected a thing.

When the verb of the principal clause is in a past or conditional tense, the imperfect subjunctive is used in the dependent clause to express a simultaneous or future action. The past perfect subjunctive is used if the action had already taken place.

Credevo che m'invitasse a ballare.
   I thought he was going to invite me to dance.

Credevamo che fossero già tornati dal ballo in maschera.
   We thought they had already returned from the masquerade ball.

Dubitavamo che trovasse la mashera adatta.
   We doubted that she would find the right mask.

The following chart summarizes the sequence of tenses.

INDEPENDENT CLAUSE	RELATION BETWEEN CLAUSES	DEPENDENT CLAUSE
Present indicative/ Future/Imperative	concurrent action	present subjunctive
	past action	past subjunctive
	future action	present subjunctive/ future
Any past tense Conditional	concurrent action	imperfect subjunctive
	past action	perfect subjunctive
	future action	imperfect subjunctive/ past conditional

D. PAROLE! PAROLE! PAROLE!

Morire (to die), like its English counterpart, appears in many idiomatic expressions.

Sto morendo di fame.
   I'm starving to death.

Stanotte sono morto di freddo.
   Last night I froze to death.

Oggi fa un freddo da morire.
   Today is freezing cold.

Ho una sete da morire.
   I'm dying of thirst.

Sono stanco da morire.
   I'm dead tired.

Vorrei morire se non è vero.
   I'll be damned if it's not true.

Chi non muore si rivede!
   Look who's here!

Ci andrò anche a costo di morire.
   I'll go even if it kills me.

Meglio/Peggio di così si muore!
   You can't have better/worse than that! (It couldn't be better/worse!)

Giovanni muore per quella ragazza.
   Giovanni is mad about that girl.

Si sa dove si nasce, non dove si muore!
   We know our birthplace, but we do not know where our end shall be!

Muoio dalla curiosità!
   I'm dying of curiosity!

Muoio dalla voglia/dal desiderio di andare in Italia!
   I'm dying to go to Italy!

Sono morto dallo spavento!
   I dropped dead of fright!

Sto morendo di noia.
   I'm bored to death.

Mi farai morire!
   You'll be the death of me!

Le mie speranze sono morte!
   My hopes died away!

364

Questa strada muore a Roma.
This road comes to an end in Rome.

Quell'uomo ha visto morire tutti i figli.
That man outlived all his children.

Più facile di così si muore!
Nothing could be easier than that!

E. L'ANGOLO DEGLI AFFARI

LE TRADIZIONI ITALIANE (ITALIAN TRADITIONS)

Italians have countless traditions, many of which have their origins in religious feasts that have been held for centuries. At times the traditions vary from region to region.

Carnevale, the Mardi Gras, is an old and honored tradition in Italy. In every city and in every town throughout the peninsula this period is celebrated with various festivities, some of which, like those of the Mardi Gras in New Orleans, Louisiana, have become world-famous.

Carnevale festivities begin days or even weeks prior to the actual day of *martedì grasso* (literally, Fat Tuesday). The day after *martedì grasso,* Ash Wednesday, marks the commencement of Lent, the forty-day period of penitence and contrition which culminates in the celebration of Easter. For this reason, the period of *Carnevale* is meant to be a time in which people can celebrate, get all their vices out of their systems, so to speak, before they begin their period of abstinence.

Probably the most internationally known *Carnevale* occurs in Venice. Walking through the streets of this beautiful and unique city is even more spectacular during *Carnevale.* Thousands of people flock to the city to dress in beautiful and elaborate costumes. Venice is known for its masks, and this becomes evident when one sees the elaborate and beautiful masks worn by people on the streets of Venice. Often the masks are frozen in frightening grimaces in order to ward off any evil spirits. Historically, however, masks worn at *Carnevale* served more of a social function than a religious one. They were worn by revellers who did not wish to be recognized. In past centuries, for instance, the masks served nobles well, as they engaged in acts of merriment and debauchery in the streets without being recognized.

Although the tradition of the mask is pretty widely diffused at *Carnevale,* different traditions preside in other cities in Italy. In the city of Viareggio, in Tuscany, papier-mâché floats are constructed and then paraded across the *lungomare,* the long promenade close to the sea. The floats usually have an allegorical meaning and are ridden by people in costumes. This Medieval tradition is taken to very elaborate heights. The floats appear in a procession amidst a storm of *coriandoli* (confetti). Like those of other cities, the Viareggio Carnival culminates in various parties, the largest of which takes place in the streets. There is music and dancing until the wee hours. The hallmark of the Viareggio Carnival, however, lies in the construction of the allegorical floats. Talented artisans dedicate months to the making of these floats prior to the advent of the festivities.

In Acireale, Sicily, the tradition of building floats has also been adopted, but the focus is slightly different. The traditions of the Acireale Carnival originated in the seventeenth century. The parade in Acireale is a much more colorful one, as floats are covered in flowers, mostly carnations.* Acireale's festivities are quite lively, and include animated games such as sack races and the *albero della cuccagna,* literally, the tree of the greasy pole, in which competitors must race to climb a pole that is covered in grease.

The period of *Pasqua,* Easter, is full of traditions. Italy is well known for its food, and the country's different regions hold many gastronomical traditions. Easter is a time for sweets, and in Italy's *pasticcerie,* or pastry shops, one can find a variety of desserts during the weeks leading up to Easter. In many parts of Italy one can find a dessert that is made of large, deep-fried ribbons of dough covered in powdered sugar. This delicious treat is called *crostoli* in Northern regions such as Veneto and Friuli-Venezia Giulia, *chiacchiere* in Sicily, and may have other names in other regions. Another *pasticceria* favorite is the *colomba* (dove), a dove-shaped sponge cake. Finally, Italian pastry shops are filled with giant chocolate Easter eggs that are made on the premises by expert pastry chefs.

The most typical Easter feast has lamb as its main dish, although traditions vary. The day following Easter, many Italians often go off to the country to enjoy a picnic on Easter Monday, *lunedì in albis* or *pasquetta.*

If there is one tradition that unites all Italians it is that of *Ferragosto,* the fifteenth of August. On this day, and in most cases, for at least a two-week period surrounding this day, virtually all of Italy comes to a stand-

---

* The *garofano* (carnation) is the national flower of Italy.

still, as Italians leave their homes and flock to the country's beaches, mountain resorts, and campgrounds. Italians take their holiday period very seriously, and in fact, if one travels to Italy in mid-August and plans to visit museums, to shop, or even to dine out, one will be extremely disappointed. During the period of *Ferragosto* even the largest Italian centers become ghost towns. Shops and businesses close for periods of up to a month.

Like Easter, Christmas, *Natale,* is a time of many traditions. Most cities and towns are heavily decorated throughout the Christmas season. It is difficult to believe that Italy is operating at a deficit when one sees the amount of lights and other decorations put up by municipal governments in order to mark the season. In modern times Christmas has become an extremely commercial holiday in Italy as in much of the Western world, and consequently, stores tend to remain open seven days a week in many parts of Italy for the weeks leading up to Christmas.* However, Christmas gifts tend to be more sentimental than expensive in Italy.

Christmas dinner menus tend to vary in Italy. However, often the traditions are similar: families gather on Christmas Eve to have a late supper before attending Midnight Mass. In Southern Italy, this supper consists of many fish courses. Following Mass, families will return home to open the gifts they have exchanged. The next family gathering occurs at lunch on Christmas day. *Lasagna* is a popular Christmas dish in some families; for others, a meat course is mandatory. Turkey is beginning to become popular, probably due to American influence. Typical Christmas desserts are *panettone,* a sponge-cake with raisins and candied fruits, or *pandoro,* a similar cake minus the fruit and garnished with powdered sugar. Many variations of this dessert exist. Some are injected and covered with chocolate cream, chantilly cream, or other fillings. *Torrone* is also a popular sweet. It is generally made with caramellized almonds and then shaped into bars. There are many variations of this as well.

The Christmas holidays are longer in Italy than they are in America. New Year's Eve, *l'ultimo dell'anno* (the last of the year), is celebrated in much the same fashion as North America. However, Italians do not return to their regular schedule after January 1st as Americans do. Holidays continue until the end of the first week of January. On January

---

* Laws regarding store openings and closings are very strict in Italy. Generally, stores must only remain open five days a week, and must not remain open for more than eight hours a day. They must be closed on Sundays, and one other day. During the Christmas holidays many *comuni* (town halls) relax their laws and allow stores to open every day.

6th, Italians celebrate *Epifania,* the Epiphany. On this day, which is celebrated in commemoration of the Three Magi's arrival at the birthplace
of Jesus, children are given small gifts, and are told that if they have not
been good, they will receive coal instead of a gift. The legendary figure
who distributes gifts on this day is the *Befana,* an old, witch-like woman
with a hooked nose.

Italy is a country steeped in tradition. Part of the fascination of
discovering this remarkable country lies in learning the different
traditions, in discovering their common elements and their variations.
Here is the list of Italian public holidays: New Years Day (January 1),
Epiphany (January 6), Easter Monday (varies), Liberation Day
(April 25), Labor Day (May 1), Assumption or the day of Ferragosto
(August 15), All Saints Day (November 1), Immaculate Conception
(December 8), Christmas (December 25), Boxing Day or Santo Stefano
(December 26).

ESERCIZI

A. *Trasformare le seguenti frasi in frasi ipotetiche. Seguire l'esempio.*
(Rewrite the following sentences, following the example.)

ESEMPIO: Se tu decidi di andare alla sfilata, vengo con te.
               Se tu decidessi di andare alla sfilata, verrei con te.

1. *Se piove, non vado in centro.*
2. *Se ci fermiamo al bar, prendo qualcosa.*
3. *Se non racconta una barzelletta, muore.*
4. *Se andate insieme alla festa di Carnevale, vi divertite di sicuro.*
5. *Se ci sono i carabinieri, gli fanno sicuramente la multa.*
6. *Se ascolti, ti racconto una bella barzelletta.*
7. *Se i bambini entrano nel bar, ti buttano addosso i coriandoli.*
8. *Se posso, vengo all'aeoporto a prenderti.*

B. *Completare le seguenti frasi ipotetiche con due verbi opportuni.* (Fill in
the blanks, using the imperfect subjunctive and the simple conditional.)

1. *Se ci _____ la sfilata, noi _____ in centro.*
2. *Se quella maschera non _____ così tanto, io la _____ subito.*

368

3. Se _____ brutto tempo, noi _____ a casa.
4. Se Silvio _____ più lentamente, i suoi amici _____ tutto quello che dice.
5. Se non _____ Carnevale, noi _____ la tua reazione.
6. Se mi _____ una barzelletta, te ne _____ una pure io.
7. Se voi _____ alla festa, _____ i bambini e i loro costumi di Carnevale.
8. Se tu _____ i soldi, me li _____?

C. *Completare gli spazi vuoti con il congiuntivo o il condizionale, usando i seguenti verbi.* (Choosing from the following verbs, fill in the blanks with the subjunctive or the conditional.)

venire   dire   sapere   accompagnare
avere   raccontare   perdere   arrivare

1. *Avreste visto i bambini in costume, se _____ prima.*
2. *Se _____ che tu non c'eri, io non sarei venuto.*
3. *Se alla festa _____ anche Barbara, ci sarei venuto anch'io.*
4. *Se avessi avuto la macchina, vi _____ io a vedere la sfilata.*
5. *Se tu me lo _____ prima, sarei venuta anch'io al bar.*
6. *Se si fossero alzati presto, non _____ l'autobus.*
7. *Se ci fossimo accorti che le barzellette non le piacciono, noi non le _____.*
8. *Se _____ i soldi, saremmo andati anche noi al cinema.*

D. *Tradurre.* (Translate.)

1. May God bless you, children!
2. I am not sure whether they have seen the children sounding horns and throwing confetti of various colors in the air.
3. Alessandra, don't get upset. Today you're really not in the mood. As they say: "At the Carnival, any prank goes!"
4. We're bored to death! This party is so boring!
5. I'll be damned if it's not true!
6. I haven't eaten all day. I'm starving to death. What's there to eat?

SECONDO RIPASSO (SECOND REVIEW)

A. *Completare usando il condizionale presente o passato di un verbo appropriato, scegliendo tra i seguenti.*

desiderare	avere	andare	volere x 2	venire
partire	immaginare	dovere	essere	piacere

1. *Mi _____ investire in beni immobili.*
2. *Io _____ un'altra domanda. La casa ha il riscaldamento autonomo?*
3. *Tu _____ proprio andare dal medico. L'asma può essere una condizione molto seria.*
4. *Loro _____ intrattenere rapporti d'affari con la ditta Lineatre di Poggibonsi.*
5. *Quando Le ho parlato al telefono non _____ mai _____ che Lei fosse di origine italiana.*
6. *La nostra compagnia _____ che il candidato avesse un'esperienza consolidata da almeno cinque anni nell'industria alimentare.*
7. *Sua moglie _____ anche a vivere in Italia?*
8. *Enzo mi ha detto che loro _____ subito e che sarebbero arrivati alla stazione di servizio verso le nove.*
9. *Noi _____ comprare una casa nuova: _____ possibile avere un prestito?*
10. *—Perché non sei andata dal dottore?*
    —Ci _____, ma non ho potuto.

B. *Completare le frasi usando il passato remoto di uno dei seguenti verbi.*

essere	venire	riuscire x 2	avere	lavorare
diventare	seguire	succedere	fare	vestirsi

1. *Noi finalmente _____ ad incontrarci.*
2. *Non fu la prima volta che loro _____ da queste parti. C'erano già stati qualche anno fa.*
3. *Nel 1141 la famiglia Ricasoli _____ proprietaria del castello.*
4. *Bettino Ricasoli _____ a Camillo Benso di Cavour.*
5. *Dopo che provò per oltre vent'anni, finalmente _____ a raggiungere la mescolanza giusta. _____ un vino eccezionale!*
6. *Quell'anno tutti _____ come Brigitte Bardot e Audrey Hepburn.*
7. *Dal 1953 al 1966 io _____ come direttore delle vendite presso la National Cheese Company Limited di Toronto.*

8. Marco _____ molti corsi di informatica e lavorò molto con i computer.

9. Nel Medioevo i padroni di questi palazzi _____ chiaramente più interessati a tenere lontano i loro nemici che all'estetica delle loro abitazioni.

10. I lavori _____ inizio ai primi del 400.

C. Completare le seguenti frasi usando il congiuntivo (presente o passato) o l'indicativo. Scegliere fra i seguenti verbi.

cercare   andare   essere   ritornare x 2
venire x 2 stare   disegnare partecipare

1. Abbiamo l'impressione che gli abiti da sera _____ intramontabili.

2. Io spero che si _____ al buon gusto di un tempo.

3. Sono sicura che domani nessuno _____ alla sfilata di moda.

4. Si dice che quella modella negli ultimi tempi _____ ad una decina di défilé.

5. È ovvio che con questi modelli noi _____ agli anni Sessanta e Settanta.

6. Io credo che loro _____ un direttore delle vendite con vasta esperienza amministrativa.

7. Oggi Franco non è venuto a lavorare. Immagino che non _____ bene.

8. Ho saputo che domani voi _____ a Firenze.

9. —Chi ha disegnato la facciata di questa chiesa?
   —Penso che l'_____ Leon Battista Alberti.

10. Mi hanno detto che quella macchina _____ con aria condizionata e air bag.

D. Completare le seguenti frasi con un verbo al congiuntivo imperfetto. Scegliere tra i seguenti verbi.

fare x 2   essere   alzarsi   avere   assumere
parlare   dire   iniziare   potere

1. Oh, io pensavo che tu _____ americano!

2. Loro vorrebbero che io _____ subito a lavorare, ma non posso.

3. Signor Centuori, desidererei che Lei mi _____ un favore.

4. Se noi L'_____, Lei potrebbe cominciare a lavorare a gennaio?

5. Noi preferiremmo che Lei _____ correntemente sia l'italiano che l'inglese.

6. —*A che ora si alzavano la mattina?*
   —*Credo che _____ molto presto per andare a lavorare.*
7. —*Secondo te, lui diceva la verità?*
   —*Dubito che _____ la verità. Non mi sembra il tipo.*
8. *Se io _____, andrei subito in Italia.*
9. *Se questa macchina _____ l'aria condizionata, io la comprerei subito.*
10. *Preferirei che voi non _____ domanda per questo posto.*

E. *Tradurre.*

1. Some fat-free products are not healthy because they are high in sodium.
2. We suggested some measures to combat inflation. We are certain they will work.
3. The modem is used to access the Internet.
4. After having worked on the computer for a whole day, one feels tired.
5. When the manager arrived, the meeting had already started.
6. What those doctors say does not convince me.
7. Those real estate agents earn as much as I do. It's not fair!
8. This type of work doesn't interest me at all. I am looking for another job.
9. When I saw her, I threw myself into her arms. I had not seen her since September.
10. —Is it true that you won a million dollars?
    —Ah, if only it were true!
11. Lucia and Maurizio are on familiar terms. Aren't they?
12. I told him that he must stand up to people. I hope he will follow my advice.
13. After what happened, I wanted to kick myself.
14. Now more than ever we need to save.
15. Last night his house was packed with people.

LEGGIAMO!

ARANCE CON LE ALI *

Journalist Pino Nano, using the example of a Calabrian businessman, demonstrates how today's southern Italy, although less industrialized than its richer northern counterpart, is quite modernized and as avid about progress and industrial development as any other part of the western world.

Clementine: il termine è assai comune. Lo è soprattutto in Calabria. Si tratta di una qualità pregiata di mandarini. Vengono prodotti soltanto nella piana di Sibari[1] *e Corigliano.*[2] *Sono mandarini dolcissimi, senza semi,*[3] *aromatici, dalla buccia*[4] *sottilissima. Sotto il profilo organolettico non c'è qualità migliore di questa. Ma c'è di più: il prodotto matura soltanto in questa particolarissima zona della Calabria. I tentativi di produrlo altrove sono falliti sul nascere. La sola piana di Sibari vanta*[5] *oggi una produzione complessiva pari al 40 per cento della produzione lorda*[6] *nazionale. Ma per anni nessuno, o quasi, ha mai saputo della loro esistenza sul mercato. I produttori locali si sono quindi dovuti accontentare di molto poco, vendendo il prodotto sotto casa a due lire,*[7] *o nella migliore delle ipotesi direttamente nei campi. È storia vecchia anche questa, storia di una agricoltura povera, priva di strumenti di promozione vera, ma soprattutto priva di grandi sponsor industriali. Altrove le piantagioni*[8] *di clementine che ci sono oggi in Calabria si sarebbero trasformate in una vera e propria miniera.*[9] *Ma forse non è mai troppo tardi. La cronaca ci avverte che siamo in presenza di una grande svolta.*[10] *Per molti versi una svolta storica. Dal 20 al 30 dicembre, quindi per tutto il periodo natalizio, questi mandarini, targati*[11] *"made in Calabria," voleranno sugli aerei dell'Alitalia [. . .]*

Questo voler affidare all'Alitalia l'immagine di una Calabria vera, la Calabria che produce [. . .], sarà certamente un'operazione pubblicitaria che sul piano economico nessuno potrà mai monetizzare con precisione. Sarebbe stupido negarlo: l'operazione è assolutamente ambiziosa. A deciderla, e a volerla con tutte le sue forze, è stato un giovane imprenditore di Corigliano, Nicola Rizzo, un manager che ha scelto di dedicare la sua vita al mondo dell'agricoltura calabrese [. . .]

---

* Pino Nano, *"Arance con le ali." Non solo mafia.* Cosenza: Edigraf, 1993, pp. 117–20.

Nel giro di[12] pochi anni [Nicola Rizzo] ha messo su un'azienda agricola che mezza Italia oggi gli invidia. È vero, è l'azienda del padre, l'azienda di famiglia, ma con l'arrivo di Nicola le regole interne sono cambiate, e al posto delle vecchie ed antiche abitudini contadine Nicola ha preteso che fossero i computer a regolare la vita dell'impresa.

Ai vecchi contadini ha sostituito gli agronomi,[13] ai vecchi modi di trattare la terra ha preferito le sofisticate tecniche di ingegneria agraria, alle vecchie produzioni e alle vecchie colture ha preferito l'innovazione [. . .]

Come avrà fatto a convincere l'Alitalia a tuffarsi in una operazione simile?

Nicola Rizzo sorride in maniera disarmante, poi risponde con una semplicità che nasconde grande competenza e grande padronanza: "È semplice, ho offerto all'Alitalia i nostri prodotti. Ho chiesto che accettassero le nostre clementine come frutta da servire a bordo. E naturalmente ho offerto le nostre clementine ad un prezzo assolutamente concorrenziale.[14] Gratis. Proprio così. La nostra associazione regalerà all'Alitalia quasi 5 mila clementine selezionate e confezionate: in cambio abbiamo chiesto che venissero distribuite su tutti i voli diretti in Europa" [. . .]

Oggi l'esperimento riguarda i paesi Europei, domani [. . .] potrebbe essere adottato su tutti i voli intercontinentali. Questo significa che in ogni parte del mondo, su questi bellissimi aerei dell'Alitalia, potrebbero volare milioni di mandarini calabresi.

VOCABOLARIO

1. Sybaris (ancient Calabrian city, proverbial for luxury; destroyed in 510 B.C.). The Piana di Sibari is the largest coastal plain in Calabria.
2. Corigliano Calabro, town of approximately 36,000 inhabitants, 75 km from the city of Cosenza.
3. seedless
4. peel
5. boasts
6. gross
7. literally, "two lire" (at a low price)
8. plantations

9. mine
10. turning point
11. literally, "with the plate" (labeled)
12. in the space of
13. agronomists
14. competitive

ANSWER KEY

LEZIONE 1

A. 1. *il biologo, i biologi* 2. *lo sportello, gli sportelli* 3. *il computer, i computer* 4. *il lago, i laghi* 5. *l'amico, gli amici* 6. *la società, le società* 7. *lo psicologo, gli psicologi* 8. *la banca, le banche* 9. *il greco, i greci* 10. *il fuoco, i fuochi* 11. *il bagaglio, i bagagli* 12. *la valigia, le valigie* 13. *la bugia, le bugie* 14. *la serie, le serie* 15. *la crisi, le crisi*

B. 1. *Il signor Paolo Rossi, rappresentante di una ditta americana, telefona all'ufficio Alitalia.* 2. *Vorrei fare una prenotazione per Roma.* 3. *Devo partire il mese prossimo. Vorrei restare in Italia un mese.* 4. *Signorina, mi prenoti un posto per il 16 maggio.* 5. *Ci sono dei posti liberi per il 24 aprile?* 6. *Che tipo di aereo è? Un Airbus?* 7. *Ecco il biglietto, il passaporto, gli scontrini e la carta d'imbarco.* 8. *Con me ho anche il mio computer portatile.* 9. *Un attimo di attenzione, per cortesia.* 10. *Siete pregati di mettere lo schienale in posizione verticale.*

C. 1. *parla* 2. *partiamo* 3. *paghiamo* 4. *vedete (vedono)* 5. *preferiscono* 6. *viaggi* 7. *dimentichi* 8. *ricordo*

D. 1. *Signor Verdi, c'è un volo domani? —No, c'è un volo il mese prossimo, il due agosto.* 2. *Quando parti (parte) per l'Italia? —Parto fra cinque giorni.* 3. *Telefoni a Diana stasera? —No, le telefono sabato.* 4. *Quale rivista italiana Le piace leggere? —Mi piacciono L'Espresso e Panorama.* 5. *C'è un volo per Milano domani? —No, il lunedì non ci sono voli per Milano.* 6. *È vero che la Sicilia è la più bella regione d'Italia?* 7. *Abbiamo prenotato per il signor Giannini una camera (stanza) bella ed elegante in uno stupendo hotel (albergo) medievale.* 8. *Potrei vedere quelle cravatte blu, per favore.* 9. *Come si dice "decollo" in inglese? —Dunque . . . si dice . . . mi dispiace ma la parola non viene in mente neanche a me. Aspetta, adesso ricordo. Si dice "take-off."* 10. *Ci dobbiamo sbrigare. Dobbiamo essere all'aeroporto alle cinque. La partenza è alle sei e sono già le quattro e mezzo (quattro e mezza; quattro e trenta).*

LEZIONE 2

A. 1. *vi preparate* 2. *si mettono* 3. *si ferma* 4. *si salutano, si abbracciano* 5. *mi tengo* 6. *mi rinfresco, mi riposo*

B. 1. *è partito, è arrivato* 2. *sono sceso, sono salito* 3. *vi siete fermati* 4. *abbiamo dichiarato* 5. *ha viaggiato, ha voluto* 6. *ci siamo visti, siamo andati* 7. *abbiamo scritto, abbiamo letto* 8. *è costato* 9. *è durato* 10. *è piaciuto*

C. *è entrata, ha dato, si è presa, ha lasciato, si è fermata, è andata, si è rinfrescata, si è riposata, si è svegliata, si è fatta, si è messa, è scesa, è andata*

D. 1. *Al Duty Free abbiamo comprato dei regali per i bambini.* 2. *Le dispiace se fumo? —No, naturalmente! (Naturalmente no)* 3. *A bordo non mi sono annoiato e in dogana tutto è andato bene.* 4. *Ieri sera siamo corsi all'aeroporto.* 5. *—Signore, ha qualcosa da dichiarare?* 6. *Preferisco viaggiare con la mia famiglia. Non mi piace viaggiare (da) solo.* 7. *È una chiacchiera. Non è vero.* 8. *Giovanni, ti devi sbrigare (devi sbrigarti) perche è tardi.* 9. *Signorina, qual è lo scopo del Suo viaggio? È qui in vacanza?* 10. *Ha (è) nevicato tutto il giorno ed avevano paura di volare.*

LEZIONE 3

A. 1. *Se ci dirai dove abiti, verremo a trovarti.* 2. *Gino, andrete in Italia quest'estate?* 3. *Quando ci vedremo, ti porterò degli opuscoli.* 4. *Il mio ufficio offrirà diversi supporti informativi ed assistenziali.* 5. *Ha detto che non appena sapranno la notizia, ve la comunicheranno.*

B. 1. *potrò* 2. *verrò* 3. *incomincerà* 4. *sarà* 5. *cercherò*

C. 1. *telefonerà, sarà arrivato (arriverà)* 2. *rientreranno (saranno rientrati), darò* 3. *avrà finito* 4. *spedirò* 5. *sarà, passerò*

D. 1. *nostri* 2. *la loro* 3. *mia, tua* 4. *Suo* 5. *la sua*

E. 1. *Sono i miei zii.* 2. *È mio nipote.* 3. *È mio cognato* 4. *È mia cugina.* 5. *È mia madre.*

F. 1. *I loro amici sono italiani?—No, sono americani.* 2. *Dove abitano i tuoi genitori?—Abitano in via Bloor (a Bloor Street). Non molto lontano da qui.* 3. *È tuo/Suo questo libro?—No, è il libro di Teresa.* 4. *Il signor Green non c'è? Potrei lasciargli un messaggio?* 5. *Mi dispiace. Ho sbagliato numero.* 6. *Per le telefonate interurbane, non dimenticare di fare il prefisso.* 7. *Potrei parlare con la signorina Bonomo, interno 5543?* 8. *Non sono a casa. Siete pregati di lasciare*

*(per favore lasciate) un messaggio dopo il segnale. 9. Chi era al telefono?
—Era Giovanni. Mi ha chiuso il telefono! 10. John mi ha appena
telefonato. Mi ha detto che la moglie aspetta un bambino. 11. Preferisce
(preferisci) aspettare in linea? 12. Aspetto una telefonata
importante.*

LEZIONE 4

A. 1. *li vogliamo*   2. *ottenerlo*   3. *lo so (sapevo)*   4. *le abbiamo viste*   5. *vi*
   6. *ti*   7. *La*   8. *l'ho visto*

B. 1. *mi, ti*   2. *le*   3. *gli ho parlato*   4. *gli abbiamo dato*   5. *telefonarLe,
   mi*   6. *ci*

C. 1. *Sì, le abbiamo spiegato le condizioni salariali. 2. Sì, l'ho fatta. 3. Sì, li
   ha preparati. 4. Sì, gli ho consegnato la lettera. 5. Sì, l'hanno firmato.
   6. Sì, ne abbiamo parlato.*

D. 1. *Le colleghe delle nostre sorelle sono molto pessimiste. 2. Le mani dei
   pianisti erano sicure ed agili. 3. I nuovi programmi erano perfetti per le
   neo-mamme. 4. Quelle artiste/Quegli artisti hanno creato dei veri e
   propri capolavori.*

E. 1. *Mi puoi aiutare (puoi aiutarmi) a prepararmi per il colloquio?
   2. Mamma, voglio venire con te, non con lui. 3. Ha telefonato alla sua
   amica? —Sì, le ha telefonato. 4. Hai trovato le chiavi della macchina?
   —No, le sto ancora cercando. 5. Le moto giapponesi sono le migliori.
   6. Quanti candidati hai intervistato oggi? —Ne abbiamo intervistati tre.
   7. Bambini, mi dovete dare una mano. 8. Ho dormito come un ghiro.
   9. Il tuo datore di lavoro ha registrato sul libretto di lavoro le tue
   mansioni? 10. Qual è lo stato attuale dei posti di lavoro?*

LEZIONE 5

A. 1. *Te la compro io per il pranzo? 2. Gli ospiti glieli portano. 3. La
   signora Merlini glielo offre. 4. Noi gliela diamo. 5. Gli sposi glieli
   mandano.*

B. 1. *Sì, glieli ho già portati. 2. Sì, gliel'abbiamo data. 3. Sì, me li ha
   comprati. 4. Sì, gliela voglio regalare. 5. Sì, gliel'hanno mandato.
   6. Sì, ve lo racconterò. 7. Me l'ha regalata Luigi. 8. Sì, gliel'ho detto.*

C. 1. *glielo porto*   2. *me lo metto*   3. *ricordartelo*   4. *me l'ha proibito*
   5. *gliel'ho chiesto*   6. *te la*   7. *Glielo*   8. *gliene abbiamo parlato*

D. 1. *Sta' più attento.* 2. *Telefoni al Suo dottore.* 3. *Fate il lavoro più in fretta.* 4. *Siate più gentili con il pubblico.* 5. *Non firmare il contratto.*

E. 1. *Dammelo subito.* 2. *Non crearci (non ci creare) problemi, per favore!* 3. *Spiegateglielo con più calma!* 4. *Diccelo subito e non farci perdere più tempo!* 5. *Spediscimi il contratto immediatamente!* 6. *Per favore, fammene nove copie.* 7. *Parlategliene voi!* 8. *Fammi il favore di telefonare all'ufficio di collocamento!* 9. *Fa' cucinare a lui!* 10. *Non farglieli lavare! (Non glieli fare lavare!)*

F. 1. *Smettila! Non mi scocciare/seccare! (Non scocciarmi/seccarmi!)* 2. *Perché non me l'hai detto? —Mamma, te l'ho detto ieri!* 3. *Fabrizio, per favore trovami le chiavi della macchina e portale a tuo padre.* 4. *Professor Veltri, potrebbe darmi (mi potrebbe dare) una copia del Suo libro? —Sì, signor Frizi, gliela porto domani.* 5. *Per favore, mandami (mi mandi) le informazioni il più presto possibile. Mandamele (Me le mandi) per fax.* 6. *—Per favore, mi mandi (mandami) tre copie del contratto. —OK. Gliene (te ne) mando tre.* 7. *Oggi andiamo dai Rossi. Ci hanno invitati (invitato) per cena.* 8. *Giulio, è ora di smetterla con questa storia!* 9. *Povero Pierino! Tutti lo prendono in giro.* 10. *Rino, fa' battere dalla segretaria questa lettera, controllala e falla firmare al cliente!* 11. *Ci hanno fatto divertire.* 12. *Mi faccio pettinare dal parrucchiere.*

LEZIONE 6

A. 1. *Sì, gli piace.* 2. *Sì, ci è piaciuta.* 3. *Sì, mi piace.* 4. *Sì, gli sono piaciuti.* 5. *Sì, le è piaciuto.*

B. 1. *Sì, l'ha visto e gli è piaciuto.* 2. *Sì, li hanno visti e gli sono piaciuti.* 3. *Sì, l'abbiamo vista e ci è piaciuta.* 4. *Sì, l'ha vista e le è piaciuta.* 5. *Sì, le ho viste e mi sono piaciute.*

C. 1. *Vorrei vedere che cosa c'è sugli altri canali.* 2. *Dobbiamo guardare gli annunci pubblicitari?* 3. *Loro non possono accettare l'indecenza di certe pubblicità.* 4. *Ieri sera noi non abbiamo voluto guardare la televisione.* 5. *Carla, appena ha finito di cenare, vuole guardarsi la televisione in pace.*

D. 1. *Io non guarderò mai questo programma televisivo. Non mi piace! Non mi è mai piaciuto! Non mi piacerà mai!* 2. *A nessuno piace andare dal dentista.* 3. *A me piace viaggiare. Anche a mia sorella piace viaggiare. Né a me né a mia sorella piace stare a casa.* 4. *Io faccio sempre più del necessario.* 5. *Quando loro parlano, noi non capiamo niente (un'acca).* 6. *Ieri sera non ho voluto guardare la televisione. Ho preferito leggere il* giornale. 7. *Ieri Carla non è potuta venire alla riunione. È dovuta andare a Roma.* 8. *Non possiamo permetterci di perdere questa occasione.* 9. *Vorrei comprare questo computer per mio figlio. Sono sicuro che gli piacerà.* 10. *Quella gente ha protestato (protestava) perché la pubblicità offendeva la loro dignità.*

LEZIONE 7

A. 1. *buon* 2. *buono* 3. *buona* 4. *buon* 5. *begli* 6. *grande* 7. *grande* 8. *grandi*

B. 1. *Io vado spesso in Italia.* 2. *Le aule sono veramente affollate.* 3. *È impossibile far entrare fisicamente gli studenti nelle aule.* 4. *Lo studente ha fatto malissimo all'esame.* 5. *Lui lavora piano ma ha tanta pazienza.* 6. *Di solito, lui va a lezione il lunedì.*

C. 1. *L'abbiamo accompagnato per un bel tratto.* 2. *C'è voluto del bello e del buono per convincerlo ad andare a scuola.* 3. *Quello studente l'ha fatta bella!* 4. *Al seminario non abbiamo fatto una bella figura!* 5. *Vado a lezione regolarmente.* 6. *Non ho capito un bel niente/nulla quando sono andato a lezione.* 7. *Ha fatto malissimo all'esame.* 8. *Ho sentito dire che la Bocconi è un'ottima università.*

LEZIONE 8

A. 1. *quegli* 2. *quella* 3. *quelle* 4. *quell'* 5. *quel* 6. *quei*

B. 1. *quella* 2. *quella* 3. *quello* 4. *quello* 5. *quelli* 6. *quelle*

C. 1. *Sì, ci siamo stati.* 2. *Sì, ci vado spesso.* 3. *Sì, ci andranno.* 4. *Sì, ci abbiamo pensato.* 5. *Sì, ci è riuscita*

D. 1. *Quanto tempo c'è voluto per andare a Murano in vaporetto?* 2. *C'era tanta nebbia che non ci vedevamo per niente (affatto).* 3. *Ci vuole molta pazienza nella vita.* 4. *Penso spesso al mio viaggio a Venezia.* 5. *Sono molto stanco(a). Ieri notte non ho potuto chiudere occhio.*

LEZIONE 9

A. 1. *ha visitato* 2. *è morto* 3. *è diventata* 4. *è arrivato* 5. *ha salutato*

B. 1. *facevano* 2. *andavamo* 3. *mangiavo, guardavo* 4. *erano* 5. *invitavate* 6. *bevevi*

C. 1. *era, è atterrato* 2. *è arrivato* 3. *erano* 4. *ha avuto* 5. *sono morte*

380

D. 1. *Nel 1980 avevo vent'anni.* 2. *Pioveva a dirotto (a catinelle).* 3. *La settimana scorsa abbiamo conosciuto John.* 4. *Ieri non ho partecipato alla riunione.* 5. *Li conosco solo di vista.*

LEZIONE 10

A. 1. *vendere* 2. *mancare* 3. *investire, avendo* 4. *tradurre* 5. *parlando*
   6. *essendo stato*
B. 1. *rappresentante* 2. *crescente* 3. *assistente* 4. *amante* 5. *cantante*
C. 1. *diciassette* 2. *trentotto* 3. *sessantatré* 4. *cinquecentoquindici*
   5. *mille* 6. *novantuno* 7. *tremilaquattrocento*
   8. *cinquantacinquemilaquattrocentotrenta* 9. *un milione*
   10. *quattrocentocinquantaquattromilatrecentoventinove*
E. 1. *Ancora non conosco il francese molto bene. Lo sto imparando ora (adesso).* 2. *Signor Parker, come sa, questa è una delle più importanti fiere (è una delle fiere più importanti) del mondo* 3. *Non conosco Milano, ma conosco Roma molto bene.* 4. *Sai (sa) che i prodotti italiani sono conosciuti in tutto il mondo per il loro stile è il loro design? —Sì, lo so.* 5. *Vorrei riscuotere quest'assegno, per favore (per piacere).* 6. *Questa è la quinta volta che vengo in Italia.* 7. *Papa Giovanni Paolo Secondo ha visitato gli Stati Uniti.* 8. *Cento di questi giorni, mia cara (mio caro)!* 9. *Sono stati (furono) licenziati su due piedi.* 10. *Ieri sera finalmente gliene ho dette quattro.*

PRIMO RIPASSO

A. 1. *Gli sposi hanno ricevuto molti telegrammi di auguri.* 2. *Ecco a Lei, il biglietto e la nuova carta d'imbarco. L'imbarco è previsto fra qualche minuto.* 3. *Gli articoli elencati sono in vendita solo sui voli internazionali.* 4. *Siete pregati di allacciare le cinture di sicurezza, di mettere i bagagli a mano sotto la poltrona davanti a voi e di porre lo schienale in posizione verticale.* 5. *"Signora Pozzi, sono Max Creech, l'amico di Suo figlio Andrea."* 6. *Mark, sono a tua disposizione. Il mio ufficio offre diversi supporti informativi e assistenziali. Quando ci vediamo ti porto degli opuscoli informativi.* 7. *Questo è un messaggio automatico. In questo momento non sono a casa. Lasciate il vostro nome e numero di telefono e vi richiamerò il più presto possibile.* 8. *Antonio, cambia gli asciugamani nel bagno perché sono sporchi!* 9. *Quelle auto giapponesi sono molto belle.* 10. *Oggi il professor Rossi mi ha dato un bel voto.*

B. 1.—*Vuoi vedere questo opuscolo?* —*Certo, lo vedo volentieri.* 2. *Gianni, chi ti ha dato questi documenti?* 3. —*Hai riempito tutti i moduli per la domanda di lavoro?* —*Sì, li ho riempiti.* 4. *Ho perso la mia borsa. Dobbiamo trovarla subito.* 5. —*Hai spiegato le condizioni di lavoro a Linda?* —*Sì, gliele ho spiegate.* 6. *Dottor Valesi, la settimana scorsa Le ho spedito la mia domanda di lavoro. L'ha ricevuta?* 7. —*Hai intervistato molti candidati oggi?* —*No, ne ho intervistati solo due.* 8. —*Quando mi dai quei libri?* —*Te li do domani. Va bene?* 9. —*Domani arriva il dottor Neri.* —*Davvero? Ma chi gliel'ha detto, signora?* 10. —*Passerete anche dal centro storico della città?* —*Certo. Ci passeremo più tardi.*

C. 1. *venite* 2. *prendermi* 3. *abbi* 4. *mettiti* 5. *sii* 6. *finisca* 7. *arrivi* 8. *vacci* 9. *accompagnala* 10. *dica*

D. 1. *preferisce* 2. *hai fatto, è partito, è arrivato, mi sono organizzata, mi sono fatta* 3. *ci dimentichiamo* 4. *è potuta, è durata* 5. *avrà* 6. *è, dormendo* 7. *volevo* 8. *erano* 9. *stavano* 10. *dare*

E. 1. *Stasera verremo a trovarti per fare quattro chiacchiere. Sarai a casa?* 2.—*Sapevi che mia moglie aspetta un bambino?* —*No, non lo sapevo. È il tuo primo bambino?* 3. —*Signor Roppa, quando mi farà portare i mobili che ho ordinato?* —*Glieli farò portare subito.* 4. *Michele, è ora di finirla con questa storia, capisci?* 5. *A Franco non piacciono quegli annunci pubblicitari. A te piacciono?* 6. —*Ti sono piaciute quelle macchine?* —*No, non mi sono piaciute.* 7. *Quando loro parlano inglese, io non capisco un'acca.* 8. *Abbiamo lavorato sodo per finire il lavoro prima della data di scadenza.* 9. *Loro non hanno viaggiato da soli. Li ho accompagnati io per un bel tratto.* 10. —*Conosci quei signori?* —*No, li conosco solo di vista.*

LEZIONE 11

A. 1. *comprerei* 2. *andremmo* 3. *investirebbe* 4. *sarebbe* 5. *potrebbe*

B. 1. *Io ci sarei andato, ma non ho potuto.* 2. *Noi li avremmo investiti, ma non abbiamo potuto.* 3. *Loro ci sarebbero rimasti, ma non hanno potuto.* 4. *Io l'avrei scambiata, ma non ho potuto.* 5. *Noi vi avremmo telefonato, ma non abbiamo potuto.*

C. 1. *che* 2. *più, di* 3. *quanto* 4. *più di* 5. *più di quell' (tanto quanto quell')* 6. *più di* 7. *il più, della* 8. *migliori* 9. *minimo, massimo* 10. *migliore*

D. 1. *Vorremmo investire dei soldi (qualche soldo) in Italia. Vorremmo comprare una casa o (oppure) un appartamento.* 2. *Io guadagno (tanto) quanto i miei genitori.* 3. *Ho pagato la casa meno di quel (quello) che pensi.* 4. *Quella casa è ultramoderna. Non mi piace.* 5. *Loro prendono tutto per scontato.* 6. *Gli ha dato di volta il cervello. Ha pagato quella casa più di un milione di dollari.* 7. *Noi facciamo ginnastica tutti i giorni (ogni giorno).* 8. *Ragazzi (Bambini), prestate attenzione a quello (quel/ciò) che dice (sta dicendo) l'insegnante.*

LEZIONE 12

A. 1. *che* 2. *cui(il quale)* 3. *cui* 4. *quale* 5. *quello che (ciò che)*
6. *chi* 7. *quali* 8. *quello che (ciò che)* 9. *quello che (ciò che)* 10. *chi*

B. 1. *Oggi ho comprato del latte.* 2. *Oggi ho comprato della carne.* 3. *Oggi ho comprato dello zucchero.* 4. *Oggi ho comprato delle medicine.* 5. *Oggi ho comprato alcuni libri.* 6. *Oggi ho comprato qualche pomodoro.*

C. 1. *abbastanza* 2. *chi* 3. *alcune* 4. *qualche* 5. *un po'* 6. *nessun*
7. *nessuna* 8. *qualche* 9. *poco* 10. *qualche*

D. 1. *Dottore, vorrei farLe (Le vorrei fare) una domanda.* 2. *I nostri prodotti sono in vendita in tutte le farmacie.* 3. *Oggi non mi sento in forma.* 4. *Io tengo molto a quei ragazzi (bambini).* 5. *Ciò (quel/quello) che lui dice non mi convince.* 6. *Oggi il nostro ospite è il dottor Francesco Perna.*

LEZIONE 13

A. 1. *No, l'avevo già spedito.* 2. *No, l'avevo già iniziata.* 3. *No, ero già sposata.* 4. *No, gli avevo già parlato.* 5. *No, l'avevo già vista.* 6. *No, avevo già dormito.*

B. 1. *avevo . . . visto* 2. *eri . . . uscito* 3. *eravamo . . . stati* 4. *avevo promesso* 5. *si era sentita* 6. *avevano . . . parlato*

C. *firme, arredamento, bagno, versatilità, materiali, qualità, prezzo, internazionali, avanguardia, pregi, tempi, tradizione*

D. 1. *Quel lavello sta molto bene con quell'arredamento.* 2. *Il film che ho visto ieri sera mi ha fatto dormire (addormentare).* 3. *—Dov'è Pietro? —Non vedi? Sta dormendo. Dorme sempre come un ghiro.* 4. *Stasera sono così (tanto) stanco che dormo in piedi.* 5. *Conosci il proverbio "Chi dorme non piglia pesci?"* 6. *Non fanno altro che dormire sugli allori.* 7. *Hanno suggerito qualche provvedimento per combattere l'inflazione.*

8. *Devi vendere questo articolo a qualsiasi costo.* 9. *Qui ognuno deve (tutti devono) portare occhiali di protezione.* 10. *Non abbiamo pagato tanto, vero?* 11. *Ci hanno promesso molto di più sul fatturato.* 12. *Venite a vedere i nostri prodotti e troverete senz'altro qualcosa di bello.*

LEZIONE 14

A. 1. *fu, furono* 2. *chiuse, chiusero* 3. *conobbe, conobbero* 4. *decise, decisero* 5. *lesse, lessero* 6. *capì, capirono* 7. *andò, andarono* 8. *prese, presero* 9. *vide, videro* 10. *venne, vennero*

B. 1. *venne, cercò* 2. *fecero, degustarono* 3. *diventò* 4. *successe (succedette)* 5. *fu* 6. *passò*

C. 1. *ebbe comprato* 2. *ebbe provato* 3. *ebbero finito* 4. *ebbero eliminato* 5. *ebbe acquistato*

D. 1. *Il mio antenato, Bettino Ricasoli, fu l'ideatore della ricetta originale del Chianti Classico.* 2. *La qualità del vino è diversa da quella di una volta (del passato)?* 3. *Si sa che una vite vecchia non produce molta uva, ma l'uva che produce è di ottima qualità.* 4. *Glielo dico io! Io non ho peli sulla lingua.* 5. *Il nome di quella persona ce l'ho proprio sulla lingua.* 6. *Questa villa si affitta (è in affitto) per due milioni al mese. (È possibile avere in affitto questa villa per due milioni al mese).* 7. *I vini erano (venivano) conservati in botti in legno.* 8. *Potrebbe (potresti) darmi qualche informazione storica (alcune informazioni storiche) su questi castelli?* 9. *Finalmente riuscì a scoprire il segreto.* 10. *Cercammo rifugio tra questi meravigliosi colli.*

LEZIONE 15

A. 1. *Il caffè è stato portato in Europa dagli esploratori.* 2. *Il computer mi è stato regalato da mia nonna.* 3. *Le rovine di Pompei saranno visitate dagli studenti tramite l'Internet.* 4. *In Italia il mercato dei computer è dominato dall'Olivetti.* 5. *Antonio sarà aiutato dal signor Liberman con l'installazione di alcuni programmi.* 6. *Il suo computer era ammirato da tutti.*

B. 1. *Si va all'università alle nove ogni mattina.* 2. *Non si ha bisogno del loro aiuto.* 3. *Ci si collega all'Internet via modem.* 4. *Si spera di riuscire a fare una visita virtuale della Scala di Milano.* 5. *Si comprano computer usati.* 6. *Quando si è troppo stanchi, non si deve guidare.*

C. 1. *Oggi non si può vivere senza un computer.* 2. *Dalla finestra si può vedere Pompei. 3. Non si può essere sempre felici (contenti). 4. Questo computer non funziona molto bene. 5. Con quello che (ciò che) si guadagna oggi non si può mantenere una famiglia. 6. Non aiutano mai. Stanno sempre con le mani in mano. 7. Dopo quello che (ciò che) è successo, volevo mordermi le mani. 8. Quando il signor Jones e il professor Mastri si sono incontrati, si sono dati la mano.*

LEZIONE 16

A. 1. *ritorni* 2. *abbia* 3. *stia* 4. *vengano* 5. *vada* 6. *cominciate*
   7. *siamo*
B. 1. *abbia* 2. *vestiremo* 3. *sono* 4. *possa* 5. *è* 6. *voglia* 7. *piace*
C. 1. *Io ho l'impressione che gli abiti da sera siano intramontabili. 2. Noi siamo contenti che loro stiano bene. 3. Io preferisco che tu compri questa borsetta. 4. I miei genitori vogliono che io non mi cotoni i capelli. 5. Io so che questa modella di guadagna dieci milioni di dollari a sfilata. 6. Tu pensi che questo modello di Valentino si ispiri ad un film di Amy Hickering? 7. Benché questi pantaloni a zampa d'elefante costino molto, io li compro lo stesso.*
D. 1. *È ovvio che non le piacciono questi sandali. 2. Benché questa maglietta sia bella, non la compro (comprerò). 3. Spero di poter andare alla sfilata di moda stasera. 4. Lei porta una maglietta, una gonna lunga di camoscio, e un bel paio di sandali marrone (marroni). 5. Abbiamo preso i ladri con le pive nel sacco. 6. Mi hanno detto un sacco di bugie. Non li voglio più vedere. 7. È stato Giovanni a vuotare il sacco. 8. Credo che porti una gonna di organza bianca. 9. Quel vestito di lino ti sta molto bene. 10. Credo che il (un) vestito e la (una) cravatta siano più appropriati.*

LEZIONE 17

A. 1. *lavorasse* 2. *stesse* 3. *fosse* 4. *andassero* 5. *facesse* 6. *avesse*
B. 1. *Oh, pensavo che uscisse il giorno dopo. 2. Oh, pensavo che studiassi economia e commercio. 3. Oh, pensavo che vivesse a Torino. 4. Oh, pensavo che parlasse anche il francese. 5. Oh, pensavo che partisse domani. 6. Oh, pensavo che finisse a mezzogiorno. 7. Oh, pensavo che fosse ingegnere.*
C. 1. *Desidereremmo che il candidato avesse esperienza nell'industria alimentare. 2. Vorrei che Lei cominciasse a lavorare all'inizio del mese.*

3. *I miei genitori vorrebbero che io studiassi l'italiano.* 4. *Io preferirei che tu ti trasferissi a Milano.* 5. *Vorrei che voi seguiste un corso di informatica.* 6. *Desidererei che Lei inviasse subito il suo curriculm vitae.*

D. 1. *No, non mi piace più.* 2. *Non voglio fare né il direttore delle vendite né il direttore del personale.* 3. *No, non ho mai lavorato a tempo pieno.* 4. *Non c'è nessuno.* 5. *No, il salario che offrono non è affatto competitivo.* 6. *Domani non faccio niente.* 7. *No, non è ancora arrivato.* 8. *No, neanch'io (nemmeno io) farò domanda per quel posto.*

E. 1. *Pensavo che tu fossi direttore delle vendite.* 2. *—Lei avrà (Le daremo) una retribuzione adeguata (appropriata/incentivante) per il Suo lavoro. —Avrò (mi darete) anche i rimborsi spese?* 3. *Vorrei darLe un'idea dello stipendio che percepirà nel caso dovessimo offrirLe il posto.* 4. *Se chiamano (telefonano), può (puoi/potrebbe/potresti) dirgli (dire loro) che sono uscito?* 5. *Finalmente ho trovato un (il) lavoro che mi piace. Meglio tardi che mai.* 6. *—Ti trasferisci davvero (veramente) a Milano? —Sì, mi piacerebbe lavorare in Italia.* 7. *Non ho mai sentito parlare di questa ditta (compagnia/azienda).* 8. *Per questo lavoro non abbiamo assunto nessun uomo.* 9. *—Ha mai lavorato all'estero? —No. Mai.* 10. *Nessuno ci ha fatto un'offerta più ragionevole.*

LEZIONE 18

A. 1. *lo (l') abbiano conosciuto* 2. *li abbia invitati, siano andati/abbiano accettato* 3. *siano andati* 4. *l'abbiano visitato* 5. *l'abbia disegnata* 6. *sia stata* 7. *l'abbia comprata* 8. *non sia potuto*

B. 1. *Credo che abbiano seguito l'itinerario.* 2. *Mi hanno detto che Rosalba ha voluto conoscere la storia del David di Michelangelo.* 3. *Mi dispiace che non abbiate avuto molto tempo a vostra disposizione.* 4. *Tutti sanno che la mostra dei capolavori del Botticelli è stata inaugurata l'8 maggio.* 5. *Non capisco perché abbia voluto visitare anche gli uffici amministrativi.* 6. *Sembra che Michelangelo sia nato a Caprese.* 7. *Sono convinto che l'hanno studiato a scuola.* 8. *È ovvio che queste cose tu le hai lette nei libri.*

C. 1. *foste . . . stati (state)* 2. *avessero visitata* 3. *avesse scolpita* 4. *fossero andati* 5. *avessimo . . . visto*

D. 1. *Ci siamo fermati per prendere un boccone. Ho mangiato troppo è adesso (ora) mi sento pieno.* 2. *Questo è il Battistero? È qui che sono conservate le opere di Donatello?* 3. *Dietro quel monumento c'è un edificio che risale al Rinascimento.* 4. *Credo che questa sia la galleria d'arte più importante (la più importante galleria d'arte) in (d') Italia.*

5. *Era pieno giorno quando siamo usciti (uscite).* 6. *Ieri abbiamo visitato una delle chiese più famose (una delle più famose chiese) di Firenze. Era piena zeppa di gente.* 7. *Ha delle ciglia molto lunghe.* 8. *Le fondamenta di questo palazzo (edificio) furono gettate nel sedicesimo secolo.* 9. *I membri del comitato hanno avuto (tenuto) una riunione ieri.* 10. *Sta' attento! I muri hanno orecchie.*

LEZIONE 19

A. 1. *Enzo ha detto che il giorno dopo sarebbe uscito presto.* 2. *Amedeo ha detto che avevano tempo per fare tutto con calma.* 3. *Teresa dice sempre che non vuole noleggiare un'auto troppo grande.* 4. *Il vigile disse ad Amedeo che non poteva posteggiare lì.* 5. *Mio padre disse al vigile che sua moglie (mia madre) era andata al tabacchino.* 6. *Mio padre ha detto al vigile che stava aspettando sua moglie (mia madre) e che (lei) sarebbe ritornata subito.* 7. *Il vigile mi ha risposto che se io non mi fossi spostato, mi avrebbe fatto la multa.* 8. *Amedeo ha detto che aveva paura che quel giorno non gli andava niente per il verso giusto.*

B. *Un carabiniere fa segno ad Amedeo di fermarsi. Il carabiniere gli dice di fargli vedere la patente e la carta di circolazione. Amedeo chiede se c'era qualche cosa che non andava. Il carabiniere ha risposto che aveva i faretti antinebbia accesi. Amedeo ha chiesto se era in contravvenzione. Il carabiniere ha detto di sì e gli ha chiesto se la macchina fosse la sua. Amedeo ha risposto che l'aveva noleggiata e che doveva ancora familiarizzarsi con tutti i bottoni. Ha anche chiesto al carabiniere di evitargli la multa. Il carabiniere ha detto che gli dispiaceva, ma che non poteva far nulla. Gli ha anche detto di fare più attenzione la volta dopo.*

C. *giro, quasi, multa, carabiniere (poliziotto, vigile), che, parcheggiare (sostare), stavo, ragioni, multa, male, bella, guida, stazione, di (che arrivi)*

D. 1. *Il mio direttore mi ha concesso tre giorni di licenza.* 2. *Ecco qui il Suo modulo di prenotazione. Questa macchina ha l'aria condizionata. L'assicurazione per il furto e contro i danni è inclusa nel prezzo del noleggio.* 3. *Loro nutrono una forte antipatia per quella gente.* 4. *Dubito veramente che gli piacerà quella macchina.* 5. *Lui si dimostra sempre forte nelle avversità della vita.* 6. *Puoi dirlo di nuovo! Oggi non mi va niente per il verso giusto!*

A. 1. *Se piovesse, non andrei in centro.* 2. *Se ci fermassimo al bar,*
    prenderei qualcosa. 3. *Se non raccontasse una barzelletta, morirebbe.*
    4. *Se andaste insieme alla festa di carnevale, vi divertireste di sicuro.*
    5. *Se ci fossero i carabinieri, gli farebbero sicuramente la multa.* 6. *Se*
    ascoltassi, ti racconterei una bella barzelletta. 7. *Se i bambini entrassero*
    nel bar, ti butterebbero addosso i coriandoli. 8. *Se potessi, verrei*
    all'aeroporto a prenderti.

B. 1. *fosse, andremmo* 2. *costasse, comprerei* 3. *facesse, staremmo*
    4. *parlasse, capirebbero* 5. *fosse, capiremmo* 6. *raccontassi, racconterei*
    7. *veniste, vedreste* 8. *avessi, daresti*

C. 1. *foste arrivati (arrivate)* 2. *avessi saputo* 3. *fosse venuta* 4. *vi avrei*
    accompagnato (accompagnati) 5. *avessi detto* 6. *avrebbero perso*
    7. *avremmo raccontate* 8. *avessimo (avessimo avuto)*

D. 1. *Bambini, che Dio vi benedica!* 2. *Non sono sicuro che (se) abbiano*
    visto i bambini che suonavano trombette e che buttavano nell'aria
    coriandoli di vari (molti) colori. 3. *Alessandra, non te la prendere (non*
    t'arrabbiare)! Oggi non sei proprio in vena. Come si dice: "A Carnevale
    ogni scherzo vale!" 4. *Stiamo morendo di noia. Questa festa è troppo*
    noiosa. 5. *Vorrei morire, se non è vero.* 6. *Non ho mangiato tutto il*
    giorno. Sto morendo di fame. Cosa c'è da mangiare?

SECONDO RIPASSO

A. 1. *piacerebbe* 2. *avrei* 3. *dovresti* 4. *vorrebbero* 5. *avrei . . .*
    immaginato 6. *vorrebbe* 7. *verrebbe* 8. *sarebbero partiti*
    9. *desidereremmo, sarebbe* 10. *sarei andata*

B. 1. *riuscimmo* 2. *vennero* 3. *divenne (diventò)* 4. *succedette*
    (successe) 5. *riuscì, fu* 6. *si vestirono* 7. *lavorai* 8. *seguì* 9. *furono*
    10. *ebbero*

C. 1. *siano* 2. *ritorni* 3. *andrà* 4. *abbia partecipato*
    5. *ritorniamo/siamo ritornati* 6. *cerchino* 7. *stia* 8. *verrete*
    9. *abbia disegnata* 10. *viene*

D. 1. *fossi* 2. *iniziassi* 3. *facesse* 4. *assumessimo* 5. *parlasse*
    6. *si alzassero* 7. *dicesse* 8. *potessi* 9. *avesse* 10. *faceste*

E. 1. *Alcuni prodotti senza grassi non sono sani perché hanno un contenuto*
    superiore di sodio. 2. *Abbiamo suggerito qualche provvedimento*
    (alcuni/dei provvedimenti) per combattere l'inflazione. Siamo certi che
    funzioneranno 3. *Il modem è/viene usato per accedere all'Internet.*

4. *Dopo aver lavorato al computer per un giorno intero, ci si sente stanchi.* 5. *Quando è arrivato il direttore la riunione era già cominciata.* 6. *Quello che dicono quei dottori non mi convince.* 7. *Quegli agenti immobiliari guadagnano quanto me. Non è giusto!* 8. *Questo tipo di lavoro non mi interessa affatto. Cerco un altro lavoro.* 9. *Quando l'ho vista, mi sono gettato fra le sue braccia. Non la vedevo da settembre.* 10. *—È vero che tu hai vinto un milione di dollari? —Magari fosse vero!* 11. *Lucia e Maurizio si danno del tu. Vero?* 12. *Gli ho detto che deve imparare a tenere testa alla gente. Spero che segua il mio consiglio.* 13. *Dopo quello che è successo, volevo mordermi le mani.* 14. *Adesso più che mai abbiamo bisogno di risparmiare.* 15. *Ieri sera la sua casa era piena zeppa di gente.*

APPENDIXES

A. ABBREVIATIONS AND MEASUREMENTS

1. ABBREVIATIONS

a.	*anno* (year)
ab.	*abitanti* (inhabitants, population)
abb.	1. *(comm.) abbuono* (allowance, discount)
	2. *(giorn.) abbonamento* (subscription)
abbr.	1. *abbreviato* (abbreviated)
	2. *abbreviazione* (abbreviation)
a.c.	1. *anno corrente* (this year)
	2. *assegno circolare* (bank or banker's draft)
acc.	*(cred.) acconto* (account)
agg.	*(pers.) aggiunto* (assistant, deputy)
all.	*allegato* (enclosure)
amm.	1. *amministatore* (administrator)
	2. *amministrazione* (administation, management)
ASS.	1. *assicurazione* (insurance)
	2. *assegno* (cheque)
a/v	*a vista* (on demand, at sight)
B.I.	*Banca d'Italia* (bank of Italy)
c.	*cento* (one hundred)
	conto (account)
c.c.	*conto corrente* (current account)
C.ia	*compagnia* (company)
cod.	*codice* (code)
c.s.	*come sopra* (as above)
c/s	*con spese* (with expenses)
Dir.	*direttore* (director)
dott.	*dottore* (doctor)
dr.ssa	*dottoressa* (female doctor)
ecc.	*eccetera* (et cetera)
es.	*esempio* (example)
fo (f.to)	*firmato* (signed)

g.	*giorno* (day)
h	*ora* (hour)
I	*Italia* (Italy)
id.	*lo stesso* (the same)
impr.	*impresa* (enterprise)
L	*Lira* (Italian currency)
m	*mese* (month)
mens.	*mensile* (monthly)
min	*minuto* (minute)
mitt.	*mittente* (sender)
or	*orario* (hourly schedule/timetable)
p. (pag.)	*pagina* (page)
par.	*paragrafo* (paragraph)
p.c.c.	*per copia conforme* (carbon copy)
p.e.	*per esempio* (for example)
p.f.	*per favore* (please)
p.v.	*prossimo venturo* (next month)
racc.	*raccomandata* (registered)
rep.	*reparto* (department)
ric.	*ricevuta* (receipt)
rif.	*riferimento* (reference)
seg.	*seguente* (following)
segr.	*segretario* (secretary)
Sig.	*Signore* (Mr.)
Sig.ra	*Signora* (Mrs.)
Sig.na	*Signorina* (Miss)
ver.	*versamento* (payment)
V/s.	*Vostro* (your, yours)

2. MEASUREMENTS

pollice	inch
piede	foot = 12 pollici (inches)
1 centimetro	1 cm = 0.3937 inch
1 metro	(meter) = 3.280 feet (39.37 inches)
1 chilometro	km = 1000 meters
1.61 km	= 1 mile
1 chilogramma	1 kg = 2.2046 pounds
28 grammi	28 grams = 1 ounce
1 litro (liter) =	1.0567 liquid quarts

B. GRAMMAR SUMMARY

1. SUBJECT PRONOUNS

	SINGULAR		PLURAL
I	*io*	we	*noi*
you (fam.)	*tu*	you (fam. or form.)	*voi*
he, she	*lui, lei*	they	*loro*
you (formal)	*Lei*	you (formal)	*Loro*

2. DISJUNCTIVE PRONOUNS

	SINGULAR		PLURAL
me	*me*	us	*noi*
you (fam.)	*te*	you (fam. or form.)	*voi*
him	*lui*	them	*loro*
her	*lei*		
you (formal)	*Lei*	you (formal)	*Loro*

3. REFLEXIVE PRONOUNS

	SINGULAR		PLURAL
myself	*mi*	ourselves	*ci*
yourself (fam)	*ti*	yourselves (fam. or form.)	*vi*
him/her/it/oneself/	*si*	themselves	*si*
yourself (formal)	*si*	yourselves (formal)	*si*

4. DIRECT OBJECT PRONOUNS

	SINGULAR		PLURAL
me	*mi*	us	*ci*
you (fam.)	*ti*	you (fam. and form.)	*vi*
him, it (m.n.)	*lo*	them (m.)	*li*
her, it (f.n.)	*la*	them (f.)	*le*
you (formal)	*La*	you (form. m.)	*Li*
		you (form. f.)	*Le*

5. INDIRECT OBJECT PRONOUNS

	SINGULAR			PLURAL
to me	*mi*		to us	*ci*
to you (fam.)	*ti*		to you (fam. or form.)	*vi*
to him	*gli*		to them	*gli*
to her	*le*			
to you (form.)	*Le*		to you (form.)	*gli*

6. DOUBLE OBJECT PRONOUNS

IND. OBJ.	+ *LO*	+ *LA*	+ *LI*	+ *LE*	+ *NE*
mi	*me lo*	*me la*	*me li*	*me le*	*me ne*
ti	*te lo*	*te la*	*te li*	*te le*	*te ne*
gli/le/Le	*glielo*	*gliela*	*glieli*	*gliele*	*gliene*
ci	*ce lo*	*ce la*	*ce li*	*ce le*	*ce ne*
vi	*ve lo*	*ve la*	*ve li*	*ve le*	*ve ne*
gli	*glielo*	*gliela*	*glieli*	*gliele*	*gliene*
loro	*lo . . . loro*	*la . . . loro*	*li . . . loro*	*le . . . loro*	*ne . . . loro*

7. PLURAL OF NOUNS AND ADJECTIVES

GENDER	SINGULAR	PLURAL
MASCULINE	*-o*	*-i*
MASC./FEM.	*-e*	*-i*
FEMININE	*-a*	*-e*

8. INDEFINITE ARTICLES

	MASCULINE	FEMININE
before a consonant	*un*	*una*
before *s* + consonant or *z*	*uno*	*una*
before a vowel	*un*	*un'*

9. DEFINITE ARTICLES

GENDER before nouns beginning with a . . .		SINGULAR	PLURAL
MASCULINE	consonant	*il*	*i*
MASCULINE	*s* + consonant or *z*	*lo*	*gli*
MASCULINE	vowel	*l'*	*gli*
FEMININE	consonant	*la*	*le*
FEMININE	vowel	*l'*	*le*

10. PREPOSITIONS + DEFINITE ARTICLES

PREPOSITION	+ LO	+ L'	+ GLI	+ IL	+ I	+ LA	+ LE
di	dello	dell'	degli	del	dei	della	delle
a	allo	all'	agli	al	ai	alla	alle
da	dallo	dall'	dagli	dal	dai	dalla	dalle
in	nello	nell'	negli	nel	nei	nella	nelle
su	sullo	sull'	sugli	sul	sui	sulla	sulle
con	con lo	con l'	con gli	col	coi	con la	con le

11. POSSESSIVE ADJECTIVES

	MASCULINE SINGULAR	MASCULINE PLURAL	FEMININE SINGULAR	FEMININE PLURAL
my	il mio	i miei	la mia	le mie
your (fam.)	il tuo	i tuoi	la tua	le tue
his, her, its	il suo	i suoi	la sua	le sue
your (form.)	il Suo	i Suoi	la Sua	le Sue
our	il nostro	i nostri	la nostra	le nostre
your (form./fam.)	il vostro	i vostri	la vostra	le vostre
their	il loro	i loro	la loro	le loro
your (form.)	il Loro	i Loro	la Loro	le Loro

12. COMPARATIVES

più . . . di/che	more . . . than
meno . . . di/che	less . . . than
così . . . come (come)	as . . . as
tanto . . . quanto (quanto)	as much . . . as

13. IRREGULAR COMPARATIVES AND SUPERLATIVES

ADJECTIVE	COMPARATIVE	RELATIVE SUPERLATIVE	ABSOLUTE SUPERLATIVE
buono (good)	migliore (better)	il migliore (the best)	ottimo (very good)
cattivo (bad)	peggiore (worse)	il peggiore (the worst)	pessimo (very bad)
grande (big)	maggiore (bigger, greater)	il maggiore (the biggest, the greatest)	massimo (very big, great)
piccolo (small)	minore (smaller)	il minore (smallest)	minimo (very small)

14. IRREGULAR ADJECTIVE *BELLO* (BEAUTIFUL)

GENDER before nouns beginning with a . . .		SINGULAR	PLURAL
MASCULINE	a consonant	*bel*	*bei*
MASCULINE	*s* + consonant or *z*	*bello*	*begli*
MASCULINE	a vowel	*bell'*	*begli*
FEMININE	a consonant	*bella*	*belle*
FEMININE	a vowel	*bell'*	*belle*

When *bello* follows a noun for emphasis, it has the following four forms:

	SINGULAR	PLURAL
MASCULINE	*bello*	*belli*
FEMININE	*bella*	*belle*

15. ADJECTIVE AND PRONOUN *QUESTO* (THIS)

The adjective and pronoun *questo* has forms: *questo* (m. s.), *questa* (f. s.), *questi* (m. pl.), and *queste* (f. pl.). If followed by a noun that starts with a vowel, the singular masculine and feminine forms *questo* and *questa* could be written with an apostrophe.

16. IRREGULAR ADJECTIVE *QUELLO* (THAT)

GENDER before nouns beginning with a . . .		SINGULAR	PLURAL
MASCULINE	a consonant	*quel*	*quei*
MASCULINE	*s* + consonant or *z*	*quello*	*quegli*
MASCULINE	a vowel	*quell'*	*quegli*
FEMININE	a consonant	*quella*	*quelle*
FEMININE	a vowel	*quell'*	*quelle*

When *quello* follows a noun for emphasis, it has the following four forms:

	SINGULAR	PLURAL
MASCULINE	*quello*	*quelli*
FEMININE	*quella*	*quelle*

17. ADJECTIVE *BUONO* (GOOD)

When *buono* follows the noun it modifies, it has the following four forms:

	SINGULAR	PLURAL
MASCULINE	*buono*	*buoni*
FEMININE	*buona*	*buone*

When it precedes the noun it modifies, the singular forms of *buono* resemble those of the indefinite articles and follow the same rules:

MASCULINE	FEMININE
buon before most nouns	*buona* before nouns beginning with a consonant
buono before nouns beginning with s + consonant or z	*buon'* before nouns beginning with a vowel

18. ADJECTIVE *GRANDE* (BIG)

Grande may precede or follow the noun it modifies. When it follows the noun, it has two forms: *grande* (m., f. singular) and *grandi* (m., f. plural) When it precedes the noun, however, there are several possibilities:

SINGULAR	PLURAL
gran or *grande* before masculine and feminine nouns beginning with a consonant	*grandi* for all masculine and feminine nouns
grand' or *grande* before masculine and feminine nouns beginning with a vowel	

19. RELATIVE PRONOUNS

RELATIVE PRONOUN	RULES OF USAGE
che	invariable, replaces a subject or direct object, never used with a preposition
cui	invariable, replaces object of a preposition
il quale, la quale, i quali, le quali	may replace subject, direct object, or object of a preposition (in which case both preposition and definite article must be used); agrees with person, animal, or thing to which it refers.

20. DOUBLE NEGATIVES

non . . . più	no more, no longer
non . . . ancora	not yet
non . . . affatto	not at all
non . . . niente/nulla	nothing
non . . . nessuno	no one, nothing
non . . . mai	never
non . . . né . . . né	neither . . . nor

21. NUMBERS

CARDINAL

uno	venti	centodue
due	ventuno	centotrè
tre	ventidue	duecento
quattro	ventitrè	trecento
cinque	ventiquattro	quattrocento
sei	venticinque	cinquecento
sette	ventisei	seicento
otto	ventisette	settecento
nove	ventotto	ottocento
dieci	ventinove	novecento
undici	trenta	mille
dodici	quaranta	duemila
tredici	cinquanta	tremila
quattordici	sessanta	quattromila
quindici	settanta	diecimila
sedici	ottanta	centomila
diciassette	novanta	un milione
diciotto	cento	un miliardo
diciannove	centouno	un bilione

ORDINAL

primo	settimo	tredicesimo
secondo	ottavo	quattordicesimo
terzo	nono	ventesimo
quarto	decimo	trentesimo
quinto	undicesimo	centesimo
sesto	dodicesimo	millesimo

C. VERB CHARTS

1. FORMS OF THE REGULAR VERBS

PRIMA CONIUGAZIONE	SECONDA CONIUGAZIONE	TERZA CONIUGAZIONE	

INFINITO PRESENTE

parlare	ripetere	partire	capire

INFINITO PASSATO

avere parlato	avere ripetuto	essere partito (-i, -a, -e)	avere capito

GERUNDIO PRESENTE

parlando	ripetendo	partendo	capendo

GERUNDIO PASSATO

avendo parlato	avendo ripetuto	essendo partito	avendo capito

PARTICIPIO PRESENTE

parlante	ripetente	partente	capente

PARTICIPIO PASSATO

parlato	ripetuto	partito	capito

INDICATIVO PRESENTE

io parlo	io ripeto	io parto	io capisco
tu parli	tu ripeti	tu parti	tu capisci
lui parla	lui ripete	lui parte	lui capisce
lei parla	lei ripete	lei parte	lei capisce
Lei parla	Lei ripete	Lei parte	Lei capisce
noi parliamo	noi ripetiamo	noi partiamo	noi capiamo
voi parlate	voi ripetete	voi partite	voi capite
loro parlano	loro ripetono	loro partono	loro capiscono
Loro parlano	Loro ripetono	Loro partono	Loro capiscono

IMPERFETTO

io parlavo	io ripetevo	io partivo	io capivo
tu parlavi	tu ripetevi	tu partivi	tu capivi
lui parlava	lui ripeteva	lui partiva	lui capiva
lei parlava	lei ripeteva	lei partiva	lei capiva
Lei parlava	Lei ripeteva	Lei partiva	Lei capiva
noi parlavamo	noi ripetevamo	noi partivamo	noi capivamo
voi parlavate	voi ripetevate	voi partivate	voi capivate
loro parlavano	loro ripetevano	loro partivano	loro capivano
Loro parlavano	Loro ripetevano	Loro partivano	Loro capivano

PRIMA CONIUGAZIONE	SECONDA CONIUGAZIONE	TERZA CONIUGAZIONE	

PASSATO REMOTO

io parlai	io ripetei	io partii	io capii
tu parlasti	tu ripetesti	tu partisti	tu capisti
lui parlò	lui ripetè	lui partì	lui capì
lei parlò	lei ripetè	lei partì	lei capì
Lei parlò	Lei ripetè	Lei partì	Lei capì
noi parlammo	noi ripetemmo	noi partimmo	noi capimmo
voi parlaste	voi ripeteste	voi partiste	voi capiste
loro parlarono	loro ripeterono	loro partirono	loro capirono
Loro parlarono	Loro ripeterono	Loro partirono	Loro capirono

FUTURO

io parlerò	io ripeterò	io partirò	io capirò
tu parlerai	tu ripeterai	tu partirai	tu capirai
lui parlerà	lui ripeterà	lui partirà	lui capirà
lei parlerà	lei ripeterà	lei partirà	lei capirà
Lei parlerà	Lei ripeterà	Lei partirà	Lei capirà
noi parleremo	noi ripeteremo	noi partiremo	noi capiremo
voi parlerete	voi ripeterete	voi partirete	voi capirete
loro parleranno	loro ripeteranno	loro partiranno	loro capiranno
Loro parleranno	Loro ripeteranno	Loro partiranno	Loro capiranno

PASSATO PROSSIMO

io ho parlato	io ho ripetuto	io sono partito/a	io ho capito
tu hai parlato	tu hai ripetuto	tu sei partito/a	tu hai capito
lui ha parlato	lui ha ripetuto	lui è partito	lui ha capito
lei ha parlato	lei ha ripetuto	lei è partita	lei ha capito
Lei ha parlato	Lei ha ripetuto	Lei è partito/a	Lei ha capito
noi abbiamo parlato	noi abbiamo ripetuto	noi siamo partiti/e	noi abbiamo capito
voi avete parlato	voi avete ripetuto	voi siete partiti/e	voi avete capito
loro hanno parlato	loro hanno ripetuto	loro sono partiti/e	loro hanno capito
Loro hanno parlato	Loro hanno ripetuto	Loro sono partiti/e	Loro hanno capito

TRAPASSATO PROSSIMO

io avevo parlato	io avevo ripetuto	io ero partito/a	io avevo capito
tu avevi parlato	tu avevi ripetuto	tu eri partito/a	tu avevi capito
lui aveva parlato	lui aveva ripetuto	lui era partito	lui aveva capito
lei aveva parlato	lei aveva ripetuto	lei era partita	lei aveva capito
Lei aveva parlato	Lei aveva ripetuto	Lei era partito/a	Lei aveva capito
noi avevamo parlato	noi avevamo ripetuto	noi eravamo partiti/e	noi avevamo capito
voi avevate parlato	voi avevate ripetuto	voi eravate partiti/e	voi avevate capito
loro avevano parlato	loro avevano ripetuto	loro erano partiti/e	loro avevano capito
Loro avevano parlato	Loro avevano ripetuto	Loro erano partiti/e	Loro avevano capito

PRIMA CONIUGAZIONE	SECONDA CONIUGAZIONE	TERZA CONIUGAZIONE	

TRAPASSATO REMOTO

io ebbi parlato	io ebbi ripetuto	io fui partito/a	io ebbi capito
tu avesti parlato	tu avesti ripetuto	tu fosti partito/a	tu avesti capito
lui ebbe parlato	lui ebbe ripetuto	lui fu partito	lui ebbe capito
lei ebbe parlato	lei ebbe ripetuto	lei fu partita	lei ebbe capito
Lei ebbe parlato	Lei ebbe ripetuto	Lei fu partito/a	Lei ebbe capito
noi avemmo parlato	noi avemmo ripetuto	noi fummo partiti/e	noi avemmo capito
voi aveste parlato	voi aveste ripetuto	voi foste partiti/e	voi aveste capito
loro ebbero parlato	loro ebbero ripetuto	loro furono partiti/e	loro ebbero capito
Loro ebbero parlato	Loro ebbero ripetuto	Loro furono partiti/e	Loro ebbero capito

FUTURO ANTERIORE

io avrò parlato	io avrò ripetuto	io sarò partito/a	io avrò capito
tu avrai parlato	tu avrai ripetuto	tu sarai partito/a	tu avrai capito
lui avrà parlato	lui avrà ripetuto	lui sarà partito	lui avrà capito
lei avrà parlato	lei avrà ripetuto	lei sarà partita	lei avrà capito
Lei avrà parlato	Lei avrà ripetuto	Lei sarà partito/a	Lei avrà capito
noi avremo parlato	noi avremo ripetuto	noi saremo partiti/e	noi avremo capito
voi avrete parlato	voi avrete ripetuto	voi sarete partiti/e	voi avrete capito
loro avranno parlato	loro avranno ripetuto	loro saranno partiti/e	loro avranno capito
Loro avranno parlato	Loro avranno ripetuto	Loro saranno partiti/e	Loro avranno capito

CONGIUNTIVO
PRESENTE

che io parli	che io ripeta	che io parta	che io capisca
che tu parli	che tu ripeta	che tu parta	che tu capisca
che lui parli	che lui ripeta	che lui parta	che lui capisca
che lei parli	che lei ripeta	che lei parta	che lei capisca
che Lei parli	che Lei ripeta	che Lei parta	che Lei capisca
che noi parliamo	che noi ripetiamo	che noi partiamo	che noi capiamo
che voi parliate	che voi ripetiate	che voi partiate	che voi capiate
che loro parlino	che loro ripetano	che loro partano	che loro capiscano
che Loro parlino	che Loro ripetano	che Loro partano	che Loro capiscano

IMPERFETTO

che io parlassi	che io ripetessi	che io partissi	che io capissi
che tu parlassi	che tu ripetessi	che tu partissi	che tu capissi
che lui parlasse	che lui ripetesse	che lui partisse	che lui capisse
che lei parlasse	che lei ripetesse	che lei partisse	che lei capisse
che Lei parlasse	che Lei ripetesse	che Lei partisse	che Lei capisse
che noi parlassimo	che noi ripetessimo	che noi partissimo	che noi capissimo
che voi parlaste	che voi ripeteste	che voi partiste	che voi capiste
che loro parlassero	che loro ripetessero	che loro partissero	che loro capissero
che Loro parlassero	che Loro ripetessero	che Loro partissero	che Loro capissero

PASSATO

che io abbia parlato	che io abbia ripetuto	che io sia partito/a	che io abbia capito
che tu abbia parlato	che tu abbia ripetuto	che tu sia partito/a	che tu abbia capito

PRIMA CONIUGAZIONE	SECONDA CONIUGAZIONE	TERZA CONIUGAZIONE	
che lui abbia parlato	che lui abbia ripetuto	che lui sia partito	che lui abbia capito
che lei abbia parlato	che lei abbia ripetuto	che lei sia partita	che lei abbia capito
che Lei abbia parlato	che Lei abbia ripetuto	che Lei sia partito/a	che Lei abbia capito
che noi abbiamo parlato	che noi abbiamo ripetuto	che noi siamo partiti/e	che noi abbiamo capito
che voi abbiate parlato	che voi abbiate ripetuto	che voi siate partiti/e	che voi abbiate capito
che loro abbiano parlato	che loro abbiano ripetuto	che loro siano partiti/e	che loro abbiano capito
che Loro abbiano parlato	che Loro abbiano ripetuto	che Loro siano partiti	che Loro abbiano capito

TRAPASSATO

che io avessi parlato	che io avessi ripetuto	che io fossi partito/a	che io avessi capito
che tu avessi parlato	che tu avessi ripetuto	che tu fossi partito/a	che tu avessi capito
che lui avesse parlato	che lui avesse ripetuto	che lui fosse partito	che lui avesse capito
che lei avesse parlato	che lei avesse ripetuto	che lei fosse partita	che lei avesse capito
che Lei avesse parlato	che Lei avesse ripetuto	che Lei fosse partito/a	che Lei avesse capito
che noi avessimo parlato	che noi avessimo ripetuto	che noi fossimo partiti/e	che noi avessimo capito
che voi aveste parlato	che voi aveste ripetuto	che voi foste partiti/e	che voi aveste capito
che loro avessero parlato	che loro avessero ripetuto	che loro fossero partiti/e	che loro avessero capito
che Loro avessero parlato	che Loro avessero ripetuto	che Loro fossero partiti/e	che Loro avessero capito

CONDIZIONALE
PRESENTE

io parlerei	io prenderei	io partirei	io capirei
tu parleresti	tu prenderesti	tu partiresti	tu capiresti
lui parlerebbe	lui prenderebbe	lui partirebbe	lui capirebbe
lei parlerebbe	lei prenderebbe	lei partirebbe	lei capirebbe
Lei parlerebbe	Lei prenderebbe	Lei partirebbe	Lei capirebbe
noi parleremmo	noi prenderemmo	noi partiremmo	noi capiremmo
voi parlereste	voi prendereste	voi partireste	voi capireste
loro parlerebbero	loro prenderebbero	loro partirebbero	loro capirebbero
Loro parlerebbero	Loro prenderebbero	Loro partirebbero	Loro capirebbero

PASSATO

io avrei parlato	io avrei ripetuto	io sarei partito/a	io avrei capito
tu avresti parlato	tu avresti ripetuto	tu saresti partito/a	tu avresti capito
lui avrebbe parlato	lui avrebbe ripetuto	lui sarebbe partito	lui avrebbe capito
lei avrebbe parlato	lei avrebbe ripetuto	lei sarebbe partita	lei avrebbe capito
Lei avrebbe parlato	Lei avrebbe ripetuto	Lei sarebbe partito/a	Lei avrebbe capito
noi avremmo parlato	noi avremmo ripetuto	noi saremmo partiti/e	noi avremmo capito
voi avreste parlato	voi avreste ripetuto	voi sareste partiti/e	voi avreste capito
loro avrebbero parlato	loro avrebbero ripetuto	loro sarebbero partiti/e	loro avrebbero capito

PRIMA CONIUGAZIONE	SECONDA CONIUGAZIONE	TERZA CONIUGAZIONE	
Loro avrebbero parlato	Loro avrebbero ripetuto	Loro sarebbero partiti/e	Loro avrebbero capito

IMPERATIVO

(tu) parla	(tu) ripeti	(tu) parti	(tu) capisci
(Lei) parli	(Lei) ripeta	(Lei) parta	(Lei) capisca
(noi) parliamo	(noi) ripetiamo	(noi) partiamo	(noi) capiamo
(voi) parlate	(voi) ripetete	(voi) partite	(voi) capite
(Loro) parlino	(Loro) ripetano	(Loro) partano	(Loro) capiscano

THE VERB *AVERE*

INFINITO PRESENTE	INFINITO PASSATO	GERUNDIO PRESENTE	GERUNDIO PASSATO	PARTICIPIO PRESENTE	PARTICIPIO PASSATO
avere	avere avuto	avendo	avendo avuto	avente	avuto

INDICATIVO

PRESENTE	IMPERFETTO	PASSATO REMOTO	FUTURO
io ho	to avevo	to ebbi	io avrò
tu hai	tu avevi	tu avesti	tu avrai
lui ha	lui aveva	lui ebbe	lui avrà
lei ha	lei aveva	lei ebbe	lei avrà
Lei ha	Lei aveva	Lei ebbe	Lei avrà
noi abbiamo	noi avevamo	noi avemmo	noi avremo
voi avete	voi avevate	voi aveste	voi avrete
loro hanno	loro avevano	loro ebbero	loro avranno
Loro hanno	Loro avevano	Loro ebbero	Loro avranno

PASSATO PROSSIMO	TRAPASSATO PROSSIMO	TRAPASSATO REMOTO	FUTURO ANTERIORE
io ho avuto	io avevo avuto	io ebbi avuto	io avrò avuto
tu hai avuto	tu avevi avuto	tu avesti avuto	tu avrai avuto
lui ha avuto	lui aveva avuto	lui ebbe avuto	lui avrà avuto
lei ha avuto	lei aveva avuto	lei ebbe avuto	lei avrà avuto
Lei ha avuto	Lei aveva avuto	Lei ebbe avuto	Lei avrà avuto
noi abbiamo avuto	noi avevamo avuto	noi avemmo avuto	noi avremo avuto
voi avete avuto	voi avevate avuto	voi aveste avuto	voi avrete avuto
loro hanno avuto	loro avevano avuto	loro ebbero avuto	loro avranno avuto
Loro hanno avuto	Loro avevano avuto	Loro ebbero avuto	Loro avranno avuto

CONGIUNTIVO

PRESENTE	IMPERFETTO	PASSATO	TRAPASSATO
che io abbia	che io avessi	che io abbia avuto	che io avessi avuto
che tu abbia	che tu avessi	che tu abbia avuto	che tu avessi avuto
che lui abbia	che lui avesse	che lui abbia avuto	che lui avesse avuto

che lei abbia	che lei avesse	che lei abbia avuto	che lei avesse avuto
che Lei abbia	che Lei avesse	che Lei abbia avuto	che Lei avesse avuto
che noi abbiamo	che noi avessimo	che noi abbiamo avuto	che noi avessimo avuto
che voi abbiate	che voi aveste	che voi abbiate avuto	che voi aveste avuto
che loro abbiano	che loro avessero	che loro abbiano avuto	che loro avessero avuto
che Loro abbiano	che Loro avessero	che Loro abbiano avuto	che Loro avessero avuto

CONDIZIONALE

IMPERATIVO

PRESENTE	PASSATO	
io avrei	io avrei avuto	
tu avresti	tu avresti avuto	(tu) abbi
lui avrebbe	lui avrebbe avuto	
lei avrebbe	lei avrebbe avuto	
Lei avrebbe	Lei avrebbe avuto	(Lei) abbia
noi avremmo	noi avremmo avuto	(noi) abbiamo
voi avreste	voi avreste avuto	(voi) abbiate
loro avrebbero	loro avrebbero avuto	
Loro avrebbero	Loro avrebbero avuto	(Loro) abbiano

THE VERB *ESSERE*

INFINITO PRESENTE	INFINITO PASSATO	GERUNDIO PRESENTE	GERUNDIO PASSATO	PARTICIPIO PRESENTE	PARTICIPIO PASSATO
essere	essere stato (-i, -a, -e)	essendo	essendo stato (-i, -a, -e)	ente	stato (-i, -a, -e)

INDICATIVO

PRESENTE	IMPERFETTO	PASSATO REMOTO	FUTURO
io sono	io ero	io fui	io sarò
tu sei	tu eri	tu fosti	tu sarai
lui è	lui era	lui fu	lui sarà
lei è	lei era	lei fu	lei sarà
Lei è	Lei era	Lei fu	Lei sarà
noi siamo	noi eravamo	noi fummo	noi saremo
voi siete	voi eravate	voi foste	voi sarete
loro sono	loro erano	loro furono	loro saranno
Loro sono	Loro erano	Loro furono	Loro saranno

PASSATO PROSSIMO	TRAPASSATO PROSSIMO	TRAPASSATO REMOTO	FUTURO ANTERIORE
io sono stato/a	io ero stato/a	io fui stato/a	io sarò stato/a
tu sei stato/a	tu eri stato/a	tu fosti stato/a	tu sarai stato/a
lui è stato	lui era stato	lui fu stato	lui sarà stato
lei è stata	lei era stata	lei fu stata	lei sarà stata
Lei è stato/a	Lei era stato/a	Lei fu stato/a	Lei sarà stato/a

noi siamo stati/e	noi eravamo stati/e	noi fummo stati/e	noi saremo stati/e
voi siete stati/e	voi eravate stati/e	voi foste stati/e	voi sarete stati/e
loro sono stati/e	loro erano stati/e	loro furono stati/e	loro saranno stati/e
Loro sono stati/e	Loro erano stati/e	Loro furono stati/e	Loro saranno stati/e

CONGIUNTIVO

PRESENTE	IMPERFETTO	PASSATO	TRAPASSATO
che io sia	che io fossi	che io sia stato/a	che io fossi stato/a
che tu sia	che tu fossi	che tu sia stato/a	che tu fossi stato/a
che lui sia	che lui fosse	che lui sia stato	che lui fosse stato
che lei sia	che lei fosse	che lei sia stata	che lei fosse stata
che Lei sia	che Lei fosse	che Lei sia stato/a	che Lei fosse stato/a
che noi siamo	che noi fossimo	che noi siamo stati/e	che noi fossimo stati/e
che voi siate	che voi foste	che voi siate stati/e	che voi foste stati/e
che loro siano	che loro fossero	che loro siano stati/e	che loro fossero stati/e
che Loro siano	che Loro fossero	che Loro siano stati/e	che Loro fossero stati/e

CONDIZIONALE

PRESENTE	PASSATO	IMPERATIVO	
io sarei	io sarei stato/a		
tu saresti	tu saresti stato/a	(tu) sii	
lui sarebbe	lui sarebbe stato		
lei sarebbe	lei sarebbe stata		
Lei sarebbe	Lei sarebbe stato/a	(Lei) sia	
noi saremmo	noi saremmo stati/e	(noi) siamo	
voi sareste	voi sareste stati/e	(voi) siate	
loro sarebbero	loro sarebbero stati/e	(Loro) siano	
Loro sarebbero	Loro sarebbero stati/e		

2. SOME COMMON IRREGULAR VERBS

ANDARE TO GO

present indicative	vado, vai, va, andiamo, andate, vanno
future indicative	andrò, andrai, andrà, andremo, andrete, andranno
present subjunctive	vada, vada, vada, andiamo, andiate, vadano
present conditional	andrei, andresti, andrebbe, andremmo, andreste, andrebbero
imperative	va', vada, andiamo, andate, vadano

BERE TO DRINK

past participle	bevuto
present indicative	bevo, bevi, beve, beviamo, bevete, bevono
imperfect indicative	bevevo, bevevi, beveva, bevevamo, bevevate, bevevano

404

past absolute	*bevvi, bevesti, bevve, bevemmo, beveste, bevvero*
future indicative	*berrò, berrai, berrà, berremo, berrete, berranno*
present subjunctive	*beva, beva, beva, beviamo, beviate, bevano*
imperfect subjunctive	*bevessi, bevessi, bevesse, bevessimo, beveste, bevessero*
present conditional	*berrei, berresti, berrebbe, berremmo, berreste, berrebbero*

CHIEDERE TO ASK

past participle	*chiesto*
past absolute	*chiesi, chiedesti, chiese, chiedemmo, chiedeste, chiesero*

CHIUDERE TO CLOSE

past participle	*chiuso*
past absolute	*chiusi, chiudesti, chiuse, chiudemmo, chiudeste, chiusero*

CONOSCERE TO KNOW

past participle	*conosciuto*
past absolute	*conobbi, conoscesti, conobbe, conoscemmo, conosceste, conobbero*

DARE TO GIVE

present indicative	*do, dai, dà, diamo, date, danno*
past absolute	*diedi, desti, diede, demmo, deste, diedero*
future indicative	*darò, darai, darà, daremo, darete, daranno*
present subjunctive	*dia, dia, dia, diamo, diate, diano*
conditional present	*darei, daresti, darebbe, daremmo, dareste, darebbero*
imperative	*da', dia, diamo, date, diano*

DECIDERE TO DECIDE

past participle	*deciso*
past absolute	*decisi, decidesti, decise, decidemmo, decideste, decisero*

DIRE TO SAY

past participle	*detto*
present indicative	*dico, dici, dice, diciamo, dite, dicono*
imperfect indicative	*dicevo, dicevi, diceva, dicevamo, dicevate, dicevano*
past absolute	*dissi, dicesti, disse, dicemmo, diceste, dissero*
present subjunctive	*dica, dica, dica, diciamo, diciate, dicano*
imperfect subjunctive	*dicessi, dicessi, dicesse, dicessimo, diceste, dicessero*
imperative	*di', dica, diciamo, dite, dicano*

DOVERE TO HAVE TO

present indicative	*devo, devi, deve, dobbiamo, dovete, devono*
future indicative	*dovrò, dovrai, dovrà, dovremo, dovrete, dovranno*
present subjunctive	*debba, debba, debba, dobbiamo, dobbiate, debbano*
present conditional	*dovrei, dovresti, dovrebbe, dovremmo, dovreste, dovrebbero*

FARE TO DO

past participle	*fatto*
present indicative	*faccio, fai, fa, facciamo, fate, fanno*
imperfect indicative	*facevo, facevi, faceva, facevamo, facevate, facevano*
past absolute	*feci, facesti, fece, facemmo, faceste, fecero*
future indicative	*farò, farai, farà, faremo, farete, faranno*
present subjunctive	*faccia, faccia, faccia, facciamo, facciate, facciano*
present conditional	*farei, faresti, farebbe, faremmo, fareste, farebbero*
imperfect subjunctive	*facessi, facessi, facesse, facessimo, faceste, facessero*
imperative	*fa', faccia, facciamo, fate, facciano*

LEGGERE TO READ

past participle	*letto*
past absolute	*lessi, leggesti, lesse, leggemmo, leggeste, lessero*

METTERE TO PUT

past participle	*messo*
past absolute	*misi, mettesti, mise, mettemmo, metteste, misero*

NASCERE TO BE BORN

past participle	*nato*
past absolute	*nacqui, nascesti, nacque, nascemmo, nasceste, nacquero*

PIACERE TO LIKE

past participle	*piaciuto*
present indicative	*piaccio, piaci, piace, piacciamo, piacete, piacciono*

PORRE TO PUT

past participle	*posto*
present indicative	*pongo, poni, pone, poniamo, ponete, pongono*
imperfect indicative	*ponevo, ponevi, poneva, ponevamo, ponevate, ponevano*
past absolute	*posi, ponesti, pose, ponemmo, poneste, posero*
future indicative	*porrò, porrai, porrà, porremo, porrete, porranno*

present subjunctive	*ponga, ponga, ponga, poniamo, poniate, pongano*
imperfect subjunctive	*ponessi, ponessi, ponesse, ponessimo, poneste, ponessero*
conditional present	*porrei, porresti, porrebbe, porremmo, porreste, porrebbero*
imperative	*poni, ponga, poniamo, ponete, pongano*

POTERE TO BE ABLE TO

present indicative	*posso, puoi, può, possiamo, potete, possono*
future indicative	*potrò, potrai, potrà, potremo, potrete, potranno*
present subjunctive	*possa, possa, possa, possiamo, possiate, possano*
present conditional	*potrei, potresti, potrebbe, potremmo, potreste, potrebbero*

RIMANERE TO STAY, TO REMAIN

present indicative	*rimango, rimani, rimane, rimaniamo, rimanete, rimangono*
past absolute	*rimasi, rimanesti, rimase, rimanemmo, rimaneste, rimasero*
future indicative	*rimarrò, rimarrai, rimarrà, rimarremo, rimarrete, rimarranno*
present subjunctive	*rimanga, rimanga, rimanga, rimaniamo, rimaniate, rimangano*
conditional present	*rimarrei, rimarresti, rimarrebbe, rimarremmo, rimarreste, rimarrebbero*
imperative	*rimani, rimanga, rimaniamo, rimanete, rimangano*

RISPONDERE TO ANSWER

| past participle | *risposto* |
| past absolute | *risposi, rispondesti, rispose, rispondemmo, rispondeste, risposero* |

SAPERE TO KNOW

present indicative	*so, sai, sa, sappiamo, sapete, sanno*
past absolute	*seppi, sapesti, seppe, sapemmo, sapeste, seppero*
future indicative	*saprò, saprai, saprà, sapremo, saprete, sapranno*
present subjunctive	*sappia, sappia, sappia, sappiamo, sappiate, sappiano*
present conditional	*saprei, sapresti, saprebbe, sapremmo, sapreste, saprebbero*
imperative	*sappi, sappia, sappiamo, sappiate, sappiano*

SCRIVERE TO WRITE

| past participle | *scritto* |
| past absolute | *scrissi, scrivesti, scrisse, scrivemmo, scriveste, scrissero* |

SEDERSI TO SIT DOWN

present indicative   *mi siedo, ti siedi, si siede, ci sediamo,*
     vi sedete, si siedono

SPEGNERE TO TURN OFF

participio passato   *spento*
imperative   *spegni, spenga, spegniamo, spegnete, spengano*

STARE TO STAY

present indicative   *sto, stai, sta, stiamo, state, stanno*
past absolute   *stetti, stesti, stette, stemmo, steste, stettero*
future indicative   *starò, starai, starà, staremo, starete, staranno*
present subjunctive   *stia, stia, stia, stiamo, stiate, stiano*
present conditional   *starei, staresti, starebbe, staremmo, stareste,*
     starebbero
imperfect subjunctive   *stessi, stessi, stesse, stessimo, steste, stessero*
imperative   *sta', stia, stiamo, state, stiano*

TENERE TO HOLD, TO KEEP, TO HAVE

present indicative   *tengo, tieni, tiene, teniamo, tenete, tengono*
past absolute   *tenni, tenesti, tenne, tenemmo, teneste,*
     tennero
future indicative   *terrò, terrai, terrà, terremo, terrete, terranno*
present subjunctive   *tenga, tenga, tenga, teniamo, teniate, tengano*
conditional present   *terrei, terresti, terrebbe, terremmo, terreste,*
     terrebbero
imperative   *tieni, tenga, teniamo, tenete, tengano*

TRADURRE TO TRANSLATE

past participle   *tradotto*
present indicative   *traduco, traduci, traduce, traduciamo,*
     traducete, traducono
imperfect indicative   *traducevo, traducevi, traduceva, traducevamo,*
     traducevate, traducevano
past absolute   *tradussi, traducesti, tradusse, traducemmo,*
     traduceste, tradussero
future indicative   *tradurrò, tradurrai, tradurrà, tradurremo,*
     tradurrete, tradurranno
present subjunctive   *traduca, traduca, traduca, traduciamo,*
     traduciate, traducano
imperfect subjunctive   *traducessi, traducessi, traducesse,*
     traducessimo, traduceste, traducessero
conditional present   *tradurrei, tradurresti, tradurrebbe,*
     tradurremmo, tradurreste, tradurrebbero
imperative   *traduci, traduca, traduciamo, traducete,*
     traducano

USCIRE TO GO OUT

present indicative   *esco, esci, esce, usciamo, uscite, escono*
present subjunctive   *esca, esca, esca, usciamo, usciate, escano*
imperative   *esci, esca, usciamo, uscite, escano*

VEDERE TO SEE

past participle	*visto, veduto*
past absolute	*vidi, vedesti, vide, vedemmo, vedeste, videro*
future indicative	*vedrò, vedrai, vedrà, vedremo, vedrete, vedranno*
present conditional	*vedrei, vedresti, vedrebbe, vedremmo, vedreste, vedrebbero*

VENIRE TO COME

past participle	*venuto*
present indicative	*vengo, vieni, viene, veniamo, venite, vengono*
future indicative	*verrò, verrai, verrà, verremo, verrete, verranno*
present subjunctive	*venga, venga, venga, veniamo, veniate, vengano*
present conditional	*verrei, verresti, verrebbe, verremmo, verreste, verrebbero*
imperative	*vieni, venga, veniamo, venite, vengano*

VOLERE TO WANT

present indicative	*voglio, vuoi, vuole, vogliamo, volete, vogliono*
future indicative	*vorrò, vorrai, vorrà, vorremo, vorrete, vorranno*
present conditional	*vorrei, vorresti, vorrebbe, vorremmo, vorreste, vorrebbero*
present subjunctive	*voglia, voglia, voglia, vogliamo, vogliate, vogliano*

3. VERBS CONJUGATED LIKE *CAPIRE*

abbellire to make beautiful
abolire to abolish
accudire to see, to attend (to)
aderire to stick, to adhere (to)
agire to act, to operate
aggredire to attach, to assault
ammonire to warn, to advise, to admonish
arricchire to enrich
arrossire to blush, to flush
asserire to assert, to affirm
assorbire to absorb
attribuire to attribute, to assign
bandire to proclaim, to banish
chiarire to clarify
colpire to hit, to strike
compatire to commiserate (with), to pity, to be sorry for
concepire to conceive
condire to season, to flavour
contribuire to contribute

costruire to construct, to build
definire to define
demolire to demolish
digerire to digest
dimagrire to get thin, to lose weight
diminuire to diminish, to decrease
distribuire to distribute
esaurire to use up, to exhaust
esibire to show, to exhibit, to display
fallire to fail, to be unsuccessful, to go bankrupt
favorire to favor
ferire to wound, to injure
finire to finish, to end
fiorire to flower, to bloom
fornire to supply, to provide
garantire to guarantee, to warrant
gradire to appreciate, to accept
guarire to cure, to recover
impallidire to (turn) pale

impaurire to frighten, to scare
impazzire to go crazy
impedire to prevent, to stop
indebolire to weaken
indispettire to irritate, to annoy
infastidire to annoy, to bother
influire to influence, to affect
ingerire to swallow, to ingest
inghiottire to swallow
ingrandire to enlarge
inserire to insert
intuire to sense, to guess (at), to intuit
istituire to found, to institute, to set up
istruire to instruct, to teach
perire to die, to perish
preferire to prefer
progredire to (make) progress, to proceed
proibire to forbid, to prohibit
pulire to clean
punire to punish
rapire to rob, to kidnap
reagire to react
restituire to return, to give back
riferire to tell, to relate, to refer

ringiovanire to make (look) (feel) younger, to rejuvenate
riunire to reunite
riverire to revere, to respect
sbalordire to shock, to astonish
sbigottire to dismay, to amaze
scolpire to sculpt, to carve
seppellire to bury
sgualcire to crumple, to wrinkle
smarrire to mislay, to lose
smentire to deny, to retract
sostituire to replace
sparire to disappear, to vanish
spedire to send, to mail
stabilire to establish, to set
starnutire to sneeze
stupire to stupefy, to amaze
subire to suffer, to endure, to undergo
suggerire to suggest
tossire to cough
tradire to betray
trasferire to transfer
ubbidire to obey
unire to unite, to join

4. VERBS WHICH FOLLOW THE 1-3-3 PATTERN IN THE *PASSATO REMOTO*

pattern *chiedere*
irregular stem + *-i chiesi*
regular *chiedesti*
regular *chiese*
regular *chiedemmo*
regular *chiedeste*
irregular stem + *-ero chiesero*

assumere assunsi
avere ebbi
bere bevvi, bevesti, . . .
cadere caddi
chiedere chiesi
chiudere chiusi
conoscere conobbi
correre corsi

crescere crebbi
discutere discussi
leggere lessi
mettere misi
nascere nacqui
piacere piacqui
rimanere rimasi
rispondere risposi
rompere ruppi
sapere seppi
scrivere scrissi
vedere vidi
venire venni
vincere vinsi
volete volli

5. VERBS WITH AN IRREGULAR PAST PARTICIPLE

VERBO	PARTICIPIO PASSATO	VERBO	PARTICIPIO PASSATO
aprire	aperto	parere	parso
bere	bevuto	perdere	perso or perduto
chiedere	chiesto	prendere	preso
chiudere	chiuso	rimanere	rimasto
correre	corso	rispondere	risposto
dare	dato	rompere	rotto
decidere	deciso	scegliere	scelto
dire	detto	scendere	sceso
discutere	discusso	scoprire	scoperto
essere/stare	stato	scrivere	scritto
fare	fatto	succedere	successo
leggere	letto	togliere	tolto
mettere	messo	vedere	visto or veduto
morire	morto	venire	venuto
nascere	nato	vincere	vinto
offrire	offerto	vivere	vissuto

6. VERBS AND EXPRESSIONS WHICH REQUIRE THE SUBJUNCTIVE

a. Impersonal Verbs and Expressions

bisogna it is necessary
è bene it is good
è difficile it is difficult
è essenziale it is essential
è giusto it is right
è importante it is important
è impossibile it is impossible
è improbabile it is improbable
è incredibile it is incredible
è indispensabile it is indispensable
è inutile it is useless
è male it is bad
è meglio it is better
è naturale it is natural

è necessario it is necessary
è normale it is normal
è ora it is time
è peccato it is a pity
è possibile it is possible
è probabile it is probable
è raro it is rare
è strano it is strange
è una vergogna it is a shame
è utile it is useful
occorre it is necessary
pare it seems
può darsi it could be
sembra it seems

b. Other Verbs and Expressions

augurare to wish
avere l'impressione to have the impression
avere paura to be afraid
avere timore to fear
chiedersi (se) to ask oneself (if)
credere to believe
desiderare to wish/to desire

dispiacere to be sorry/to regret
domandarsi (se) to ask oneself (if)
dubitare to doubt
esigere to demand
essere contento to be happy
essere felice to be happy
immaginare to imagine

insistere to insist
meravigliarsi to be surprised
non capire to not understand
non essere certo to not be certain
non essere convinto to not be convinced
non essere sicuro to not be sure
non sapere (se) to not know (if)
non vedere l'ora to look forward to/not to be able to wait
pensare to think
piacere to like/to please

preferire to prefer
pregare to ask for, to beg
pretendere to want/to require/to expect
proporre to propose/to suggest
sospettare to suspect
sperare to hope
suggerire to suggest
supporre to suppose/to immagine
temere to fear
volere to want

7. VERBS FOLLOWED DIRECTLY BY AN INFINITIVE

amare to love
bastare to have only to
bisognare to be necessary
desiderare to wish/to desire
dovere to have to
lasciare to leave
osare to dare

piacere to like
potere to be able to
preferire to prefer
sapere to know
vedere to see
volere to want

8. VERBS FOLLOWED BY THE PREPOSITION *"A"*

abituarsi a to get used to
affrettarsi a to hasten to/to hurry to
aiutare a to help
assistere a to be present at
assomigliare a to look like
badare a to look after
cominciare a to start/to begin
continuare a to continue
convincere a to convince to
costringere a to force to
decidersi a to decide to
divertirsi a to enjoy
giocare a to play
imparare a to learn to
incoraggiare a to encourage to

insegnare a to teach to
interessarsi a to be interest in
invitare a to invite to
mandare a to send to
mettersi a to begin/to start/to set to
obbligare a to force to
partecipare a to participate in
pensare a to think of/about
preparare a to prepare to
provare a to try to
ricordare a to remind
rinunciare a to renounce
riprendere a to begin/start again to
riuscire a to succeed in
tenere a to want

9. VERBS FOLLOWED BY THE PREPOSITION *"DI"*

accettare di to accept
accorgersi di to notice
ammettere di to admit
augurarsi di to hope
avere bisogno di to need
avere fretta di to be in a hurry
avere intenzione di to intend
avere l'impressione di to have the
    impression/a feeling
avere paura di to be afraid
avere vergogna di to be ashamed
avere voglia di to feel like
cercare di to try
chiedere di to ask for/to
consigliare di to advise
credere di to believe
decidere di to decide
dimenticare di to forget
dimenticarsi di to forget
dire di to say
essere in grado di to be in a position to
fare a meno di to do without

fidarsi di to trust
fingere di to pretend
finire di to finish
immaginare di to imagine
lamentarsi di to complain about
meravigliarsi di to be surprised/amazed
    at/by
non vedere l'ora di to look forward to
ordinare di to order
pentirsi di to repent of
permettere di to allow/to permit/to let
pregare di to beg
preoccuparsi di to worry
promettere di to promise
rendersi conto di to realize
ringraziare di to thank
sentirsela di to feel up to
smettere di to stop
sperare di to hope
stancarsi di to get tired
temere di to fear
tentare di to try

D. LETTER WRITING

Following are several samples that may be useful as you compose your own letters.

In seguito alla nostra conversazione telefonica del 10 ottobre, ci è gradito poterVi conferire un ordine per 100 stampanti, art. 348 A. Vi preghiamo di spedirci merce indicata con cortese sollecitudine.

Following our telephone conversation of October 10th, we would like to order 100 printers, ref. 348 A. We would appreciate it if you could send them as soon as possible.

Vi ringraziamo per le informazioni richiesteci riguardo alle nostre forniture per ufficio. Alleghiamo il ns. listino prezzi. Siamo lieti di poterVi confermare consegna prima della fine del mese.

Thank you for requesting information on our office furnishings. Please find enclosed our price list. We are happy to confirm that we will be able to make a delivery before the end of the month.

Siamo spiacenti di doverVi comunicare che non ci è possibile accettare i 50 portacenere di cristallo da Voi inviatici, in quanto risultano danneggiati. Riteniamo che il danno sia avvenuto durante il trasporto.

Vi restituiamo pertanto a vostro carico la merce, con la speranza di ricevere la nuova spedizione entro il 15 novembre. Se non Vi è possibile garantire consegna per data indicata, Vi preghiamo di contattarci al più presto.

We are sorry to inform you that we cannot accept your shipment of fifty crystal ashtrays, which were damaged in transport.

We are returning them at your expense, in the hope of receiving a new shipment by November 15th. In the event that you cannot deliver by said date, please contact us immediately.

Pordenone, 10 ottobre 1996

Spett. Ditta
Creazioni Chic
Viale Marconi, 23
32100 Belluno

Ci è pervenuta la vostra spedizione del 27 settembre al cui contenuto dovremmo contrapporre delle obiezioni.

Quando consulterete la nostra ordinazione del 28 agosto scoprirete che la merce indicata non combacia con ciò che ci è stato inviato. Noi avevamo richiesto 200 paia di orecchini, ma ne abbiamo ricevute solo 20. Visto che ci stiamo preparando per la stagione natalizia, vorremmo che ci inviaste al più presto possibile le 180 paia che abbiamo ordinato e prapagato.

Oltre a ciò vorremmo farvi notare che non siamo soddisfatti del modo in cui avete impacchettato la merce. Il pacco è stato preparato in modo molto disordinato. Di conseguenza gli orecchini si sono mischiati. Vi preghiamo di prestare massima attenzione nel preparare la prossima spedizione.

In attesa di una pronta risposta e della prossima spedizione, distintamente vi salutiamo.

GIOIELLI 2000

Allegati: 1 copia lettera di ordinazione del 28 agosto
1 copia fattura commerciale #6695192

Pordenone, October 10, 1996

Creazioni Chic
Viale Marconi, 23
32100 Belluno

We have received your shipment of September 27 and we would like to bring to your attention some objections we have regarding its content.

When you consult our order of August 28, you will discover that the merchandise indicated does not match what has been sent to us. We had requested 200 pair of earrings, but we have only received 20. Seeing that we are preparing for the Christmas season, we would like you to send us the 180 pairs that we ordered and pre-paid as soon as possible.

In addition to this we would like to have you note that we are not satisfied with the way you packed the merchandise. The packing was done in a very disorganized manner, and consequently the earrings have gotten mixed up. We ask you to pay very close attention when you prepare the next shipment.

In anticipation of a prompt reply and of the next shipment, we send our distinct regards.

GIOIELLI 2000

Enclosures: 1 copy of order letter dated August 28
             1 copy of sales invoice #6695192

Belluno, 17 ottobre 1996

Spett. Società
Gioielli 2000
33170 Pordenone

Rispondiamo con questo fax alla Vostra lettera del 10 ottobre del cui contenuto siamo molto dispiaciuti. Di quanto accaduto non possiamo che scusarci e garantiamo un rimedio immediato alla nostra svista. L'ordinazione di 180 paia di orecchini che aspettate è stata preparata con molta cura ed è stata spedita oggi stesso. Dovreste ricevere la merce nel giro di 24 ore.

In considerazione dei nostri ottimi rapporti di affari che datano da sei anni, speriamo che accetterete le nostre più sentite scuse. Sperando che questo incidente increscioso non turbi la qualità dei nostri rapporti di affari, porgiamo cordiali saluti.

CREAZIONI CHIC

Belluno, October 17, 1996

Gioielli 2000
33170 Pordenone

With this fax we reply to your letter of October 10, a letter which conveyed information we regretted to hear. We cannot but apologize for what has happened, and we guarantee an immediate solution to our oversight. The order of 180 pairs of earrings that you are waiting for has been prepared with great care and has been sent off today. You should be receiving the merchandise within the next 24 hours.

In consideration of our excellent business relationship of six years, we hope that you will accept our most heartfelt apologies. Hoping that this unfortunate incident does not alter the cordial nature of our business dealings, we extend our warm greetings.

CREAZIONI CHIC

Gentili signori,

Tra pochi giorni nella nostra città si aprirà un nuovo negozio specializzato in abbigliamento e in attrezzatura sportiva. Troverete tutto per le vostre esigenze sportive, da calzature atletiche di altissima qualità a palloni di calcio approvati dalla FIFA, a tute sportive delle migliori marche. Potrete constatare il nostro vastissimo assortimento solo venendo a visitarci. Il nostro inventario è veramente sbalorditivo; per la prima volta in Italia potrete fare spese in un vero iper-mercato dello sport.

Il nostro negozio si chiama "Gol," e vi sentirete veramente dei vincitori venendo a trovarci. Troverete non solo merce di altissima qualità, ma dei prezzi competitivi e dei venditori esperti ed entusiasti che sapranno offrirvi ottimi consigli.

"Gol" aprirà le sue porte il primo febbraio prossimo alle otto e trenta in Via Roma, 50. Saremmo molto lieti di vedervi alla nostra apertura. Vi ringraziamo anticipatamente dell'attenzione.

In attesa di una vostra visita, vogliate gradire i nostri migliori saluti.

GOL

Naples, January 18, 1996

Dear ladies and gentlemen,

In a few days' time a new specialty store will open in our city, an athletic clothing and sporting goods store. You will find everything for your sporting needs, from athletic footwear of the highest quality to FIFA-approved soccer balls and jogging suits of the finest brand names. You'll be able to see our vast assortment for yourselves only by coming to visit us. Our inventory is truly amazing; for the first time in Italy you'll be able to shop in a true sports supermarket.

The name of our store is "Gol," and you'll really be able to feel like winners when you come to visit us. You'll find not only merchandise of the highest quality, but also competitive prices and expert and enthusiastic salespeople who will be able to offer excellent advice.

"Gol" will open its doors on February 1, at 8:30 a.m., at Via Roma, 50. We would be very happy to see you at our opening. We thank you in advance for your attention. Awaiting your visit we extend to you our best regards.

GOL

_____

Milano, 30 giugno 1995

Spett. Soc. Grimaldi Informatica
Via XX settembre, 22
00100 Roma

Con la presente mi permetto di offrirVi il mio giudizio professionale su Carmela Passafiume, mia ex-studentessa e assistente. Sono stato informato che la Signora si è rivolta alla vostra Direzione per ottenere un posto in qualità di rappresentante dei Vostri prodotti in Australia. Oso dire che, a mio avviso, Carmela Passafiume sarebbe un'ottima scelta per la vostra azienda.

Permettemi di descrivere la mia associazione con la signora Passafiume. Da studentessa, ha assistito ai miei corsi di inglese e ha dimostrato un'eccezionale padronanza della lingua. In quest'ultimo semestre mi ha servito in qualità di assistente in un corso di traduzione italiano-inglese, inglese-italiano, e sia io che i miei studenti l'abbiamo trovata capacissima. Oltre ad avere una padronanza superiore dell'inglese, la signora Passafiume è una persona responsabile ed efficiente, e riesce sempre a portare a termine qualsiasi progetto di lavoro.

Sperando di aver reso il Vostro compito più facile e ringraziandoVi della gentile attenzione, Vi pongo i miei distinti saluti.

Prof. Agnes Bean

Milan, June 30, 1995

Spett. Soc. Grimaldi Informatica
Via XX settembre, 22
00100 Roma

This letter is to offer you my professional opinion of my ex-student and assistant Ms. Passafiume. I have been informed that Ms. Passafiume has applied to your management to obtain a position as a sales representative for your products in Australia. I can confidently say that in my opinion Carmela Passafiume would be an excellent choice for your firm.

Allow me to describe my association with Ms. Passafiume. As a student, she attended my English courses and showed an exceptional mastery of the language. Last semester she served as my assistant in an Italian-English, English-Italian translation course, and both the other students and I found her extremely capable. In addition to having mastered English, Ms. Passafiume is responsible and efficient, and always succeeds in bringing to completion any kind of work project.

Hoping to have made your task somewhat easier and thanking you for your kind attention I extend to you my distinct regards.

Prof. Agnes Bean

GLOSSARY

ITALIAN-ENGLISH

A

a *at, to*
  ad un passo *a few steps from here*
  ad una ad una *one by one, one after the other*
  al più presto possibile *as soon as possible*
  all'improvviso *all of a sudden, suddenly*
  a condizione che *on condition that*
  a dire il vero *to tell (you) the truth, to be honest*
  a meno che *unless*
  a patto che *provided that*
  a pochi passi *a few steps from here*
  a proposito *by the way*
  a qualsiasi costo *at any cost*
  a risentirci *good-bye for now, until next time*
  a tua disposizione *at your disposal*
  a buon mercato *at a cheap price*
  A più tardi. *See you later.*
  A presto! *See you soon.*
  A domani. *See you tomorrow.*
  a destra *on the right*
  a sinistra *on the left*
  all'agenzia immobiliare *at a real estate agency*
  alla questura *at the police station*
  all'ufficio del cambio *at the currency exchange office*
  andare a piedi *to go on foot*
  allo stesso tempo *at the same time*
abbastanza *enough, rather*
abbigliamento *clothes, clothing*
  articoli di abbigliamento *articles of clothing*
  negozio di abbigliamento *clothing store*
abbracciarsi *to hug*
abitare *to live*
  abitare al primo piano *to live on the second floor*
  abitare in Italia *to live in Italy*
  abitare a Roma *to live in Rome*
abitazione a *residence, dwelling-place*
abito *outfit, suit, dress*
  abito confezionato *ready-to-wear suit*
  abito da mezza stagione *between seasons suit*
  abito da sera *evening wear*
abituarsi a *to get used to*
abitudine *habit*
accademia *academy*
accademicamente *academically*
accademico *academic*
accanto *beside, near, by*
  Il museo è accanto alla pinacoteca. *The museum is beside the art gallery.*
accedere *to approach, to enter*

accelerare *to accelerate*
accendere *to turn on, to light*
  accendere la televisione *to turn on the television*
  accendere la radio *to turn on the radio*
accendino *lighter*
accennare *to beckon, to mention, to refer to, to hint at*
accertamento *assurance; assessment; control*
accesso *entry, admittance*
accettare *to accept*
accettazione *acceptance, reception, check-in*
  banco d'accettazione *check-in counter*
accomodarsi *to sit down, to make oneself comfortable*
  Si accomodi. *Sit down. Make yourself comfortable.*
accompagnare *to accompany*
accontentare *to satisfy, to please*
accordo *agreement, arrangement*
accorgersi *to notice, to realize*
accudire *to attend to*
accumulare *to accumulate*
aceto *vinegar*
acido *acid, sour*
acqua *water*
  acqua minerale *mineral water*
  acqua tonica *tonic water*
  acqua calda *hot water*
acquistare *to buy, to purchase*
acquisto *purchase*
adattare *to adapt, to adjust*
adatto *suitable, suited, right*
addebitare *to charge, to debit*
addebito *debit*
addormentarsi *to fall asleep*
addosso *on one's back*
adesso *now*
aereo *(adj.) aerial*
  compagnia aerea *airline*
aereo *(n.) airplane*
aeronautico *aeronautical, aircraft*
aeroporto *airport*
aerostazione *air terminal*
affacciarsi *to appear at, to lean out of, to go and look out of*
affare *(m.) business*
  viaggio d'affari *business trip*
affatto *at all*
  Non sono affatto stanco. *I am not tired at all.*
affettati *cold cuts*
affidare *to entrust, to assign, to grant, to give a loan to*

affinché *so that*
affittacamere *landlord, landlady*
affittare *to rent*
   affittare un appartamento *to rent an apartment*
   affittasi *for rent*
   Ha camere da affittare? *Do you have rooms for rent?*
affitto *(n.) rent*
   cercare un appartamento in affitto *to look for an apartment for rent*
   dare in affitto *to let, to rent*
affollato *crowded*
affrancare *to put a stamp on*
   affrancare una lettera *to put a stamp on a letter*
affresco *fresco*
affrontare *to face, to confront*
agente *(m.) agent*
   agente di viaggio *travel agent*
   agente immobiliare *real estate agent*
   agente di vendita *sales agent*
agenzia *agency*
   agenzia di viaggio *travel agency*
   agenzia immobiliare *real estate agency*
   agenzia di pubblicità *advertising agency*
aggettivo *adjective*
aggiustare *to fix*
   aggiustare la macchina *to fix the car*
aglio *garlic*
ago *needle*
agosto *August*
agrario *agrarian, agricultural*
agricolo *agricultural*
agricoltore *farmer*
agricoltura *agriculture*
agriturismo *farm holiday*
agronomo *agronomist*
aiutare *to help*
aiuto *help*
ala *wing*
alba *dawn*
albergo *hotel*
   albergo a tre stelle *three-star hotel*
   albergo di prima categoria *first-class hotel*
albero *tree*
   albero della cuccagna *greasy pole*
album *album*
   l'ultimo album *the latest album*
alcolico *alcoholic*
alcuni *some*
alimentare *food-, alimentary*
alimentazione *diet, feeding*
allacciare *to fasten, to tie*
allacciarsi le scarpe *to tie one's shoes*
allattamento *feeding, nursing*
allegare *to attach*
allegato *attachment*
allegorico *allegoric*
allenamento *training*
allenatore *coach*
allergia *allergy*
allergico *allergic*
allievo *pupil*

alloggio *accommodation, lodging*
allontanare *to send away, to keep away, to dismiss*
allora *then, at that moment, in that case, therefore, so, what then*
alluce *big toe*
alluvione *flood, inundation*
almeno *at least*
alpino *alpine*
altezza *height*
alto *tall, high*
altrettanto *likewise*
altrimenti *otherwise*
altro *other*
altrove *elsewhere*
alzare *to raise, to lift, to build*
   alzarsi *to get up*
amante *lover*
amare *to love*
ambasciata *embassy*
ambiente *surroundings, environment, background, sphere*
ambito *circuit, limits, circle*
ambizioso *ambitious*
ambulanza *ambulance*
americano *American*
amichevole *friendly*
amicizia *friendship*
amico *friend*
ammalarsi *to get sick*
ammettere *to admit, to receive, to grant*
amministrativo *administrative*
amministratore *administrator, director*
amministrazione *administration*
ammirare *to admire*
ammiratore *admirer*
ammissione *admission*
ammobiliato *furnished*
   appartamento ammobiliato *furnished apartment*
amore *love*
ampio *wide, broad*
analisi *(f.) analysis, test*
   analisi del sangue *blood test*
analizzare *to analyze*
anatomia *anatomy*
anche *too, also*
ancora *still, yet, once more, another*
andare *to go*
   andare al lavoro *to go to work*
   andare dal dottore *to go to the doctor*
   andare a messa *to go to mass*
   andare in centro *to go downtown*
   andare al ristorante *to go to a restaurant*
   andare al mare *to go to the sea/ocean/shore*
   andare alla spiàggia *to go to the beach*
   andare a piedi *to walk*
   andare al negozio *to go to the store*
   andare al cìnema *to go to the movies*
   andare al concerto *to go to a concert*
   andare in vacanza *to go on vacation*
   andare alla posta *to go to the post office*

andare alla questura *to go to the police station*
andare a teatro *to go to the theatre*
andare all'opera *to go to the opera*
Va bene! *Okay!*
Va' piano *Go slow.*
andare a fondo *to get to the bottom, to fall through*
andare a ruba *to sell like hotcakes*
andare avanti *to go forward, to go ahead*
andare contromano *to go in the wrong direction*
andare d'accordo *to agree, to get on well*
andare di moda *to be in, to be fashionable*
andare per la propria (sua) strada *to go one's own way*
andata *departure, going*
   biglietto di andata *one-way ticket*
   biglietto di andata e ritorno *round-trip ticket*
angelo *angel*
angolo *angle, corner*
anguria *watermelon*
annata *year, crop, harvest, annual amount*
anno *year*
   lanno prossimo *next year*
   lanno scorso *last year*
   avere . . . anni *to be . . . years old*
annoiarsi *to get bored*
annunciare *to announce*
annuncio *announcement, advertisement*
   annunci economici *classified ads*
   annuncio personale *personal advertisement*
   annuncio pubblicitario *advertisement, ad*
annuo *annual, yearly*
antenato *ancestor*
antico *old, ancient, out-of-date*
antidolorifico *pain killer*
antinebbia *anti-fog*
antipasto *hors-d'oeuvre, appetizer*
antipatia *dislike*
anulare *ring finger*
anzi *in fact, better still, as a matter of fact*
ape *bee*
aperitivo *aperitif*
aperto *open*
concerto all'aperto *open-air concert*
apparecchiare *to prepare, to get ready*
   apparecchiare la tavola *to set the table*
apparecchiatura *equipment, preparation*
apparecchio *apparatus, set, aircraft*
apparire *to appear, to seem*
appartamento *apartment, flat*
   appartamento ammobiliato *furnished apartment*
   affittare un appartamento *to rent an apartment*
appartenere *to belong*
appello *appeal*
appena *hardly, scarcely, only, just*
appetito *appetite*
   Buon appetito! *Enjoy your meal!*
applaudire *to applaud, to clap*
applicazione *application, diligence*
appoggio *support, assistance*

apprezzamento *esteem, evaluation, opinion*
apprezzare *to appreciate, to evaluate, to appraise*
appropriato *appropriate*
approssimativamente *approximately*
approvazione *approval*
appuntamento *appointment*
   fissare un appuntamento *to make an appointment*
appunto *note, remark*
aprile *(m.) April*
aprire *to open*
   aprire un conto *to open an account*
aquila *eagle*
arancia *orange*
   spremuta d'arancia *freshly squeezed orange juice*
aranciata *orange drink*
arbitro *referee*
architetto *architect*
architettonico *architectural, architectonic*
architettura *architecture*
archivio *archives, file, filing cabinet*
arcobaleno *rainbow*
area *area, surface, zone*
argomento *reason, topic, subject, contents, cause, motive*
aria *air*
   aria condizionata *air conditioning*
arma *weapon, arm*
armadio *wardrobe, armoire*
   armadio a muro *closet*
aroma *aroma, fragrance*
aromatico *aromatic*
arredamento *interior design, furnishing, furniture*
arredare *to furnish*
   arredare una casa *to furnish a house*
   La stanza è arredata. *The room is furnished.*
arredo *furnishings, fittings*
arrestare *to arrest*
arrivare *to arrive*
   arrivare in tempo *to arrive on time*
arrivederci *Goodbye (fam.)*
arrivederLa *Goodbye (formal)*
arrivo *arrival*
arte *(f.) art*
Belle Arti *Fine Arts*
articolo *article, item*
   articoli di regalo *gift items*
   articoli di abbigliamento *articles of clothing*
artigianato *craftsmanship*
artista *(m. f.) artist*
artistico *artistic*
ascensore *elevator*
asciugamano *towel*
asciugare *to dry*
   asciugarsi i capelli *to dry one's hair*
asciugatrice *clothes dryer*
ascoltare *to listen, to hear*
   ascoltare la radio *to listen to the radio*
   ascoltare una canzone *to listen to a song*
ascoltatore *listener*

ascolto *listening*
asilo *kindergarten, nursery school*
asino *donkey*
asma *asthma*
aspettare *to wait, to wait for*
  aspettare in fila *to wait in line*
  aspettare l'autobus *to wait for the bus*
aspetto *waiting, wait; look, appearance*
  sala d'aspetto *waiting room*
aspirina *aspirin*
assaggiare *to taste*
assai *very, enough, a lot of*
assegnato *assigned*
assegno *check*
  libretto degli assegni *checkbook*
  riscuotere un assegno *to cash a check*
assenteismo *absenteeism*
assicurare *to secure, to assure, to insure*
  assicurare un pacco *to insure a parcel*
assicurativo *insurance-*
assicurazione *insurance*
  assicurazione per il furto *anti-theft
    insurance*
  assicurazione medica *medical insurance*
  assicurazione contro i danni *collision damage
    waiver*
assistente *(m. f.) assistant*
  assistente di volo *flight attendant*
  assistente del personale *staff assistant*
  assistente di bordo *flight attendant*
assistenziale *welfare-*
assistere *to assist; to attend*
  assistere ad uno spettacolo *to attend a show*
associazione *association, society, company*
assolutamente *absolutely, definitely*
assumere *to adopt, to undertake, to employ, to
    hire*
  essere assunto *to be hired*
assunzione *undertaking, hiring*
astinenza *abstinence*
ateneo *university*
attendere *to wait for, to attend, to look after*
  attendere in linea *to wait in line*
attentamente *carefully, attentively*
attento *attentive*
  Sta' attento! *Be careful!*
attenzione *attention*
atterraggio *landing*
atterrare *to land*
attesa *waiting, expectation*
attillato *close-fitting*
attimo *instant, moment*
  Un attimo, per favore. *One moment, please.*
attività *activity*
  attività professionale *professional activity*
attivo *active*
attore *(m.) actor*
attorno *around, about*
attraverso *across, through, over*
attrezzatura *equipment*
attrice *(f.) actress*
attuale *present, current*

attualità *current event*
  servizio di attualità *news report*
attualmente *at present, now*
augurare *to wish*
augurio *wish, greeting*
  Tanti auguri! *Best wishes!*
aula *classroom*
aumentare *to increase, to augment*
aumento *increase*
aurora *dawn*
australiano *Australian*
auto *car, automobile*
  auto aziendale *car company*
autobus *(m.) bus*
  aspettare l'autobus *to wait for the bus*
  biglietto per l'autobus *bus ticket*
  prendere l'autobus *to take the bus*
automatico *automatic*
  cambio automatico *automatic transmission*
automobilismo *car racing*
autonoleggio *car rental office*
autonomo *autonomous*
autore *author*
autorimessa *garage*
autorità *authority*
autorizzato *authorized*
autostrada *highway*
autunno *autumn, fall*
avanzato *advanced, forward*
avere *to have*
  avere sete *to be thirsty*
  avere una promozione *to get promoted*
  avere occasione di *to have the opportunity to*
  avere pazienza *to be patient*
  avere appena il tempo di *to just have time for*
  avere fame *to be hungry*
  avere un bel posto *to have a good job, position*
  avere fretta *to be in a hurry*
  avere l'esaurimento nervoso *to have a nervous
    breakdown*
  avere fiducia in *to trust*
  avere la febbre *to have a fever*
  avere mal di gola *to have a sore throat*
  avere mal di stomaco *to have a stomach ache*
  avere paura *to be afraid*
  avere . . . anni *to be . . . years old*
  avere bisogno di *to need*
  avere cura di *to take care of*
  avere forti dubbi *to have strong doubts*
  avere forti motivi *to have strong reasons*
  avere il tempo *to have time*
  avere inizio *to begin*
  avere intenzione di *to intend*
  avere l'impressione *to have the impression*
  avere la lingua lunga *to be quick with a nasty
    reply*
  avere le mani bucate *to be a spendthrift*
  avere le mani di ricotta *to be butter-fingered*
  avere le mani lunghe *to be light-fingered*
  avere paura *to be afraid*
  avere qualcosa da dichiarare *to have something
    to declare*

avere qualcosa sulla punta della lingua *to have something on the tip of the tongue*
avere ragione *to be right*
avere un appuntamento *to have an appointment*
avere un impegno *to have an engagement*
avere un sacco di lavoro *to have a lot of work*
avere un sacco di soldi *to have a lot of money*
avere una fame da lupi *to be as hungry as a wolf, to be famished*
avere una sete da morire *to be dying of thirst*
avere voglia di *to feel like*
averne le tasche piene di *to be fed up*
avversario *rival, adversary*
avvertire *to inform, to notify, to warn*
avviare *to direct, to guide, to start, to set up*
avvicinarsi *to approach, to draw near*
avviso *announcement, advertisement, notice, advice, opinion, message*
avviso di chiamata *call waiting*
avviso economico *newspaper ad*
avvocato *lawyer*
azienda *company, firm*
aziendale *company-, business-*
azione *action, deed, movement, influence, lawsuit, share*
azionista *shareholder, stockholder*

B

baffo *moustache*
avere i baffi *to have a moustache*
bagaglio *luggage*
bagaglio a mano *hand luggage*
bagno *bathroom*
fare il bagno *to go swimming*
farsi il bagno *to take a bath*
balcone *balcony*
ballare *to dance*
ballare il liscio *to dance to a slow song*
ballare il rock *to dance to rock and roll*
ballerina/ballerino *female dancer/male dancer*
ballo *dance, dancing, ballet*
balsamo *balsam*
balsamo per i capelli *hair conditioner*
bambino *baby, child, son*
banale *banal, ordinary, trivial*
banana *banana*
banca *bank*
bancarella *stand*
bancario *banking, bank-*
banchiere *banker*
banco *desk, counter*
banco d'accettazione *check-in counter*
bancomat *instant teller*
banconota *banknote, bill*
bandiera *flag*
bar *bar, cafe*
baracca *shed*

barba *beard*
farsi la barba *to shave*
sapone per la barba *shaving cream*
barbiere *(m.) barber*
barista *(m. f.) bartender*
barocco *baroque*
barzelletta *joke*
basilare *basic, fundamental*
basilica *basilica*
basso *short, low*
bassa stagione *low season*
bastare *to be enough, to suffice, to last, to be sufficient*
basta! *stop it, that's enough*
battere *to beat*
battere a macchina *to type*
battesimo *baptism*
battuta *blow, beat, cue, witty remark, witty reply, phrase, shooting party*
bellezza *beauty*
bello *beautiful*
È una bella giornata. *It's a beautiful day.*
benché *although, even if, even though*
bene *well*
beneficenza *charity*
beni capitali *capital goods*
beni di consumo *consumer goods*
beni d'investimento *investment goods*
beni immobili *fixed property, real assets*
benvenuto *welcome*
benzina *gasoline*
benzina super *super*
benzina normale *regular gas*
benzina senza piombo *unleaded gas*
benzina verde *unleaded gas*
buono benzina *gas coupon*
fare benzina *to fill up*
benzinaio *gas station attendant*
bere *to drink*
bersaglio *target, mark*
bevanda *drink, beverage*
bianchetto *whiteout, liquid paper*
bianco *white*
biblioteca *library*
bicchiere *(m.) glass*
bicchiere d'acqua minerale *glass of mineral water*
bicicletta *bicycle*
bigliettaio *ticket-collector*
biglietteria *ticket booth*
biglietto *ticket*
biglietto di andata e ritorno *round-trip ticket*
biglietto di andata *one-way ticket*
biglietto di prima classe *first-class ticket*
biglietto per l'autobus *bus ticket*
biglietti di grosso/piccolo taglio *big/small bills*
biglietto aereo *airplane ticket*
biglietto da visita *business card*
biglietto della lotteria *lottery ticket*
biglietto di condoglianze *message of sympathy*
biglietto d'invito *invitation card*

biglietto omaggio *free ticket*
biglietto scaduto *expired ticket*
bimbo *child, baby*
binario *train track*
    Su quale binario arriva il treno? *Which track is the train arriving on?*
biologia *biology*
biologo *biologist*
biondo *blond*
    capelli biondi *blond hair*
birra *beer*
bis *encore*
    concedere il bis *to give an encore*
    chiedere il bis *to ask for an encore*
biscotto *biscuit*
bisogno *need*
    avere bisogno di *to need*
bistecca *steak*
    Voglio la mia bistecca ben cotta/al sangue. *I want my steak well done/rare.*
blocchetto *paper pad*
blu *blue*
bocca *mouth*
bocconcino *mozzarella ball*
boicottaggio *boycott*
bolletta *bill; receipt*
    pagare la bolletta *to pay the bill*
bollo *stamp*
    carta da bollo *government-stamped paper*
    marca da bollo *tax stamp*
boom economico *economic boom*
    boom edilizio *housing boom*
borsa *purse, bag; stock market*
    borsa a mano *hand luggage*
    borsa di studio *scholarship*
borsetta *purse*
botte *barrel*
botteghino *ticket booth*
bottiglia *bottle*
    bottiglia di vino *bottle of wine*
bottone *button*
boutique *boutique*
braccio *arm*
bravo *capable, good, nice*
breve *brief, short*
brezza *breeze*
brillante *brilliant, bright*
brillare *to shine*
brindisi *toast*
bronzo *bronze*
bruciore *burning sensation*
    bruciore allo stomaco *heartburn*
brutto *ugly, bad, mean, awful*
buca *hole*
    buca delle lettere *mailbox*
bucato *laundry*
buccia *skin, peel, bark*
buco *hole*
bugia *lie*
buono *(adj.) good*
    Buon viaggio! *Have a nice trip!*
    Buon appetito! *Enjoy your meal!*

Buon giorno. *Good morning. Good afternoon.*
Buon compleanno! *Happy Birthday!*
Buon onomastico! *Happy Name Day! Happy Saint's Day!*
Buona notte. *Good night.*
Buona sera. *Good evening.*
Buona fortuna. *Good luck.*
a buon mercato *at a cheap price*
buon affare *good bargain*
buono *(n.) coupon, bond*
    buono benzina *gas coupon*
burro *butter*
busta *envelope*
    busta paga *pay-envelope*
buttare *to throw*
    buttare via il denaro *to throw away one's money*

C

cabina *cabin, booth*
    cabina telefonica *telephone booth*
cadere *to fall, to drop*
caffè *(m.) cafe, coffee*
    caffè espresso *espresso coffee*
    caffè corretto *laced coffee*
    caffè macchiato *coffee with a dash of milk*
    caffè lungo *weak coffee*
    caffè ristretto *extra strong coffee*
    caffellatte *(m) coffee with milk*
calcio *soccer*
calcolatore *calculator*
caldo *hot*
    Fa caldo. *It's hot.*
calma *calm, peace*
calmante *(n.m.) sedative*
caloroso *warm, heated*
calpestare *to trample on*
calzascarpe *(m.) shoe horn*
calzatura *footwear*
calzolaio *shoemaker*
calzoleria *shoe store*
calzoncini *shorts*
calzoni *trousers*
cambiale *(f.) promissory note*
cambiamento *change*
cambiare *to change*
    cambiare casa *to move*
    cambiare canale *to change channel*
    cambiare dollari in lire *to exchange dollars into liras*
    cambiare l'olio *to change the oil*
    cambiare il filtro *to change the filter*
cambio *gear; exchange*
    cambio automatico *automatic transmission*
    Quanto è il cambio oggi? *What is the exchange rate today?*
    Il cambio è alto/basso. *The exchange rate is high/low.*
    tasso del cambio *exchange rate*
    sportello dei cambi *exchange window*
camera *room, chamber*

camera di commercio *Chamber of Commerce*
camera da letto *bedroom*
camera senza bagno *room without bathroom*
camera con doccia *room with shower*
camera singola/doppia *single/double room*
camera matrimoniale *double room*
Ha camere da affittare? *Do you have rooms for rent?*
prenotare una camera *to reserve a room*
cameriera *maid, waitress*
cameriere *(m.) waiter*
camicetta *blouse*
camicia *shirt*
camion *truck*
camminare *to walk, to work, to progress*
camoscio *suede*
scarpe di camoscio *suede shoes*
campagna *country*
campana *bell*
campanile *bell tower*
campionario *samples, sample collection*
campionato *championship*
campione *champion, sample, specimen*
campo *field, branch, battleground, sector*
campo agricolo *agricultural sector*
campo d'atterraggio *landing-ground*
campo di giuoco *playing field*
campo di tennis *tennis court*
campo sportivo *playing field*
canadese *Canadian*
canale *(m.) channel*
cambiare canale *to change channels*
cancellare *to erase, to wipe out, to cancel*
cancellazione *(f.) cancellation*
candidato *candidate*
cane *dog*
cane da caccia *hunting dog*
cantante *(m. f.) singer*
cantare *to sing*
cantautore *(m.) song writer and singer*
cantina *wine cellar*
canto *song*
canzone *(f.) song*
capace *skillful, able, capable*
capacità *ability, capacity*
cercare qualcuno con capacità manageriali *to look for someone with managerial ability*
capello *hair*
capelli corti *short hair*
avere i capelli lunghi *to have long hair*
capelli ricci *curly hair*
capelli lisci *straight hair*
capelli ondulati *wavy hair*
capelli biondi *blond hair*
capelli castani *brown hair*
tagliarsi i capelli *to get a haircut*
tagliarsi capelli a spazzola/a zero *to get a brush cut/a crew cut*
asciugarsi i capelli *to dry one's hair*

tingersi i capelli biondi *to dye one's hair blond*
Come vuole i capelli? *How do you like your hair?*
balsamo per i capelli *hair conditioner*
capire *(isc) to understand*
capitale *capital*
capofabbrica *plant manager*
capogruppo *group leader*
capolavoro *masterpiece*
capo operaio *foreman*
capotecnico *technical director*
capoturno *head of a shift*
cappello *hat*
cappotto *coat*
cappuccino *cappuccino*
capufficio *director, boss*
carabiniere *(m.) carabiniere (see cultural note)*
caratteristico *characteristic, typical, distinctive*
carbone *(m.) charcoal*
carta carbone *carbon paper*
carburante *(m.) gas, fuel*
carico *load*
carne *meat*
carne in scatola *canned meat*
carnevale *Carnival*
carnevalesco *carnival-like*
caro *dear, expensive*
Ha qualcosa di meno caro? *Do you have something less expensive?*
carota *carrot*
carpentiere *carpenter*
carrello *trolley*
carriera *career*
fare carriera *to have a successful career*
carro *cart, chariot*
carta *paper*
carta d'imbarco *boarding pass*
cara da lettere *writing-paper*
carta telefonica *telephone cord*
carta carbone *carbon paper*
carta carburante turistica *highway toll card*
carta da bollo *government-stamped paper*
carta igienica *toilet paper*
carta geografica *map*
carta stradale *road map*
carta da imballaggio *packing paper*
carta da lettere *letter-paper*
carta da lettere intestata *headed letter-paper*
carta d'identità *identity card*
carta di credito *credit card*
carta di credito telefonica *phone card*
carta straccia *waste paper*
carta stradale *route map*
carta telefonica prepagata *prepaid phone card*
cartella *folder*
cartolina *postcard, card*
cartoni animati *cartoons*
casa *house*
a casa *at home, home*
cambiare casa *to move*
restare a casa *to stay home*
casella *box*

casella postale *post-office box*
cassa *cash register*
   Si accomodi alla cassa. *Please go to the cashier's window.*
cassaforte *(f.) safe*
cassetta *cassette, box*
   cassetta di sicurezza *safety deposit box*
   cassetta postale *mailbox*
cassetto *drawer*
cassiere/a *(m.f.) cashier, treasurer*
castano *brown*
   capelli castani *brown hair*
castello *castle*
catalogo *catalogue*
categoria *category*
   albergo di prima categoria *first-class hotel*
cattedrale *cathedral*
cavo *cable, rope*
CD *CD (compact disc)*
   l'ultimo CD *the latest CD*
celebre *famous, well-known*
cemento *cement, concrete*
cena *supper*
cenare *to have supper*
censimento *census*
centigradi *centigrade*
cento *hundred*
   Il tasso di interesse è al dieci percento. *The interest rate is at ten percent.*
centrale *central*
centralinista *(m.f.) operator*
centralino *(place) operator, telephone exchange*
   Chiama il centralino. *Call the operator.*
centro *center*
   in centro *downtown*
   andare in centro *to go downtown*
   centro commerciale *commercial center*
   centro storico *historic city centre*
cera *wax*
ceramica *ceramics, pottery, baked clay*
cercare *to look for*
   cercare lavoro *to look for a job*
   cercare un appartamento in affitto *to look for an apartment for rent*
cereale *cereal*
cerotto *band-aid*
certamente *certainly*
certificato *certificate, warrant, bill*
   certificato d'assicurazione *certificate of insurance*
   certificato di deposito *deposit warrant*
   certificato di garanzia *manufacturer's certificate*
   certificato di ispezione *bill of sight*
   certificato di prestito *loan certificate*
certo *certain*
   essere certo *to be certain*
cervello *brain*
cetriolo *cucumber*
che *what, which; that, whom*
chi *who, whom*
   Pronto! Chi parla? *Hello! Who is speaking?*

chiacchiera *chat, small talk, rumor*
chiamare *to call*
   chiamarsi *to be called*
   Come ti chiami/si chiama? *What's your name? (fam./formal)*
   Mi chiamo Antonio. *My name is Anthony.*
chiamata *call*
chiaramente *clearly*
chiarire *to clarify*
chiaro *clear*
chiave *(f.) key, range*
   chiavi della camera *keys of the room*
chiedere *to ask*
   chiedere il bis *to ask for an encore*
   chiedere indicazioni *to ask for directions*
   chiedere scusa *to apologize*
chiesa *church*
chilo *kilo*
   Cinquemila lire al chilo. *Five thousand liras a kilo.*
chilometraggio *mileage*
   chilometraggio illimitato *unlimited mileage*
chilometro *kilometer*
chimica *chemistry*
chiosco *newsstand, stand*
chirurgo *surgeon*
chissà *who knows; I wonder*
chitarra *guitar*
   suonare la chitarra *to play the guitar*
chiudere *to close*
chiuso *closed*
ci *(adv.) here, there*
ciao *(fam.) Hi! Hello! Bye!*
ciascuno *every, everyone, each person*
cibo *food*
ciclismo *cycling*
cieco *blind*
cielo *sky*
cifra *figure, sum, amount*
ciglio *eyelash, eyebrow, edge, rim*
ciliegia *cherry*
cima *top, summit, end, tip*
cincin *cheers*
cinema *(m.) movie theater*
   andare al cinema *to go to the movies*
cinese *Chinese*
cinque *five*
cinquecento *five hundred*
cintura *belt*
   cintura di sicurezza *seat belt*
cioccolato *chocolate*
   gelato al cioccolato *chocolate ice cream*
cioè *that is, namely, or rather*
cipolla *onion*
circa *approximately, about, regarding*
   È distante circa un chilometro. *It's approximately a kilometer away.*
circolazione *circulation*
città *city*
   girare la città *to tour the city*
   pianta della città *map of the city*
civetta *little owl, flirt*

civile *civil, civilian, civilized, polite*
clacson *hooter, horn*
classe *(f.) class*
  viaggiare in prima classe *to travel first class*
  classe turistica *economy class*
classico *classical*
  musica classica *classical music*
cliente *client, customer, shopper*
  cliente fisso *regular customer*
  cliente potenziale *prospective client*
clientela *clientele, customers*
clima *climate*
coda *tail, queue*
codice *(m.) code, statute-book*
  codice postale *postal code*
  codice civile *civil code*
  codice commerciale *commercial code*
  codice d'avviamento postale *zip code*
  codice stradale *the rules of the road*
cognato/a *brother/sister-in-law*
cognome *surname*
coincidere *to coincide*
colazione *breakfast*
  fare colazione *to have breakfast*
collega *colleague, fellow worker*
collegamento *connection, liaison*
collegare *to connect*
collettivo *collective*
collezione *collection*
  collezione di francobolli *stamp collection*
collo *neck*
collocamento *placing, arrangement, position*
colloquio *talk, interview*
colonna *column, pillar*
colorato *colored*
colore *(m.) color*
  rullino a colori *color film*
colpa *fault, blame*
colpo *blow, stab, shot, attempt, fit*
coltello *knife*
coltivare *to cultivate, to till*
coltivatore *grower, till, cultivator, patron*
comandare *to order, to command*
combattere *to fight, to strive*
come *how, as, like*
  come da contratto *as per contract*
  come mai *how come?*
  come no *of course, by all means!*
comico *comical, funny*
cominciare *to start*
comitiva *party, group, company*
commedia *comedy*
commerciale *commercial, business-, trade-, sales-*
commercialista *graduate in economics and commerce, business consultant, expert in commercial law*
commerciante *dealer, trader, shopkeeper, merchant, businessman*
  commerciante al minuto *retail dealer*
  commerciante all'ingrosso *wholesale dealer*
  commerciante in proprio *sole trader*
  commerciante straniero *a foreign trader*

commercio *commerce, trade, business*
  commercio bancario *banking business*
  commercio d'esportazione *export trade*
  commercio di importazione *import trade*
  commercio internazionale *international trade*
  commercio interno *domestic trade*
commesso/a *salesman, saleswoman*
commissariato *police station*
comodamente *comfortably*
comodità *commodity*
comodo *(adj.) comfortable, convenient, handy*
compagnia *company, corporation, business, firm, society*
  compagnia d'assicurazione *insurance company*
  compagnia aerea *airline*
compartecipazione *co-partnership*
compatibile *compatible, consistent*
competenza *competence, expertise*
competitivo *competitive*
competitore *competitor*
competizione *competition*
compilare *to fill in, to compile*
  Deve compilare alcuni moduli. *You have to fill in some forms.*
compito *assignment, business, task*
compleanno *birthday*
  Buon compleanno! *Happy birthday!*
complementare *complementary*
complessivo *global, inclusive, gross*
complesso *musical group*
  complesso *(adj.) complex*
completamente *completely*
completare *to complete, to fill in*
completo *complete, comprehensive, thorough*
complicato *complicated, complex*
comporre *to compose, to dial*
comportamento *behavior, conduct*
composizione *composition*
comprare *to buy, to purchase*
  comprare il giornale *to buy the newspaper*
compratore *buyer, shopper*
compravendita *buying and selling*
comprensione *understanding*
compreso *included; understood*
  Il servizio è compreso? *Is the service charge included?*
comproprietà *joint ownership*
comproprietario *part-owner, joint owner*
computer *computer*
comunale *municipal*
  guardia comunale *municipal (traffic) policeman*
comune *municipality, town hall*
comunicare *to communicate, to announce*
comunicazione *communication, announcement, message, memo*
concedere *to concede, to allow*
  concedere il bis *to give an encore*
concerto *concert*
  concerto all'aperto *open-air concert*
  andare al concerto *to go to a concert*

conciliare *to conciliate, to reconcile*
  Concilia? *Will you pay the fine now?*
concordare *to agree*
concorrente *competitor, candidate*
concorrenza *competition*
concorrenziale *competitive*
concorso *competition, contest, aid, help*
concreto *concrete*
condimento *dressing, sauce, seasoning*
condire *to season, to flavor, to dress*
condizionale *conditional, probation*
condizionato *conditional, qualified,*
  contingent
condizione *condition, position, qualification, pro-*
  vision
condoglianza *sympathy, condolence*
condominio *condominium*
conduttore *driver, tenant, conductor*
conferenza *conference, lecture*
conferma *confirmation*
confermare *to confirm*
confermato *confirmed*
confezionare *to package, to manufacture*
confezionato *manufactured, ready-made*
confuso *confused*
congratulazioni *congratulations*
coniglio *rabbit*
coniugato *married*
coniuge *spouse*
conoscenza *knowledge*
conoscere *to know, to be acquainted with, to*
  meet
consapevolezza *awareness*
consegnare *to turn in, to deposit, to trust*
conseguenza *consequence*
conservato *preserved*
considerare *to consider*
consigliare *to advise, to suggest*
consiglio *advice, suggestion*
consociato *consociate*
consolidato *consolidated*
consultare *to consult*
consumare *to consume, to use*
  Questa macchina consuma molta benzina?
  Does this car use a lot of gas?
consumatore *consumer*
consumo *consumption*
contabile *bookkeeper*
contabilità *bookkeeping*
contante *ready, cash*
  soldi in contanti *cash money*
contare *to count*
contattare *to contact*
contatto *contact*
contento *happy, glad, pleased, satisfied*
contestare *to contest, to challenge*
continuare *to continue*
conto *count, bill, account*
  conto sociale *joint account*
  conto corrente *checking account*
  aprire un conto *to open an account*
  Il conto, per favore. *The bill, please.*

contorno *sidedish*
  contorno di verdura *side dish of vegetables*
contratto *contract, agreement*
  contratto d'acquisto *purchase contract*
  contratto di cessione *transfer deed*
  contratto di compravendita *contract of sale*
  contratto di lavoro *contract of employment*
contravvenzione *(f.) infraction; fine, ticket*
  pagare una contravvezione *to pay a fine*
contribuire *to contribute*
contributo *contribution*
contro *against*
  pomata contro le scottature *suntan lotion*
controfirma *countersignature*
controllare *to check, to control*
controllo *control, check, verification*
controllore *controller, inspector, conductor*
convalescenza *convalescence*
conversazione *conversation*
convincere *to convince*
copertina *jacket, cover*
coperto *(n.) cover charge*
coperto *(adj.) covered*
copia *copy*
coppia *couple*
coraggio *courage*
coraggioso *courageous*
corpo *body*
corrente *current, present*
correre *to run*
corretto *correct*
  caffè **corretto** *laced coffee*
corridoio *aisle*
corriera *bus, coach*
corriere *(m.) courier*
corrispondenza *correspondence*
corsa *run*
corso *course*
cortese *polite, courteous*
cortesia *courtesy*
corto *short*
  capelli corti *short hair*
cosa *(int. pron.) What?*
cosa *(n.) thing*
così *so, thus*
  così così *so so*
  É proprio così! *That's the way it is!*
cosiddetto *so-called*
costante *constant*
costantemente *constantly*
costare *to cost*
costituzione *constitution*
costo *cost, charge*
costoso *costly, expensive*
costringere *to force, to oblige*
costruire *to build*
costruttore *builder*
costruzione *construction, building*
costume *custom, habit, costume*
  costume da bagno *bathing suit*
cotone *cotton*
cotto *cooked*

cravatta *tie*
creare *to create*
credenza *belief, kitchen cupboard*
credere *to believe*
credito *credit*
creditore *creditor*
crema *cream*
crescere *to increase, to grow, to bring up*
crescita *growth, increase, advance*
crimine *(m.) crime*
crisi *(f.) crisis*
cristallo *crystal*
criticare *to criticize*
crociera *cruise*
    fare una crociera *to go on a cruise*
crollare *to collapse, to crash*
cronaca *commentary, news, column*
    cronaca mondana *gossip column*
    cronaca nera *crime news*
cuccetta *couchette*
cucchiaino *teaspoon, coffee spoon*
cucchiaio *spoon*
cucina *kitchen, stove*
cucinare *to cook*
cugino *cousin*
culla *cradle, birthplace*
cultura *culture*
culturale *cultural*
cuoco *cook*
cuore *heart*
cupola *dome, crown, cupola*
cura *cure*
    seguire una cura dimagrante *to follow a diet*
curriculum vitae *curriculum vitae, resumé*
cuscino *pillow*
custodire *to keep, to safeguard, to watch*
custodito *guarded*
    parcheggio custodito *guarded parking lot*

D

da *from, since, at, to, by*
    Da quanto tempo è in Italia? *How long have you been in Italy?*
    Vado dal dottore. *I am going to the doctor*
    Da dove vieni? *Where are you from?*
    camera da letto *bedroom*
dado *cube, dice*
    dado di manzo *beef bouillon*
    dado di pollo *chicken bouillon*
danno *damage*
    assicurazione contro i danni *collision damage waiver*
dappertutto *everywhere*
dare *to give*
    dare un film *to show a movie*
    dare una festa *to have a party*
    dare in affitto *to let, to rent*
    dare indicazioni *to give directions*
    Dammi una mano! *Give me a hand.*
    dare ascolto *to listen*

dare cuore *to encourage*
dare fastidio *to bother*
dare il permesso *to give permission*
dare informazioni *to give information*
dare lavoro a qualcuno *to give work/a job to someone*
dare su *to look onto, to face*
dare per scontato *to take for granted*
dare torto *to blame*
dare una mano *to give a hand*
darsi del tu *to be on familiar terms*
data *date*
    data di pubblicazione *publication date*
    data di nascita *birth date*
    data d'annullamento *cancellation date*
dati *data, figures*
dato *given, datum*
datore *giver*
    datore di lavoro *employer*
davanti *in front of, before*
    Il museo è davanti alla chiesa. *The museum is in front of the church*
davanzale *windowsill*
davvero *really, indeed, truly*
    Davvero? *Really?*
dazio *customs duty*
debito *debit*
debitore *debtor*
debole *weak*
decalogo *decalogue*
decidere *to decide*
decina *ten, about ten*
decisamente *decidedly*
decisione *decision*
deciso *definite, fixed*
decollo *take-off*
decoratore *decorator*
decorazione *decoration*
dedicare *to dedicate*
défilé *fashion show*
definizione *definition*
degustare *to taste, to sample*
delegato *delegate, representative*
delizioso *delightful*
democratico *democratic*
denaro *money, tender*
    denaro liquido *cash*
dente *tooth*
dentifricio *toothpaste*
dentro *inside, in, within*
denuncia *denunciation*
    fare denuncia *to file a complaint*
denunciare *to denounce; to declare*
deperibile *perishable*
dépliant *leaflet, folder*
depositare *to deposit*
deposito *deposit*
deroga *derogation*
derubare *to rob*
    Mi hanno derubato. *I have been robbed*
descrivere *to describe*
descrizione *description*

desiderare *to want, to desire*
  Desidera? *What would you like?*
desiderio *wish*
destinatario *addressee, receiver*
destinazione *(f.) destination*
destra *right*
  girare a destra *to turn right*
  sulla destra *on the right*
detersivo *detergent*
dettaglio *detail, retail*
detto *said, above-mentioned*
di *of*
  Di dov'è Lei? *Where are you from? (form.)*
diabete *(m.) diabetes*
dialettale *dialect-, dialectal*
dicembre *(m.) December*
dietro *behind, after*
difetto *deficiency, defect, flaw*
differenza *difference, discrepancy*
differibile *deferrable, postponable*
difficile *difficult, hard*
difficoltà *difficulty*
diffidare *to distrust*
digestivo *digestive*
digitale *digital*
dignità *dignity*
dilettante *(m.) amateur*
dimagrante *slimming*
  seguire una cura dimagrante *to follow a diet*
dimenticare *to forget*
dimettersi *to resign, to step down*
diminuzione *decrease, drop, fall*
dimostrazione *demonstration, proof, show*
dipartimento *department*
dipendente *dependent, employer*
dipendere *to depend*
dipingere *to paint; to describe*
diploma *diploma*
diplomarsi *to obtain a diploma*
diplomatico *diplomatic*
dire *to say*
  Mi dica. *May I help you?*
direttore *manager, editor, director*
  direttore d'orchestra *conductor*
  direttore amministrativo *administrative director*
  direttore commerciale *sales manager*
  direttore dei lavori *works manager*
  direttore del marketing *marketing director*
  direttore del personale *personnel manager*
  direttore della produzione *production manager*
  direttore delle vendite *sales manager*
  direttore di filiale *branch manager*
  direttore di sede *head-office manager*
  direttore di stabilimento *plant manager*
  direttore di zona *district manager*
  direttore generale *general manager*
direzione *direction, leadership, management*
dirigente *executive, manager*
dirigenziale *managerial*
  lavorare nel settore dirigenziale *to work in the managerial sector*

dirigere *to direct, to manage, to supervise*
diritto *right*
disaccordo *disagreement*
disastro *disaster*
disastroso *disastrous*
disavanzo *deficit, loss*
discesa *descent*
disciplina *discipline*
disco *record*
discorso *talk*
discoteca *discotheque*
discussione *discussion, debate*
discutere *to discuss, to debate, to argue*
disegnare *to draw, to design*
disinfettante *(m.) disinfectant*
disoccupato *unemployed*
  essere disoccupato *to be unemployed*
dispiacere *to dislike, regret*
  Mi dispiace. *I'm sorry.*
disponibile *available, on hand*
disponibilità *availability*
disposizione *disposal*
disposto *prepared, ready, willing*
disputare *to dispute, to contest, to play*
distante *distant*
  É distante un chilometro. *It's a kilometer away.*
distanza *distance*
distare *to be distant*
distinguere *to distinguish*
distribuire *to distribute, to deliver*
distribuzione *distribution, delivery*
dito *finger*
ditta *business, firm, house, trade, company*
divano *sofa*
diventare *to become*
diversità *difference*
diverso *different, several*
divertirsi *to enjoy oneself*
dividere *to divide*
doccia *shower*
  camera con doccia *room with shower*
documentario *documentary*
documentazione *(f.) documentation, file*
documento *document, paper*
dogana *customs (n.)*
doganale *customs (adj.)*
doganiere *customs officer*
dolce *(adj.) sweet*
dollaro *dollar*
  A quanto è il dollaro oggi? *What is the exchange rate for the dollar today?*
dolore *(m.) pain*
domanda *question, request, claim, demand, application*
  fare domanda per un lavoro *to apply for a job*
  domanda d'impiego *application for a job*
  domanda di denaro *request for money*
  domanda di fondi *application for funds*
  domanda di lavoro *application for a job*

domani *tomorrow*
   A domani. *See you tomorrow.*
   Domani è il due luglio. *Tomorrow is July second.*
domenica *Sunday*
domestico *domestic*
domicilio *residence*
donazione *(f.) donation*
donna *woman*
dopo *after*
   dopo tutto *after all*
dopobarba *aftershave lotion*
doppia *double*
   camera doppia *double room*
dormire *to sleep*
   pillole per dormire *sleeping pills*
   dormire come un ghiro *to sleep like a log*
   dormire tra due guanciali *to have nothing to worry about*
dormiveglia *drowsiness*
dose *(f.) dose, ration*
dote *(f.) dowry*
dottore *(m.) doctor*
   andare dal dottore *to go to the doctor*
dove *where*
dovere *to have to, must*
dozzina *dozen*
   una dozzina di uova *a dozen eggs*
dramma *(m.) drama; dramatic literature; theatre*
durata *duration*
dubbio *doubt*
   senza dubbio *without any doubt*
dubitare *to doubt*
due *two*
dunque *so, therefore*
duomo *cathedral*
duplicato *duplicate*
durante *during*
durare *to last*
duro *hard*

E

e *and*
e-mail *e-mail*
eccedere *to exceed*
eccellente *excellent*
eccessivo *excessive*
eccetto *except*
eccezionale *exceptional*
ecco *here is/are; there is/are*
   Ecco a Lei. *Here you are.*
   Ecco fatto. *All done!*
economia *economy*
   economia di massa *economy of scale*
   economia di mercato *market economy*
economico *economic*
   annunci economici *classified ads*
   avviso economico *newspaper ad*
edilizia *building industry*

editore *publisher*
editoriale *editorial*
educazione *upbringing, education, good manners*
   educazione fisica *physical education*
effettivamente *actually*
effettivo *actual, real, true, regular*
effetto *effect, impact*
efficiente *efficient*
elaborare *to draft, to prepare*
elaboratore *elaborator, computer*
elegante *elegant*
elegantemente *elegantly*
eleganza *elegance*
elementare *elementary*
elencare *to list*
elenco *list*
   elenco telefonico *telephone book*
elettrico *electric*
eliminare *to eliminate*
embargo *embargo*
emettere *to issue*
emigrazione *emigration*
energia *energy*
enfasi *emphasis*
enologo *oenologist*
enoteca *stock of vintage wines*
ente *board, body, agency*
entrare *to enter*
entrata *entrance*
epoca *epoch, age, era*
equilibrio *balance, stability*
equipaggio *crew*
equivalente *equivalent*
equo *equitable, fair, just*
   equo canone *controlled rent*
erba *grass*
erede *heir*
eredità *heritage, inheritance*
ereditare *to inherit*
errore *error, mistake*
esagerare *to exaggerate*
esame *(m.) examination; survey*
esaminare *to examine*
esattamente *exactly*
esattore *toll collector, bill collector*
esaurito *worn out, out of print, out of stock, sold out*
esclusiva *exclusive right, exclusive*
escursione *(f.) excursion*
eseguire *to execute, to carry out, to fulfill*
esempio *example*
esemplare *exemplary*
esentare *to exempt, to frank*
esente *exempt, free*
esenzione *exemption*
esercente *shopkeeper*
esigenza *requirement, demand, claim*
esigibile *demandable, collectable, receivable*
esonerare *to exempt*
espansione *expansion*
esperienza *experience*
   avere esperienza *to have experience*

esperimentare *to experiment*
esperimento *experiment*
esperto *experienced, expert*
esplorare *to explore*
esponente *exponent*
esporre *to expose, to exhibit*
esportazione *exportation*
espositore *exhibitor*
esposizione *exhibition*
espressione *(f.) expression*
espresso *(adj.) express*
   lettera espresso *express letter*
   caffè espresso *espresso coffee*
   treno espresso *express train*
essenziale *essential*
essere *to be*
   essere gentile *to be nice*
   essere disoccupato *to be unemployed*
   essere assunto *to be hired*
   essere licenziato *to be fired*
   essere in ritardo *to be late*
   essere in orario *to be on time*
   essere sicuro *to be sure*
   essere certo *to be certain*
   essere di servizio *to be on duty*
   essere vivace *to be active*
   essere in ufficio *to be in the office*
   essere stressato *to be under stress*
   essere occupato *to be busy*
   essere contento *to be happy*
estate *(f.) summer*
estero *foreign country*
   francobollo per l'estero *stamp for a foreign country*
   valuta estera *foreign currency*
estero *(adj.) foreign, overseas*
età *age, period*
etichetta *ticket, label*
etnico *ethnic*
europeo *European*
evasore *evader*
   evasore fiscale *tax evader*
eventualmente *possibly*
evidente *evident*
evidenziatore *(m.) highlighter*
evitare *to avoid*
ex *ex, former, late*
extra *extra, plus*
   extraeuropeo *extra-European*

F

fabbrica *factory*
fabbricare *to manufacture*
facchino *porter*
faccia *face*
facciata *facade, front, face*
facile *easy*
facilitare *facility, ease*
facilmente *easily*
facoltà *faculty, authority*

facoltativo *optional*
fallimento *failure, crash, bankruptcy*
fallire *to fail, to crash, to go bankrupt*
familiare *familiar*
familiarizzarsi *to become familiar*
fantasma *ghost*
fare *to do, to make*
   fare del proprio meglio *to do one's best*
   fare domanda d'impiego *to apply for a job*
   fare ginnastica *to exercise*
   fare tutto il possibile *to do all that is possible*
farina *flour*
fascicolo *file, brochure, issue*
fase *phase*
fattoria *farm*
fattura *invoice, bill of sale*
fatturato *turnover*
favorevole *favorable*
felice *happy*
ferie *holidays*
fiera *fair, show*
filiale *branch office*
filosofia *philosophy*
finanziamento *loan*
finanziare *to finance, to sponsor*
finanziere *customs officer*
fiore *flower*
firma *signature*
fisco *national revenue*
fisica *physics*
fiume *river*
folla *crowd*
fondamento *foundation*
   le fondamenta *the foundation of a house, of a building*
   i fondamenti *the foundations of a science, of a discipline, of a theory*
fondatore *founder*
forchetta *fork*
fornire *to provide, to supply, to furnish*
fornitore *supplier*
fornitura *supply*
forno *oven*
   forno microonde *microwave oven*
forse *maybe*
forte *strong*
fortunato *lucky*
fotocopiare *to photocopy*
fotocopiatrice *photocopier*
fragile *fragile*
francobollo *postage stamp*
frontiera *border*
funzionare *to function, to operate, to work*
fuoco *fire*
fuori *outside*
furgoncino *delivery van*
furto *theft*
fusione *melting, amalgamation*
futuro *future*

G

galateo *etiquette, good manners*
galleria *tunnel, galley*
gara *competition, contest, race*
garante *guarantor, sponsor, warrantor*
garanzia *guarantee, warrant*
gatto *cat*
gelo *freeze*
generale *general*
genere *kind, sort, line*
gente *people*
gentiluomo *gentleman*
gestione *administration, management*
gestire *to manage, to operate, to run*
gestore *manager, operator*
già *already*
giallo *yellow*
giocare *to play*
giornalaio *news vendor*
giornalismo *journalism*
giovane *young man*
giovare *to be useful*
giro turistico *sightseeing tour*
gita *tour, trip*
giudice *judge*
giuramento *oath*
goccia *drop*
godere *to enjoy*
gondola *gondola*
gotico *Gothic*
governare *to govern*
gradazione *graduation, scale, shade*
   gradazione alcoolica *alcoholic contents*
gradire *to like, to accept*
grande magazzino *department store*
grano *wheat, corn*
gratis *free*
grattacielo *skyscraper*
gratuitamente *freely, free*
gratuito *free*
greco *Greek*
grezzo *raw, crude, unmanufactured*
grossista *wholesaler*
gru *crane*
guadagnare *to gain, to earn*
guadagno *gain, profit, return*
guanciale *pillow*
guidatore *driver*
gusto *taste*

H

hobby *hobby*
holding *holding company*
hostess *stewardess*
hotel *hotel*

I

idea *idea*
ideare *to conceive, to devise*
identificare *to identify*
identità *identity*
idioma *(m.) language, idiom*
idrico *water-, hydric*
ieri *yesterday*
illeggibile *illegible*
illuminato *illuminated*
imballaggio *packaging, packing*
imbottire *to pad*
imbrogliare *to cheat*
immaginare *to imagine*
immagine *image*
immediatamente *immediately*
immigrante *immigrant*
immobile *building, house*
imparare *to learn*
impaziente *impatient*
impazzire *to go crazy*
impegnato *bound, busy, engaged, taken*
impegno *engagement, obligation, care*
imperfezione *imperfection*
impero *empire*
impiantare *to establish, to start*
impianto *installation, plant*
   impianto idrico *waterworks*
impiegato *employee*
impiego *employment*
imponente *imposing, impressive*
imporre *to impose*
importante *important*
importanza *importance*
importare *to import*
importazione *importation, import*
impossibile *impossible*
imposta *tax, duty, toll*
imprenditore *entrepreneur, contractor*
impresa *enterprise, business, company, trade*
impressione *impression, imprint*
improvvisamente *suddenly*
improvviso *sudden*
incaricare *to assign, to entrust*
incarico *assignment, task, commission*
incentivare *to stimulate, to enliven*
inchiesta *investigation, inquiry, survey*
incidente *accident*
incidere *to carve, to record, to have an effect*
includere *to include*
incominciare *to begin, to start*
incontro d'affari *a business meeting*
incredibile *incredible*
indecenza *indecency*
indimenticabile *unforgettable*
indirizzo *address*
indispensabile *indispensable, necessary*
individuo *individual*
indossatrice *fashion model*
indovinello *riddle, puzzle*
industria *industry, trade*

industriale *industrial*
inefficace *ineffective*
inefficienza *inefficiency*
infanzia *infancy, childhood*
inferiore *inferior*
infezione *infection*
infine *in the end, at last*
inflazione *inflation*
influenza *influence, bearing*
influire *to exert an influence*
informare *to inform, to communicate*
informativo *informative*
ingegnere *engineer*
ingegneria *engineering*
ingiustizia *injustice*
ingrandire *to enlarge, to increase*
iniziale *initial*
iniziare *to begin, to open*
iniziativa *initiative*
inizio *start, beginning*
innovazione *innovation*
inoltre *besides, also, moreover*
inquilino *tenant, renter*
inquinamento *pollution*
insalata *salad*
inscatolare *to pack in boxes*
insegna *sign, signboard*
insegnante *teacher*
insegnare *to teach*
insieme *together*
insignificante *insignificant*
insoddisfazione *(f.) dissatisfaction*
insolito *unusual*
insostituibile *irreplaceable*
instabilità *instability*
installare *to install*
installazione *(f.) installation*
insufficiente *insufficient*
intelligenza *intelligence*
intendere *to understand*
intenditore *(m.) expert, connoisseur*
intenzione *(f.) intention*
interessare *to interest*
interesse *(m.) interest*
interiore *(m.) interior*
internazionale *international*
interprete *(m. f.) interpreter, translator*
interrompere *to interrupt*
intervenire *to intervene*
intervento *intervention*
intervistare *to interview*
intervistatore *(m.) interviewer*
intestino *intestine*
intimo *intimate*
intrattenere *to entertain*
introdurre *to introduce, to insert*
inventario *inventory*
investimento *investment*
investire *to invest, to run over*
inviare *to send*
inviato *correspondent*
  inviato speciale *special correspondent*

invidia *envy*
invitare *to invite*
invito *invitation*
ipoteca *mortgage*
ipotesi *hypothesis*
ironia *irony*
iscriversi *to register, to enroll*
isola *island*
ispettore *(m.) inspector*
istituire *to institute*
istituzione *(f.) institution*
itinerario *itinerary*

K

know-how *know-how*

L

labbro *lip*
laboratorio *laboratory*
laborioso *hard-working, laborious*
laccato *lacquered, varnished*
lago *lake*
lana *wool*
lanciare *to fling, to launch*
lasciare *to leave, to desert, to give up*
latte *(m.) milk*
latticino *dairy product*
laurea *degree*
laureato *graduate*
lavabo *wash basin*
lavanderia *laundry*
lavastoviglie *(f.) dishwasher*
lavorare *to work*
lavoratore *(m.) worker, laborer*
lavorazione *(f.) manufacture, processing, produc-*
    tion, work(ing)
leader *leader*
leadership *leadership*
legale *legal*
legge *(f.) law*
legno *wood*
lentamente *slowly*
lento *slow*
leone *(m.) lion*
lettera *letter*
letto *bed*
  letto matrimoniale *double bed*
lettore *(m.) reader*
lettura *reading*
lezione *(f.) lesson, class*
libero *free*
libertà *freedom, liberty*
libreria *bookcase, bookstore*
libretto *booklet*
  libretto delle istruzioni *instruction manual*
  libretto universitario *student's record booklet*
libro *book*
licenza *permission, licence, permit, leave*

licenziare *to dismiss, to fire*
licenziarsi *to resign*
liceo *high school*
   liceo classico *high school specializing in classical studies*
   liceo scientifico *high school specializing in scientific studies*
limitato *limited, restricted*
limite *(m.) boundary, limit*
limitrofo *neighbouring*
limone *(m.) lemon*
linea *line*
lingua *tongue*
linguaggio *language*
linguistico *linguistic*
liquidare *to liquidate, to pay off*
liquidazione *liquidation, payment*
liquore *(m.) liquor*
lista *list*
   lista d'attesa *waiting list*
   lista dei vini *wine list*
livello *level*
logico *logic*
longevità *longevity*
lontano *far-away*
lordo *filthy, soiled, gross*
losco *sinister, grim*
lotteria *lottery, sweepstake*
luce *(f.) light*
lucente *bright, brilliant*
lucido *shining, glossy, polished*
lucro *lucre, gain*
lungomare *(m.) waterfront*
luogo *place, spot*
lupo *wolf*
lusso *luxury*

M

macchiato *spotted*
macchina *car, machine*
   macchina da scrivere *typewriter*
macchinario *machinery*
macellaio *butcher*
maestoso *majestic*
maestro *master, teacher*
magari *I wish, if only*
magazzino *warehouse, store*
magistrato *magistrate*
magistratura *magistrature*
maglia *stitch, knitting, undershirt, jersey*
maglietta *undershirt, light jersey, t-shirt*
maglione *(m.) sweater, pullover*
magnifico *magnificent*
mago *magician*
malanno *misfortune*
malattia *illness, sickness*
maledetto *cursed, damned*
malessere *discomfort, uneasiness*
manager *manager*
manageriale *managerial*

mancanza *lack, scarcity*
mancare *to be lacking of, to be missing*
mancia *gratuity, tip*
mandare *to send*
mandarino *tangerine*
mania *obsession*
maniera *manner, way, way of behavior*
manifesto *poster*
maniglia *handle*
manodopera *manpower, labour*
manovale *(m.) unskilled worker*
mansione *(f.) duty, task, office*
mantenere *to maintain, to preserve*
manuale *(m.) manual, workbook*
mappa *map*
marca *brand, brand name, make*
marcio *rotten, spoiled*
marinaio *sailor, seaman*
marketing *marketing*
marmo *marble*
martire *martyr*
maschera *mask*
maschile *masculine*
maschio *boy, male, man*
massello *ingot, block*
massimo *maximum*
matematica *mathematics*
materia *matter, subject*
materiale *(m.) material, equipment*
   materiale aeronautico *aeronautical equipment*
   materiale da costruzione *building materials*
   materiale edile *building materials*
   materiale grezzo *raw material*
matrimonio *marriage*
mattonella *tile*
maturazione *(f.) maturation, ripening, maturity*
maturità *maturity, ripeness*
maturo *mature, ripe*
meccanico *mechanic*
medaglia *medal*
media *average*
medico *doctor*
medioevo *Middle Ages*
Mediterraneo *Mediterranean*
membro *member*
memorandum *memorandum*
meno male *thank goodness*
mensile *monthly*
mente *(f.) mind*
mentre *while*
meraviglia *wonder*
meravigliosamente *wonderfully, marvellously*
meraviglioso *wonderful, marvellous*
mercato *market*
   Mercato Comune Europeo *European Common Market*
   mercato di libera concorrenza *free market*
   mercato favorevole agli acquisti *buyers' market*
   mercato favorevole alle vendite *sellers' market*
merce *(f.) goods, merchandise*
mescolanza *mixture, blend*
mescolare *to mix, to blend*

mese *(m.) month*
messa *Mass*
messaggio *message*
mestiere *(m.) trade, craft, job*
metano *methane*
meteorologico *meteorologic*
meteorologo *meteorologist*
metodo *method*
metropolitana *subway*
mettere *to put, to place*
mezzadria *share cropping*
mezzadro *sharecropper*
mezzo *half*
mezzogiorno *noon*
mietitura *reaping, harvesting*
migliaio *thousand, about a thousand*
miglio *mile*
migliorare *to improve*
migliore *better*
mignolo *little finger*
miliardario *billionaire*
miliardo *billion*
milionario *millionaire*
mille *thousand*
minatore *(m.) miner*
mini *miniskirt*
miniera *mine*
  miniera d'oro *gold mine*
minigonna *miniskirt*
minimo *minimum*
ministero *ministry*
ministro *minister*
minoranza *minority*
minore *minor*
minuto *minute*
mira *aim*
miracolo *miracle*
miscela *mixture*
misura *measure, size*
misurare *to measure*
mittente *(m.f.) sender*
mobilia *furniture*
moda *fashion*
modello *design, model, style*
moderno *modern*
modico *moderate, reasonable*
modo *manner*
modulo *form*
molle *soft, tender*
mondiale *world-*
moneta *coin, money*
monopolio *monopoly*
montaggio *assembly*
montagna *mountain*
monte *(m.) mount*
monumento *monument*
mordere *to bite*
  mordersi le mani *to bite one's hands*
morire *to die*
  morire dalla curiosità *to die of curiosity*
  morire dalla voglia/dal desiderio di *to be dying*
    to do something

morire dallo spavento *to be scared to death*
morire di fame *to be very hungry*
morire di freddo *to be very cold*
morire di noia *to be very bored*
mortale *mortal, deadly*
mosaico *mosaic*
mosca *fly*
mostra *show, display, exhibition*
motivo *motive, reason*
motore *(m.) motor, engine*
mucca *cow*
mucchio *heap, pile*
muco *mucus*
multa *fine, penalty*
multinazionale *(f.) multinational company*
muro *wall*
mutuo *loan*
  mutuo a breve scadenza *short-term loan*
  mutuo a lunga scadenza *long-term loan*
  mutuo ipotecario *mortgage loan*

N

nascita *birth*
nascondere *to hide, to conceal*
nastro *ribbon*
Natale *(m.) Christmas*
natalizio *Christmas-*
natura *nature*
naturale *natural*
naturalmente *naturally*
nave *(f.) ship, vessel*
navigare *to navigate, to seal*
nazionale *national*
nazione *(f.) nation*
nebbia *fog*
negare *to deny*
negligenza *negligence*
negoziabile *negotiable*
negoziante *(m.f.) merchant*
negozio *shop, store*
nemico *enemy*
nemmeno *not even*
neppure *not even*
netto *net*
neve *(f.) snow*
nevicata *snowfall*
noce *nut*
noia *boredom*
noleggiare *to rent (a car), to lease, to hire*
nome *(m.) name*
nomina *nomination, appointment*
nonostante *despite, in spite of*
nord *north*
norma *rule, regulation, standard*
normalmente *normally*
nota *mark, note, remark*
notare *to note, to notice*
nota bene *nota bene*
notevole *noteworthy, remarkable*
notifica *notice, notification, summons*

notiziario *newsletter, newscast*
notte *(f.) night*
nove *nine*
novembre *(m.) November*
novità *novelty, innovation, change*
nozze *(f.,pl.) wedding*
nulla *nothing*
numero *number*
   numero di telefono *telephone number*
numeroso *numerous*
nuovamente *again*
nuovo *new, other, further*
nuvola *cloud*

O

o *or*
obbligare *to oblige, to force*
obbligatorio *mandatory, compulsory*
obiettivo *objective*
occasionale *occasional*
occasione *(f.) occasion*
occhiali *eyeglasses*
   occhiali di protezione *safety glasses*
occhiata *glimpse, look*
occhio *eye*
occidentale *western*
occidente *(m.) west*
occupare *to occupy, to take possession of*
   occuparsi *to deal with, to engage in*
occupato *occupied, busy, engaged*
occupazione *(f.) occupation, employment, occu-*
   pancy
oceano *ocean*
odierno *present, today's*
offendere *to offend*
offerente *(m.f.) offerer, bidder*
offerta *offer, tender, supply*
officina *workshop, shop*
offrire *to offer*
oggetto *object*
oggigiorno *nowadays, today*
ognuno *everyone, everybody*
oliva *olive*
oltre *beyond, more than*
omaggio *homage, premium, giveaway*
   omaggi *compliments, free goods*
omettere *to omit*
ombrello *umbrella*
onda *wave*
ondata *tide*
opaco *opaque*
opera *work, opera*
operaio *worker, laborer, operator*
operativo *operative, effective*
operatorio *operative, surgical*
operazione *(f.) operation*
opportunità *opportunity*
opportuno *opportune*
opuscolo *booklet, pamphlet*
   opuscolo informativo *brochure*

opzione *(f.) option*
ora *hour*
orale *oral*
oralmente *orally*
orario *timetable, schedule*
ordinazione *(f.) order*
ordine *(m.) order, arrangement*
organizzare *to organize*
organizzatore *(m.) organizer*
organizzazione *(f.) organization*
orgogliosamente *proudly*
originale *original*
origine *(f.) origin, beginning*
ormai *by now, by this time*
ornare *to decorate*
oro *gold*
orologio *clock, watch*
ospitalità *hospitality*
ospitare *to accommodate, to give hospitality to*
ospite *(m.f.) host, hostess, guest, visitor*
osservare *to observe*
osso *bone*
ostaggio *hostage*
ottenere *to obtain*
   ottenere un contratto *to secure a contract*
ottenibile *obtainable*
ottimizzare *to optimize*
ottimo *excellent, very good*
otto *eight*
ottone *(m.) brass*
ovviamente *obviously*
ovvio *obvious*

P

pacchetto *packet, parcel*
pacco *package, parcel*
pace *(f.) peace*
padiglione *(m.) pavilion*
padrone *(m.) boss, owner*
paese *(m.) country, town, village*
paga *salary, paycheck*
pagabile *payable, due*
pagamento *payment*
pagare *to pay*
pallido *pale*
pane *(m.) bread*
   pane e coperto *bread and cover charge*
panettone *(m.) light Christmas cake*
pannello *panel*
panorama *view*
panoramico *panoramic*
pantaloncini *shorts*
pantaloni *trousers*
papa *pope*
paradiso *paradise, heaven*
paragone *(m.) comparison*
parcella *honorarium*
parcheggiare *to park*
parecchio *several, a lot of*
parete *(f.) wall*

pari *equal, same*
parlamento *parliament*
parlare *to speak*
parola *word*
parolaccia *dirty word*
parquet *parquet (flooring)*
partecipare *to participate*
partecipazione *(f.) participation*
particolare *particular*
partito *party*
Pasqua *Easter*
passare *to pass*
passeggiare *to walk, to stroll, to go for a walk*
passione *(f.) passion*
pasticcino *pastry*
pasticcio *mess, trouble*
patente *(f.) license*
patrimonio *estate, property*
patrocinatore *(m.) supporter, sponsor*
patto *pact, condition, agreement*
pausa *pause*
paziente *patient*
pedaggio *toll*
pedagogia *pedagogy*
pedonale *pedestrian*
pelletteria *leather goods shop*
penisola *peninsula*
penna *pen*
pensiero *thought*
pensionabile *pensionable, eligible for a pension*
percentuale *percentage*
percepire *to perceive, to receive*
percezione *perception*
perché *why, because*
perciò *so, therefore*
perdere *to lose*
perfetto *perfect*
perfino *even*
periferico *suburban*
permanenza *permanence, stay*
permesso *permission*
permettere *to permit, to allow*
però *but, however,*
perplesso *puzzled, undecided*
persona *person*
personale *staff*
personalmente *personally*
pesante *heavy*
pesare *to weigh*
peso *weight*
pessimista *(m.) pessimist*
pettinare *to comb*
petto *chest, breast*
pezzo *piece*
piacevole *pleasant*
piangere *to cry*
pianificazione *(f.) planning*
piano *floor, plan, programme*
piantagione *(f.) plantation*
pianterreno *ground floor*
piazza *square, place*

pieno *full*
pigiare *to press, to push*
pigro *lazy*
pilota *pilot*
pioggia *rain*
piovere *to rain*
pistola *gun*
pittoresco *picturesque*
più *more*
piuttosto *rather*
plastica *plastic*
podere *(m.) estate, farm*
poi *then, later*
poiché *since*
politica *politics*
politico *political*
poliziotto *policeman*
polizza *receipt, voucher, policy*
pollice *(m.) thumb*
polmone *(m.) lung*
poltrona *armchair, seat*
pontefice *(m.) Pontiff*
popolare *popular*
popolo *people*
porre *to put, to place*
porta *door*
portalettere *(m.,f.) mailman*
portatile *(m.) laptop computer*
portatile *portable*
portiere *(m.) doorkeeper, porter, goalie*
porto *port*
porzione *(f.) portion*
positivo *positive*
posizione *(f.) position*
possedere *to possess, to own*
posto *place, position, job, seat*
potente *powerful*
potere *(v.) to be able to*
potere *(n.) power*
    potere di acquisto *purchasing power*
povero *poor*
pratica *experience, file*
praticità *functional capacity, practicality*
prato *meadow*
preavviso *notice, warning*
precisamente *precisely*
precisione *(f.) precision*
preciso *precise*
prefisso *area code*
pregiato *esteemed, valuable*
pregio *esteem, merit*
prelevare *to withdraw*
premere *to press, to push*
preoccuparsi *to be worried*
preoccupazione *worry*
prepagato *prepaid*
prerequisito *prerequisite*
presentare *to show, to present, to introduce*
    presentarsi *to introduce oneself*
presente *present*
presenza *presence*
presidente *(m.) president*

presidente del consiglio *Prime Minister,*
Premier
presidente del consiglio d'amministrazione
chairman of the board of directors
presidente della Camera dei Deputati *speaker*
of the Chamber of Deputies
pressappoco *about, roughly*
presso *near, with, care of*
prestabilito *pre-arranged*
prestito *loan*
prestigioso *prestigious*
presumere *to imagine, to presume*
prevalenza *priority*
prevedere *to foresee*
preventivo *estimate*
previsione *(f.) forecast*
previsto *foreseen, expected*
prezzo *price*
primato *primacy, record*
primavera *spring*
principale *(adj.) main, principal*
principale *(n.m.) boss*
principalmente *mainly*
principe *(m.) prince*
probabilmente *probably*
problema *(m.) problem*
procedura *procedure*
processo *process, procedure, trial*
procurare *to obtain, to give*
prodotto *product*
produrre *to produce, to make, to manufacture*
produttivo *productive*
produttore *(m.) producer*
produzione *(f.) production*
professionale *professional*
professione *(f.) profession*
professore *(m.) professor, teacher*
profilo *profile, outline*
profitto *profit*
progetto *project*
programma *(m.) program*
   programma di videoscrittura *wordprocessing*
programmatore *(m.) planner, programmer*
programmazione *(f.) programming, scheduling*
proibire *to prohibit*
prole *(f.) children*
promemoria *memo, reminder*
promettere *to promise*
promosso *promoted*
promuovere *to promote*
proporre *to propose*
proporzione *(f.) proportion*
proposta *proposal*
proprietà *property*
proprietario *owner*
proroga *extension (of time)*
protagonista *(m.f.) protagonist*
proteggere *to protect*
proteina *protein*
protesta *protest*
protezione *(f.) protection*
prova *test, attempt, trial, proof, rehearsal*

provocare *to provoke*
provvedere *to provide, to look after, to take steps*
provvedimento *measure, action, steps*
psicologo *psychologist*
pubblicitario *advertising-*
pubblicizzare *to publicize*
pulire *to clean*
pullman *coach*
pulsante *(m.) button*
punta *point, tip*
punto di vista *point of view*
purché *provided that*
pure *too, also*
puro *pure*
purtroppo *unfortunately*

Q

qua *here*
quaderno *exercise book*
qualifica *title, qualification*
qualità *quality*
qualsiasi *any*
quantità *quantity*
quasi *almost*
quattrini *money*
quattro *four*
questionario *questionnaire*
questione *(f.) matter, problem, question*
quindi *therefore*
quinquennale *five-year*
quintale *(m.) quintal; hundred kilograms*
quota *quota, dues, share, altitude*
quotare *to assess, to value*
quotazione *(f.) quotation*
quotidiano *daily*

R

raccogliere *to pick up*
raccolta *collecting, collection, harvesting*
raccomandare *to recommend*
raccomandata *registered letter*
raccomandazione *(f.) recommendation*
raccontare *to tell*
racconto *narration, story, account*
radioascoltatore *(m.) radio listener*
radiogiornale *(m.) radio news bulletin*
raffinato *refined*
raggio *ray*
raggiungere *to reach*
ragione *(f.) reason*
ragioneria *commercial or business secondary*
school
ragioniere *(m.) accountant*
rame *(m.) copper*
ramo *branch*
rapporto *report, connection.*
rappresentante *(m.) agent, sales representative*
raro *rare*

rassomigliare *to look like*
rata *installment*
razionale *rational*
razza *race*
re *(m.) king*
realizzare *to realize, to make*
realmente *really*
realtà *reality*
reazione *(f.) reaction*
recapito *address*
recente *recent*
recessione *(f.) recession*
reclamare *to complain*
reclamo *complaint*
record *record*
redattore *editor*
reddito *income, revenue*
referenza *reference*
regalo *gift, present*
regina *queen*
regione *(f.) region*
registrare *to record, to register*
regola *rule*
regolo *rule, slide rule*
relazione *(f.) connection, relation, report, account*
religioso *religious*
rendere *to give back, to repay*
reparto *department*
reputazione *(f.) reputation*
requisito *requirement*
residenza *residence*
residenziale *residential*
respirare *to breathe*
respiro *breath*
responsabile *responsible*
responsabilità *responsibility*
restaurare *to restore*
restituire *to send back, to give back*
resto *rest, remainder, change*
retribuzione *(f.) remuneration, salary, pay*
revisione *(f.) revision, check-up, audit*
riagganciare *to hang up*
rialzo *increase, rise*
riassumere *to re-employ*
riassunto *summary*
ribasso *decline, fall, drop*
ricamato *embroidered*
ricambio *return, turnover*
ricco *rich*
ricerca *inquiry, research*
ricevere *receive*
ricevimento *reception*
ricevuta *receipt*
richiedere *to demand, to ask*
richiesta *request*
riciclabile *recyclable*
riconoscere *to recognize*
ricordo *memory, souvenir*
ricorso *petition, appeal, claim*
ridere *to laugh*

ridurre *to reduce*
riempire *to fill up*
rifare *to do again*
riferimento *reference*
riferirsi *to refer*
rifinito *finished, polished*
rifiutare *to refuse*
rifugio *refuge*
rigido *rigid, harsh*
rilevare *to point out*
rimanere *to remain, to stay*
rimborsare *to reimburse*
rimborso *reimbursement, refund*
rimpiazzare *to replace*
rimprovero *reproach*
rinforzare *to strengthen*
rinfresco *reception, refreshments*
ringraziare *to thank*
rinunciare *to renounce*
rinviare *to send back*
riparare *to repair*
ripartire *to leave again*
ripetere *to repeat*
ripetizione *(f.) repetition*
riposarsi *to rest*
riposo *rest*
riproduzione *(f.) reproduction*
risalire *to go up again*
riscaldamento *heating*
rischiare *to risk*
riservato *reserved*
risolvere *to resolve*
risparmiare *to save*
rispedire *to send again*
rispetto *respect*
rispondere *to answer*
risposta *answer*
ritardo *delay*
ritenuta *deduction*
ritirare *to withdraw*
rito *rite*
ritornare *to return*
ritorno *return*
riunione *(f.) meeting*
riuscire *to succeed*
rivedere *to see again*
rivelare *to reveal*
rivestire *to cover*
rivista *magazine*
rivolgersi *to turn*
romanzo *novel*
rovina *ruin*
rumore *(m.) noise*

S

S.p.A. (**società per azioni**) *joint-stock company*
sabbia *sand*
sacchetto *bag*
sacco *sack, bag*
sacrilegio *sacrilege*

saggio *essay*
  saggio *wise*
sala *room, hall*
  sala da pranzo *dining room*
  sala operatoria *operating room*
  sala riunioni *meeting room*
salariale *of wages*
salario *salary*
salire *to go up*
saltare *to jump*
salto *jump*
salute *(f.) health*
salvare *to save*
sano *healthy*
santo *saint*
sardo *Sardinian*
sasso *stone*
sbagliare *to make a mistake, to be wrong*
  sbagliare in pieno *to be completely wrong*
  sbagliare numero *to dial the wrong number*
sbaglio *mistake*
sbrigarsi *to hurry up*
scadente *of poor quality*
scala *stair, ladder*
scambiare *to exchange*
  scambiare quattro parole *to exchange a few words*
scampare *to survive, to escape*
  scamparla bella *to have a narrow escape*
scandalizzare *to scandalize, to outrage*
scandalo *scandal, outrage*
scarpa *shoe*
  scarpe da tennis *tennis shoes*
scarpetta *dress shoe*
scatto *click (telephone), increase*
scavo *excavation*
scegliere *to choose*
scelta *choice*
schermo *screen*
scherzare *to joke*
scherzo *joke, prank*
schienale *(m.) back of a seat*
schioppo *gun, rifle*
sciare *to ski*
scientifico *scientific*
scienza *science*
  scienze fisiche e naturali *physical and natural science*
  scienze matematiche *mathematical science*
sciocco *silly*
sciogliere *to undo, to loosen, to melt, to release*
sciopero *strike*
scocciare *to bother, to annoy*
scolaro *pupil*
scolastico *(adj.) school—*
  anno scolastico *school year*
scommettere *to bet*
sconcertante *disconcerting*
scontare *to discount, to reduce*
sconto *discount*
scontrino *ticket, bill, cash slip*
scoperta *discovery*

scopo *goal*
scoprire *to discover*
scorso *last*
scritto *written*
scudetto *championship, shield*
scuola *school*
  scuola elementare *elementary/primary school*
  scuola media *secondary school*
  scuola superiore *high school*
se *if*
sé *himself/herself*
seccare *to bother*
secco *dry*
secolo *century*
secondo *second*
  seconda classe *second class*
  secondo piatto *second course*
sede *seat, building, center*
segnale *signal*
  segnale acustico *beep, acoustic signal*
segno *sign*
segretaria *secretary*
segreto *secret*
seguente *following*
seguire *to follow, to take*
  seguire le lezioni *to attend classes*
selettivo *selective*
selezionata *selected, chosen*
semaforo *traffic light*
sembrare *to seem*
seme *(m.) seed*
semina *sowing, seeding*
seminario *seminary*
semplice *simple, easy*
semplicemente *simply*
semplicità *simplicity*
seno *bosom, chest, breast*
sensibilità *sensitivity*
senso *sense*
sentire *to hear*
  sentire la mancanza *to miss*
  sentirsi *to feel*
senza che *without*
serata *evening*
sereno *serene, calm*
seriamente *seriously*
serio *serious*
serratura *lock*
servizio *service*
  servizio di segreteria *telephone answering service*
  servizio traduzione *translation service*
sessanta *sixty*
sesso *sex*
sessuale *sexual*
sessualità *sexuality*
sesto *sixth*
seta *silk*
settanta *seventy*
sette *seven*
settecentesca *of the eighteenth century, eighteenth-century*

settimo *seventh*

settore *(m.) sector, area, zone*

sexy *sexy*

sfilare *to parade, to fashion*

sfilata *parade*

    sfilata di moda *fashion show*

sfogliare il giornale *to skim through the newspaper*

sfottere *to tease, to make fun of*

sfuggire *to run away, to escape, to elude, to slip out*

sgualcire *to crumple, to crease*

sguardo *look, glance*

siccome *since, as, because*

siciliano *Sicilian*

sicuramente *certainly, of course, undoubtedly*

sicurezza *security*

sicuro *sure*

significare *to mean*

significato *meaning*

signora *Mrs.*

signore *(m.) Mr., sir*

signori *ladies and gentlemen, gentlemen*

signorina *Miss*

simbolo *symbol*

simile *similar, alike*

sindacale *labor union—, of the labor union*

sindacato *labor union*

sindaco *mayor*

sino *until*

sinonimo *synonym*

sintomo *symptom*

sistema *system*

sistemarsi *to find employment*

sito *place, site*

situato *situated, located*

situazione *(f.) situation*

slogan *slogan*

smentire *to deny*

smettere *to stop*

smoking *tuxedo*

soccorritore *(m.) rescuer, helper*

società *society, firm, company*

soddisfatto *satisfied*

soffermarsi *to stop, to linger, to pause*

soffiare *to blow, to puff*

soffiato *blown*

soffice *soft*

soffitto *ceiling*

sofisticato *sophisticated*

software *software*

sognare *to dream*

solidarietà *solidarity*

solido *solid*

solitamente *usually*

sollievo *relief*

solo *(adj.) alone*

solo *(adv.) only*

soluzione *(f.) solution*

somma *amount, sum*

sondaggio *survey, poll*

sonno *sleep*

sopportare *to bear, to sustain*

soprattutto *above all, most of all*

sorprendere *to surprise*

sorpresa *surprise*

sorridere *to smile*

sospettare *to suspect*

sospiro *sigh*

sosta *stop, halt, pause, break*

sostanzialmente *substantially*

sostare *to stop, to halt*

sostegno *support*

sostenere *to support, to sustain*

sostituto *substitute*

sottile *thin, fine*

sotto *under*

    sotto contratto *under contract*

sottoporsi *to undergo, to go through*

spaghettata *spaghetti dinner*

spavento *fear, fright, scare*

spazio *space*

spazioso *spacious*

specializzato *specialized, skilled*

specializzazione *(f.) specialization*

specificato *specified*

spedizione *(f.) shipping, shipment*

spendere *to spend*

speranza *hope*

sperimentare *to experiment*

spese *(f.,pl.) expenses*

spesso *often*

spessore *thickness*

spettabile *Messrs (normally not translated), dear*

spettacolare *spectacular*

spettatore *(m.) spectator*

spia *spy*

spiegare *to explain*

spillo *pin*

spina *plug*

spiritoso *witty, funny*

splendido *splendid, shiny, bright*

splendore *(m.) splendor*

sporta *shopping bag*

sportello *door (of a car), counter*

sposato *married*

spostare *to move, to shift*

sprecare *to waste*

sproporzione *(f.) disproportion*

spuntino *snack*

squisito *exquisite*

stabilimento *establishment, factory, plant*

stabilire *to establish, to settle*

stadio *stadium, stage*

stagflazione *(f.) stagflation*

stamattina *this morning*

stampante *(f.) printer*

    stampante laser *laser printer*

stand *stand*

stanotte *tonight*

statale *state —, of the state*

statistica *statistics*

stato *state*

    stato civile *civil status*

stato di famiglia *certificate identifying the members of a family*
Stati Uniti *United States*
statua *statue*
statunitense *American*
stazione di servizio *gas/service station*
stenografia *stenography*
stereotipo *stereotype*
stesso *same*
stilare *to draw up*
stile *style*
stipsi *constipation*
stoffa *material, fabric*
storia *history*
storico *historic*
strada *road, street*
straniero *(n.) foreigner*
straniero *(adj.) foreign*
strano *strange*
straordinario *extraordinary*
stratificato *stratified*
strato *layer, coat*
stress *stress*
stressante *stressful*
stretta *hold, grip, grasp*
stretta di mano *handshake*
striminzito *pulled in, poor, shabby*
striscia *stripe, slip*
strisce pedonali *pedestrian stripes*
strumento *tool, instrument*
struttura *structure*
studente *(m.) student*
studentessa *female student*
studi umanistici *classical studies, the humanities*
studio *study, den, office*
studioso *(n.) scholar*
studioso *(adj.) diligent*
stufa *stove, heater*
stufa a gas *gas heater*
stufa a legno *wood-burning stove*
stufa elettrica *electric heater*
stufo *sick and tired*
stupidaggine *(f.) stupidity, stupid remarks, nonsense*
stupido *stupid*
su *on, by*
su domanda *by request*
su misura *fit to measure*
subito *right away*
succedere *to happen, to occur*
sudafricano *South African*
sudata *sweat*
sufficienza *sufficiency*
suggerire *to suggest*
suono *sound*
superare *to exceed, to surpass, to overcome*
superato *obsolete*
superficiale *superficial*
superficie *(f.) surface*
superiore *superior*
supermercato *supermarket*

supplementare *supplementary*
supplemento *supplement*
supporre *to suppose*
supporto *support*
surfing *surfing*
suscitare *to cause, to bring about, to provoke, to stir up*
suvvia *come one*
sveglia *alarm clock, time for getting up, wake-up call*
sviluppare *to develop*
sviluppo *development*
sviluppo professionale *professional development*
svizzero *Swiss*
svogliato *lazy, indolent, idle, disorganized*
svolgere *to develop, to carry on, to unwind*

T

tacere *to keep quiet*
tagliare *to cut*
tailleur *suit*
tale *such*
tangente *(f.) money extorted by racketeers, bribe*
tangentopoli *a city of bribes*
tappeto *carpet*
tardi *late*
targa *license plate*
tartaruga *turtle*
tasca *pocket*
taschino *(breast/inside) pocket*
tavola *table plank, board*
tecnico *technical*
tecnologia *technology*
telecommunicazione *(m.) telecommunication*
telefax *fax*
telefonare *to phone*
telefonare 'collect' *to phone collect*
telefonicamente *by telephone, on the phone, telephonically*
telefonino *cellular phone*
telegiornale *(m.) newscast*
telegramma *(m.) telegram*
teleselezione *(f.) direct dialing*
tema *(m.) theme, composition, subject, topic*
temperatura *temperature*
tempio *temple*
tempo *time*
temporale *(n.m.) storm*
tendenza *tendency*
tenere *to hold, to keep*
tenere le distanze *to keep the distances*
tenere le mani a posto *to keep one's hands to oneself*
tenere testa a qualcuno *to stand up to someone*
tenersi forte *to hold on*
tensione *(f.) tension*
tentativo *try, attempt*
termine *(m.) end, limit*
terrazza *terrace*

terreno *land*
terziario *tertiary*
tesi *(f.) thesis*
   tesi di laurea *degree thesis*
tessile *(adj.) textile*
tessuto *textile, fabric, material*
test *test*
tetto *roof*
ticket *prescription charge*
tifoso *fan*
   tifoso di calcio *soccer fan*
timido *shy, timid*
tipologia *typology*
titolo *title*
   titolo di studio *degree, education, qualification*
   titolo principale *headline*
toccare *to touch, to be one's turn*
tono *tone, volume*
tornare *to return, to get back, to come back*
tornito *polished*
torre *(f.) tower*
torrone *(m.) torrone, nougat*
torto *wrong*
   avere torto *to be wrong*
toscano *Tuscan*
tosse *(f.) cough*
totocalcio *soccer lottery*
tra *between, among*
   tra poco *in a little while*
tradizione *(f.) tradition*
tradurre *to translate*
traduzione *(f.) translation*
traffico *traffic*
tragedia *tragedy*
tramite *through, by means of*
tramonto *sunset*
tranquillo *calm, quiet*
transito *transit*
transizione *(f.) transition*
trascorrere *to spend, to pass*
trascrivere *to transcribe, to copy*
trascurare *to neglect*
trascuratezza *negligence*
trasferimento *transfer, move*
trasferirsi *to move*
trasformare *to transform*
trasparente *transparent*
trasporto *transport, transportation*
trattamento *treatment*
trattare *to treat, to deal with*
trattativa *negotiation*
tratto *stroke, line*
travestirsi *to disguise*
trebbiare *to thresh*
tremendo *tremendous, terrible, dreadful, awful*
trionfale *triumphal*
triste *sad*
triviale *vulgar*
trombetta *trumpet*
tubo *pipe, tube*
tuffarsi *to dive, to plunge*
tuffo *dive*

tugurio *hovel*
turbare *to disturb, to trouble*
turbolento *turbulent*
turno *shift, turn*
   turno di lavoro *shift*
tuttavia *yet, nevertheless, however*

U

ubbidire *to obey*
ubriaco *drunk*
uccello *bird*
ufficiale *(adj.) official*
ufficio *office*
   ufficio anagrafe *registry office*
   ufficio di collocamento *employment office*
uguale *equal*
ulteriore *further, ulterior*
ulteriormente *farther, further*
ultimamente *lately, recently*
umanistico *humanistic*
umorismo *humor*
unico *unique*
unificazione *(f.) unification*
unità *unity*
universale *universal*
universitario *university—*
uomo *man*
   uomo d'affari *businessman*
urgente *urgent*
usare *to use*
uscita *exit*
usufruire *to benefit from, to take advantage of*
usuraio *loan shark*
utente *(m. f.) user, consumer*
utile *useful, helpful*
utilizzare *to use, to employ*

V

valere *to be worth*
valore *(m.) value*
valutazione *(f.) appraisal, evaluation, estima-tion*
vantaggio *advantage*
vaporetto *steamer, steamboat*
variare *to vary, to change*
vario *varied, diversified, various*
vasca *basin, bathtub, pool's length*
   vasca da bagno *bathtub*
vaso *vase*
vasto *vast, huge*
vecchio *old, aged*
vedere *to see*
veduta *view*
veicolo *vehicle*
velluto *velvet*
veloce *fast*
venatura *vein, grain*
vendemmia *vintage, grape harvest*

vendemmiare *to harvest grapes*
vendemmiatore *(m.) vintager, grape harvester*
vendere *to sell*
vendita *sale*
  in vendita *on sale, for sale*
  vendita a contanti *cash sale*
  vendita a credito *credit sale*
  vendita a domicilio *door-to-door sale*
  vendita a rate *sale by installments*
  vendita al dettaglio *sale by retail, over-the-counter sale*
  vendita al miglior offerente *sale to the highest bidder*
  vendita al minuto *sale by retail*
  vendita all'asta *auction-sale*
  vendita all'ingrosso *wholesale*
  vendita condizionata *conditional sale*
  vendita di liquidazione *clearance sale*
  vendita di rimanenze *a bargain sale*
  vendita di seconda mano *second-hand sale, re-sale*
  vendita giornaliera *daily sales*
  vendita immobiliare *a sale of real property*
  vendita netta *net sales*
  vendita privata *sale by private treaty*
  vendita sotto costo *underselling*
veneziano *Venetian*
venire *to come*
  venire alle mani *to come to blows*
  venire ammesso *to be admitted to*
  venire in mente *to come to mind*
  venire meno *to faint*
  venire meno alla propria parola *to break one's word*
ventilato *ventilated, aired, airy*
ventilatore *(m.) fan*
veramente *really, truly*
verbale *verbal*
verbo *verb*
verde *green*
verità *truth*
verniciare *to paint, to varnish*
versatilità *versatility*
verso *toward*
verticale *vertical*
vestiario *clothing*
vestito *suit*
  vestito da sera *evening dress*
vetraio *glass maker, glass worker*
vetreria *glassworks*
vetrina *shop-window*
vetro *glass*
via marittima *by sea*
viaggio *trip*
  viaggio aereo *flight*
  viaggio di nozze *honeymoon*
viavai *(m.) coming and going, confusion*
vicinanza *proximity, closeness*

vietato *forbidden, prohibited*
vigilia *(m.) eve, night before, day before*
vigneto *vineyard*
villa *villa, country house*
villino *small detached house*
vincere *to win, to beat, to conquer*
vino *wine*
  vino da dessert *dessert wine*
  vino da pasto *table wine*
  vino dolce *sweet wine*
  vino frizzante *sparkling wine*
  vino in bottiglia *bottled wine*
  vino invecchiato *mellow wine*
  vino leggero *light wine*
  vino pregiato *vintage wine*
  vino rosato *rosé*
  vino secco *dry wine*
virtuale *virtual*
  realtà virtuale *virtual reality*
virus *virus*
visita *visit*
visitatore *(m.) visitor*
vista *view, sight*
vita *life*
vite *(f.) grapevine*
vittima *(m.) victim*
vitto *food, board*
vivere *to live*
vizio *vice*
voce *(f.) voice*
voglia *wish, desire*
volare *to fly*
volentieri *gladly*
volgere *to turn*
volo *flight*
volpe *(f.) fox*
volume *(m.) volume*
voto *mark*
vuoto *empty*

Y

yen *yen*

Z

zaino *knapsack*
zampa *foot, hoof, paw*
zia *aunt*
zio *uncle*
zoccolo *clog*
zona *zone, area*
  zona doganale *customs area*
  zona pedonale *pedestrian zone/area*
zucchero *sugar*

ENGLISH-ITALIAN

A

abandoned *abbandonato*
about *circa, pressappoco*
above *sopra*
  above all *soprattutto*
absenteeism *assenteismo*
absolutely *assolutamente*
abstinence *astinenza*
academic *accademico*
academically *accademicamente*
academy *accademia*
accent *accento*
accept (to) *accettare*
accident *incidente, accidente*
accommodate (to) *ospitare*
accommodation *alloggio*
accompany (to) *accompagnare*
accountant *ragioniere*
accumulate (to) *accumulare*
acid *acido*
across *attraverso*
action *azione*
active *attivo*
activity *attività*
actual *effettivo*
actually *effettivamente*
adapt (to) *adattare*
address *indirizzo, recapito*
adjective *aggettivo*
adjust (to) *adattare*
administration *amministrazione, gestione*
administrative *amministrativo*
administrator *amministratore*
admire (to) *ammirare*
admirer *ammiratore*
admission *ammissione*
admit (to) *ammettere*
adopt (to) *assumere*
advanced *avanzato*
advantage *vantaggio*
advertisement *annuncio pubblicitario, avviso*
advertising- *pubblicitario*
advice *consiglio*
advise (to) *consigliare*
aeronautical *aeronautico*
  aeronautical equipment *materiale aeronautico*
after *dopo*
  after all *dopo tutto*
again *nuovamente*
age *età*
agency *agenzia*
  advertising agency *agenzia di pubblicità*
agent *rappresentante*
ago *fa*
  a month ago *un mese fa*
agree (to) *andare d'accordo, concordare*
agreement *accordo*
agricultural *agrario, agricolo*

agriculture *agricoltura*
agronomist *agronomo*
aim *mira*
air *aria*
  air conditioning *aria condizionata*
airport *aeroporto*
alarm *allarme*
  alarm clock *sveglia*
alcoholic *alcolico*
all *tutto*
allegoric *allegorico*
allergy *allergia*
allow (to) *permettere*
almost *quasi*
alone *solo (adj.)*
Alpine *alpino*
already *già*
also *anche*
although *benché*
ambitious *ambizioso*
American *statunitense, americano*
amount *somma, importo, totale*
analysis *analisi*
analyse (to) *analizzare*
ancestor *antenato*
angel *angelo*
announce (to) *annunciare, comunicare*
announcement *avviso*
annoy (to) *scocciare*
annual *annuo*
answer *risposta*
answer (to) *rispondere*
anti-fog *antinebbia*
any *qualsiasi*
apartment *appartamento*
apologize (to) *chiedere scusa*
apparatus *apparecchio*
appeal *appello*
appear (to) *apparire*
  appear at (to) *affacciarsi*
appetite *appetito*
applaud (to) *applaudire*
application *applicazione*
  application for a job *domanda d'impiego, domanda di lavoro*
  application for funds *domanda di fondi*
apply *fare domanda*
  apply (to) for a job *fare domanda d'impiego*
appointment *appuntamento*
appraisal *valutazione*
appraise (to) *apprezzare*
appreciate (to) *apprezzare*
approach (to) *accedere, avvicinarsi*
appropriate *appropriato*
approval *approvazione*
approximately *approssimativamente*
architectural *architettonico*
architecture *architettura*
archives *archivio*

area *area*
  area code *prefisso*
argue (to) *discutere*
armchair *poltrona*
armourer *armaiolo*
aroma *aroma*
aromatic *aromatico*
around *attorno*
arrest (to) *arrestare*
arrive (to) *arrivare*
  arrive on time *arrivare in tempo*
ask (to) *chiedere*
assign (to) *assegnare, incaricare*
assigned *assegnato*
assignment *incarico*
assignment, business, task *compito*
association *associazione*
asthma *asma*
attach (to) *allegare*
attachment *allegato*
attend *frequentare*
  attend (to) classes *seguire le lezioni*
  attend (to) to *accudire*
attention *attenzione*
auction-sale *vendita all'asta*
Australian *australiano*
author *autore*
authority *autorità*
authorized *autorizzato*
autumn *autunno*
availability *disponibilità*
available *disponibile*
average *media*
avoid (to) *evitare*
awareness *consapevolezza*

B

baby *bambino, bimbo*
bag *sacchetto*
basin *vasca*
balance *equilibrio*
balcony *balcone*
banal *banale*
bank *banca*
banker *banchiere*
banking, bank- *bancario*
banknote *banconota*
baptism *battesimo*
bargain *affare, offerta speciale, occasione*
  bargain sale *vendita di rimanenze*
baroque *barocco*
barrel *botte*
basic *basilare*
basilica *basilica*
bathing suit *costume da bagno*
bay *baia*
be (to) *essere*
  be (to) a spendthrift *avere le mani bucate*
  be (to) admitted to *venire ammesso*
  be (to) afraid *avere paura*

be (to) as hungry as a wolf *avere una fame da lupi*
be (to) back in style *tornare di moda*
be (to) butter-fingered *avere le mani di ricotta*
be (to) completely wrong *sbagliare in pieno*
be (to) dead tired *essere stanco da morire*
be (to) dying to do something *morire dalla voglia/dal desiderio di*
be (to) enough *bastare*
be (to) famished *avere una fame da lupi*
be (to) fashionable *andare di moda*
be (to) fed up *averne la tasche piene*
be (to) in *andare di moda*
be (to) in shape *sentirsi in forma*
be (to) lacking of *mancare*
be (to) light-fingered *avere la mani lunghe*
be (to) missing *mancare*
be (to) on familiar terms *darsi del tu*
be (to) out of fashion *uscire passare di moda*
be (to) quick with a nasty reply *avere la lingua lunga*
be (to) right *avere ragione*
be (to) scared to death *morire dallo spavento*
be (to) sufficient *bastare*
be (to) useful *giovare*
be (to) very bored *morire di noia*
be (to) very cold *morire di freddo*
be (to) very hungry *morire di fame*
be (to) very thirsty *avere una sete da morire*
be (to) worried *preoccuparsi*
be (to) worth *valere*
bear (to) *sopportare*
beat (to) *sconfiggere*
beauty *bellezza*
beckon (to) *accennare*
become (to) *diventare*
  become (to) familiar *familiarizzarsi*
bed *letto*
  double bed *letto matrimoniale*
bee *ape*
before *davanti, prima*
begin (to) *incominciare, iniziare, avere inizio*
behavior *comportamento*
believe (to) *credere*
bell *campana*
  bell tower *campanile*
belong (to) *appartenere*
belt *cintura*
benefit (to) from *usufruire*
besides *inoltre*
bet (to) *scommettere*
better *migliore*
between *tra*
beyond *oltre*
bicycle *bicicletta*
bill *fattura, conto, bolletta, banconota*
  bill board *cartellone pubblicitario*
  bill collector *esattore*
  bills payable *effetti passivi*
  bill (to) *fatturare, inviare fatture a*
billion *miliardo*
biologist *biologo*

biology *biologia*
bird *uccello*
biscuit *biscotto*
bite (to) *mordere*
    bite (to) one's hands *mordersi le mani*
blame (to) *dare torto*
blind *cieco*
blow *colpo*
blow (to) *soffiare*
blown glass *vetro soffiato*
board *ente*
body *corpo, ente*
bone *osso*
book *libro*
booklet *libretto, opuscolo*
boredom *noia*
boss *padrone, principale*
bother (to) *seccare, scocciare, dare fastidio*
    Don't bother me! *Non mi seccare!/Non scocciarmi!*
bottle *bottiglia*
    bottle of wine *bottiglia di vino*
bound *impegnato*
boundary *limite*
boutique *boutique*
boy *ragazzo, maschio*
boycott *boicottaggio*
brain *cervello*
branch *ramo, filiale, succursale*
brand *marca*
brass *ottone*
bread and cover charge *pane e coperto*
break (to) *rompere*
    break (to) one's word *venire meno alla propria parola*
breath *respiro*
breathe (to) *respirare*
breeze *brezza*
brief *breve*
bright *lucente, brillante, vivace*
brilliant *brillante*
bring (to) *portare*
    bring (to) about *suscitare*
brochure *opuscolo informativo*
bronze *bronzo*
builder *costruttore*
building *construzione, edificio, immobile*
    building industry *edilizia*
    building materials *materiale da construzione, materiale edile*
business *affare, affari, lavoro, commercio, azienda*
    business address *indirizzo d'ufficio*
    business card *biglietto di visita*
    business consultant *commercialista*
    business day *giorno lavorativo*
    business deal *transazione commerciale*
    business executive *dirigente commerciale*
    business hours *ore d'ufficio*
    businessman *uomo d'affari*
    business manager *direttore commerciale*
    business meeting *incontro d'affari*

    business school *scuola commerciale*
    business trip *viaggio d'affari*
    business world *mondo degli affari*
busy *occupato*
but *però, ma*
butcher *macellaio*
button *bottone, pulsante*
buy (to) *comprare*
buying and selling *compravendita*
buyer *acquirente, direttore dell'ufficio acquisti*
buyers' market *mercato favorevole agli acquisti*
bye *ciao*

C

cable *cavo*
calculator *calcolatore, calcolatrice*
call *chiamata, telefonata*
    call transferring *trasferimenti di chiamata*
    wake up call *sveglia*
    call waiting *avviso di chiamata*
calm *calma*
cancellation date *data d'annullamento*
candidate *candidato*
capable *abile*
capital *capitale*
car *auto, macchina*
    car company *auto aziendale*
carefully *accuratamente*
carnival *carnevale*
carnival-like *carnevalesco*
carpenter *carpentiere*
carpet *tappeto*
carry on (to) *svolgere*
cart *carro*
carve (to) *incidere*
cash *contanti, denaro liquido*
    cash account *conto cassa*
    cash assets *attivo liquido*
    cash sale *vendita per contanti*
    cash (to) *incassare, riscuotere*
    to cash a check *incassare un assegno*
castle *castello*
cat *gatto*
catalogue *catalogo*
cathedral *cattedrale*
cause (to) *suscitare, causare*
ceiling *soffitto*
cellar *cantina*
cellular phone *telefonino*
cement *cemento*
census *censimento*
centigrade *centigrado*
central *centrale*
century *secolo*
ceramics *ceramica*
cereal *cereale*
certainly *certamente*
certificate *certificato*
    certificate of insurance *certificato d'assicurazione*

manufacturer's certificate *certificato di garanzia*
    loan certificate *certificato di prestito*
chairman *presidente*
    chairman of the board of directors *presidente del consiglio d'amministrazione*
challenge (to) *contestare, sfidare*
Chamber of Commerce *camera di commercio*
champion *campione*
change *cambiamento, spiccioli, resto*
change (to) *cambiare, variare*
characteristic *caratteristico*
charge (to) *addebitare*
charity *beneficenza*
chat *chiacchiera*
check-in *accettazione*
cheers *cincin*
chemistry *chimica*
chest *petto*
child *bambino, bimbo*
choice *scelta*
choose (to) *scegliere*
Christmas *Natale*
Christmas- *natalizio*
circulation *circolazione*
civil *civile*
    civil engineer *ingegnere civile*
    civil rights *diritti civili*
    civil suit *causa civile*
clap (to) *applaudire*
clarify (to) *chiarire*
classroom *aula*
clean (to) *pulire*
clear *chiaro*
clearance *sdoganamento*
    clearance papers *documenti di sdoganamento*
    clearance sale *vendita di liquidazione*
clearly *chiaramente*
client *cliente*
    regular client *cliente fisso*
    prospective client *cliente potenziale*
clientele *clientela*
climate *clima*
clock *orologio*
    alarm clock *sveglia*
close (to) *chiudere*
clothing *abbigliamento*
    clothing trade *commercio di articoli di abbigliamento*
cloud *nuvola*
coach *corriera, pullman*
code *codice*
    civil code *codice civile*
    commercial code *codice commerciale*
    zip code *codice d'avviamento postale*
coffee *caffè*
coin *moneta*
coincide (to) *coincidere*
collapse (to) *crollare*
colleague *collega*
collection *raccolta, collezione*
collective *collettivo*

colored *colorato*
column *colonna*
comb (to) *pettinare*
come (to) *venire*
    come (to) to mind *venire in mente*
    come (to) to blows *venire alle mani*
comical *comico*
command *comandare*
commerce *commercio*
commercial *commerciale, stacco pubblicitario*
    commercial or business secondary school *ragioneria*
communicate (to) *comunicare*
communication *comunicazione*
company *impresa, società, compagnia*
    insurance company *compagnia d'assicurazione*
comparison *paragone*
compatible *compatibile*
competence *competenza*
competition *competizione, gara, concorrenza*
competitive *competitivo, concorrenziale*
competitor *competitore, concorrente*
compile (to) *compilare*
complain (to) *reclamare*
complaint *reclamo*
complementary *complementare*
complete *completo*
complete (to) *completare*
completely *completamente*
complicated *complicato*
compose (to) *comporre*
composition *composizione*
conceive (to) *ideare*
concrete *concreto*
condition *condizione*
conditional *condizionale*
conference *conferenza*
confirm (to) *confermare*
confirmation *conferma*
confirmed *confermato*
confused *confuso*
congratulations *congratulazioni*
connect (to) *collegare*
connection *collegamento, relazione*
consequence *conseguenza*
consider (to) *considerare*
consociate *consociato*
consolidated *consolidato*
constant *costante*
constantly *costantemente*
constitution *costituzione*
consult (to) *consultare*
consumer *consumatore*
consumption *consumo*
contact *contatto*
contact (to) *contattare*
contest (to) *contestare, disputare*
continue (to) *continuare*
contract *contratto*
    contract of employment *contratto di lavoro*
contribute (to) *contribuire*
control *controllo*

controller *controllore*
convalescence *convalescenza*
conversation *conversazione*
convince (to) *convincere*
cook *cuoco*
cook (to) *cucinare*
copartnership *compartecipazione*
copper *rame*
copy *copia*
correspondent *inviato*
cost *costo*
cost (to) *costare*
costly *costoso*
cotton *cotone*
cough *tosse*
   cough (to) *tossire, avere le tosse*
count (to) *contare*
country *nazione, paese, campagna*
couple *coppia*
courage *coraggio*
courageous *coraggioso*
course *corso*
courtesy *cortesia*
cover (to) *rivestire*
cow *mucca*
cradle *culla*
crash (to) *crollare*
cream *crema*
crease (to) *sgualcire*
create (to) *creare*
credit *credito*
   credit card *carta di credito*
creditor *creditore*
crew *equipaggio*
crisis *crisi*
criticize (to) *criticare*
crowd *folla*
crowded *affolato*
crumple (to) *sgualcire*
cry (to) *piangere*
crystal *cristallo*
cultivate (to) *coltivare*
cultural *culturale*
culture *cultura*
current *corrente*
cirriculum vitae *curriculum vitae, resumé*
customs *dogana*
   customs agent *agente doganale, doganiere*
   customs area *zona doganale*
   customs declaration *dichiarazione doganale*
   customs duties *dazi doganali*
   customs examination *controllo doganale*
   customs warehouse *magazzino doganale*
cut (to) *tagliare*

D

daily *quotidiano*
   daily paper *quotidiano*
   daily sales *vendita giornaliera*
   daily wage *paga giornaliera*

dairy product *latticino*
damage *danno*
dance (to) *ballare*
data *dati*
dawn *alba, aurora*
daydream (to) *sognare a occhi aperti*
deal with (to) *trattare, occuparsi di*
dealer *commerciante*
   retail dealer *commerciante al minuto*
   wholesale dealer *commerciante all'ingrosso*
debate (to) *discutere*
debit *addebito*
   debit memo *nota d'addebito*
debit (to) *addebitare*
debt *debito*
debtor *debitore*
decidedly *decisamente*
decision *decisione*
decorate (to) *ornare*
decoration *decorazione*
decrease *diminuzione*
dedicate (to) *dedicare*
deed *azione*
deferrable *differibile*
deficiency *difetto*
definite *deciso*
definition *definizione*
degree *laurea*
delay *ritardo*
deduction *ritenuta*
delegate *delegato*
delightful *delizioso*
deliver (to) *portare, distribuire*
demand (to) *richiedere*
demandable *esigibile*
democratic *democratico*
demonstration *dimostrazione*
deny (to) *negare, smentire*
department *dipartimento, reparto*
   department store *grande magazzino*
depend (to) *dipendere*
dependent *dipendente*
deposit *deposito, versamento*
   deposit account *conto di deposito*
   deposit slip *modulo di versamento*
deposit (to) *depositare*
derogation *deroga*
descent *discesa*
describe (to) *descrivere*
description *descrizione*
detail *dettaglio*
develop (to) *sviluppare, svolgere*
development *sviluppo*
devise (to) *ideare*
dial (to) *comporre il numero*
   dial (to) the wrong number *sbagliare numero*
dialectal *dialettale*
die (to) *morire*
   die (to) of curiosity *morire dalla curiosità*
diet *alimentazione, dieta*
   diet (to) *essere a dieta*
difference *diversità, differenza*

difficult *difficile*
difficulty *difficoltà*
digital *digitale*
dignity *dignità*
dine (to) *pranzare*
dining room *sala da pranzo*
diploma *diploma*
diplomatic *diplomatico*
direct (to) *avviare, dirigere*
direct *diretto*
   direct dialing *teleselezione*
direction *direzione*
disagreement *disaccordo*
disaster *disastro*
disastrous *disastroso*
deficit *disavanzo*
discipline *disciplina*
discount *sconto*
discount (to) *scontare*
discovery *scoperta*
discover (to) *scoprire*
discuss (to) *discutere*
discussion *disussione*
disguise (to) *travestirsi*
dishwasher *lavastoviglie*
disposal *disposizione*
disproportion *sproporzione*
dispute (to) *disputare*
dissatisfaction *insoddisfazione*
distance *distanza*
distinguish (to) *distinguere*
distribute (to) *distribuire*
distribution *distribuzione*
distrust (to) *diffidare*
disturb (to) *turbare*
dive *tuffo*
dive (to) *tuffarsi*
divide (to) *dividere*
do (to) *fare*
   do (to) all that is possible *fare tutto il possibile*
   do (to) one's best *fare del proprio meglio*
   do (to) again *rifare*
   do (to) nothing at all *fare un bel niente/nulla*
doctor *medico, dottore*
document *documento*
dog *cane*
dollar *dollaro*
dome *cupola*
domestic *domestico*
donation *donazione*
donkey *asino*
door *porta*
   door (of a car) *sportello*
   door-to-door distribution *distribuzione porta a porta*
   door-to-door sale *vendita a domicilio*
doorkeeper *portiere*
double *doppio*
double (to) *raddoppiare*
doubt (to) *dubitare*
dowry *dote*
draft (to) *elaborare*

draw (to) *disegnare*
   draw up (to) an agreement/contract *stilare un accordo*
drawer *cassetto*
dream (to) *sognare*
dressing *condimento*
drink *bevanda*
driver *guidatore, conduttore*
drop *goccia*
drowsiness *dormiveglia*
drunk *ubriaco*
dry *secco*
   dry wine *vino secco*
duplicate *duplicato*
during *durante*
duration *duarata*
duty *dovere, mansione, dazio, imposta*

E

eagle *aquila*
earn (to) *guadagnare*
easily *facilmente*
Easter *Pasqua*
easy *facile*
economic *economico*
   economic boom *boom economico*
   economic development *sviluppo economico*
   economic growth *sviluppo economico*
   economic recovery *ripresa economica*
   economic situation *situazione economica*
   economic system *sistema economico*
economy *economia*
   economy of scale *economia di massa*
   market economy *economia di mercato*
editor *redattore*
eight *otto*
electric *elettrico*
   electric sign *insegna luminosa*
   electric heater *stufa elettrica*
elegance *eleganza*
elegant *elegante*
elegantly *elegantemente*
elementary *elementare*
   elementary school *scuola elementare*
eliminate (to) *eliminare*
elsewhere *altrove*
embargo *embargo*
embroidered *ricamato*
emergency *emergenza*
   emergency exit *uscita di sicurezza*
emigration *emigrazione*
emphasis *enfasi*
empire *impero*
employ (to) *impiegare*
employee *impiegato*
employer *datore di lavoro*
employment *impiego, occupazione*
   employment agency *ufficio di collocamento*
   employment interview *intervista d'assunzione*
   employment rate *tasso d'occupazione*

employ (to) *assumere, impiegare, usare*
employment *occupazione*
empty *vuoto*
encourage (to) *dare cuore, incoraggiare*
end *fine, scopo*
   end of fiscal year *fine dell'anno finanziario*
end (to) *finire*
enemy *nemico*
energy *energia*
engage in (to) *occuparsi*
engaged *occupato*
   to be engaged (to someone) *essere il/la Fidanzato/a di*
engagement *impegno*
engineer *ingegnere*
engineering *ingegneria*
enjoy (to) *godere*
enlarge (to) *ingrandire*
enough *abbastanza*
enter (to) *entrare, accedere*
enterprise *impresa*
entertain (to) *intrattenere*
entrance *entrata*
entrepreneur *imprenditore*
entrust (to) *affidare, incaricare*
entry *entrata*
envy *invidia*
epoch *epoca*
equal *uguale, pari*
equipment *attrezzatura*
equivalent *equivalente*
erase *cancellare*
error *errore*
essay *saggio*
essential *essenziale*
establish (to) *impiantare, stabilire*
establishment *stabilimento, fabbrica*
estate *proprietà, possedimento, podere*
esteem *apprezzamento, pregio*
esteem (to) *stimare, apprezzare*
esteemed *pregiato*
estimate *preventivo*
ethnic *etnico*
etiquette *galateo*
European *europeo*
   European Common Market *Mercato Comune Europeo*
evader *evasore*
   tax evader *evasore fiscale*
evident *evidente*
evaluate (to) *apprezzare*
eve *vigilia*
even *anche, perfino, addirittura*
   even if *benché*
   even though *benché*
evening *sera*
   evening dress *vestito da sera*
   evening school *scuola serale*
   evening wear *abito da sera*
everyone *ognuno, ciascuno*
everywhere *dappertutto*
exactly *esattamente*

examination *esame*
examine *esaminare*
excavation *scavo*
exceed (to) *eccedere, superare*
excellent *eccellente, ottimo*
except *eccetto*
exceptional *eccezionale*
exercise book *quaderno*
excessive *eccessivo*
exchange (to) *scambiare*
   exchange a few words *scambiare quattro parole*
exclusive right *esclusiva*
example *esempio*
executive *dirigente*
exemplary *esemplare*
exempt *esente*
exemption *esenzione*
exempt (to) *esentare, esonerare*
exercise (to) *fare ginnastica*
exert (to) *eseratare*
   exert an influence *influire*
exhibit (to) *esporre*
exhibition *esposizione*
exhibitor *espositore*
expansion *espansione*
experience *esperienza*
experienced *esperto*
experiment *esperimento*
experiment (to) *esperimentare, sperimentare*
expert *intenditore*
explain (to) *spiegare*
explore (to) *esplorare*
exponent *esponente*
exportation *esportazione*
expose (to) *esporre*
expression *espressione*
extension *proroga*
extra *extra*
extraordinary *straordinario*
eye *occhio*
eyeglasses *occhiali*
eyelash *ciglio*

F

fabric *tessuto*
facade *facciata*
face *faccia*
facilities *infrastrutture, attrezzature*
face (to) *affrontare*
facility *facultà*
factory *fabbrica*
faculty *facoltà*
failure *fallimento*
fail (to) *fallire*
faint (to) *venire meno, svenire*
fair *fiera*
fall (to) *cadere*
familiar *familiare*
famous *celebre*

fan *ventilatore, tifoso*
farm *fattoria*
farmer *agricoltore*
farming *agricoltura*
fashion *moda*
  fashion designer *stilista*
  fashion model *indossatrice*
  fashion show *sfilata di moda, défilé*
fast *veloce*
fault *colpa*
favorable *favorevole*
fax *telefax, fax*
feel (to) *sentirsi*
  like a lion *sentirsi un leone*
  feel like (to) *avere voglia di*
female *femminile*
  female labor *manodopera femminile*
field *campo*
fight (to) *combattere*
figure *cifra*
file *fascicolo*
fill (to) *riempire*
  fill in (to) *completare*
  fill up (to) *riempire*
find (to) *trovare*
  find (to) employment *sistemarsi, trovare
    impiego*
fine *multa*
finished *rifinito*
fire *fuoco*
five *cinque*
five-year *quinquennale*
fix (to) *aggiustare*
fixed *fisso*
  fixed capital *capitale fisso*
  fixed income *reddito fisso*
  fixed prices *prezzi fissi*
flag *bandiera*
flight *volo*
  flight attendant *assistente di bordo*
flood *alluvione*
floor *piano, pavimento*
flour *farina*
flower *fiore*
fly *mosca*
fly (to) *volare*
fog *nebbia*
follow (to) *seguire*
following *seguente, successivo*
food *cibo, alimentazione, vitto*
  food prices *prezzi dei prodotti alimentari*
  food products *prodotti alimentari*
footwear *calzatura*
forbid (to) *proibire, vietare*
forbidden *proibito, vietato*
force (to) *costringere*
forecast *previsione*
foreign *straniero, estero*
  foreign company *società estera*
  foreign currency *valuta estera*
  foreign exchange *cambio estero*
  foreign market *mercato estero*

foreign money order *vaglia per l'estero*
  foreign stocks *titoli esteri*
  foreign trade *commercio estero*
foreman *capooperaio*
foresee (to) *prevedere*
foreseen *previsto*
forget (to) *dimenticare*
fork *forchetta*
form *modulo*
foundation *fondamento*
four *quattro*
fox *volpe*
fragile *fragile*
free *gratis, gratuito, libero*
  free market *mercato di libera concorrenza*
freedom *libertà*
freely *gratuitamente*
freeze *gelo*
friendly *amichevole*
friendship *amicizia*
full *pieno*
furnish (to) *fornire, arredare, ammobiliare*
  furnish a house *arredare una casa*
furnisher *fornitore*
furnishings *mobilia*
furniture *mobilia, mobili*
further *ulteriore*

G

gain *guadagno*
gain (to) *guadagnare*
garage *autorimessa, garage*
gas *benzina*
  gas station *stazione di servizio, distributore di
    benzina*
gasoline *benzina*
general *generale*
gentleman *gentiluomo*
get (to) *prendere*
  get bored (to) *annoiarsi*
  get (to) on well *andare d'accordo*
  get (to) sick *ammalarsi*
  get (to) used *abituarsi*
ghost *fantasma*
gift *regalo*
give (to) *dare*
  give (to) a loan to *fare un prestito a*
  give (to) hospitality to *ospitare*
  give a hand *dare una mano*
  give back *rendere, restituire*
  give information *dare informazioni*
  give permission *dare il permesso*
  give work/a job to someone (to) *dare lavoro a
    qualcuno*
gladly *felicemente*
glass *bicchiere, vetro*
glassware *articoli di vetro*
glimpse *occhiata*
global *complessivo*
go (to) *andare*

go (to) for a walk *passeggiare, fare una passeggiata*
go (to) in the wrong direction *andare contromano*
go (to) one's own way *andare per la sua strada*
go (to) ahead *andare avanti*
go (to) crazy *impazzire*
go (to) forward *andare avanti*
go (to) off one's mind *dare di volta il cervello a qualcuno*
go (to) up *salire*
goal *scopo, rete, goal*
gold *oro*
   gold mine *miniera d'oro*
gondola *gondola*
good *buono*
   good bargain *buon affare*
   good day *buongiorno*
   good evening *buonasera*
   good faith *buona fede*
   good luck *buona fortuna*
goods *beni, merci, prodotti*
   capital goods *beni capitali*
   consumer goods *beni di consumo*
   investment goods *beni d'investimento*
Gothic *gotico*
govern (to) *governare*
gradation *gradazione*
graduate *laureato*
   graduate in economics and commerce *commercialista*
grant (to) *ammettere, concedere*
grapevine *vite*
grass *erba*
gratuity *mancia*
Greek *greco*
ground floor *pianterreno*
group leader *capogruppo*
grower *coltivatore*
growth *crescita*
guarantor *garante*
guarantee *garanzia*
guide (to) *guidare*
gun *pistola*

H

habit *abitudine*
half *mezzo*
hallmark *marchio*
hand luggage *bagaglio a mano*
handle *maniglia*
handmade *fatto a mano, lavorato a mano*
handshake *stretta di mano*
hang up (to) *riagganciare*
happen (to) *succedere*
happy *felice*
hard *duro*
hard-working *laborioso*
harvest (to) *raccogliere*
   harvest (to) grapes *vendemmiare*

have (to) *avere*
   have (to) a lot of money *avere un sacco di soldi*
   have (to) a lot of work *avere un sacco di lavoro*
   have (to) a narrow escape *scamparla bella*
   have (to) an appointment *avere un appuntamento*
   have (to) an effect *incidere*
   have (to) an engagement *avere un impegno*
   have (to) nothing to worry about *dormire tra due guanciali*
   have (to) something to declare *avere qualcosa da dichiarare*
   have (to) something on the tip of the tongue *avere qualcosa sulla punta della lingua*
   have (to) strong doubts *avere forti dubbi*
   have (to) strong reasons *avere forti motivi*
   have (to) the impression *avere l'impressione*
   have (to) time *avere il tempo*
   have (to) to *dovere*
health *salute*
healthy *sano*
heap *mucchio*
hear (to) *sentire dire*
heart *cuore*
heating *riscaldamento*
heavy *pesante*
height *altezza*
heir *erede*
help *aiuto*
help (to) *aiutare*
here *qua*
heritage *eredità*
hide (to) *nascondere*
high school *scuola superiore*
highway *autostrada*
hire (to) *assumere*
hint (to) **at** *accennare*
hire (to) *assumere*
historic *storico*
   historic city center *centro storico*
history *storia*
hobby *hobby*
hold (to) *tenere*
   hold (to) on *tenersi forte*
   hold (to) out *tenere duro/forte*
holder *possessore, intestatario, titolare*
hole *buco*
holidays *ferie*
home *casa, sede*
honeymoon *viaggio di nozze*
honorary *onorario*
hope *speranza*
hope (to) *sperare*
hors-d'oeuvre *antipasto*
hospitality *ospitalità*
host *ospite*
hostage *ostaggio*
hot *caldo, rovente*
   hot water *acqua calda*
hour *ora*
hug (to) *abbracciarsi*
humor *umorismo*

hunt (to) *cacciare*
  hunting dog *cane da caccia*
hurry (to) **up** *sbrigarsi*
hypothesis *ipotesi*

I

idea *idea*
identify (to) *identificare*
identity *identità*
if *se*
illegible *illeggibile*
illness *malattia*
illuminated *illuminato*
image *immagine*
imagine (to) *immaginare*
immediately *immediatamente*
immigrant *immigrante*
impatient *impaziente*
imperfection *imperfezione*
import *importazione*
  import firm *impresa di import*
  import goods *merce d'importazione*
  import license *licenza d'importazione*
  import permit *permesso d'importazione*
  import surcharge *soprattassa d'importazione*
  import tax *dazio d'importazione*
import (to) *importare*
importance *importanza*
important *importante*
importation *importazione*
impose (to) *imporre*
imposing *imponente*
impossible *impossibile*
impression *impressione*
improve (to) *migliorare*
include (to) *includere*
income *reddito*
increase *aumento, crescita, rialzo*
increase (to) *aumentare, crescere*
incredible *incredibile*
indecency *indecenza*
indispensable *indispensabile*
individual *individuo*
industrial *industriale*
industry *industria*
ineffective *inefficace*
inefficiency *inefficienza*
infancy *infanzia*
infection *infezione*
inferior *inferiore*
inflation *inflazione*
influence *influenza*
inform (to) *informare, avvertire*
informative *informativo*
inherit (to) *ereditare*
initial *iniziale*
initiative *iniziativa*
injustice *ingiustizia*
innovation *innovazione*
inquiry *ricerca*

insert (to) *introdurre, inserire*
inside *dentro*
insignificant *insignificante*
inspector *ispettore*
instability *instabilità*
install (to) *installare*
installation *installazione, impianto*
installment *rata*
institute (to) *istituire*
institution *istituzione*
insufficient *insufficiente*
insurance *assicurazione*
intelligence *intelligenza*
intend (to) *avere intenzione di*
intention *intenzione*
interest *interesse*
interest (to) *interessare*
interior *interiore*
international *internazionale*
interpreter *interprete*
interrupt (to) *interrompere*
intervene (to) *intervenire*
intervention *intervento*
interview (to) *intervistare*
interviewer *intervistatore*
intestine *intestino*
intimate *intimo*
introduce (to) *introdurre*
  introduce (to) oneself *presentarsi*
inventory *inventario*
investigation *inchiesta*
investment *investimento*
invest (to) *investire*
invitation *invito*
invite (to) *invitare*
invoice *fattura*
irony *ironia*
irreplaceable *insostituibile*
island *isola*
issue (to) *emettere*
itinerary *itinerario*

J

jacket *giacca; copertina* (of a book)
job *lavoro, impiego*
  job evaluation *valutazione del lavoro*
  job market *mercato del lavoro*
  job opportunities *possibilità d'impiego*
  job sheet *foglio d'istruzioni*
joint *congiunto*
  joint account *conto sociale*
  joint association *associazione in
    partecipazione*
  joint director *codirettore*
  joint owner *comproprietario*
  joint ownership *comproprietà*
  joint stock *capitale sociale*
  joint-stock company *S.p.A. (società per
    azioni)*
joke *barzelletta, scherzo*

joke (to) *scherzare*
journalism *giornalismo*
judge *giudice*
jump *salto*
jury *giuria*
justification *giustificazione, scusa*
justify (to) *giustificare*
jump (to) *saltare*

K

keep (to) *tenere, mantenere*
   keep (to) a cool head *conservare il sangue freddo*
   keep (to) one's hands to oneself *tenere le mani a posto*
   keep (to) quiet *tacere*
   keep (to) the distances *tenere le distanze*
key *chiave*
kind *genere, specie, qualità*
kindergarten *asilo*
king *re*
kitchen *cucina*
knapsack *zaino*
knockdown *abbassamento (di prezzi)*
know-how *know-how*
know (to) *conoscere, sapere*
knowledge *conoscenza*

L

label *etichetta*
laboratory *laboratorio*
labor *lavoro*
   Labor day *festa del lavoro*
   labor dispute *controversia sindacale*
   labor force *forze del lavoro*
   labor union *sindacato*
lack *mancanza*
lacquered *laccato*
lake *lago*
land *terreno*
land (to) *atterrare*
landing *atterraggio*
   landing ground *campo d'atterraggio*
language *linguaggio, idioma*
last *passato, scorso*
last (to) *durare, bastare*
late *tardi*
lately *ultimamente*
laugh (to) *ridere*
laundry *bucato, lavanderia*
law *legge*
lawyer *avvocato*
lazy *pigro*
leader *leader*
leadership *leadership*
leaflet *dépliant*
lean (to) **out of** *affacciarsi*
learn (to) *imparare*

lease (to) *noleggiare, affittare*
leather *pelle*
   leader goods shop *pelleteria*
leave (to) *lasciare, partire*
legal *legale*
lemon *limone*
lesson *lezione*
letter *lettera*
level *livello*
library *biblioteca*
license *patente*
lie *bugia*
life *vita*
light *(adj.)* *leggero, chiaro*
light *(n.)* *luce*
like *uguale, simile*
like (to) *piacere, desiderare*
limited *limitato*
line *linea*
linguistic *linguistico*
lion *leone*
lip *labbro*
liquidation *liquidazione*
liquidate (to) *liquidare*
liquor *liquore*
list *lista, elenco*
   waiting list *lista d'attesa*
   wine list *lista dei vini*
list (to) *elencare*
listen (to) *dare ascolto*
listener *ascoltatore*
listening *ascolto*
little *piccolo*
live *abitare, vivere*
load *carico*
loan *mutuo*
   short-term loan *mutuo a breve scadenza*
   long-term loan *mutuo a lunga scadenza*
   mortgage loan *mutuo ipotecario*
lock *serratura*
lock (to) *chiudere a chiave*
logic *logico*
longevity *longevità*
look (to) *sembrare, parere*
   look (to) at *guardare*
   look (to) for *cercare*
   look (to) like *rassomigliare*
   look (to) onto *dare su*
lose (to) *perdere*
lottery *lotteria*
love *amore*
love (to) *amare*
lover *amante*
low *basso, minimo*
   low-cost *a buon mercato*
   low season *bassa stagione*
   low wages *salari bassi*
lucky *fortunato*
luggage *bagaglio*
lung *polmone*
luxury *lusso*
   luxury articles *articoli di lusso*

M

magazine *rivista*
magician *mago*
magistrate *magistrato*
magistrature *magistratura*
magnificent *magnifico*
maid *cameriera*
mailman *portalettere*
main *principale*
mainly *principalmente*
majestic *maestoso*
make (to) fun of *sfottere*
manage (to) *gestire, dirigere*
manager *manager, direttore, gestore*
  sales manager *direttore commerciale*
  works manager *direttore dei lavori*
  personnel manager *direttore del personale*
  production manager *direttore della produzione*
  sales manager *direttore delle vendite*
  branch manager *direttore di filiale*
  head-office manager *dirretore di sede*
  plant manager *direttore di stabilimento*
  district manager *direttore di zona*
  general manager *direttore generale*
managerial *manageriale*
mandatory *obbligatorio*
manner *modo, maniera*
manpower *manodopera*
manual *manuale*
manufacture *lavorazione*
manufacture (to) *fabbricare*
manufactured *confezionato*
map *mappa*
marble *marmo*
mark (grade) *voto*
market *mercato*
  market analysis *analisi di mercato*
  market crash *tracollo del mercato*
  market economy *economia di mercato*
  market price *prezzo di mercato*
  market trend *tendenza di mercato*
market (to) *vendere, commercializzare*
marketing *marketing, distribuzione, compraven-dita*
markup *aumento di prezzo, rialzo*
marriage *matrimonio*
married *coniugato, sposato*
martyr *martire*
masculine *maschile*
mask *maschera*
Mass *messa*
material *stoffa, materiale*
mathematics *matematica*
matter *questione, materia, argomento, problema*
maturation *maturazione*
mature *maturo*
maturity *maturità*
maximum *massimo*
maybe *forse*

mayor *sindaco*
meadow *prato*
mean (to) *significare*
meaning *significato*
measure *provvedimento, misura*
measure (to) *misurare*
mechanic *meccanico*
medal *medaglia*
Mediterranean *Mediterraneo*
meet (to) *incontrare, conoscere*
meeting *riunione*
  meeting room *sala riunioni*
member *membro*
memo *memorandum, promemoria*
memorandum *memorandum, nota, comuni-cazione*
memory *ricordo*
  memory book *agenda, taccuino*
mention (to) *menzionare*
merchant *negoziante*
mess *pasticcio*
message *messaggio*
meteorologic *meterologico*
meteorologist *meterologo*
methane *metano*
method *metodo*
microwave oven *forno microonde*
Middle Ages *medioevo*
milk *latte*
millionaire *miliardario*
mind *mente*
mine *miniera*
miner *minatore*
minimum *minimo*
ministry *ministero*
miniskirt *mini, minigonna*
minister *ministro*
minor *minore*
minority *minoranza*
minute *minuto*
miracle *miracolo*
misfortune *malanno*
Miss *signorina*
miss (to) someone *sentire la mancanza di qual-cuno*
mistake *sbaglio, errore*
mix (to) *mescolare*
mixture *miscela, mescolanza*
modern *moderno*
moderate *modico, moderato*
moment *attimo*
money *moneta, denaro, soldi, quattrini*
  money market *mercato monetario*
  money order *vaglio postale*
monopoly *monopolio*
month *mese*
monthly *mensile*
monument *monumento*
more *più*
mortal *mortale*
mortgage *ipoteca*
  mortgage debt *debito ipotecario*

mortgage loan *prestito ipotecario, mutuo ipotecario*
mortgage tax *imposta ipotecaria*
mortgage (to) *ipotecare*
mosaic *mosaico*
motive *motivo*
motor *motore*
mount *monte*
mountain *montagna*
mouth *bocca*
move (to) *trasferirsi, spostare*
movie theater *cinema*
Mr. *signore*
Mrs. *signora*
mucus *muco*
multinational *multinazionale*
multinational organization *impresa multinazionale*
municipality *comune*
mutual *mutuo, reciproco*
mutual fund *fondo comune di investimento*
must (to) *dovere*

N

name *nome*
narration *racconto*
nation *nazione*
national *nazionale*
nationality *nazionalità, cittadinanza*
natural *naturale*
naturally *naturalmente*
nature *natura*
navigate (to) *navigare*
near *presso, vicino*
near (to) *avvicinarsi*
neck *collo*
needle *ago*
neglect (to) *trascurare*
negligence *trascuratezza*
negligence *negligenza*
negotiable *negoziabile*
negotiation *trattativa, negoziazione*
neighboring *limitrofo*
net *netto*
net assets *attivo netto*
net earnings *reddito netto*
net income *reddito netto*
net price *prezzo netto*
net sales *vendita netta*
new *nuovo*
news *notizia, informazioni*
news bulletin *notiziario*
news service *agenzia d'informazioni*
news vendor *giornalaio*
newsstand *chiosco*
next *prossimo, seguente*
night *notte*
nine *nove*
noise *rumore*
nomination *nomina*

non-deductible *non deducibile*
non-delivery *mancata consegna*
noon *mezzogiorno*
normally *normalmente*
north *nord*
note *nota, appunto, promemoria*
note (to) *notare*
noteworthy *notevole*
notice *notifica*
nothing *nulla, niente*
notice *preavviso*
notice (to) *notare, accorgersi*
novel *romanzo*
novelty *novità*
November *novembre*
nowadays *oggigiorno*
number *numero*
number (to) *numerare*
numerous *numeroso*
nut *noce*

O

oath *giuramento*
obey (to) *ubbidire*
object *oggetto*
objection *obiezione*
objective *obiettivo*
oblige (to) *obbligare, costringere*
observe (to) *osservare*
obtain (to) *ottenere*
obsolete *superato*
obsession *mania*
obtain (to) *procurare*
obtain (to) a diploma *diplomarsi*
obvious *ovvio*
obviously *ovviamente*
occasion *occasione*
occasional *occasionale*
occupation *occupazione, impiego, lavoro*
occupied *occupato*
occupy (to) *occupare*
occur (to) *succedere*
ocean *oceano*
oenologist *enologo*
offend (to) *offendere*
offer *offerta*
offer (to) *offrire*
offerer *offerente*
office *ufficio, studio*
office furniture *mobili per ufficio*
office hours *ore d'ufficio*
office personnel *personale d'ufficio*
office work *lavoro d'ufficio*
official *ufficiale*
officious *ufficioso*
often *spesso*
old *vecchio, antico*
olive *oliva*
only *solo*
opaque *opaco*

open *aperto*
opening *apertura, inizio, posto vacante*
open (to) *iniziare*
operating room *sala operatoria*
operation *operazione*
operative *operativo, operatorio*
opinion *opinione, parere*
opportune *opportuno*
opportunity *opportunità*
optimize (to) *ottimizzare*
optional *facoltativo*
or *o*
oblige (to) *obbligare*
oral *orale*
orally *oralmente*
order *ordine, ordinazione*
order (to) *ordinare, commissionare, comandare*
organization *organizzazione*
organize (to) *organizzare*
organizer *organizzatore*
origin *origine*
original *originale*
other *altro*
otherwise *altrimenti*
outside *fuori*
oven *forno*
overestimate *sopravvalutazione*
overheating *surriscaldamento*
overweight *sovrappeso*
owe (to) *dovere, essere debitore*
owing *dovuto, arretrato*
overcome (to) *superare*
own (to) *possedere*
owner *proprietario*
ownership *proprietà*

P

package (to) *confezionare*
packaging *imballaggio*
packing paper *carta da imballaggio*
pact *patto*
pad *tampone*
pad (to) *imbottire*
pain *dolore*
paint (to) *verniciare*
pale *pallido*
panel *pannello*
panoramic *panoramico*
paper *carta*
   paper clip *serracarte, clip, fermaglio*
   paper currency *carta moneta*
   paper weight *fermacarte*
parade *sfilata*
parade (to) *sfilare*
paragraph *paragrafo*
park (to) *parcheggiare*
parliament *parlamento*
parcel *pacco, pacchetto, involto*
parquet (flooring) *parquet*
participation *partecipazione*

participate (to) *partecipare*
particular *particolare*
party *partito, festa, comitiva*
pass *lasciapassare, biglietto gratuito*
pass (to) *passare*
passion *passione*
pastry *pasticcino*
patient *paziente*
pause *pausa*
pavilion *padiglione*
pay *paga, retribuzione*
   pay envelope *busta paga*
   payroll *libro paga*
pay (to) *pagare*
payable *pagabile*
payment *pagamento*
peace *pace*
pedagogy *pedagogia*
pedestrian *pedonale*
pen *penna*
peninsula *penisola*
pension *pensione*
   pension plan *piano di pensionamento*
pensionable *pensionabile*
people *gente*
perceive (to) *percepire*
percentage *percentuale*
perception *percezione*
perfect *perfetto*
perishable *deperibile*
permanence *permanenza*
permission *permesso, licenza*
permit (to) *permettere*
person *persona*
personal *personale*
   personal advertisement *annuncio personale*
personality *personalità*
personally *personalmente*
personnel *personale*
pessimist *pessimista*
phase *fase*
philosophy *filosofia*
phone (to) *telefonare*
   phone collect (to) *telefonare 'collect'*
   phone card *carta di credito telefonica*
photocopier *fotocopiatrice*
physical education *educazione fisica*
physics *fisica*
pick up (to) *raccogliere*
picturesque *pittoresco*
piece *pezzo*
pillow *cuscino, guanciale*
pilot *pilota*
pin *spillo*
pipe (smoking) *tubo (pipa)*
place *posto, sito, luogo*
placing *collocamento*
plan *piano, programma*
plan (to) *pianificare, progettare*
plane *aereo*
plank *tavola*
planner *programmatore*

planning *pianificazione*
plant *fabbrica, stabilimento*
  plant inventory *inventario di fabbrica*
  plant manager *capofabbrica*
plantation *piantagione*
plastic *plastica*
plate *lastra, targa*
play (to) *giocare, suonare*
playing field *campo di giuoco, campo*
  sportivo
pleasant *piacevole*
pleased *contento*
plug *spina*
plunge (to) *tuffarsi*
pocket *tasca*
point *punta, punto*
  point of departure *punto di partenza*
  point of view *punto di vista*
point (to) *indicare*
point out (to) *rilevare*
police *polizia*
policeman *poliziotto*
policy *polizza, tattica*
polished *tornito*
polite *cortese*
political *politico*
politics *politica*
pontiff *pontefice*
poor *povero*
pope *papa*
popular *popolare*
port *porto*
portable *portatile*
porter *facchino*
portion *porzione*
position *posizione, posto, impiego*
positive *positivo*
post *posta, corrispondenza*
post (to) *impostare, imbucare*
postage *affrancatura*
postcard *cartolina*
poster *manifesto*
power *potere*
powerful *potente*
precaution *precauzione*
precedent *precedente*
precise *preciso*
precisely *precisamente*
precision *precisione*
prepaid *prepagato*
prepare (to) *preparare*
prepared *disposto*
prerequisite *prerequisito*
prescription *ricetta*
presence *presenza*
present *(adj.) presente, attuale*
preserved *conservato*
president *presidente*
press (to) *premere, pigiare*
prestigious *prestigioso*
price *prezzo*
prince *principe*

printer *stampante*
  laser printer *stampante laser*
priority *prevalenza*
probably *probabilmente*
problem *problema*
procedure *procedura*
process *processo*
produce (to) *produrre*
producer *produttore*
product *prodotto*
production *produzione*
productive *produttivo*
profession *professione*
professional *professionale*
  professional activity *attività professionale*
  professional development *sviluppo profession-*
  ale
professor *professore*
profile *profilo*
profit *profitto*
project *progetto*
program *programma*
programming *programmazione*
prohibit (to) *proibire*
promise (to) *promettere*
promoted *promosso*
promote (to) *promuovere*
property *proprietà*
proportion *proporzione*
proposal *proposta*
propose (to) *proporre*
protagonist *protagonista*
protect (to) *proteggere*
protection *protezione*
protein *proteina*
protest *protesta*
provide (to) *provvedere*
provoke (to) *provocare, suscitare*
proximity *vicinanza*
psychologist *psicologo*
publicize (to) *pubblicizzare*
publisher *editore*
pupil *allievo, scolaro*
purchase *acquisto*
purchase (to) *comprare, acquistare*
  purchase contract *contratto d'acquisto*
purchasing power *potere di acquisto*
pure *puro*
purse *borsetta*
put (to) *mettere*
puzzled *perplesso*

Q

qualification *qualità, qualificazione, qualifica,*
  requisito, titolo
qualified *qualificato, dotato dei requisiti richiesti*
quality *qualità*
quantity *quantità*
queen *regina*
question *domanda*

questionnaire *questionario*
quintal *quintale*
quota *quota*
quote (to) *citare*
quotation *quotazione*

R

rabbit *coniglio*
race *razza*
radio *radio*
   radio listener *radioascoltatore*
   radio news bulletin *radiogiornale*
rain *pioggia*
rain (to) *piovere*
rainbow *arcobaleno*
raise (to) *alzare*
rare *raro*
rather *piuttosto*
rational *razionale*
raw *grezzo*
   raw material *materiale grezzo*
ray *raggio*
reach (to) *raggiungere*
reaction *reazione*
read (to) *leggere*
reader *lettore*
reading *lettura*
ready *pronto*
   ready-to-wear suit *abito confezionato*
reality *realtà*
realize (to) *accorgersi, rendersi conto,*
   realizzare
really *realmente, veramente*
reaping *mietitura*
reason *ragione, argomento*
receipt *ricevuta, polizza*
   receipt form *modulo di ricevuta*
receivable *esigibile*
receive (to) *ricevere*
receiver *destinatario*
recent *recente*
reception *ricevimento, rinfresco*
recession *recessione*
recognize (to) *riconoscere*
recommend (to) *raccomandare*
recommendation *raccomandazione*
reconcile (to) *conciliare*
record *record*
record (to) *incidere, registrare*
recyclable *riciclabile*
reference *refernza, riferimento*
reduce (to) *ridurre*
refer (to) *riferirsi*
refer (to) *accennare*
refined *raffinato*
refuge *rifugio*
refund *rimborso*
region *regione*
refuse (to) *rifiutare*
register (to) *iscriversi*

registered letter *raccomandata*
regret (to) *dispiacere*
reimburse (to) *rimborsare*
reimbursement *rimborso*
relief *sollievo*
religious *religioso*
remain (to) *rimanere*
remuneration *retribuzione*
renounce (to) *rinunciare*
rent (to) *noleggiare*
repeat (to) *ripetere*
repetition *ripetizione*
replace (to) *rimpiazzare*
report *rapporto*
reproach *rimprovero*
reproduction *riproduzione*
reputation *reputazione*
request *richiesta, sollecito*
requirement *requisito*
reserved *riservato*
residence *domicilio, residenza, abitazione*
residential *residenziale*
resign (to) *dimettersi*
resolve (to) *risolvere*
respect *rispetto*
responsibility *responsabilità*
responsible *responsabile*
rest *riposo*
rest (to) *riposare, riposarsi*
restore (to) *restaurare*
return *ritorno*
return (to) *ritornare, tornare*
   return (to) empty-handed *tornarsene con le*
   pive nel sacco
reveal (to) *rivelare*
revision *revisione*
ribbon *nastro*
rich *ricco*
riddle *indovinello*
right *diritto*
rigid *rigido*
ring *anello*
risk (to) *rischiare*
rite *rito*
rival *avversario*
river *fiume*
road *strada*
roof *tetto*
room *camera, stanza, sala*
rotten *marcio*
ruin *rovina*
rule *regola, norma*
run *corsa*
run (to) *correre*
   run away (to) *sfuggire*

S

sack *sacco*
sacrilege *sacrilegio*
sad *triste*

safety *sicurezza*
  safety glasses *occhiali di protezione*
said *detto*
sailor *marinaio*
saint *santo*
salad *insalata*
salary *salario*
sale *vendita, svendita*
  sale by installments *vendita a rate*
  sale by private treaty *vendita privata*
  sale by retail *vendita al minuto*
  over-the-counter sale *vendita al dettaglio*
  sale to the highest bidder *vendita al miglior offerente*
  sales agent *agente di vendita*
  sales manager *direttore commerciale*
same *stesso*
sample *campione, esemplare*
sand *sabbia*
Sardinian *sardo*
satisfied *soddisfatto*
save (to) *salvare, risparmiare*
say (to) *dire*
scandal *scandalo*
scandalize (to) *scandalizzare*
scholar *studioso*
scholarship *borsa di studio*
school *scuola*
science *scienza*
scientific *scientifico*
screen *schermo*
season (to) *condire*
seat *sedile, posto, sede*
second *secondo*
  second class *seconda classe*
  second course *secondo piatto*
  second-hand sale *vendita di seconda mano*
secret *segreto*
secretary *segretaria*
sector *settore*
secure (to) **a contract** *ottenere un contratto*
security *sicurezza*
see (to) *vedere*
  see (to) something with someone's eyes *toccare con mano*
  see (to) again *rivedere*
seed *seme*
seem (to) *sembrare, apparire*
selective *selettivo*
sell (to) *vendere*
  sell (to) like hotcakes *andare a ruba*
seminary *seminario*
send (to) *inviare, mandare*
  send (to) back *restituire*
sender *mittente*
sense *senso*
sensitivity *sensibilità*
serene *sereno*
serious *serio*
seriously *seriamente*
set (to) **the table** *apparecchiare la tavola*
seven *sette*

seventh *settimo*
seventy *settanta*
sexual *sessuale*
sexuality *sessualità*
sexy *sexy*
share *azione*
share (to) *ripartire, condividere*
sharebroker *agente di cambio*
sharecropping *mezzadria*
sharecropper *mezzadro*
shareholder *azionista*
shed *baracca*
shift *turno, turno di lavoro*
shine (to) *brillare*
shining *lucido*
ship *nave*
shipment *spedizione*
shop *negozio*
shopping *compere, spesa, shopping*
  shopping center *centro degli acquisti*
shorts *calzoncini, pantaloncini*
show *mostra*
shy *timido*
Sicilian *siciliano*
sick *malato, stufo*
sigh *sospiro*
sign *segno, insegna, cartello*
sign (to) *firmare*
signal *segnale*
signature *firma*
silk *seta*
  silk suit *tailleur di seta*
silly *sciocco*
similar *simile*
simple *semplice*
simplicity *semplicità*
simply *semplicemente*
situated *situato*
situation *situazione*
sixth *sesto*
sixty *sessanta*
ski (to) *sciare*
skillful *capace*
skim (to) **through the newspaper** *sfogliare il giornale*
skin *pelle, buccia*
sky *cielo*
skyscraper *grattacielo*
sleep *sonno*
sleep (to) *dormire*
  sleep (to) like a log *dormire come un ghiro*
slogan *slogan*
slow *lento*
slowly *lentamente*
smile (to) *sorridere*
snack *spuntino*
  to have a snack *fare uno spuntino*
snow *neve*
snowfall *nevicata*
society *società*
soft *soffice, molle*
software *software*

461

solid *solido*
solidarity *solidarietà*
solution *soluzione*
song *canto*
sophisticated *sofisticato*
sound *suono*
sowing *semina*
space *spazio*
spacious *spazioso*
speak (to) *parlare*
   speak (to) out *vuotare il sacco*
special *speciale*
   special price *prezzo di favore*
specialization *specializzazione*
specialized *specializzato*
specialty *specialità*
specified *specificato*
spectacular *spettacolare*
spectator *spettatore*
spell (to) *compitare*
spend (to) **an arm and a leg** *spendere un occhio della testa*
splendid *splendido*
splendor *splendore*
spotted *macchiato*
spouse *coniuge*
spring *primavera*
spy *spia*
square *piazza*
stadium *stadio*
staff *personale*
   staff assistant *assistente del personale*
stagflation *stagflazione*
stair *scala*
stamp *francobollo*
stand *stand*
   stand (to) up to someone *tenere testa a qualcuno*
start *inizio*
start (to) *iniziare, incominciare*
state *stato*
statistics *statistica*
statue *statua*
stay (to) *stare, rimanere*
steak *bistecca*
steamer *vaporetto*
stenography *stenografia*
step down (to) *dimettersi*
stereotype *stereotipo*
stewardess *hostess*
still *ancora*
stimulate (to) *incentivare*
stir up (to) *suscitare*
stock *azioni, titoli*
stockholder *azionista*
stone *sasso*
stop (to) *smettere*
   Stop it! *Smetila!*
storm *temporale*
stove *stufa*
strange *strano*
strengthen (to) *rinforzare*

stress *stress*
stressful *stressante*
strike *sciopero*
strip *striscia*
strong *forte*
structure *struttura*
student *studente*
study *studio*
stupid *stupido*
stupidity *stupidità*
   a stupid thing *una stupidaggine*
style *stile*
substantially *sostanzialmente*
substitute *sostituto*
suburban *periferico*
subway *metropolitana*
succeed (to) *riuscire*
sudden *improvviso*
suddenly *all'improvviso*
suffice (to) *bastare*
sufficiency *sufficienza*
suggest (to) *suggerire*
suit *tailleur*
suitable *adatto*
sum *somma*
summary *riassunto*
sunset *tramonto*
superficial *superficiale*
superior *superiore*
supermarket *supermercato*
supervise (to) *controllare, dirigere*
supper *cena*
supplement *supplemento*
supplementary *supplementare*
support *sostegno, supporto, appoggio*
support (to) *sostenere*
supporter *patrocinatore*
suppose *supporre*
sure *sicuro*
surface *superficie*
surfing *surfing*
surgeon *chirurgo*
surname *cognome*
surpass (to) *superare*
surprise *sorpresa*
surprise (to) *sorprendere*
surroundings *ambiente*
survey *sondaggio*
suspect *sospettare*
sustain (to) *sopportare*
sweat *sudata*
sweater *maglione*
sweet *dolce*
Swiss *svizzero*
symbol *simbolo*
sympathy *condoglianza*
symptom *sintomo*
synonym *sinonimo*
system *sistema*

T

table *tavolo, tavola*
  table wine *vino da pasto*
tail *coda*
take (to) *prendere*
  take (to) advantage of *usufruire*
  take (to) for granted *dare per scontato*
  take (to) care of *avere cura di*
  take (to) heart *stare a cuore*
take-off *decollo*
talk *discorso, colloquio*
tall *alto*
tangerine *mandarino*
target *bersaglio*
taste *gusto*
taste (to) *degustare, assaggiare*
tax *tassa, imposta*
  tax allowance *sgravio fiscale*
  tax collector *esattore delle imposte*
  tax equity *giustizia fiscale*
  tax evasion *evasione fiscale*
  tax exemption *esenzione fiscale*
  tax expert *fiscalista*
  tax reduction *riduzione delle imposte*
tax (to) *tassare*
teach (to) *insegnare*
teacher *insegnante*
tease (to) *sfottere*
teaspoon *cucchiaino*
technical *tecnico*
technology *tecnologia*
telecommunication *telecomunicazione*
telegram *telegramma*
telephone *telefonata*
  telephone answering service *servizio di segreteria*
  telephone number *numero di
  telefono*
telephone (to) *telefonare*
tell (to) *raccontare*
temperature *temperatura*
temple *tempio*
tenant *inquilino*
tendency *tendenza*
tension *tensione*
terminal *aerostazione*
terrace *terrazza, terrazzo*
tertiary *terziario*
test *test, prova*
textile *tessile*
  textiles *prodotti tessili*
thank (to) *ringraziare*
theme *tema*
then *poi, allora*
therefore *quindi*
thesis *tesi*
thickness *spessore*
thin *sottile*
thought *pensiero*
thousand *mille, migliaio*
through *attraverso, tramite*

throw (to) *buttare*
  throw (to) away one's money *buttare via il
  denaro*
thumb *pollice*
ticket *scontrino, etichetta*
tie *cravatta*
tile *mattonella*
timetable *orario*
title *titolo, qualifica*
toast *brindisi*
together *insieme*
toll *pedaggio*
  toll collector *esattore*
tomorrow *domani*
tone *tono*
tongue *lingua*
tonight *stanotte*
too *pure, anche*
tool *strumento*
tooth *dente*
top *cima*
total *totale, somma totale*
touch (to) *toccare*
tour *gita, giro*
toward *verso*
towel *asciugamano*
tower *torre*
trade *mestiere*
tradition *tradizione*
traffic *traffico*
  traffic light *semaforo*
tragedy *tragedia*
trample on (to) *calpestare*
transcribe (to) *trascrivere*
transfer *trasferimento*
transform (to) *trasformare*
transit *transito*
transition *transizione*
translate (to) *tradurre*
translation *traduzione*
  translation service *servizio traduzione*
transparent *trasparente*
transportation *trasporto, mezzo di trasporto*
travel (to) *viaggiare*
treatment *trattamento*
tree *albero*
tremendous *tremendo*
triumphal *trionfale*
trivial *banale*
trolley *carrello*
trousers *calzoni, pantaloni*
truck *camion*
trumpet *trombetta*
trust *fiducia*
truth *verità*
try *tentativo*
tunnel *galleria*
turnover *fatturato*
turtle *tartaruga*
Tuscan *toscano*
tuxedo *smoking*
two *due*

typewriter *macchina da scrivere*
typology *tipologia*

U

ugly *brutto*
umbrella *ombrello*
unanimous *unanime*
unauthorized *non autorizzato*
unbinding *non vincolante*
unconditional *senza condizioni*
unfair *ingiusto*
unification *unificazione*
uncle *zio*
under *sotto*
   under construction *in costruzione*
   under no circumstance *in nessun caso*
   under oath *sotto giuramento*
underpay (to) *pagare poco*
undergo (to) *sottoporsi*
undersell (to) *vendere sottocosto*
undershirt *maglietta*
undersign (to) *sottoscrivere*
understand (to) *intendere*
understanding *comprensione*
undertake (to) *assumere*
unemployed *disoccupato*
unemployment *disoccupazione*
unforgettable *indimenticabile*
unfortunately *purtroppo*
union *unione, sindacato*
unique *unico*
United States *Stati Uniti*
unity *unità*
universal *universale*
university *(adj.) universitario*
unless *a meno che*
until *sino*
unused *non usato*
unusual *insolito*
unwind (to) *svolgere*
upbringing *educazione*
urgent *urgente*
use (to) *utilizzare*
useful *utile*
useless *inutile*
usually *di solito*

V

vacancy *posto vacante*
vacation *vacanza, ferie*
valuable *prezioso*
value *valore*
varied *vario*
varnish (to) *verniciare*
vary (to) *variare*
vase *vaso*
vast *vasto*
vehicle *veicolo*

velvet *velluto*
vendor *venditore*
Venetian *veneziano*
ventilated *ventilato*
verb *verbo*
verbal *verbale*
versatility *versatilità*
vertical *verticale*
vice *vizio, difetto*
victim *vittima*
view *panorama, veduta*
vineyard *vigneto*
vintage *vendemmia*
vintager *vendemmiatore*
virtual *virtuale*
   virtual reality *realtà virtuale*
virus *virus*
visit *visita*
visitor *visitatore*
voice *voce*
void (to) *invalidare*
volume *volume*
volunteer *volontario*
voucher *buono, scontrino*

W

wage *paga*
wall *muro*
wait (to) *aspettare*
   wait (to) on the (phone) line *attendere in linea*
   wait (to) for *attendere, aspettare*
walk (to) *camminare*
wall *parete*
wanted *cercasi, cercansi, ricercato*
warehouse *magazzino*
warm *caloroso*
warranty *garanzia*
waste *spreco, scario, rifiuti*
   waste paper *carta straccia*
waste (to) *sprecare*
water *acqua*
waterfront *lungomare*
waterworks *impianto idrico*
wave *onda*
wax *cera*
weapon *arma*
wedding *nozze*
weekly *settimanale*
welcome *benvenuto*
welfare *benessere*
   welfare officer *assistente sociale*
wheat *grano*
while *mentre*
wholesale *vendita all'ingrosso*
wholesaler *grossista*
why *perché*
wide *ampio*
win (to) *vincere*
wine *vino*
wing *ala*

wish *desiderio, augurio*
wish (to) *augurare*
withdraw (to) *prelevare, ritirare*
without *senza*
witty *spiritoso*
wolf *lupo*
wonder *meraviglia*
wonderful *meraviglioso*
wonderfully *meravigliosamente*
wood *legno*
   wood-burning stove *stufa a legno*
wool *lana*
word *parola*
   dirty word *parolaccia*
wordprocessing *programma di videoscrittura*
work *lavoro, occupazione, opera*
work (to) *lavorare, funzionare*
worker *lavoratore, operaio*
world *mondo*
worried *preoccupato*
worry *preoccupazione*

write (to) *scrivere*
written *scritto*
wrong *sbagliato, torto*

Y

year *anno, annata*
yearly *annuale*
yellow *giallo*
yesterday *ieri*
yet *tuttavia*
yours *vostro, Vostro, tuo, Suo*
   yours sincerely *distinti saluti*

Z

zero *zero*
zone *area*

INDEX